# An Introduction to ANSYS® Fluent® 2020

John E. Matsson, Ph.D., P.E.

**SDC**
PUBLICATIONS

**SDC Publications**
P.O. Box 1334
Mission, KS 66222
913-262-2664
www.SDCpublications.com
Publisher: Stephen Schroff

ISBN-13: 978-1-63057-396-6
ISBN-10: 1-63057-396-5

Printed and bound in the United States of America.

## Acknowledgements

I would like to thank Stephen Schroff of SDC Publications for his help in preparing this book for publication.

## About the Author

Dr. John Matsson is a Professor of Engineering and Chair of the Engineering Department at Oral Roberts University in Tulsa, Oklahoma. He earned M.S. and Ph.D. degrees from the Royal Institute of Technology in Stockholm, Sweden, in 1988 and 1994, respectively, and completed postdoctoral work at the Norwegian University of Science and Technology in Trondheim, Norway. His teaching areas include Finite Element Methods, Fluid Mechanics, Manufacturing Processes, and Principles of Design. He is a member of the American Society of Mechanical Engineers ASME Mid-Continent Section. Please contact the author jmatsson@oru.edu with any comments, questions, or suggestions on this book.

**Notes:**

4

**TABLE OF CONTENTS**

# TABLE OF CONTENTS

# TABLE OF CONTENTS

## CHAPTER 1.  INTRODUCTION

### A. ANSYS Workbench

ANSYS Workbench is an integrated simulation platform that includes a wide range of systems in the toolbox including analysis systems, component systems, custom systems, and design exploration, see Table 1.1.

| Analysis Systems | Component Systems | Custom Systems | Design Exploration |
|---|---|---|---|
| Design Assessment | ACP (Post) | FSI: Fluid Flow (CFX) > Static Structural | Direct Optimization |
| Eigenvalue Buckling | ACP (Pre) | FSI: Fluid Flow (FLUENT) > Static Structural | Parameters Correlation |
| Electric | Autodyn | Pre-Stress Modal | Response Surface |
| Explicit Dynamics | BladeGen | Random Vibration | Response Surface Optimization |
| Fluid Flow (CFX) | CFX | Response Spectrum | ROM Builder |
| Fluid Flow (Fluent) | Engineering Data | Thermal-Stress | Six Sigma Analysis |
| Harmonic Acoustics | External Data | | |
| Harmonic Response | External Model | | |
| IC Engine (Fluent) | Fluent | | |
| IC Engine (Forte) | Fluent (with Fluent Meshing) | | |
| Magnetostatic | Forte | | |
| Modal | Geometry | | |
| Modal Acoustics | Mechanical APDL | | |
| Random Vibration | Mechanical Model | | |
| Response Spectrum | Mesh | | |
| Rigid Dynamics | Microsoft Office Excel | | |
| Static Acoustics | Performance Map | | |
| Static Structural | Results | | |
| Steady-State Thermal | System Coupling | | |
| Thermal-Electric | Turbo Setup | | |
| Topology Optimization | Turbo Grid | | |
| Transient Structural | Vista AFD | | |
| Transient Thermal | Vista CCD | | |
| TurbomachineryFluid Flow | Vista CPD | | |
| | Vista RTD | | |

Table 1.1 Available systems in ANSYS Workbench Toolbox

ANSYS Workbench also has a Project Schematic where the details for the process of execution of the different analysis systems are available. These details of each analysis system in the project schematic include Engineering Data, Geometry, Model, Setup, Solution and Results. Furthermore, properties of schematics are available for user input.

### B. ANSYS DesignModeler

The geometry for the Fluid Flow (Fluent) flow study project can be created either in DesignModeler or alternatively using SpaceClaim. DesignModeler is a parametric modeler designed to draw 2D sketches and model 3D CAD parts. ANSYS DesignModeler has nine different toolbars as listed in Table 1.2.

| Toolbars |
|---|
| Active Plane/Sketch toolbar |
| Display toolbar |
| Feature toolbar |
| File toolbar |
| Graphics Options toolbar |
| Menus toolbar |
| Rotation Modes toolbar |
| Selection toolbar |
| Undo/Redo toolbar |

Table 1.2 Toolbars in ANSYS DesignModeler

Moreover, the Sketching Toolboxes in DesignModeler include Draw, Modify, Dimensions, Constraints and Settings as shown in Table 1.3.

| Constraints | Dimensions | Draw | Modify | Settings |
|---|---|---|---|---|
| Auto Constraints | Angle | Arc by 3 Points | Chamfer | Grid |
| Coincident | Animate | Arc by Center | Copy | Major Grid Spacing |
| Concentric | Diameter | Arc by Tangent | Corner | Minor-Steps per Major |
| Equal Distance | Display | Circle | Cut | Snaps per Minor |
| Equal Length | Edit | Circle by 3 Tangents | Drag | |
| Equal Radius | General | Construction Point | Duplicate | |
| Fixed | Horizontal | Construction Point at Intersection | Extend | |
| Horizontal | Length/Distance | Ellipse | Fillet | |
| Midpoint | Move | Line | Move | |
| Parallel | Radius | Line by 2 Tangents | Offset | |
| Perpendicular | Semi-Automatic | Oval | Paste | |
| Symmetry | Vertical | Polygon | Replicate | |
| Tangent | | Polyline | Spline Edit | |
| Vertical | | Rectangle | Split | |
| | | Rectangle by 3 Points | Trim | |
| | | Spline | | |
| | | Tangent Line | | |

Table 1.3 Sketching Toolboxes in ANSYS DesignModeler

## C. ANSYS Meshing

ANSYS Meshing produces the mesh using Mesh Methods and Mesh Controls as shown in Tables 1.4 and Table 1.5.

| Hexahedral Meshing | Tetrahedral Meshing | Surface Meshing |
|---|---|---|
| Cut cell Cartesian | ANSYS CFX-Mesh | Default quad, quad/tri or tri |
| General Sweep | Patch conforming | Uniform quad or quad tri |
| Hex-dominant | Patch independent | |
| MultiZone | | |
| Thin Sweep | | |

Table 1.4 Mesh methods in ANSYS Meshing

| Global Mesh Control | Local Mesh Control |
|---|---|
| Curvature-based refinement settings | Automatic Contact Detection |
| Element midside node settings | Body, face, edge curvature-based refinement |
| Inflation settings | Body, face, edge, vertex sizings |
| Physics preference settings | Body, face, edge, vertex sphere of influence |
| Pinch (defeaturing) settings | Body mesh method controls |
| Proximity-based refinement settings | Body of Influence |
| Quality settings | Contact Sizing |
| Relevance settings | Gap tool |
| Rigid-body behavior settings | Inflation controls |
| Smoothing settings | Mapped-face meshing controls |
| Transition/growth settings | Match mesh controls |
| | Pinch controls |
| | Solver-based refinement controls |
| | Virtual topologies |

Table 1.5 Mesh controls in ANSYS Meshing

## D. ANSYS Fluent

ANSYS Fluent is a computational fluid dynamics software package that is written in the C language. Fluent has numerous capabilities for simulations as shown in Table 1.6.

| Fluent Capabilities |
|---|
| 2D Planar flows, Axisymmetric flows, Axisymmetric flows with swirl, 3D Flows |
| Acoustics |
| Cavitation flows |
| Chemical species mixing and reaction |
| Compressible flows, Incompressible flows |
| Forced heat transfer, Mixed convection heat transfer, Natural heat transfer |
| Free surface flows |
| Ideal gases, Real gases |
| Inviscid flows, Laminar flows, Turbulent flows |
| Lumped Parameter Models |
| Melting and Solidification |
| Multiphase flows |
| Newtonian flows, Non-Newtonian flows |
| Porous media |
| Steady flows, Time-dependent flows |

Table 1.6 Some of the capabilities for ANSYS Fluent

There are eleven add on modules available in ANSYS as shown in Table 0.7.

| Fluent Addon Modules |
|---|
| Adjoint Solver |
| Dual-Potential MSMD Battery Model |
| Fiber Model |
| Fuel Cell and Electrolysis Model |
| Macroscopic Particle Model |
| MHD Model |
| PEM Fuel Cell Model |
| Population Balance Model |
| Single-Potential Battery Model |
| SOFC Model with Unresolved Electrolyte |
| Reduced Order Model |

Table 1.7 Add on modules for ANSYS Fluent

The user interface of Fluent includes the Outline View and the Task Page. The Outline View includes Setup, Solution, Results and Parameters & Customization, see Table 1.8. The different categories and variables available in setup, solution and results are shown in Tables 1.9-1.12.

| Setup | Solution | Results | Parameters & Customization |
|---|---|---|---|
| Boundary Conditions | Calculation Activities | Animations | Custom Field Functions |
| Cell Zone Conditions | Cell Registers | Graphics | Parameters |
| Dynamic Mesh | Controls | Plots | User Defined Functions |
| General | Initialization | Reports | User Defined Memory |
| Materials | Methods | Scene | User Defined Scalars |
| Models | Monitors | Surfaces | |
| Named Expressions | Report Definitions | | |
| Reference Frames | Run Calculation | | |
| Reference Values | | | |

Table 1.8 Outline view options in ANSYS Fluent

| Setup Models |
|---|
| Acoustics (Ffowcs-Williams & Hawkings, Wave Equation) |
| Discrete Phase (Numerics, Parallel, Physical Models, Tracking, UDF) |
| Electric Potential (Potential Equation) |
| Energy (Energy Equation) |
| Heat Exchanger (Dual Cell Model, Macro Model Group, Ungrouped Macro Model) |
| Multiphase (Eulerian, Mixture, Volume of Fluid, Wet Stream) |
| Radiation (Discrete Ordinates DO, Discrete Transfer DTRM, P1, Rosseland, Surface to Surface S2S) |
| Solidification and Melting (Back Diffusion, Solidification/Melting) |
| Species (Composition PDF Transport, Non-Premixed Combustion, Partially Premixed Combustion, Premixed Combustion, Species Transport) |
| Structure (Linear Elasticity) |
| Viscous (Detached Eddy Simulation DES, Inviscid, k-epsilon 2 eqn, k-omega 3 eqn, Laminar, Reynolds Stress 5 eqn, Scale-Adaptive Simulation SAS, Spalart-Allmaras 1 eqn, Transition k-kl-omega 3 eqn, Transition SST 4 eqn) |

Table 1.9 Models options in ANSYS Fluent

| Setup Reference Values |
|---|
| Area (m2) |
| Density (kg/m3) |
| Enthalpy (j/kg) |
| Length (m) |
| Pressure (pascal) |
| Ratio of Specific Heats |
| Temperature (k) |
| Velocity (m/s) |
| Viscosity (kg/m-s) |

Table 1.10 Reference values in ANSYS Fluent

| Solution | |
|---|---|
| Calculation Activities | Monitors |
| Autosave | Convergence Conditions |
| Execute Commands | Report Files |
| Cell Register Operations | Report Plots |
| Solution Animation | Residual |

Table 1.11 Calculation activities and monitors options in ANSYS Fluent

| Results | | | |
|---|---|---|---|
| **Animations** | **Graphics** | **Plots** | **Reports** |
| Scene Animation | Contours | FFT | Discrete Phase |
| Solution Animation Playback | Mesh | File | Fluxes |
| Sweep Surface | Vectors | Histogram | Forces |
| | Particle Tracks | Interpolated Data | Surface Integrals |
| | Pathlines | Profile Data | Volume Integrals |
| | Vectors | XY Plot | |

Table 1.12 Animation, graphics, plots and reports options in ANSYS Fluent

The different options that are available for the General Setup are Gravity, Mesh and Solver with the details as shown in Table 1.13.

| General | | |
|---|---|---|
| **Gravity** | **Mesh** | **Solver** |
| X (m/s2) | Check | 2D Space (Axisymmetric, Axisymmetric Swirl, Planar) |
| Y (m/s2) | Display… | Time (Steady, Transient) |
| Z (m/s2) | Report Quality | Type (Density-Based, Pressure-Based) |
| | Scale… | Velocity Formulation (Absolute, Relative) |
| | Units… | |

Table 1.13 Gravity, mesh and solver options in ANSYS Fluent

The different Solution Methods are shown in Table 1.14.

| Solution Methods | |
|---|---|
| **Pressure-Velocity Coupling** | **Pressure-Based Solver , Spatial Discretization** |
| Coupled | Gradient (Green-Gauss Cell Based, Green-Gauss Node Based, Least Squares Cell Based) |
| PISO | Pressure (Body Force Weighted, Linear, PRESTO!, Second Order, Standard) |
| SIMPLE | Momentum (First Order Upwind, Power Law, QUICK, Second Order Upwind, Third-Order MUSCL) |
| SIMPLEC | Energy (First Order Upwind, Power Law, QUICK, Second Order Upwind, Third-Order MUSCL) |
| | **Density-Based Solver , Spatial Discretization** |
| | Gradient (Green-Gauss Cell Based, Green-Gauss Node Based, Least Squares Cell Based) |
| | Flow (First Order Upwind, Second Order Upwind, Third-Order MUSCL) |

Table 1.14 Solution methods options in ANSYS Fluent

## E. References

1. ANSYS Fluent Getting Started Guide, Release 19.1, April 2018, ANSYS, Inc.
2. ANSYS FLUENT Theory Guide, Release 15.0, January 2013, ANSYS, Inc.
3. ANSYS Fluent Tutorial Guide, Release 18.0, January 2017, ANSYS, Inc.
4. ANSYS FLUENT User's Guide, Release 15.0, November 2013, ANSYS, Inc.
5. ANSYS Meshing User's Guide, Release 15.0, November 2013, ANSYS, Inc.
6. ANSYS Workbench User's Guide, Release 12.1, November 2009, ANSYS, Inc.
7. DesignModeler User Guide, Release 14.5, October 2012, ANSYS, Inc.

**F. Notes**

## CHAPTER 2.  FLAT PLATE BOUNDARY LAYER

### A. Objectives

- Creating Geometry in ANSYS Workbench for ANSYS Fluent Flow Simulation
- Setting up ANSYS Fluent Simulation for Laminar Steady 2D Planar Flow
- Setting up Mesh
- Selecting Boundary Conditions
- Running Calculations
- Using Plots to Visualize Resulting Flow Field
- Compare with Theoretical Solution using Mathematica Code

### B. Problem Description

In this chapter, we will use ANSYS Fluent to study the two-dimensional laminar flow on a horizontal flat plate. The size of the plate is considered as being infinite in the spanwise direction and therefore the flow is 2D instead of 3D. The inlet velocity for the 1 m long plate is 5 m/s and we will be using air as the fluid for laminar simulations. We will determine the velocity profiles and plot the profiles. We will start by creating the geometry needed for the simulation.

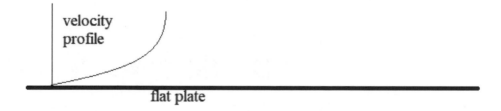

### C. Launching ANSYS Workbench and Selecting Fluent

1. Start by launching ANSYS Workbench. Double click on Fluid Flow (Fluent) that is located under Analysis Systems in Toolbox.

Figure 2.1 Selecting Fluid Flow

19

**D. Launching ANSYS DesignModeler**

2.  Select Geometry under Project Schematic in ANSYS Workbench. Right-click on Geometry and select Properties. Select 2D Analysis Type under Advanced Geometry Options in Properties of Schematic A2: Geometry. Right-click on Geometry in Project Schematic and select to launch New DesignModeler Geometry. Select Units>>Millimeter as the length unit from the menu in DesignModeler.

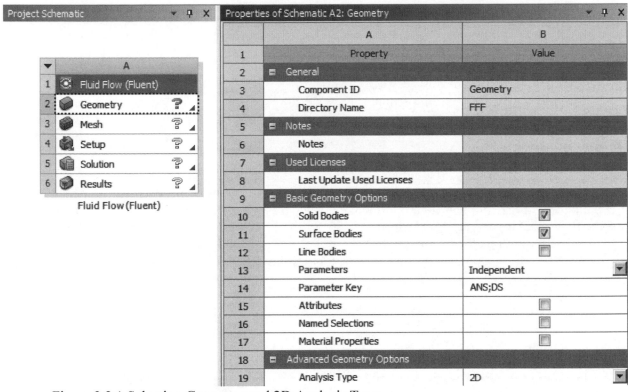

Figure 2.2a) Selecting Geometry and 2D Analysis Type

Figure 2.2b) Launching DesignModeler

Figure 2.2c) Selecting the length unit

3.  Next, we will be creating the geometry in DesignModeler. Select XYPlane from the Tree Outline on the left-hand side in DesignModeler. Select Look at Sketch 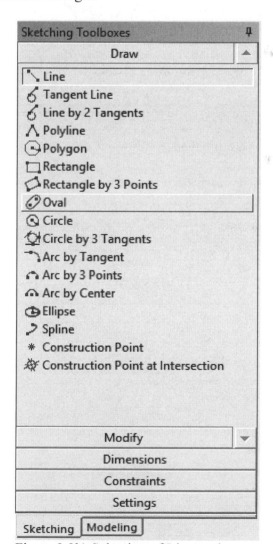. Click on the Sketching tab in the Tree Outline and select the Line sketch tool.

Draw a horizontal line 1,000 mm long from the origin to the right. Make sure you have a *P* at the origin when you start drawing the line. Also, make sure you have an *H* along the line so that it is horizontal and a *C* at the end of the line.

Select Dimensions within the Sketching options. Click on the line and enter a length of 1,000 mm. Draw a vertical line upward 100 mm long starting at the end point of the first horizontal line. Make sure you have a *P* when starting the line and a *V* indicating a vertical line. Continue with a horizontal line 100 mm long to the left from the origin followed by another vertical line 100 mm long.

The next line will be horizontal with a length 100 mm starting at the endpoint of the former vertical line and directed to the right. Finally, close the rectangle with a 1,000 mm long horizontal line starting 100 mm above the origin and directed to the right.

Figure 2.3a) Selection of XYPlane

Figure 2.3b) Selection of Line tool

Figure 2.3c) Rectangle with dimensions

| Details View | |
|---|---|
| **Details of Sketch1** | |
| Sketch | Sketch1 |
| Sketch Visibility | Show Sketch |
| Show Constraints? | No |
| **Dimensions: 4** | |
| ☐ H1 | 1000 mm |
| ☐ H3 | 100 mm |
| ☐ V2 | 100 mm |
| ☐ V4 | 100 mm |

Figure 2.3d) Dimensions in Details View

4.  Click on the Modeling tab under Sketching Toolboxes. Select Concept>>Surfaces from Sketches in the menu. Control select the six edges of the rectangle as Base Objects and select Apply in Details View. Click on Generate in the toolbar . The rectangle turns gray. Right click in the graphics window and select Zoom to Fit and close DesignModeler.

Figure 2.4a) Selecting Surfaces from Sketches

| Details View | | 무 |
|---|---|---|
| **Details of SurfaceSk1** | | |
| Surface From Sketches | SurfaceSk1 | |
| Base Objects | Apply | Cancel |
| Operation | Add Material | |
| Orient With Plane Normal? | Yes | |
| Thickness (> =0) | 0 mm | |

Figure 2.4b) Applying Base Objects

Figure 2.4c) Completed rectangle in DesignModeler

## E. Launching ANSYS Meshing

5. We are now going to double click on Mesh under Project Schematic in ANSYS Workbench to open the Meshing window. Select Mesh in the Outline of the Meshing window. Right click and select Generate Mesh. A coarse mesh is created. Select Unit Systems>>Metric (mm, kg, N …) from the bottom of the graphics window.

Figure 2.5a) Launching mesh

Figure 2.5b) Generating mesh

Figure 2.5c) Coarse mesh

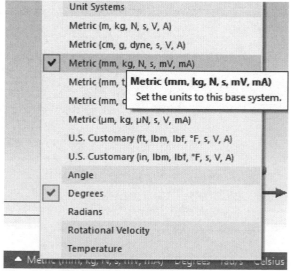

Figure 2.5d) Selection of units in graphics window

Select Mesh>> Controls>>Face Meshing from the menu. Click on the yellow region next to Geometry under Scope in Details of Face Meshing. Select the rectangle in the graphics window. Click on the Apply button for Geometry in Details of "Face Meshing". Select Mesh>>

Controls>>Sizing from the menu and select Edge  above the graphics window.

Figure 2.5e) Selection of face meshing    Figure 2.5f) Sizing

Select the upper longer horizontal edge of the rectangle, control select the lower horizontal edges and the vertical edges for a total of 5 edges. Click on Apply for the Geometry in "Details of Edge Sizing". Under Definition in "Details of Edge Sizing", select Element Size as Type, 1.0 mm for Element Size, and Hard as Behavior. Select the second Bias Type - - — —— and enter 12.0 as the Bias Factor.

Figure 2.5g) Details of edge sizing for three of the horizontal edges and the vertical edges

Repeat the selection of Mesh>>Controls>>Sizing from the menu once again but this time select the upper horizontal edge to the left of the origin. Enter the same Element Size, Behavior, and Bias Factor but the first Bias Type —— — - - . Click on Home>>Generate Mesh in the menu and select Mesh in the Outline. The finished mesh is shown in the graphics window.

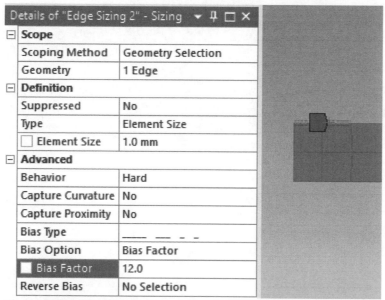

Figure 2.5h) Details of edge sizing for the remaining horizontal edge

Figure 2.5i) Details of finished mesh

---

**Why did we create a biased mesh?** The reason for using a biased mesh is that we need a finer mesh close to the wall where we have velocity gradients in the flow. We also included a finer mesh where the boundary layer starts to develop on the flat plate.

---

We are now going to rename the edges for the rectangle. Select the left edge of the rectangle, right click and select Create Named Selection. Enter *inlet* as the name and click on the OK button.

Repeat this step for the right vertical edge of the rectangle and enter the name *outlet*. Create a named selection for the lower longer horizontal right edge and call it *wall*. Finally, control-select the remaining three horizontal edges and name them *ideal wall*. An ideal wall is an adiabatic and frictionless wall.

Figure 2.5j) Named selections

Select File>>Export...>>Mesh>>FLUENT Input File>>Export from the menu. Select Save as type: FLUENT Input Files (*.msh). Enter "boundary-layer-mesh" as file name and click on the Save button. Select File>>Save Project from the menu. Name the project "Flat Plate Boundary Layer". Close the ANSYS Meshing window. Right click on Mesh in Project Schematic and select Update.

## F. Launching ANSYS Fluent

6. We are now going to double click on Setup under Project Schematic in ANSYS Workbench to open Fluent. Launch the Dimension 2D and Double Precision solver of Fluent. Check the Double Precision. Set the number of Solver Processes equal to the number of computer cores. To check the number of physical cores, press the Ctrl + Shift + Esc keys simultaneously to open the Task Manager. Go to the Performance tab and select CPU from the left column. You'll see the number of physical cores on the bottom-right side. Click on Show More Options. Write down the location of the working directory as you will use this information later. Click on the Start button to launch ANSYS Fluent.

> **Why do we use double precision?** Double precision will give more accurate calculations than single precision.

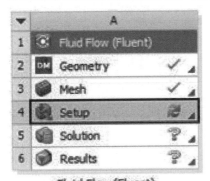

Fluid Flow (Fluent)

Figure 2.6a) Launching Setup

Figure 2.6b) Taskmanager

Figure 2.6c) Fluent Launcher

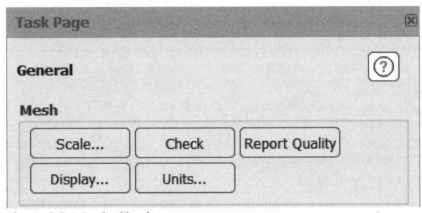

Figure 2.6d) Example of console printout for four cores

7. Check the scale of the mesh by selecting the Scale button under Mesh in General on the Task Page. Make sure that the Domain Extent is correct and close the Scale Mesh window.

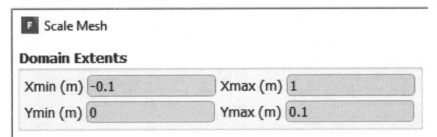

Figure 2.7a) Scale Check

**Scale Mesh**

**Domain Extents**

Xmin (m) -0.1          Xmax (m) 1
Ymin (m) 0             Ymax (m) 0.1

Figure 2.7b) Scale Mesh

8. Double click on Models and Viscous (SST k-omega). Select Laminar as Viscous Model. Click Ok to close the window. Double click on Boundary Conditions under Setup in the Outline View. Double click on *inlet* under Zone on the Task Page. Choose Components as Velocity Specification Method and set the X-Velocity (m/s) to 5. Click on the OK button to close the window. Double click on *ideal_wall* under Zones. Check Specified Shear as Shear Condition and keep zero values for specified shear stress since an ideal wall is frictionless. Click OK to close the window.

> **Why did we select Laminar as Viscous Model?** For the chosen free stream velocity 5 m/s the Reynolds number is less than 500,000 along the plate and the flow is therefore laminar. Turbulent from along a flat plate occurs at Reynolds numbers above 500,000.

Figure 2.8a) Viscous model

Figure 2.8b) Boundary Conditions for inlet

Figure 2.8c) Inlet velocity

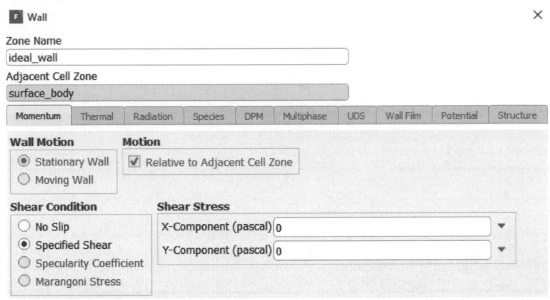

Figure 2.8d) Specified shear for ideal wall

9.  Double click on Methods under Solution in the Outline View. Select *Standard* for Pressure and *First Order Upwind* for Momentum. Double click on Reference Values under Setup in the Outline View. Select *Compute from inlet* on the Task Page.

Figure 2.9a) Solution Methods Task Page

> **Why do we use First Order Upwind method for Spatial Discretization of Momentum?** The First Order Upwind method is generally less accurate but converges better than the Second Order Upwind method. It is common practice to start with the First Order Upwind method at the beginning of calculations and continue with the Second Order Upwind method.

Figure 2.9b) Reference values

10. Double click on Initialization under Solution in the Outline View, select *Standard Initialization*, select *Compute from inlet*, and click on the *Initialize* button.

Figure 2.10 Solution Initialization

11. Double click on Monitors under Solution in the Outline View. Double click on Residual under Monitors and enter 1e-9 as *Absolute Criteria* for all Residuals. Click on the OK button to close the window.

Figure 2.11a) Residual monitors

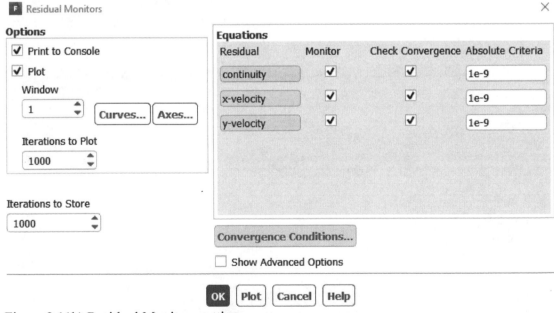

Figure 2.11b) Residual Monitors settings

**Why did we set the Absolute Criteria to 1e-9?** Generally, the lower the absolute criteria, the longer time the calculation will take and give a more exact solution. We see in Figure 2.12b) that the *x*-velocity and *y*-velocity equations have lower residuals than the continuity equation. The slopes of the residual curves for all three equations are about the same with a sharp downward trend.

12. Double click on Run Calculation under Solution and enter 5000 for *Number of Iterations*. Click on the *Calculate* button.

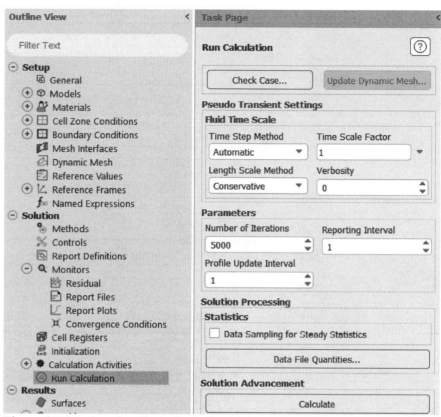

Figure 2.12a) Running the calculations

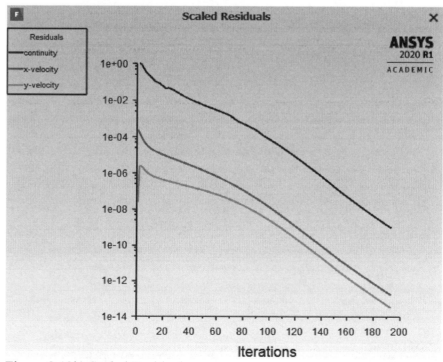

Figure 2.12b) Scaled Residuals

## G. Post-Processing

13. Select the Results tab in the menu and select Create>>Line/Rake under Surface. Enter 0.2 for x0 (m), 0.2 for x1 (m), 0 for y0 (m), and 0.02 m for y1 (m). Enter *x=0.2m* for the New Surface Name and click on Create. Repeat this step three more times and create vertical lines at x = 0.4m (length 0.04 m), x=0.6m (length 0.06 m), and x=0.8m (length 0.08 m). Close the window.

Figure 2.13a) Selecting Line/Rake from the Post-processing menu

Figure 2.13b) Line/Rake Surfaces at x=0.2 m and x=0.4m

14. Double click on Plots and XY Plot under Results in the Outline View. Uncheck Position on X Axis under Options and check Position on Y Axis. Set Plot Direction for X to 0 and 1 for Y. Select Velocity… and X Velocity as X Axis Function. Select the four surfaces x=0.2m, x=0.4m, x=0.6m, and x=0.8m.

Figure 2.14a) XY Plot setup

Figure 2.14b) Settings for Solution XY Plot

15. Click on the *Axes* button in the Solution XY Plot window. Select the X Axis, uncheck Auto Range under Options, enter 6 for Maximum Range, select general Type under Number Format and set Precision to 0. Click on the Apply button. Select the Y Axis, uncheck the Auto Range, enter 0.01 for Maximum Range, select general Type under Number Format, and click on the Apply button. Close the Axes window.

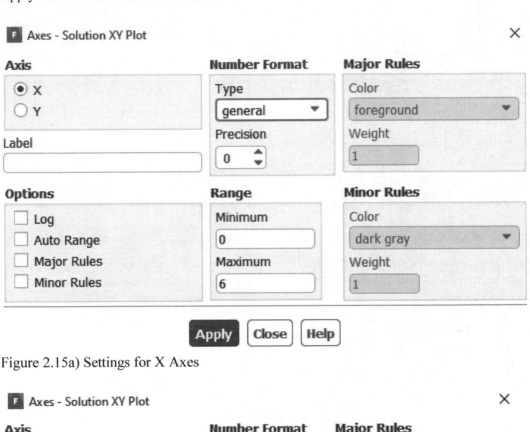

Figure 2.15a) Settings for X Axes

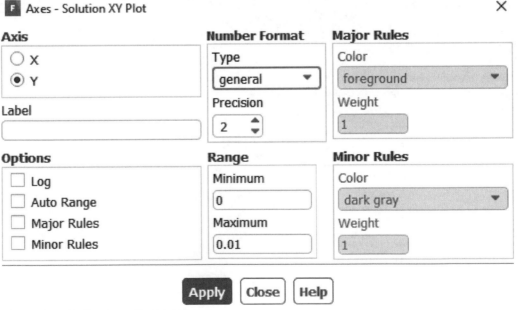

Figure 2.15b) Settings for Y Axes

16. Click on the Curves... button in the Solution XY Plot window. Select the first pattern under Line Style for Curve # 0. Select no Symbol for Marker Style and click on the Apply button.

Next select Curve # 1, select the next available Pattern for Line Style, no Symbol for Marker Style, and click on the Apply button. Continue this pattern of selection with the next two curves # 2 and # 3. Close the Curves – Solution XY Plot window. Click on the Save/Plot button in the Solution XY Plot window and close this window.

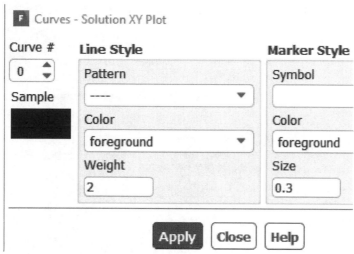

Figure 2.16a) Settings for curve # 0

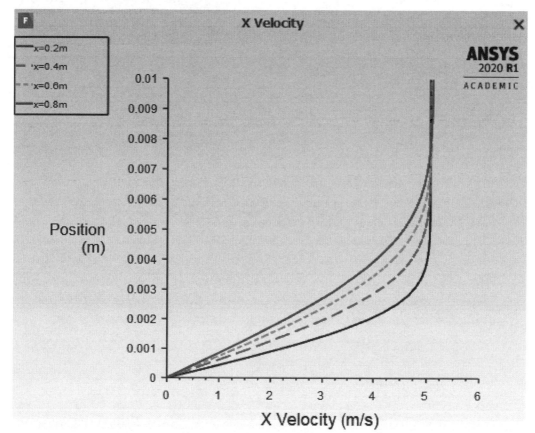

Figure 2.16b) Velocity profiles for a laminar boundary layer on a flat plate

Select the *User Defined* tab in the menu and *Custom*. Select a specific *Operand Field Functions* from the drop-down menu by selecting *Mesh...* and *Y-Coordinate*. Click on *Select* and enter the definition as shown in Figure 2.16e). You need to select *Mesh...* and *X-Coordinate* to complete the definition of the field function. Enter *eta* as *New Function Name*, click on *Define* and close the window.

Repeat this step to create another custom field function. This time, we select *Velocity...* and *X Velocity* as *Field Functions* and click on *Select*. Complete the *Definition* as shown in Figure 2.16f) and enter *u-divided-by-freestream-velocity* as *New Function Name*, click on *Define* and close the window.

Figure 2.16c) Custom Field Functions          Figure 2.16d) Operand Field Function

Figure 2.16e) Custom field function for self-similar coordinate

**Why did we create a self-similar coordinate?** It turns out that by using a self-similar coordinate, the velocity profiles at different streamwise positions will collapse on one self-similar velocity profile that is independent of the streamwise location.

Figure 2.16f) Custom field function for non-dimensional velocity

17. Double click on Plots and XY Plot under Results in the Outline View. Set X to 0 and Y to 1 as Plot Direction. Uncheck *Position on X Axis* and *Position on Y Axis* under *Options*. Select *Custom Field Functions* and *eta* for *Y Axis Function* and select *Custom Field Functions* and *u-divided-by-freestream-velocity* for *X Axis Function*.

    Place the file "*blasius.dat*" in your working directory. This file can be downloaded from *sdcpublications.com*. See Figure 2.19 for the Mathematica code that can be used to generate the theoretical Blasius velocity profile for laminar boundary layer flow over a flat plate. As an example, in this case the working directory is *C*:\Users\jmatsson. Click on *Load File*. Select Files of type: All Files (*) and select the file "*blasius.dat*" from your working directory. Select the four surfaces *x=0.2m, x=0.4m, x=0.6m, x=0.8m* and the loaded file *Theory*.

Figure 2.17a) Solution XY Plot for self-similar velocity profiles

Click on the Axes button. Select *Y Axis* in Axes-Solution XY Plot window and uncheck *Auto Range*. Set the *Minimum Range* to 0 and *Maximum Range* to 10. Set the Type to float and Precision to 0 under Number Format. Enter the Label as *eta* and click on *Apply*.

Select *X Axis* in Axes-Solution XY Plot window and enter the Label to *u/U*. Check the box for *Auto Range*. Set the Type to float and Precision to 1 under Number Format. Click on Apply and close the window.

Click on the Curves... button in the Solution XY Plot window. Select the first pattern under Line Style for Curve # 0. Select no Symbol for Marker Style and click on the Apply button.

Next select Curve # 1, select the next available Pattern for Line Style, no Symbol for Marker Style, and click on the Apply button. Continue this pattern of selection with the next two curves # 2 and # 3. Close the Curves – Solution XY Plot window. Click on the Save/Plot button in the Solution XY Plot window and close this window.

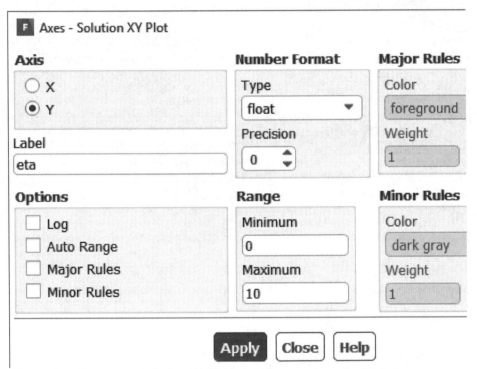

Figure 2.17b) Axes – Solution XY Plot window settings for Y Axis

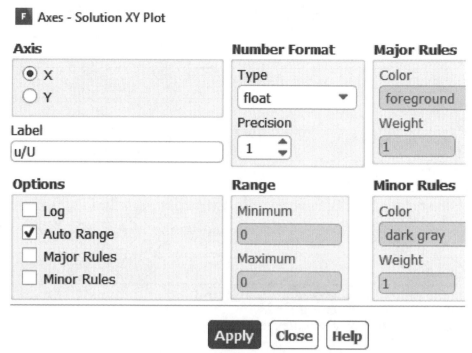

Figure 2.17c) Axes – Solution XY Plot window settings for X Axis

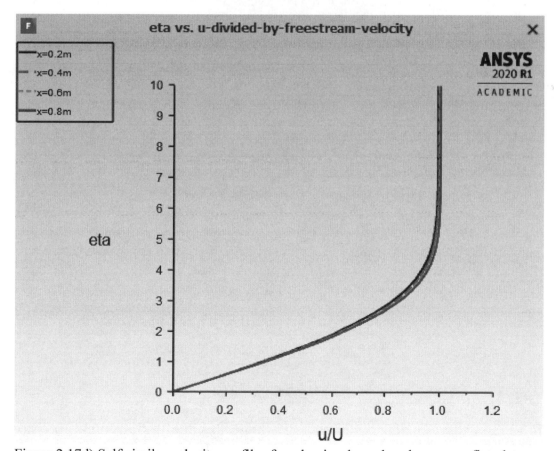

Figure 2.17d) Self-similar velocity profiles for a laminar boundary layer on a flat plate

Select the User Defined tab in the menu and Custom. Select a specific Operand Field Functions from the drop-down menu by selecting Mesh… and X-Coordinate. Click on Select and enter the definition as shown in Figure 2.17e). Enter *re-x* as New Function Name, click on Define and Close the window.

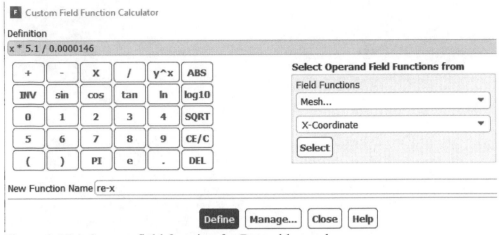

Figure 2.17e) Custom field function for Reynolds number

18. Double click on Plots and XY Plot under Results in the Outline View. Set X to 0 and Y to 1 under Plot Direction. Uncheck Position on X Axis and Position on Y Axis under Options. Select *Wall Fluxes* and *Skin Friction Coefficient* for Y Axis Function and select Custom Field Functions and *re-x* for X Axis Function.

Place the file "*Theoretical Skin Friction Coefficient*" in your working directory. Click on Load File. Select Files of type: All Files (*) and select the file "*Theoretical Skin Friction Coefficient*". Select *wall* under Surfaces and the loaded file Skin Friction under File Data. Click on the Axes button.

Figure 2.18a) Solution XY Plot for skin friction coefficient

Check the X Axis, check the box for Log under Options, enter Re-x as Label, uncheck Auto Range under Options, set Minimum to 100 and Maximum to 1000000. Set Type to float and Precision to 0 under Number Format and click on Apply.

Check the Y Axis, check the box for Log under Options, enter Cf-x as Label, uncheck Auto Range, set Minimum to 0.001 and Maximum to 0.1, set Type to float, Precision to 3 and click on Apply. Close the window. Click on Save/Plot in the Solution XY Plot window.

Click on the Curves… button in the Solution XY Plot window. Select the first pattern under Line Style for Curve # 0. Select no Symbol for Marker Style and click on the Apply button.

Next select Curve # 1, select the next available Pattern for Line Style, no Symbol for Marker Style, and click on the Apply button. Close the Curves – Solution XY Plot window. Click on the Save/Plot button in the Solution XY Plot window and close this window.

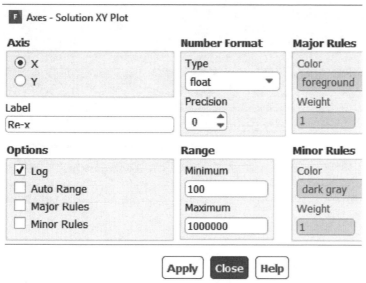

Figure 2.18b) Axes – Solution XY Plot window settings for X Axis

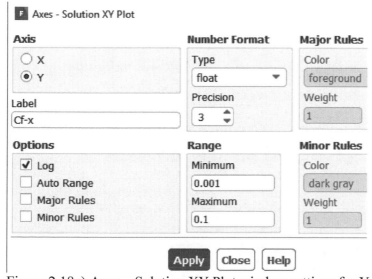

Figure 2.18c) Axes – Solution XY Plot window settings for Y Axis

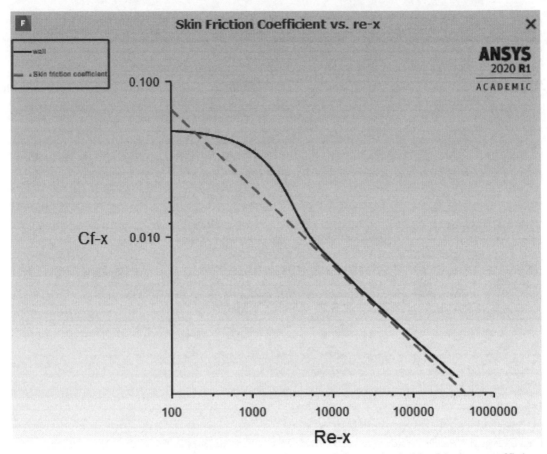

Figure 2.18d) Comparison between ANSYS Fluent and theoretical skin friction coefficient (dashed line) for laminar boundary layer flow on a flat plate

## H. Theory

19. In this chapter we have compared ANSYS Fluent velocity profiles with the theoretical Blasius velocity profile for laminar flow on a flat plate. We transformed the wall normal coordinate to a similarity coordinate for comparison of profiles at different streamwise locations. The similarity coordinate is defined by

$$\eta = y\sqrt{\frac{U}{\nu x}} \qquad (2.1)$$

where $y$ (m) is the wall normal coordinate, $U$ (m/s) is the free stream velocity, $x$ (m) is the distance from the streamwise origin of the wall and $\nu$ (m$^2$/s) is the kinematic viscosity of the fluid.

We also used the non-dimensional streamwise velocity $u/U$ where $u$ is the dimensional velocity profile. $u/U$ was plotted versus $\eta$ for ANSYS Fluent velocity profiles in comparison with the Blasius theoretical profile and they all collapsed on the same curve as per definition of self-similarity. The Blasius boundary layer equation is given by

$$f'''(\eta) + \frac{1}{2}f(\eta)f''(\eta) = 0 \tag{2.2}$$

with the following boundary conditions

$$f(0) = f'(0) = 0, f'(\infty) = 0 \tag{2.3}$$

The Reynolds number for the flow on a flat plat is defined as

$$Re_x = \frac{Ux}{\nu} \tag{2.4}$$

The boundary layer thickness $\delta$ is defined as the distance from the wall to the location where the velocity in the boundary layer has reached 99% of the free stream value. For a laminar boundary-layer we have the following theoretical expression for the variation of the boundary layer thickness with streamwise distance $x$ and Reynolds number $Re_x$.

$$\delta = \frac{4.91x}{\sqrt{Re_x}} \tag{2.5}$$

The corresponding expression for the boundary layer thickness in a turbulent boundary layer is given by

$$\delta = \frac{0.16x}{Re_x^{1/7}} \tag{2.6}$$

The local skin friction coefficient is defined as the local wall shear stress divided by dynamic pressure.

$$C_{f,x} = \frac{\tau_w}{\frac{1}{2}\rho U^2} \tag{2.7}$$

The theoretical local friction coefficient for laminar flow is determined by

$$C_{f,x} = \frac{0.664}{\sqrt{Re_x}} \qquad Re_x < 5 \cdot 10^5 \tag{2.8}$$

and for turbulent flow we have the following relation

$$C_{f,x} = \frac{0.027}{Re_x^{1/7}} \qquad 5 \cdot 10^5 < Re_x < 10^7 \tag{2.9}$$

```
sol = NDSolve[{f'''[η] + 0.5 f[η] f''[η] == 0, f[0] == f'[0] == 0, f'[10] == 1}, f, η];
myplot = Plot[f'[η] /. First[sol], {η, 0, 10}, AxesLabel → {"u/U", "η"}];
axisFlip # /. {x_Line | x_GraphicsComplex :> MapAt[#~Reverse~2 &, x, 1],
      x : (PlotRange → _) :> x~Reverse~2} &;
myplot // axisFlip

SetDirectory["C:\\Users\\jmatsson"];
mylist = Table[{f'[η] /. First[sol], η}, {η, 0, 10, 0.5}];
TableOfValues1 = Prepend[mylist, {""}];
TableOfValues1 = Prepend[TableOfValues1, {"((xy/key/label \"Blasius profile\")"}];
TableOfValues1 = Prepend[TableOfValues1, {""}];
TableOfValues1 = Prepend[TableOfValues1, {"(labels \"X Velocity\" \"η-Coordinate\")"}];
TableOfValues1 = Prepend[TableOfValues1, {"(title \"Theory\")"}];
TableOfValues1 = Append[TableOfValues1, {")"}];
Grid[TableOfValues1]
Export["blasius.dat", TableOfValues1]
```

Figure 2.19 Mathematica code for theoretical Blasius laminar boundary layer

## I. References

1. Çengel, Y. A., and Cimbala J.M., Fluid Mechanics Fundamentals and Applications, 1st Edition, McGraw-Hill, 2006.
2. Richards, S., Cimbala, J.M., Martin, K., ANSYS Workbench Tutorial – Boundary Layer on a Flat Plate, Penn State University, 18 May 2010 Revision.
3. Schlichting, H., and Gersten, K., Boundary Layer Theory, 8th Revised and Enlarged Edition, Springer, 2001.
4. White, F. M., Fluid Mechanics, 4th Edition, McGraw-Hill, 1999.

## J. Exercises

2.1 Use the results from the ANSYS Fluent simulation in this chapter to determine the boundary layer thickness at the streamwise positions as shown in the table below. Fill in the missing information in the table. $U_\delta$ is the velocity of the boundary layer at the distance from the wall equal to the boundary layer thickness and $U$ is the free stream velocity.

| $x$ (m) | $\delta$ (mm) Fluent | $\delta$ (mm) Theory | Percent Difference | $U_\delta$ (m/s) | $U$ (m/s) | $\nu$ (m²/s) | $Re_x$ |
|---|---|---|---|---|---|---|---|
| 0.2 | | | | | | .0000146 | |
| 0.4 | | | | | | .0000146 | |
| 0.6 | | | | | | .0000146 | |
| 0.8 | | | | | | .0000146 | |

Table 2.1 Comparison between Fluent and theory for boundary layer thickness

2.2 Change the element size to 2 mm for the mesh and compare the results in XY Plots of the skin friction coefficient versus Reynolds number with the element size 1 mm that was used in this chapter. Compare your results with theory.

2.3 Change the free stream velocity to 3 m/s and create an XY Plot including velocity profiles at $x = 0.1, 0.3, 0.5, 0.7$ and $0.9$ m. Create another XY Plot with self-similar velocity profiles for this lower free stream velocity and create an XY Plot for the skin friction coefficient versus Reynolds number.

2.4 Use the results from the ANSYS Fluent simulation in Exercise 2.3 to determine the boundary layer thickness at the streamwise positions as shown in the table below. Fill in the missing information in the table. $U_\delta$ is the velocity of the boundary layer at the distance from the wall equal to the boundary layer thickness and $U$ is the free stream velocity.

| $x$ (m) | $\delta$ (mm) Fluent | $\delta$ (mm) Theory | Percent Difference | $U_\delta$ (m/s) | $U$ (m/s) | $\nu$ (m$^2$/s) | $Re_x$ |
|---|---|---|---|---|---|---|---|
| 0.1 | | | | | | .0000146 | |
| 0.2 | | | | | | .0000146 | |
| 0.5 | | | | | | .0000146 | |
| 0.7 | | | | | | .0000146 | |
| 0.9 | | | | | | .0000146 | |

Table 2.2 Comparison between Fluent and theory for boundary layer thickness

**K. Notes**

## CHAPTER 3.  FLOW PAST A CYLINDER

### A.  Objectives

- Using ANSYS Workbench to Model the Cylinder and Mesh
- Inserting Boundary Conditions and Free Stream Velocity
- Running ANSYS Fluent Simulation for Laminar Transient 2D Planar Flow
- Using FFT Analysis, Velocity, Pressure and Vorticity Plots for Visualizations

### B.  Problem Description

We will study the flow of air past a cylinder and we will analyze the problem using ANSYS Fluent. The diameter of the cylinder is 50 mm and the free stream velocity is 0.06 m/s.

### C.  Launching ANSYS Workbench and Selecting Fluent

1. Start by launching ANSYS Workbench. Double click on Fluid Flow (Fluent) that is located under Analysis Systems in the Toolbox.

Figure 3.1 Selecting Fluid Flow (Fluent)

**D. Launching ANSYS DesignModeler**

2. Select Geometry under Project Schematic in ANSYS Workbench. Right-click on Geometry and select Properties. Select 2D Analysis Type under Advanced Geometry Options in Properties of Schematic A2: Geometry. Right-click on Geometry under Project Schematic and select to launch New DesignModeler Geometry. Select Units>>Millimeter as the length unit from the menu in DesignModeler.

Figure 3.2a) Selecting Geometry

| | A | | B |
|---|---|---|---|
| 1 | Property | | Value |
| 2 | General | | |
| 3 | Component ID | | Geometry |
| 4 | Directory Name | | FFF |
| 5 | Notes | | |
| 6 | Notes | | |
| 7 | Used Licenses | | |
| 8 | Last Update Used Licenses | | |
| 9 | Basic Geometry Options | | |
| 10 | Solid Bodies | | ☑ |
| 11 | Surface Bodies | | ☑ |
| 12 | Line Bodies | | ☐ |
| 13 | Parameters | | Independent |
| 14 | Parameter Key | | ANS;DS |
| 15 | Attributes | | ☐ |
| 16 | Named Selections | | ☐ |
| 17 | Material Properties | | ☐ |
| 18 | Advanced Geometry Options | | |
| 19 | Analysis Type | | 2D |
| 20 | Use Associativity | | 3D |
| 21 | Import Coordinate Systems | | 2D |

Figure 3.2b) Selecting 2D Analysis Type

Figure 3.2c) Launching DesignModeler

Figure 3.2d) Selecting the length unit

3.  Next, we will be creating the geometry for the simulation. Select XYPlane from the Tree Outline on the left-hand side. Select Look at Sketch [ ]. Click on the Sketching tab in the Tree Outline, select the Draw tab within the Sketching options, and select the Circle sketch tool.

Figure 3.3a) Selection of XYPlane

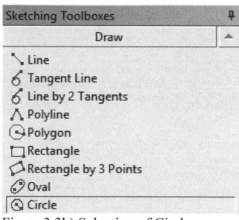

Figure 3.3b) Selection of Circle

Draw a circle centered at the origin of the coordinate system in the graphics window. Make sure that you move the cursor so that you get the letter $P$ in the graphics window indicating that your circle will be centered at the origin. Select the Dimensions tab within the Sketching options and select Diameter. Click on the circle in the graphics window and enter 50 mm for the diameter D1 under Dimensions:1 in Details View.

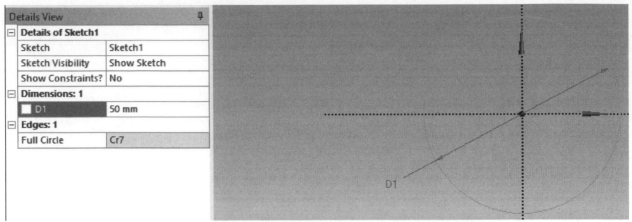

Figure 3.3c) Circle with dimension

Click on the Modeling tab in the Tree Outline and select Concepts>>Surfaces from Sketches from the menu. Click on the circle in the graphics window and select Apply as Base Objects in Details View. Click on Generate . The circle turns gray.

Figure 3.3d) Surfaces from Sketches          Figure 3.3e) Applying Base Objects

Click on the Modeling tab in the Tree Outline and select the XYPlane. Click on New Sketch . Select Rectangle by 3 Points from the Sketching tools. Click anywhere outside of the circle in the upper left corner (2$^{nd}$ quadrant) of the graphics window, followed by clicking anywhere outside of the circle in the lower left corner (3$^{rd}$ quadrant) of the graphics window (make sure you have a *V* before clicking), and finally click in the right-hand plane outside of the circle (4$^{th}$ quadrant).

Select the Dimensions tab under Sketching Toolboxes, select Horizontal and click on the vertical edges of the rectangle. Enter 1575 mm as the horizontal length of the rectangle. Select the vertical axis and the vertical edge of the rectangle on the left-hand side. Enter 575 mm as the length. Select the Vertical dimensioning tool and click on the horizontal edges of the rectangle. Enter 1250 mm as the vertical length of the rectangle. Click on the horizontal axis and the lower horizontal edge of the rectangle. Enter 625 mm as the length. Right-click in the graphics window and select Zoom to Fit.

Figure 3.3f) Applying Base Objects

Select Concept>>Surface from Sketches from the menu. Click on Sketch2 in the Tree Outline and select Apply for Base Objects in Details View. Select Operation>>Add Frozen in Details View followed by Generate.

| Details of SurfaceSk2 | |
|---|---|
| Surface From Sketches | SurfaceSk? |
| Base Objects | 1 Sketch |
| Operation | Add Frozen |
| Orient With Plane Normal? | Yes |
| Thickness (>=0) | 0 mm |

Figure 3.3g) Add frozen operation

Select Create>>Boolean from the menu. Select Subtract Operation from the Details View. Click on the mesh region around the cylinder in the graphics window and click on Apply as Target Bodies. Select the Cylinder as the Tool Body, see Figure 3.3j), and click on Generate.

Figure 3.3h) Creating a Boolean

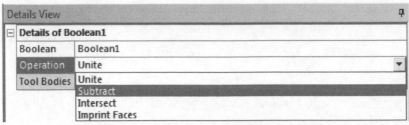

Figure 3.3i) Selecting a subtracting operation

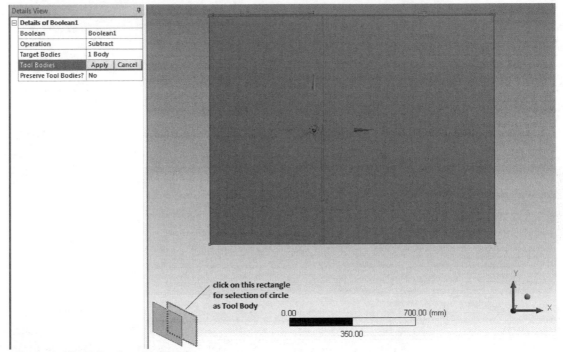

Figure 3.3j) Selecting tool body

Figure 3.3k) Mesh region around cylinder

4.  Select *XYPlane* in the Tree Outline and create a New Sketch . Select the Sketching tab and select Line under the Draw tab. Draw a vertical line in the mesh region from top to bottom to the left of the cylinder. Make sure you have a *C* when you start the line, a *V* indicating that the line is vertical and another *C* at the end of the line. The vertical line will intersect the entire mesh region. Position the line 75 mm from the vertical axis.

    Select Concepts>>Lines from Sketches from the menu. Select from the graphics window the newly created vertical line and Apply it as a Base Object in Details View. Click on Generate. Create another sketch in the *XYPlane* with a vertical line 75 mm to the right of the vertical axis and repeat all the different steps as listed above.

    Finally, repeat these steps two more times with one line from left to right intersecting the mesh region and positioned 75 mm above the cylinder and another line positioned 75 mm below the cylinder.

Figure 3.4a) First vertical line located 75 mm from the vertical axis

Figure 3.4b) Lines from sketches

55

Figure 3.4c) Lines added to the mesh region

Select Tools>>Projection from the menu. Select Edges on Face as type in Details View. Control-select all 12 line-segments for the 4 lines that you have created and Apply as the Edges in the Details View. Select the mesh region and Apply it as the Target under Details View. Click Generate.

Figure 3.4d) Selection of the projection tool

You should now have 9 different regions for meshing. Select File>>Save Project from the menu and save the project with the name "Cylinder Flow Study". Close DesignModeler.

## E. Launching ANSYS Meshing

5.  Next, we will be creating the mesh around the cylinder. We are now going to double click on Mesh in Project Schematic to open the Meshing window.

Figure 3.5a) Launching mesh

Select Mesh under Model (A3) in Project under Outline on the left-hand side. Select Mesh>> Controls>>Face Meshing from the menu. Control-select all 9 faces of the mesh. Apply the Geometry under Details of "Face Meshing".

Figure 3.5b) Selection of face meshing

Figure 3.5c) Details of face meshing

57

Select Mesh>>Controls>>Sizing from the menu, right-click in the graphics window and select Cursor Mode>>Edge. Control-select the three edges to the left and bottom of the mesh region as shown in Figure 3.5d). Apply the Geometry under Details of "Edge Sizing". Select Number of Divisions as Type under Details of "Edge Sizing". Set the Number of Divisions to 100. Set the Behavior to Hard. Select the Bias Type at the top from the drop-down menu. Enter a Bias Factor of 10.

Figure 3.5d) Details for first mesh sizing

Select Mesh>>Controls>>Sizing from the menu. Control-select the three edges to the right and bottom of the mesh region as shown in Figure 3.5e). Apply the Geometry under Details of "Edge Sizing". Select Number of Divisions as Type under Details of "Edge Sizing". Set the Number of Divisions to 150. Set the Behavior to Hard. Select the second Bias Type from the drop-down menu. Enter a Bias Factor of 10.

Figure 3.5e) Details for second mesh sizing

Select Mesh>>Controls>>Sizing from the menu. Select the horizontal upper left edge. Apply the Geometry under Details of "Edge Sizing". Select Number of Divisions as Type under Details of "Edge Sizing". Set the Number of Divisions to 100. Set the Behavior to Hard. Select the second Bias Type from the drop-down menu. Enter a Bias Factor of 10, see Figure 3.5f).

Figure 3.5f) Details for third mesh sizing

Select Mesh>>Controls>>Sizing from the menu. Select the upper horizontal right edge. Apply the Geometry under Details of "Edge Sizing". Select Number of Divisions as Type under Details of "Edge Sizing". Set the Number of Divisions to 150. Set the Behavior to Hard. Select the first Bias Type from the drop-down menu. Enter a Bias Factor of 10, see Figure 3.5g).

Figure 3.5g) Details for fourth mesh sizing

Select Mesh>>Controls>>Sizing from the menu. Control-select the 8 short edges around the cylinder and on the edges as shown in Figure 3.5h). Apply the Geometry under Details of "Edge Sizing". Select Number of Divisions as Type under Details of "Edge Sizing". Set the number of Divisions to 50. Set the Behavior to Hard.

Figure 3.5h) Details for fifth mesh sizing

Select Mesh>>Controls>>Sizing from the menu. Control-select the four edges as shown in Figure 3.5i). Apply the Geometry under Details of "Edge Sizing". Select Number of Divisions as Type under Details of "Edge Sizing". Set the Number of Divisions to 100. Set the Behavior to Hard. Select the first Bias Type from the drop-down menu. Enter a Bias Factor of 20.

Figure 3.5i) Details for sixth mesh sizing

Select Mesh>>Control>>Sizing from the menu. Control-select the four edges as shown in Figure 3.5j). Apply the Geometry under Details of "Edge Sizing". Select Number of Divisions as Type under Details of "Edge Sizing". Set the Number of Divisions to 100. Set the Behavior to Hard. Select the second Bias Type from the drop-down menu. Enter a Bias Factor of 20.
Right click on Mesh in the tree outline and select Generate Mesh.

Figure 3.5j) Details for seventh mesh sizing

Figure 3.5k) Finished mesh close to the cylinder

> **Why do we use a biased mesh?** A biased mesh enables us to create a finer mesh closer to the cylinder. This way we create a fine mesh where it is needed the most and the calculation time will be much shorter compared with a finer mesh in the whole mesh region.

6.  Select Geometry in the outline. Select the Edge Selection filter ![icon]. Control-select the 3 vertical edges on the right-hand side, right click and select Create Named Selection. Name the edges "outlet" and click OK. Name the 3 vertical edges to the left "inlet" and the edge of the cylinder with the name "cylinder". Name the 6 horizontal edges (3 at the top and 3 at the bottom) "symmetry".

Figure 3.6a) Named selections

Open Geometry in the outline, select Line Body, and select Thermal Fluid as Model Type in Details of "Line Body". In Geometry, right click the Line Body and select Suppress Body.

| Details of "Line Body" | ▾ ┨ ☐ ✕ |
|---|---|
| ⊞ **Graphics Properties** | |
| ⊟ **Definition** | |
| ☐ Suppressed | Yes |
| Coordinate System | Default Coordinate System |
| Cross Section | |
| Offset Mode | Refresh on Update |
| Offset Type | Centroid |
| Model Type | Thermal Fluid |
| Fluid Cross Area | 0. m² |
| Fluid Discretization | Upwind/Linear |
| Reference Frame | Lagrangian |
| ⊟ **Material** | |
| Assignment | |
| Fluid/Solid | Defined By Geometry (Solid) |
| ⊞ **Bounding Box** | |
| ⊞ **Properties** | |
| ⊞ **Statistics** | |

Figure 3.6b) Details of Line Body

Select File>>Export>>Mesh >>FLUENT Input File>>Export from the menu. Enter the name *cylinder-flow-mesh* and select FLUENT Input Files (*,msh) as Save as Type. Select File>>Save Project… from the menu. Close the meshing window. Right click on Mesh under Project Schematic in ANSYS Workbench and select Update.

> **Why do we export the mesh?** When we save the mesh file, we can read the mesh using standalone mode directly in ANSYS Fluent without having to design the mesh all over again each time that we run the simulation for various flow variables.

## F. Launching ANSYS Fluent

7. Double click Setup under Project Schematic in ANSYS Workbench. Check the Options box for Double Precision. Set the number of Solver Processes equal to the number of computer cores. To check the number of physical cores, press the Ctrl + Shift + Esc keys simultaneously to open the Task Manager. Select the Performance tab and select CPU from the left column.
You'll see the number of physical cores on the bottom-right side. Click on Show More Options. You can see the location of your working directory. Click OK to launch Fluent. Select Transient Time under General on the Task Page on the left-hand side.

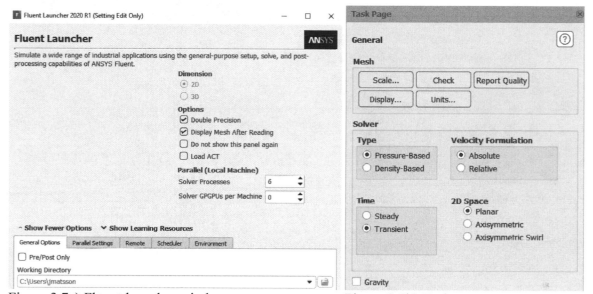

Figure 3.7a) Fluent launcher window          Figure 3.7b) Task page

> **Why do we use the Pressure-Based Solver?** The pressure-based solver is usually being used for incompressible flows such as the flow past a cylinder at low Reynolds numbers.

> **Why do we use a planar 2D Space study?** The plane 2D Space study is done under the assumption that the cylinder is infinitely long such that there is no variation of the flow along the length of the cylinder.

8. Double click on Models and Viscous (SST k-omega) under Setup in the Outline View. Select Laminar as Viscous Model. Click OK to close the window. Double click on Boundary Conditions under Setup in the Outline View. Double click on *inlet* under Zone on the Task Page.

> **Why do we use a Transient study and the Laminar model?** The flow past a cylinder is time dependent at the Reynolds number that we are using in this chapter. Vortex shedding will occur behind the cylinder and we are interested in determining the frequency and Strouhal number for the vortex shedding process. The Reynolds number is not sufficiently high to have turbulent flow and therefore we choose the Laminar as Viscous model in this case.

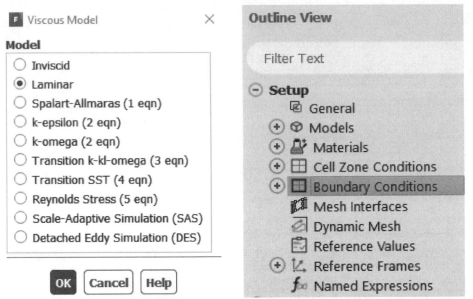

Figure 3.8a) Viscous model          Figure 3.8b) Defining boundary conditions

Select Components as Velocity Specification Method. Enter 0.06 m/s as X-Velocity. Click OK to close the Velocity Inlet window. Double-click on Methods in the Outline View under Solution. Set the Pressure-Velocity Coupling Scheme to PISO. Uncheck the box for Skewness-Neighbor Coupling. Select Green-Gauss Cell Based Gradient under Spatial Discretization.

Figure 3.8c) Velocity inlet boundary condition

**Why do we choose PISO as Pressure-Velocity Coupling Scheme?** PISO is used for transient solutions.

Figure 3.8d) Settings for solution methods

9. Double-click on Initialization in the Outline View under Solution. Select Standard Initialization under Solution Initialization on the Task Page and enter 0.06 for X-Velocity (m/s). Click on Initialize.

   Double-click on Reference Values under Setup in the Outline View. Select Compute from inlet from the drop-down menu. Set the value for Area (m2) to 0.05 and Length (m) to the same value. Select *solid-surface_body* as Reference Zone.

   Double-click on Report Definitions under Solution in the Outline View. Select New>>Force Report>>Lift… from the drop-down menu. Select Lift Coefficient as Report Output Type and set the Force Vector to X 0, Y 1 and Z 1. Select cylinder as Wall Zone. Check the boxes for Report File, Report Plot and Print to Console under Create. Click on the OK button to close the Lift Report Definition window. Close the Report Definitions window.

Figure 3.9a) Solution initialization

Figure 3.9b) Reference values

Figure 3.9c) New Force Report

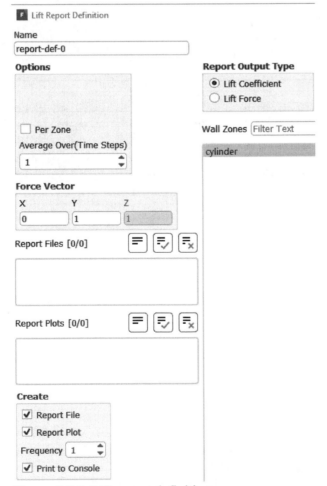

Figure 3.9d) Lift report definition

Double-click on Run Calculation under Solution on the left-hand side in the Outline View. Enter 0.2 for the Time Step Size (s) and 600 for number of Time Steps. Enter 30 for Max Iterations/Time Step and click on Calculate.

> **Why do we choose 0.2 s as Time Step Size?** The Time Step Size must be sufficiently small to resolve the wave form of the time signal as shown in Figure 3.9f).

Figure 3.9e) Calculation settings

Figure 3.9f) Scaled residuals

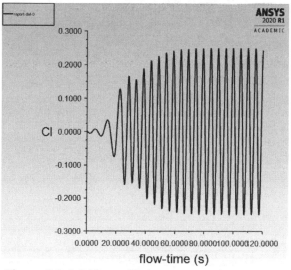

Figure 3.9g) Lift coefficient versus time

## G. Post-Processing

10. Open Plots under Results in the Outline View. Double-click on FFT. Select Load Input File in the Fourier Transform window. Select the file with the name "report-def-0-rfile.out" and click OK. Select Axes… at the bottom of the Fourier Transform window. Select Y axis, set Type to float and Precision to 1 as Number Format. Click on Apply and Close the Axes – Fourier Transform window. Click on Plot FFT in the Fourier Transform window. Check the box for Write FFT to File under Options in the Fourier Transform window and click on the Write FFT button. Save the file with All Files (*) as file type and the name "*fft-data*" in the working directory. This file can be opened in Notepad, see Figure 3.10d). The power spectral density maximum is at 0.2 Hz. The power spectral density shows the variation of power in the different frequencies that makes up the time signal and it is based on the mathematical theory for Fourier analysis.

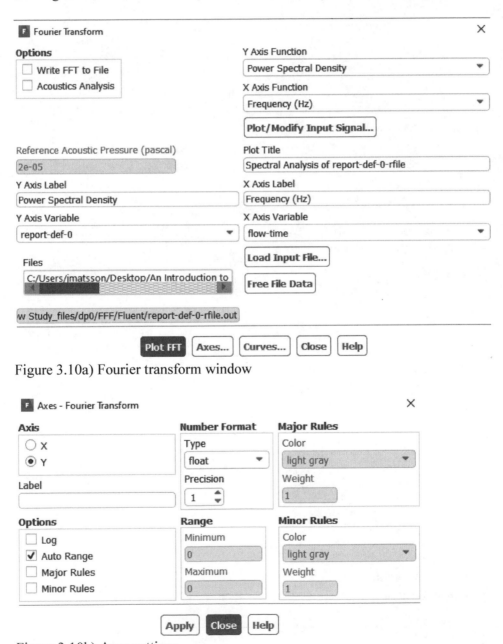

Figure 3.10a) Fourier transform window

Figure 3.10b) Axes settings

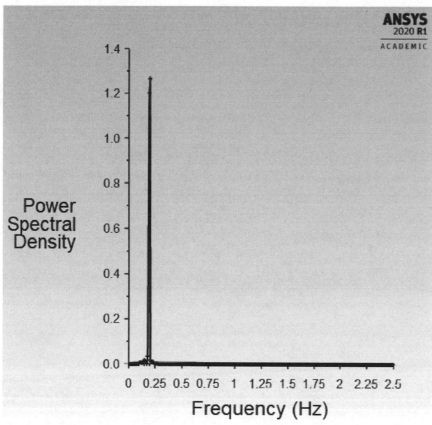

Figure 3.10c) Plot of power spectral density versus frequency

```
fft-data - Notepad
File  Edit  Format  View  Help
(title "Spectral Analysis of report-def-0-rfile")
(labels "Frequency (Hz)" "Power Spectral Density")

((xy/key/label "report-def-0")
8.3194673e-03    1.4787889e-05
1.6638935e-02    2.9278910e-05
2.4958402e-02    3.3112065e-05
3.3277869e-02    2.8574532e-05
4.1597337e-02    4.4784781e-05
4.9916804e-02    1.3838832e-04
5.8236271e-02    2.6973721e-04
6.6555738e-02    2.6485429e-04
7.4875206e-02    9.2931710e-05
8.3194673e-02    2.4445311e-04
9.1514140e-02    1.6314491e-03
9.9833608e-02    4.5275553e-03
1.0815307e-01    7.2578583e-03
1.1647254e-01    7.0704320e-03
1.2479201e-01    4.4357637e-03
1.3311148e-01    4.7372920e-03
1.4143094e-01    1.0639108e-02
1.4975041e-01    1.6352594e-02
1.5806988e-01    1.4479918e-02
1.6638935e-01    6.1218636e-03
1.7470881e-01    4.6911958e-04
1.8302828e-01    3.4843225e-02
1.9134775e-01    1.2007430e+00
1.9966722e-01    1.2653939e+00
2.0798668e-01    1.7123464e-02
2.1630615e-01    9.9544134e-03
2.2462562e-01    1.0607040e-02
2.3294508e-01    8.6749792e-03
```

Figure 3.10d) Data for plot in figure 3.10c)

Double-click on Contours in Graphics under Results in the Outline View. Enter *static-pressure* as Contour Name in the Contours window. Select Contours of Pressure… and Static Pressure. De-select all Surfaces and click on Save/Display.

Figure 3.10e) Contours plot of pressure

Select Contours of Velocity and Vorticity Magnitude. Enter vorticity-magnitude as Contour Name in the Contours window. De-select all surfaces and click on Save/Display.

Figure 3.10f) Contour plot of vorticity

Find the coefficient of drag by double-clicking on Reports under Results in the Outline View. Double-click on Forces under Reports. Click Print and write down the value for the total drag coefficient that you have calculated: 1.1663.

```
Forces - Direction Vector (1 0 0)
                         Forces (n)                                   Coefficients
Zone                     Pressure         Viscous          Total      Pressure         Viscous          Total
cylinder                 0.00010445281    2.412938e-05     0.00012858219  0.94741777    0.21886059       1.1662784
-----------------------  ---------------  ---------------  ---------------  ---------------  ---------------  ---------
Net                      0.00010445281    2.412938e-05     0.00012858219  0.94741777    0.21886059       1.1662784
```

Figure 3.10g) Forces and coefficients

## H. Theory

11. We determine the Reynolds number for the flow around the cylinder as

$$Re = Ud/v = 0.06 * 0.050 / 1.5 * 10^{-5} = 200 \tag{3.1}$$

where $U$ is the magnitude of the free stream velocity, $d$ is the diameter of the cylinder, and $v$ is the kinematic viscosity of air at room temperature. The drag coefficient from experiments for a smooth cylinder is found using the following curve-fit formula:

$$C_{D,Exp} = 1 + \frac{10}{Re^{2/3}} = 1.29 \qquad 0 \le Re \le 250,000 \tag{3.2}$$

The difference between ANSYS Fluent results from Figure 3.10g) and experiments for the drag coefficient is 10%.

The Strouhal number $S$ is one of the many non-dimensional numbers used in fluid mechanics and based on the oscillation frequency of fluid flows. In this case the Strouhal number is based on the vortex shedding frequency $f$ as shown in Figures 3.10c), 3.10d) and can be defined as

$$S = \frac{fd}{U} = \frac{0.2Hz*0.050m}{0.06 \, m/s} = 0.167 \tag{3.3}$$

This value of the Strouhal number from ANSYS Fluent can be compared with DNS (Direct Numerical Simulation) results by Henderson[3], see also Williamson and Brown[6]. The difference is 15%.

$$S_{DNS} = 0.2698 - \frac{1.0272}{\sqrt{Re}} = 0.1968 \tag{3.4}$$

## I. References

1. Cimbala, J.M., Fluent-Laminar Flow over a cylinder, Penn State University, 29 January 2008.
2. Flow Over a Cylinder, Fluent Inc., FlowLab 1.2, April 16, 2007.
3. Henderson, R., Nonlinear dynamics and pattern formation in turbulent wake transition, J. of Fluid Mech., 352, (65-112), 1997.
4. Tutorial 6. Flow Past a Circular Cylinder. Fluent Inc. January 17, 2007.
5. Validation 3. Laminar Flow Around a Circular Cylinder, Fluent Inc. September 13, 2002.
6. Williamson, C. H. K., and Brown G.L., A series in $1/\sqrt{Re}$ to represent the Strouhal-Reynolds number relationship of the cylinder wake, Journal of Fluids and Structures, 12, (1073 – 1085), 1998.

## J. Exercises

3.1 Rerun the simulation with the same free stream velocity and Reynolds number and the same mesh but use a Time Step Size of 0.25 s and 500 as the Number of Time Steps. Set Max Iterations /Time Step to 30. Determine the drag coefficient and compare with equation (3.1). Determine the Strouhal number and compare with equation (3.4). Include plots of the lift coefficient over time and power spectral density versus frequency.

3.2 Rerun the simulation shown in this chapter for a lower free stream 0.05 m/s but with the same mesh and for the same diameter 0.05 m of the cylinder. Use the same Time Step Size, Number of Time Steps and Max Iterations/Time Step as in this chapter. Determine the Reynolds number. Determine the drag coefficient and compare with equation (3.1). Determine the Strouhal number and compare with equation (3.4). Include plots of the lift coefficient over time and power spectral density versus frequency. Also, include contour plots of static pressure, vorticity and velocity magnitude.

3.3 Rerun the simulation shown in this chapter for the free stream velocities as shown in Table 2.1 with the same mesh and for the same diameter 0.05 m of the cylinder. Use the same Time Step Size, Number of Time Steps and Max Iterations/Time Step as in this chapter. Determine the drag coefficients and compare with equation (3.1). Determine the Strouhal numbers and compare with equation (3.4).

| $U$ (m/s) | $f$ (Hz) | $Re$ | $C_{D,Exp}$ | $C_{D,Fluent}$ | Percent Diff. | $S_{DNS}$ | $S_{Fluent}$ | Percent ifference |
|---|---|---|---|---|---|---|---|---|
| 0.00006 | | 0.2 | | | | | | |
| 0.0006 | | 2 | | | | | | |
| 0.006 | | 20 | | | | | | |
| 0.06 | 0.2 | 200 | 1.29 | 1.1663 | 10 | 0.1968 | 0.167 | 15 |
| 0.6 | | 2000 | | | | | | |
| 6 | | 20000 | | | | | | |
| 60 | | 200000 | | | | | | |

Table 3.1 Comparison between Fluent and theory for boundary layer thickness

3.4 Rerun the simulation shown in this chapter for the flow around a square with a size of 50 mm x 50 mm. Use the same Time Step Size, Number of Time Steps and Max Iterations/Time Step as in this chapter. Determine the Reynolds number. Determine the drag coefficient and the Strouhal number. Include plots of the lift coefficient over time and power spectral density versus frequency. Also, include contour plots of static pressure, vorticity and velocity magnitude.

(mm)

0.06 m/s

50

50

3.5 Rerun the simulation shown in this chapter for the flow around an equilateral triangle with a side length of 50 mm. Use the same Time Step Size, Number of Time Steps and Max Iterations/Time Step as in this chapter. Determine the Reynolds number. Determine the drag coefficient and the Strouhal number. Include plots of the lift coefficient over time and power spectral density versus frequency. Also, include contour plots of static pressure, vorticity and velocity magnitude.

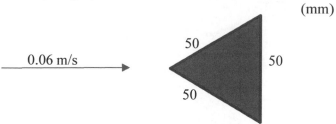

**K. Notes**

## CHAPTER 4. FLOW PAST AN AIRFOIL

## A. Objectives

- Using ANSYS Workbench to Model the NACA 2412 Airfoil and Mesh
- Inserting Boundary Conditions and Free Stream Velocity
- Running Turbulent Steady 2D Planar ANSYS Fluent Simulations
- Using Velocity and Pressure Plots for Visualizations
- Determine Lift and Drag Coefficients for Zero Angle of Attack

## B. Problem Description

The purpose of this simulation is to become familiar with a few basic aerodynamic concepts and terms such as Reynold's number, coefficients of lift, drag, and pressure. We will therefore study the flow of air past the NACA 2412 airfoil and we will analyze the problem using ANSYS Fluent. The chord length of the airfoil is 230 mm, the angle of attack is 0° and the free stream velocity is 12.7 m/s.

Another airfoil shape that has been studied extensively is the Clark-Y airfoil. One of the first measurements of pressure distributions on this airfoil was completed by Jacobs et al.[1], followed by Marchman and Werme[2] and Stern et al.[3] that made low Reynolds number measurements. Warner[4] and Matsson[5] have also determined results from tests of the Clark-Y airfoil. The NACA 2412 airfoil has been tested by Matsson et al.[6].

For the four digit series[7] of NACA airfoils, the first digit stands for the camber which is the distance between chord line and mean camber line. The second digit stands for the location of maximum camber along the chord line from the leading edge. The last two digits stand for the maximum thickness of the airfoil. For the NACA 2412 studied in this chapter, there is a 2% max camber at 40% chord length with 12% thickness.

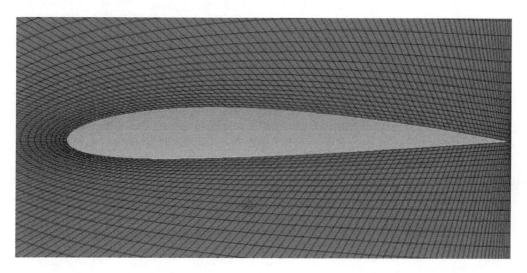

## C. Launching ANSYS Workbench and Selecting Fluent

1. Start by launching ANSYS Workbench. Double click on Fluid Flow (Fluent) that is located under Analysis Systems in Toolbox.

Figure 4.1 Selecting Fluid Flow in ANSYS Workbench

## D. Launching ANSYS DesignModeler

2. Right click Geometry and select Properties. In Properties of Schematic A2: Geometry, select Analysis Type 2D under Advanced Geometry Options. Right-click on Geometry in the Project Schematic window and select New DesignModeler Geometry. Select **Units>>Millimeter** from the menu as the desired length unit in the new DesignModeler window.

Select Create>>Point from the menu. We will use the coordinates file *NACA_2412_Airfoil* that is available for download at *sdcpublications.com*. Open the Coordinates File from Details View and click on Generate. Select Look At Face [icon]. Select Concept>>Lines From Points in the menu. Right click in the graphics window and select Point Chain. Right click in the graphics window and select Select All. Apply the Point Segments in Details View. Click on Generate. Select Concept>>Surfaces From Edges from the menu. Right click in the graphics window and Select All. Apply Edges in Details View. Click on Generate.

Figure 4.2a) Selection of units in DesignModeler (DM)

Figure 4.2b) Creating points in DM

Figure 4.2c) Creating lines from points

Figure 4.2d) Creating surfaces from edges

Figure 4.2e) NACA 2412 Airfoil in DesignModeler

3. Next, we will be sketching the mesh region around the airfoil. Create a new coordinate system by first clicking on New Plane 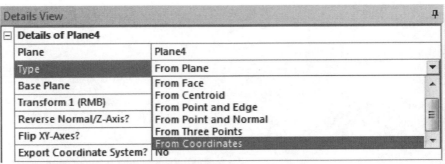. Select Type>>From Coordinates in the Details View. Enter 230 mm for FD11, Point X. Click on Generate. Select the new Plane4 in the tree outline and click on 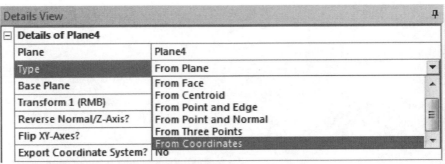 to generate a new sketch. Click on the Sketching tab and select Arc by Center from the Draw tab. Click on Look At Face/Plane/Sketch 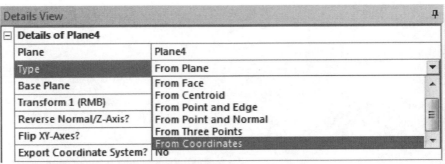. Click at the origin of the coordinate system at the trailing edge of the airfoil. Make sure that you see the letter *P* when you move the cursor over the origin of the coordinate system. Next, click on the vertical axis above the origin (make sure you have a *C*) and finally on the vertical axis below the origin (make sure you have a *C* once again), see Figure 4.3b).

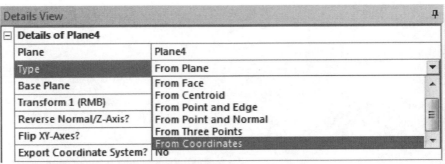

Figure 4.3a) A new plane from coordinates

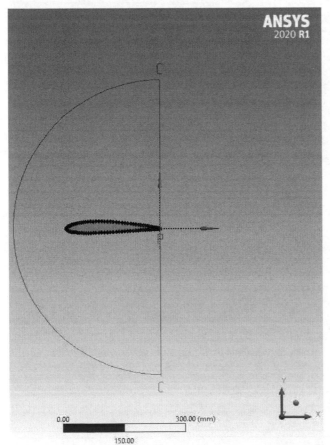

Figure 4.3b) Half-circle around the NACA 2412 airfoil

4.  Select Rectangle by 3 Points from the Draw tab. Click at the intersection of the arc and the positive vertical axis, at the intersection between the arc and the negative vertical axis, and finally click in the right-hand side plane. Select Modify and Trim from Sketching Toolboxes. Click on the lines of the rectangle that are aligned with and on top of the vertical axis.

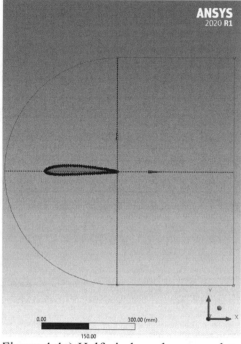

Figure 4.4a) Half-circle and rectangular mesh region around the NACA 2412 airfoil

Select Dimensions under Sketching Toolboxes, select Radius under Dimensions and select the arc in the graphics window. Set the radius of the arc to 2875 mm which gives a ratio of the radius of the arc to the chord length of 12.5. Next, select Horizontal under Dimensions from the Sketching Toolboxes and click on the vertical axis and the vertical edge of the rectangle on the right-hand side. Enter 5750 mm as the length.

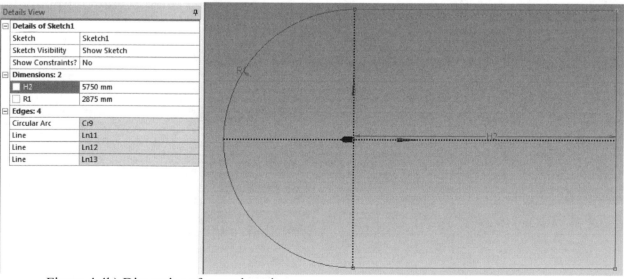

Figure 4.4b) Dimensions for mesh region

Select Concept>>Surface from Sketches. Select Sketch1 under Plane4 in the Tree Outline and Apply as Base Objects in Details View. Select Operation>>Add Frozen in Details View followed by Generate.

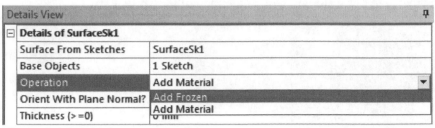

Figure 4.4c) Add frozen operation

5. Select Create>>Boolean from the menu. Select Subtract Operation from the Details View. Click on the mesh region in the graphics window and click on Apply as Target Bodies in Details View. Select the Airfoil as Tool Bodies in Details View and click on Generate, see Figure 4.5c).

Figure 4.5a) Creating a Boolean

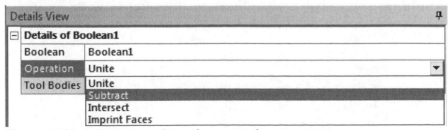

Figure 4.5b) Selecting a subtracting operation

click on this rectangle for selection of airfoil as Tool Body

3e+03 (mm)

1.5e+03

Figure 4.5c) Selection of Tool Body

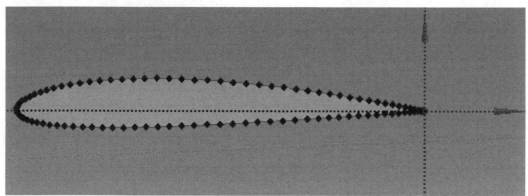

Figure 4.5d) Completed subtraction operation

6. Select Plane 4 in the tree outline and create a new sketch . Select the Sketching tab and the Line tool under Draw. Draw a line on the vertical axis from top to bottom of the mesh that intersects the entire mesh region. Select Concepts>>Lines from Sketches from the menu. Select the newly created vertical line and Apply it as a Base Object in the Details View. Click on Generate.
Repeat this step and create a new sketch with a line on the horizontal axis in Plane4 that is drawn from left to right and goes through the whole mesh region including the leading and trailing edges of the airfoil. You will need to create a Coincident Constraint using the Sketching Toolbox and insert the constraint between the new line and the horizontal axis. This is completed by selecting the Coincident Constraint and clicking on both the new line and the horizontal axis. It will be helpful to draw the horizontal line a little bit below the horizontal axis and use the constraint to fix the line with the horizontal axis.

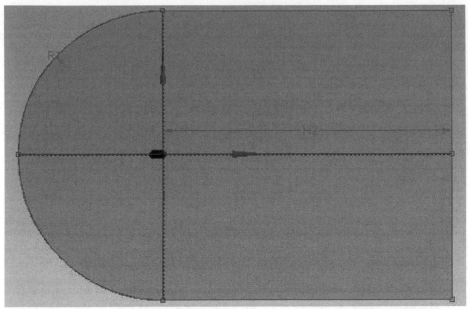

Figure 4.6 Completed vertical and horizontal lines through the mesh region

7. Select Tools>>Projection from the menu. Select Edges on Face as Type. Control-select both parts of the newly created vertical line and the two parts of the newly created horizontal line and Apply the four Edges in the Details View. Click in the yellow region next to Target in Details View. Select the mesh region around the airfoil and Apply it as the Target under Details View. Click Generate. You should now have four different mesh regions.

Figure 4.7a) Selection of the projection tool

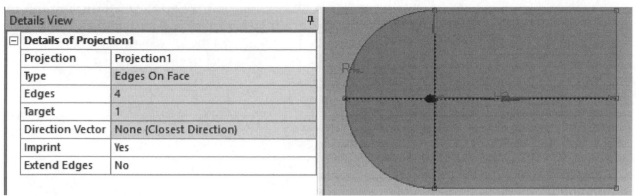

Figure 4.7b) Details view for projection

Click on the plus sign next to 2 Parts, 2 Bodies in the Tree Outline. Right click the Line Body and select Suppress Body. Select File>>Save Project from the menu and save the project with the name "NACA 2412 Airfoil Flow Study". Close DesignModeler.

## E. Launching ANSYS Meshing

8.  Double click on Mesh under Project Schematic in ANSYS Workbench. Select Mesh in the Outline of the Meshing window and select Mesh>>Controls>>Face Meshing from the menu. Control-select all four faces of the mesh. Apply the Geometry under Details of "Face Meshing".

Figure 4.8a) Selection of face meshing

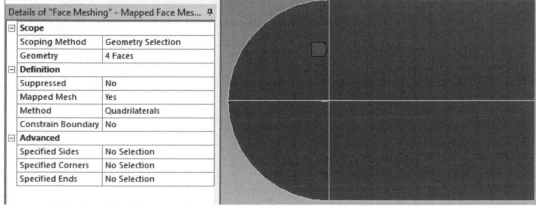

Figure 4.8b) Detail of face meshing

Select Mesh Control>>Sizing from the menu and click on the Edge Selection Filter 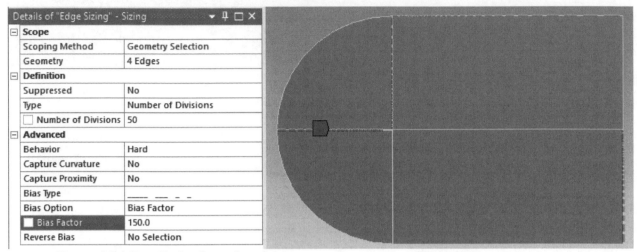. Control-select the four edges as shown in Figure 4.8c). Apply the Geometry under Details of "Edge Sizing". Select Number of Divisions as Type under Details of "Edge Sizing". Set the number of Divisions to 50. Set the Behavior as Hard. Select the first Bias Type from the drop-down menu. Enter a Bias Factor of 150.

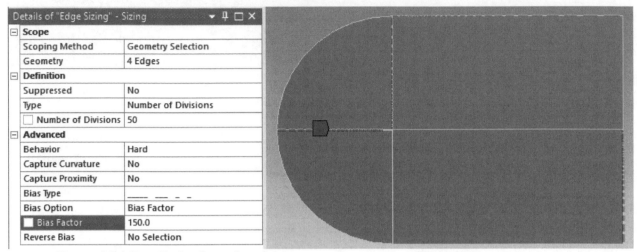

Figure 4.8c) Details for first edge sizing

Create another identical edge sizing but this time select the four remaining straight edges, see Figure 4.8d). Select the same number of divisions 50 and behavior Hard. Select the second Bias Type ═ ─ ── ═══ from the top from the drop-down menu and the same bias factor of 150.

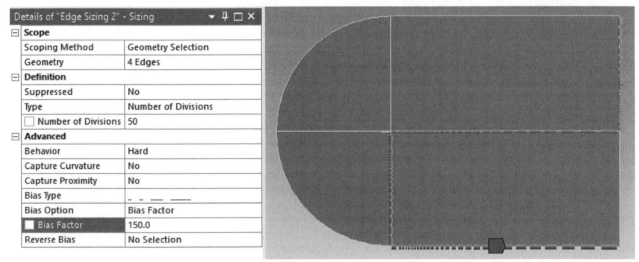

Figure 4.8d) Details for second edge sizing

> **Why do we use a biased mesh?** A biased mesh enables us to create a finer mesh closer to the airfoil. We create a fine mesh where it is needed the most and the calculation time will be much shorter compared with a finer mesh over the entire mesh region.

The final edge sizing will be for the two round edges. Set the Number of Divisions to 100 and Hard behavior. No bias will be used for the round edges. Right click on Mesh in the tree outline and select Generate Mesh.

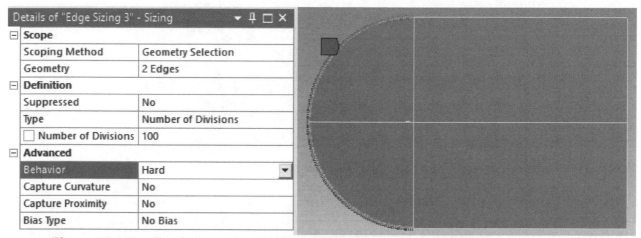

Figure 4.8e) Details of edge sizing for the two round edges

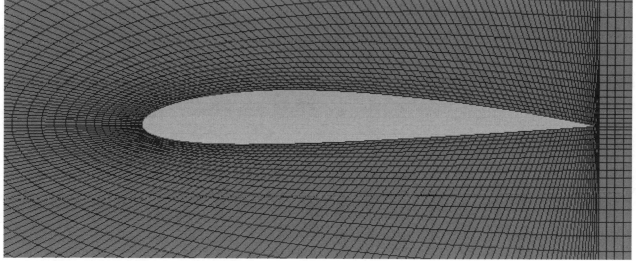

Figure 4.8f) Finished mesh close to the airfoil

9. Select Geometry in the Outline. Select the Edge Selection filter. Control-select the two vertical edges on the right-hand side of the mesh region, right click and select Create Named Selection. Name the edges "outlet" and click OK. Name the two round edges "inlet". Name the horizontal upper and lower edges "symmetry". Save the project. Select File>>Export>>Mesh>>FLUENT Input File>>Export from the menu. Enter "airfoil-flow-mesh" as file name and Save as type: FLUENT Input Files (*.msh). Close the meshing window. Right click on Mesh and select Update in ANSYS Workbench.

> **Why do we export the mesh?** When we save the mesh file, we can read the mesh using standalone mode directly in ANSYS Fluent without having to design the mesh all over again each time that we run the simulation for various flow variables.

Figure 4.9 Named selections for mesh

## F. Launching ANSYS Fluent

10. Double click on Setup under Project Schematic in ANSYS Workbench. Check the Options box Double Precision. Select the number of Solver Processes under Parallel (Local Machine) to the same number as the total number of cores for your computer. Click on Show More Options and take a note of the location for your working directory. Click Start to launch Fluent.

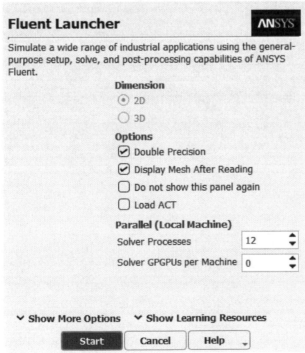

Figure 4.10a) Fluent launcher window

Select the Density-Based Solver under General on the Task Page. Double-click on Models under Setup in Outline View and double click on the Viscous (SST k-omega) on the Task Page. Select the Spalart-Allmaras (1 eqn) turbulence model. Select OK to close the Viscous Model window.

# CHAPTER 4. FLOW PAST AN AIRFOIL

Figure 4.10b) General solution setup

> **Why did we select the Density-Based Solver?** Both solver type options can be used for a variety of flow cases. Traditionally, the density-based solver has been used for compressible flow. For the flow past an airfoil that is studied in this chapter, by using the density-based solver we can choose to include the study of flows where compressibility of air is important.
> **Why do we use the Spalart-Allmaras Viscous Model?** This viscous model was designed for boundary layers in aerospace applications.

Figure 4.10c) Details for the viscous model

11. Double click on Boundary Conditions under Setup in Outline View. Double click the inlet Zone on the Task Page. Select Components as Velocity Specification Method. Enter 12.7 m/s as X-Velocity (m/s). Click OK to close the Velocity Inlet window.

Figure 4.11 Velocity inlet boundary condition

12. Double click on Monitors under Solution in the Tree. Double click on Residual under Monitor. Change the Convergence Criterion for all four residuals to 1e-8. Click on OK to exit the Residual Monitors window. Double click on Initialization under Solution under the Outline View. Select Standard Initialization as Initialization Method, select Compute from inlet and click on Initialize. Select File>>Save Project from the menu. Double click on Run Calculation under Solution in the Outline View. Set number of Iterations to 10000. Click on Calculate. Click OK when the calculations are complete.

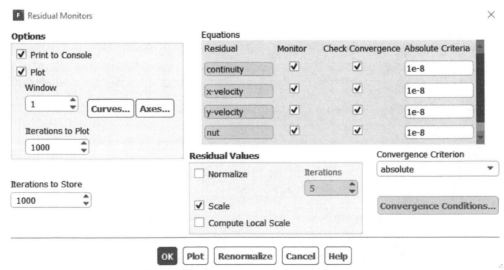

Figure 4.12a) Settings for residual monitors

**Why did we select 1e-8 as the Absolute Criteria?** We want to choose a sufficiently small value for the absolute criteria such that the drag and lift coefficients are not depending on the value of the absolute criteria that we use. As an example, using 1e-12 instead of 1e-8 will not change the results for lift and drag coefficient. Therefore, the higher value was chosen as calculation times will be shorter.

Figure 4.12b) Solution initialization

Figure 4.12c) Running calculations

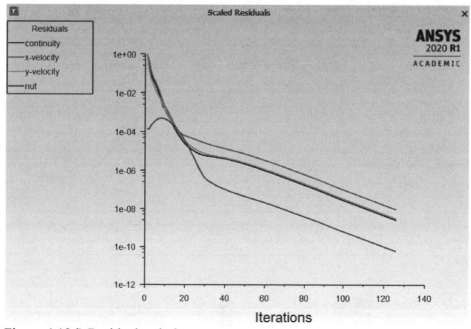

Figure 4.12d) Residuals window

89

## G. Post-Processing

13. Double click on Graphics under Results in the Outline View. Display a plot of pressure contours by double clicking on Contours under Graphics, check the box for Filled under Options, select all Surfaces and select Pressure and Static Pressure under Contours of followed by Save/Display. Create another contour plot for Velocity and Velocity Magnitude.

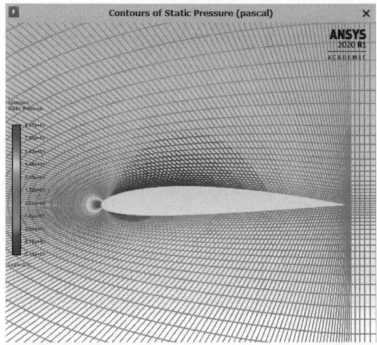

Figure 4.13a) Pressure contours around NACA 2412 airfoil

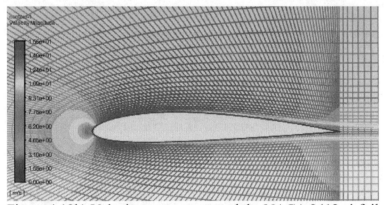

Figure 4.13b) Velocity contours around the NACA 2412 airfoil

> **Why did we select all surfaces when we created the contour plots?** When we select all surfaces, the mesh will be shown on top of the contour plot. Deselecting all surfaces will cause the mesh to disappear.

14. Double click on Reference Values under Setup in the Outline View. Select Compute from inlet. Enter the value 0.23 for Length (m) which is the chord length and enter the value 12.7 for

Velocity (m/s). Enter the value 0.3048 for Depth (m) and 0.070104 for Area (m2). The Area is equal to the Depth times the Length.

Figure 4.14a) Reference values

Find the coefficient of drag by double clicking on Reports under Results in the Outline View. Double click on Forces under Reports. Set the Direction Vector in the Force Reports window to 1 for X and 0 for Y. Click Print and write down the value for the total drag coefficient that you have calculated $C_d$ = 0.017688832. Repeat this step to find the value for the lift coefficient using 0 for X and 1 for Y for the Direction Vector in the Force Reports window. The value for the lift coefficient is $C_l$ = 0.19927406.

Figure 4.14b) Force reports

Determine the Reynolds number for the flow around an airfoil that is defined as $Re = Uc/v$ where $U$ (m/s) is the magnitude of the free stream velocity, $c$ (m) is the chord length of the airfoil, and $v$ ($m^2$/s) is the kinematic viscosity of air at room temperature. You will find that $Re = 200,000$. The angle of attack $AoA$ for the flow case that we studied in this chapter was zero degrees.

Open the Mesh by right-clicking on the Mesh in the Project Schematic in ANSYS Workbench and select Edit. Click on the plus sign next to Mesh. Change the values for Number of Divisions for the three different Edge Sizings to 60 and 120 instead of the current values 50 and 100. Right click on Mesh and select Generate Mesh.

Select File>>Export>>Mesh>>FLUENT Input File>>Export from the menu. Save the mesh with the name "fine-airfoil-flow-mesh". Select File>>Close Meshing, right click on Mesh in the Project Schematic in ANSYS Workbench and select Update. Right click on Setup in ANSYS Workbench and select Update. Double click on Setup and reinitialize the solution. Run the calculations. Enter the reference values once again and calculate the drag and lift coefficients.

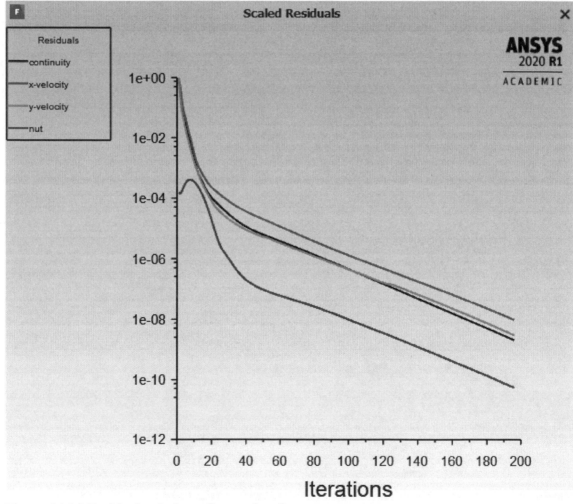

Figure 4.14c) Residuals window after mesh refinement

| $Re = 200{,}000$ | Mesh 1 | Mesh 2 | Mesh 3 | Mesh 4 | Mesh 5 | Mesh 6 |
|---|---|---|---|---|---|---|
| $C_d$ | 0.01769 | 0.01662 | 0.01551 | 0.01545 | 0.01558 | 0.01564 |
| $C_l$ | 0.19927 | 0.20069 | 0.19936 | 0.19568 | 0.20354 | 0.20174 |
| Angle of Attack | 0 | 0 | 0 | 0 | 0 | 0 |
| No. of Divisions | 50, 100 | 60, 120 | 100, 200 | 150, 300 | 200, 400 | 250, 500 |
| No. of Nodes | 15,300 | 21,960 | 60,600 | 135,900 | 241,200 | 376,500 |
| No. of Elements | 15,000 | 21,600 | 60,000 | 135,000 | 240,000 | 375,000 |

Table 4.1 Comparison of drag and lift coefficient for different mesh sizes

Figure 4.14d) Drag coefficient versus mesh refinement

---

**Why did we do mesh refinement?** Any CFD study should be accompanied by a mesh independence study where you refine the mesh until the results converge. We see in Figure 4.14d) that the drag coefficient seems to level off at around 0.0156. However, the ANSYS Student version has a maximum allowed number of elements and it can therefore sometimes be difficulty to fully achieve mesh independence.

---

## H. Theory

15. The Reynolds number for the flow over an airfoil is determined by

$$Re = \frac{Uc}{v} \tag{4.1}$$

where $U$ (m/s) is the magnitude of the free stream velocity, $c$ (m) is the chord length of the airfoil, and $v$ (m²/s) is the kinematic viscosity of air at room temperature.

The pressure distribution over the airfoil is expressed in non-dimensional form by the pressure coefficient

$$C_p = \frac{p_i - P}{\frac{1}{2}\rho U^2} \tag{4.2}$$

where $\rho$ (kg/m$^3$) is the free stream density and where $p_i$ (Pa) is the surface pressure at location $i$ and $p$ (Pa) is the pressure in the free stream. The pressure coefficient can alternatively be related to the velocity distribution $u$ (m/s) around the airfoil through

$$C_p = 1 - \left(\frac{u}{U}\right)^2 \tag{4.3}$$

The lift and drag coefficients can be determined from

$$C_l = \frac{F_l}{\frac{1}{2}\rho U^2 bc} \tag{4.4}$$

$$C_d = \frac{F_d}{\frac{1}{2}\rho U^2 bc} \tag{4.5}$$

, where $F_l$ and $F_d$ (N) are lift and drag forces and $b$ (m) is the wingspan.

## I.  References

1.  Jacobs E.N., Stack J. and Pinkerton R.M. Airfoil Pressure Distribution Investigation in the Variable Density Wind Tunnel, NACA Report No. 353, 1930.
2.  Marchman III J.F and Werme T.D., Clark-Y Airfoil Performance at Low Reynolds Numbers, AIAA-84-0052, 1984.
3.  Stern F., Muste M., Houser D., Wilson M. and Ghosh S., Measurement of Pressure Distribution and Forces acting on an Airfoil, Laboratory Experiment #3, 57:020 Mechanics of Fluids and Transfer Processes (http://css.engineering/uiowa.edu/fluidslab/pdfs/57-020/airfoil.doc)
4.  Warner E.P., Airplane Design: Performance, McGraw-Hill, New York, 1936.
5.  Matsson J., A Student Project on Airfoil Performance, Annual Conference & Exposition, Honolulu, Hawaii, 2007.
6.  Matsson J., Voth J., McCain C. and McGraw C., Aerodynamic Performance of the NACA 2412 Airfoil at Low Reynolds Number, ASEE 123rd Annual Conference & Exposition, New Orleans, LA, June 26-29, 2016.
7.  Anderson, J., Fundamentals of Aerodynamics, 6st Edition, McGraw-Hill, 2017.
8.  Abbott, I.H., Von Doenhoff, A.E., Theory of Wing Sections: Including a Summary of Airfoil Data, Dover Publications, 1959.

## J.  Exercises

4.1 Determine contours of pressure and velocity for the flow field around an airfoil with a different NACA number than the one covered in this chapter. Include the corresponding mesh refinement level, number of iterations, refine threshold, number of cells refined, drag coefficient, lift coefficient, Reynolds number and the angle of attack as shown in Table 4.1 for the NACA 2412 airfoil. Include the residuals window after the solution has converged and include a printout of the mesh around the airfoil.

4.2 Continue with Exercise 4.1 using different angles of attack *AoA* = 2, 4, 6, 8, 10, 12 degrees for the same Reynolds number. For each AoA, refine the mesh until you get a converged solution. Plot the drag and lift coefficients versus AoA and compare with experimental results for the chosen airfoil using data from Abbott and Von Doenhoff[8].

4.3 Create an O-mesh mesh around the airfoil instead of the C-mesh that was modeled in this chapter. Run the simulations for the O-mesh and compare results with the mesh used in this chapter. Use the same radius for the O-mesh as for the C-mesh in this chapter.

**K. Notes**

## CHAPTER 5.  RAYLEIGH-BENARD CONVECTION

## A.  Objectives

- Using ANSYS Workbench to Create the Mesh for 3D Rayleigh-Bénard Convection
- Inserting Wall Boundary Conditions
- Running Laminar Steady 3D ANSYS Fluent Simulations
- Using Contour Plots for Visualizations
- Compare Results with Neutral Stability Theory

## B.  Problem Description

Bénard[1] was the first scientist to experimentally study convection in a fluid layer with a free surface heated from below. Rayleigh[2] used linear stability analysis to theoretically explain and study the stability of the fluid motion between horizontal parallel plates with the hotter plate at the bottom. Chandrasekhar[3] completed the linear stability analysis for Rayleigh-Bénard convection and Koschmieder[4] showed the development of the research in this area during the following couple of decades.

There are only a few experiments including Koschmieder and Pallas[5], Hoard et al.[6] and to some extent Matsson[6] that have produced the concentric ring cells in Rayleigh-Bénard convection that according to stability theory should appear with a rigid upper boundary condition. This instability with an upper rigid wall in experiments is very sensitive to the surface roughness and flatness of the upper wall. Torres et al.[7] completed 3D numerical simulations of Rayleigh-Benard convection in a cylindrical container and verified the existence of roll cells in the form of concentric circles.

In this chapter, we will study Rayleigh-Bénard convection and we will analyze the problem using ANSYS Fluent in 3D. The enclosure is filled with water and the temperature of the cold wall is 296.5 K while the hot wall is at 298 K. The diameter of the enclosure is 100 mm and the depth 4.8 mm.

## C.  Launching ANSYS Workbench and Selecting Fluent

1.  Start by launching ANSYS Workbench. Double click on Fluid Flow (Fluent).

Figure 5.1 Selecting Fluid Flow

## D.  Launching ANSYS DesignModeler

2.  Right-click on Geometry in Project Schematic and select Properties. Select Geometry and 3D Analysis Type under Advanced Geometry Options in Properties of Schematic A2: Geometry. Right click on Geometry and open a New DesignModeler Geometry. Select **Millimeter as the Unit** from the menu in DesignModeler.

Figure 5.2a) Geometry          Figure 5.2b) Selecting 3D Analysis Type

3. Next, we will be creating the mesh region for the simulation. Select XYPlane from the Tree Outline. Select Look at Sketch . Select the Sketching tab and draw a circle from the origin. Select the Dimensions tab in Sketching Toolboxes. Click on the circle and enter a diameter of 100 mm. Select Create>>Extrude from the menu. Select Sketch1 under XYPlane in in the Tree Outline and Apply the sketch as Geometry in Details View. Enter 4.8 mm as FD1, Depth (>0). Click on Generate and Close DesignModeler.

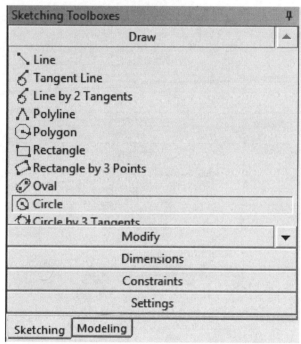

Figure 5.3a) Selection of XYPlane

Figure 5.3b) Selection of circle sketch tool

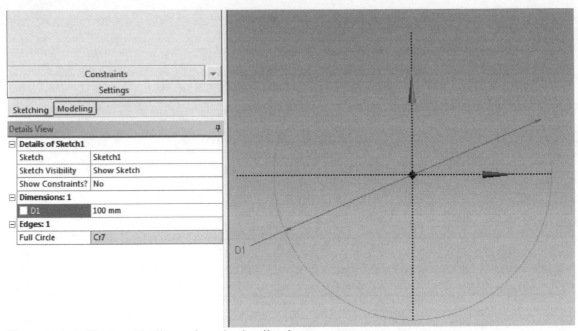

Figure 5.3c) Circle with dimensions in details view

Figure 5.3d) Selecting extrusion

Figure 5.3e) Details of extrusion

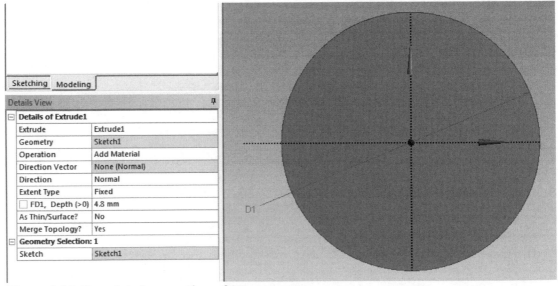

Figure 5.3f) Completed generation of 3D geometry

## E. Launching ANSYS Meshing

4.  We are now going to double click on Mesh under Project Schematic in ANSYS Workbench to open the Mechanical window. Select Mesh in the Outline. Select Unit Systems>>Metric (mm, kg, N ...) from the bottom of the graphics window. Right click on Mesh in the Outline and select Update. A coarse mesh is created.

Figure 5.4a) Starting Mesh

Figure 5.4b) Selection of Mesh in Outline

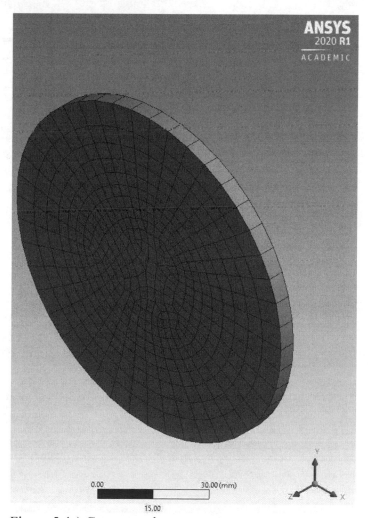

Figure 5.4c) Coarse mesh

5. Select Mesh>>Controls>>Face Meshing from the menu. Click on the cylindrical face of the mesh region in the graphics window. The face turns green. Click on the Apply button for Geometry in Details of "Face Meshing".

Select Mesh>>Controls>>Sizing from the menu and select Edge . Control click on the two circular edges of the mesh region. Click on Apply for the Geometry in "Details of Edge Sizing". Under Definition in "Details of Edge Sizing", select Number of Divisions for Type, 500 for Number of Divisions, and Hard as Behavior.

Repeat the selection of Mesh>>Controls>>Sizing from the menu and select Face . Control select the two plane faces and the cylindrical face of the mesh region. Enter 0.5 mm for Element Size and Hard Behavior.

Repeat the selection of Mesh>>Controls>>Sizing from the menu and select Body . Select the body of the mesh region. Enter 5 mm for Element Size and Hard Behavior.
Click on Update and select Mesh in the Outline. Right click in the graphics window and select Isometric View. The finished mesh is shown in the graphics window.

Figure 5.5a) Generation of Face Meshing

Figure 5.5b) Face for Face Meshing

Figure 5.5c) Mesh Control Sizing

Figure 5.5d) Round edges for sizing

| Details of "Edge Sizing" - Sizing | ▾ ⤼ ☐ ✕ |
|---|---|
| **Scope** | |
| Scoping Method | Geometry Selection |
| Geometry | 2 Edges |
| **Definition** | |
| Suppressed | No |
| Type | Number of Divisions |
| ☐ Number of Divisions | 500 |
| **Advanced** | |
| Behavior | Hard |
| Capture Curvature | No |
| Capture Proximity | No |
| Bias Type | No Bias |

Figure 5.5e) Details of edge sizing

Figure 5.5f) Faces for face sizing

| Details of "Face Sizing" - Sizing | ▾ ⤼ ☐ ✕ |
|---|---|
| **Scope** | |
| Scoping Method | Geometry Selection |
| Geometry | 3 Faces |
| **Definition** | |
| Suppressed | No |
| Type | Element Size |
| ☐ Element Size | 0.5 mm |
| **Advanced** | |
| ☐ Defeature Size | Default (3.5376e-002 mm) |
| Influence Volume | No |
| Behavior | Hard ▾ |
| Capture Curvature | No |
| Capture Proximity | No |

Figure 5.5g) Details of face sizing

| Details of "Body Sizing" - Sizing | ▾ ⤼ ☐ ✕ |
|---|---|
| **Scope** | |
| Scoping Method | Geometry Selection |
| Geometry | 1 Body |
| **Definition** | |
| Suppressed | No |
| Type | Element Size |
| ☐ Element Size | 5.0 mm |
| **Advanced** | |
| ☐ Defeature Size | Default (3.5376e-002 mm) |
| Behavior | Hard ▾ |
| Capture Curvature | No |
| Capture Proximity | No |

Figure 5.5h) Details of body sizing

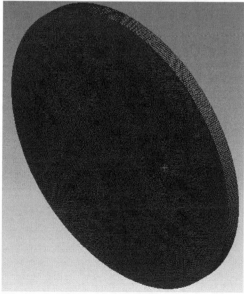

Figure 5.5i) Finished mesh

| Details of "Mesh" | ▾ ⤼ ☐ ✕ |
|---|---|
| **Display** | |
| Display Style | Use Geometry Setting |
| **Defaults** | |
| Physics Preference | CFD |
| Solver Preference | Fluent |
| Element Order | Linear |
| ☐ Element Size | Default (7.0751e-003 m) |
| Export Format | Standard |
| Export Preview Surface Mesh | No |
| ⊞ **Sizing** | |
| ⊞ **Quality** | |
| ⊞ **Inflation** | |
| ⊞ **Assembly Meshing** | |
| ⊞ **Advanced** | |
| ⊟ **Statistics** | |
| ☐ Nodes | 357390 |
| ☐ Elements | 323200 |

Figure 5.5j) Details of mesh

103

6.  Select Face 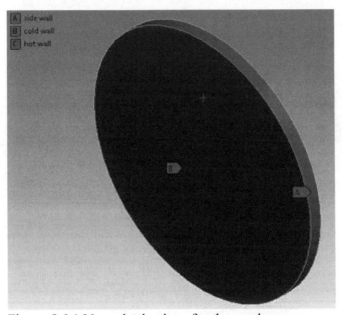 and select the cylindrical face of the mesh region, right click and select Create Named Selection. Enter *side wall* as the name and click on the OK button. Repeat this step for the upper and lower faces in the Z-direction of the mesh region and name these *cold wall* and *hot wall*, respectively.

Select File>>Export>>Mesh>>FLUENT Input File>>Export from the menu and save the mesh with the name *rayleigh-benard-3D.msh*. Select File>>Save Project from the menu and name the project "3D Rayleigh-Benard Convection". Select File>>Close Meshing to close the meshing window. Right click on Mesh in ANSYS Workbench and select Update.

Figure 5.6a) Named selections for the mesh

Figure 5.6b) Updating the mesh

## F. Launching ANSYS Fluent

7. Double click on Setup under Project Schematic in ANSYS Workbench. Check the box for Double Precision. Set the number of Processes to the number corresponding to the number of cores for your computer processor. Write down the location of the *Working Directory* that is listed under Show More Options. Click Start to launch Fluent.

Figure 5.7 ANSYS Fluent Launcher

8. Check the mesh by selecting the Check button under Mesh in General Setup. Check the scale of the mesh by selecting the Scale button. Make sure that the Domain Extent is correct and close the Scale Mesh window.

Figure 5.8a) Checking the mesh

```
Domain Extents:
  x-coordinate: min (m) = -5.000000e-02, max (m) = 5.000000e-02
  y-coordinate: min (m) = -5.000000e-02, max (m) = 5.000000e-02
  z-coordinate: min (m) = 0.000000e+00, max (m) = 4.800000e-03
Volume statistics:
  minimum volume (m3): 5.466825e-12
  maximum volume (m3): 2.678178e-10
    total volume (m3): 3.769812e-05
Face area statistics:
  minimum face area (m2): 1.138922e-08
  maximum face area (m2): 5.579537e-07
Checking mesh....................................
Done.
```

Figure 5.8b) Console output generated by mesh check

Figure 5.8c) Scale Mesh window

9.  Check the Gravity box and enter -9.81 as the Gravitational Acceleration in the Z direction. Double click on Models under Setup in Outline View. Double click on the Energy model and check the box for the Energy equation. Click OK to exit the Energy Model window.

Figure 5.9a) Gravity settings

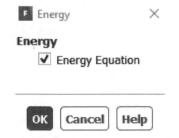

Figure 5.9b) Energy equation

10. Double click on Materials under Setup in the Outline View. Click on the Create/Edit button for Fluid on the Task Page to open the Create/Edit Materials window. Select Fluent Database…. Scroll down in the Fluent Fluid Materials window and select *water-liquid (h2o<l>)*. Click on the Copy button and Close the Fluent Database Materials window. Select *boussinesq* using the drop-down menu next to Density under Properties. Enter the value 997 (kg/m3) for the Density. Enter the value 4180 (j/kg-k) for Specific Heat, 0.607 (w/m-k) for Thermal Conductivity, and 0.000891 (kg/m-s) for Viscosity. Scroll down and enter the value 0.000247 (1/k) for the Thermal Expansion Coefficient. Click on the Change/Create button and Close the window.

> **Why did we choose the boussinesq setting?** The Boussinesq approximation is used for buoyancy driven flows. The reason for using boussinesq for density is that this will give faster convergence. Density is treated as a constant in all equations except for the buoyancy term in the momentum equation.

Double click on Boundary Conditions under Setup in the Outline View. Click on Operating Conditions on the Task Page. Set the value for the Operating Temperature to 297.395 (k) and click on OK to close the Operating Conditions box.

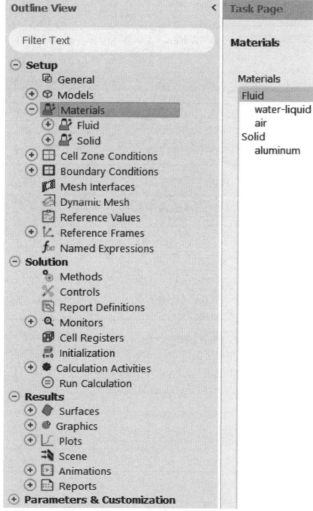

Figure 5.10a) Materials problem setup

Figure 5.10b) Create/Edit Materials window

Figure 5.10c) Operating Conditions settings

11. Open Boundary Conditions under Setup in the Outline View. Double click *cold_wall* under Boundary Conditions. Select the Thermal tab and select Temperature for Thermal Conditions. Enter the value 296.79 as Temperature (k). Click OK to exit the window. Double click *hot_wall* under Boundary Conditions and set the Temperature (k) boundary condition to 298. Double click on *side_wall* under Boundary Conditions and set the Temperature (k) boundary condition to 296.79. Double click on Cell Zone Conditions under Setup in the Outline View. Double click on solid under Cell Zone Conditions. Select *water-liquid* from the Material Name drop-down menu in the Fluid window. Click OK to exit the window.

Figure 5.11a) Cold wall temperature

Figure 5.11b) Hot wall temperature

Figure 5.11c) Side wall temperature

Figure 5.11d) Fluid selection

12. Double click on Models under Setup in Outline View. Double click on Viscous (SST k-omega) model and check the box for the Laminar model. Click OK to exit the Viscous Model window. Double click on Initialization under Solution in the Outline View. Select Standard Initialization under Initialization Methods. Enter 0.01 for Z Velocity (m/s), enter 297.395 as Temperature (k) and click on Initialize.

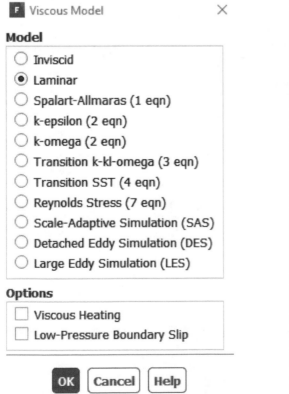

Figure 5.12a) Laminar Viscous Model

Figure 5.12b) Solution Initialization settings

13. Double click on Monitors under Solution in the Outline View and double click on Residual under Monitors. Set the Absolute Criteria to 1e-6 for all equations and click OK to close the window. Double click on Methods under Solution in the Outline View and select Body Force Weighted from the Pressure drop-down menu under Spatial Discretization. Select SIMPLE as Pressure-Velocity Coupling Scheme.

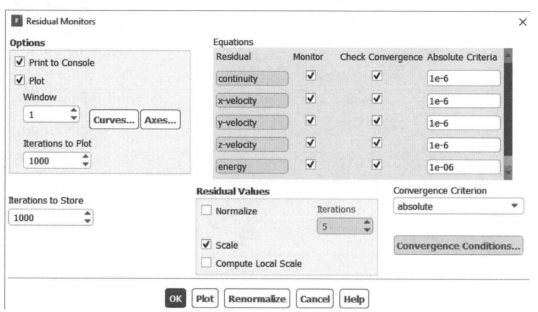

Figure 5.13a) Residual Monitors Settings

**Why did we choose Body Force Weighted and SIMPLE Solution Methods?** The reason for using SIMPLE as Pressure-Velocity Coupling algorithm is that we are studying steady laminar flow. SIMPLEC may alternatively be used as it can provide a faster solution. PISO is used for transient solutions. Coupled can also give an efficient steady state solution for single phase flows. The Body Force Weighted pressure scheme is recommended when we have large body forces such as gravity in Rayleigh-Benard convection.

Figure 5.13b) Solution Methods Settings

14. Double click Run Calculation under Solution in the Outline View. Set the number of iterations to 5000. Click on the Calculate button. Click on the OK button in the Information window that appears when the calculations are complete.

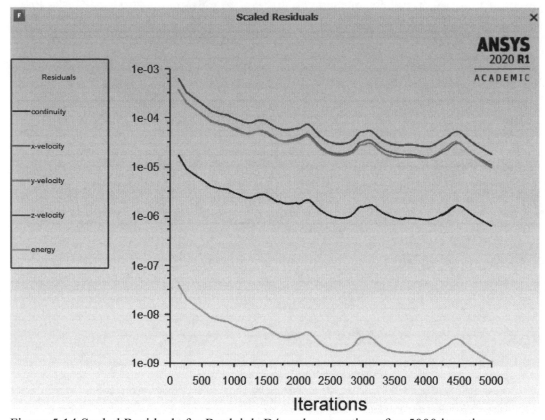

Figure 5.14 Scaled Residuals for Rayleigh-Bénard convection after 5000 iterations

## G. Post-Processing

15. Double click on Graphics under Results in the Outline View. Double click on Contours in the Graphics section. Check the Filled box under Options and select Contours of Velocity and Z Velocity.

Select New Surface>>Plane from the drop-down menu in the Contours window. Select Three Points as Method. For Point 1, set (X (m), Y (m), Z (m)) to (0, -0.05, 0.0024), for Point 2 set (X (m), Y (m), Z (m)) to (0, 0.05, 0.0024) and for point 3 set (X (m), Y(m), Z (m)) to (0.05, 0, 0.0024). Enter the name *mid-plane-z=0.0024m* as the New Surface Name. Click on Create and Close the window.

Select the new plane under Surfaces in the Contours window and check the box for Contour Lines under Options. Click on the Save/Display button and Close the window. Select the x-y plane view. Repeat this step but select Contours of Temperature and Static Temperature. Click on Colormap Options. Select float as Type for Number Format and set Precision to 1. Click on Apply and Close the Colormap window. Click on the Save/Display button. Select the x-y plane view.

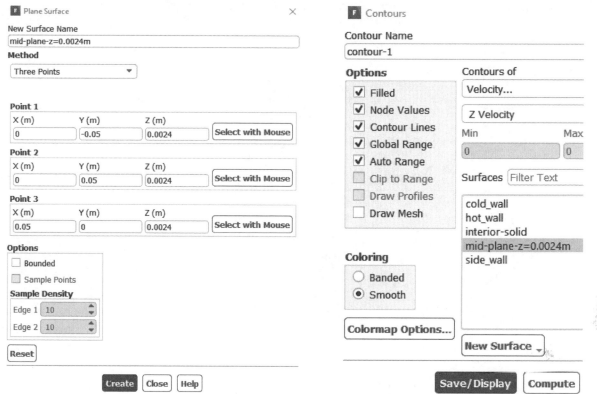

Figure 5.15a) Creation of a new x-y plane          Figure 5.15b) Contours settings

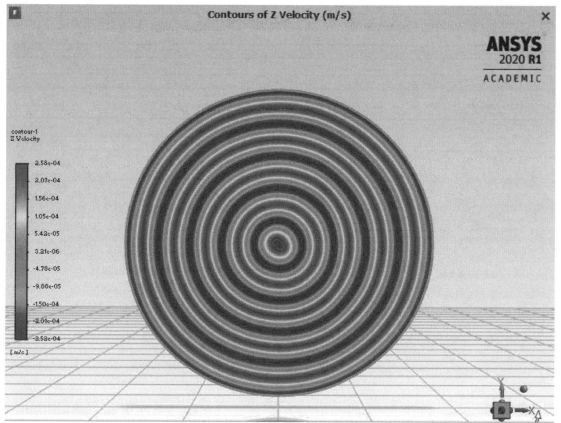

Figure 5.15c) Contours of Z Velocity in x-y plane at 5000 iterations, $Ra = 2491$

113

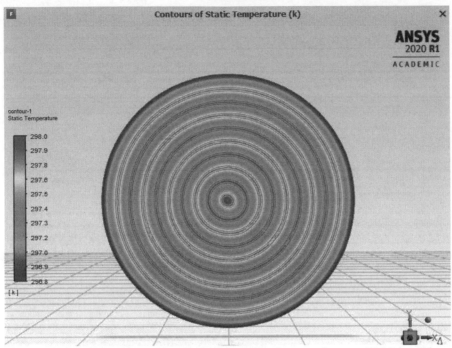

Figure 5.15d) Contours of Static Temperature in x-y plane at 5000 iterations, $Ra = 2491$

16. Select New Surface>>Plane from the drop-down menu in the Contours window. Select Three Points as Method. For Point 1, set (X (m), Y (m), Z (m)) to (0, 0, 0), for Point 2 set (X (m), Y (m), Z (m)) to (0, 0, 0.0048) and for Point 3 set (X (m), Y (m), Z (m)) to (0.05, 0, 0). Enter the name *x-z-plane-y=0* as the New Surface Name. Click on Create and Close the window. Select the new plane under Surfaces in the Contours window and check the box for Contour Lines under Options. Click on Colormap Options. Select float as Type for Number Format and set Precision to 1. Set Colormap Alignment to Top. Click on Apply and close the Colormap window. Click on the Save/Display button to display the Temperature field. Select the x-z plane view. Finally, display the Z Velocity field in the *x-z* plane, see Figure 5.16c). You will need to change Colormap Options. Select general as Type for Number Format and set Precision to 2.

Figure 5.16a) Creation of *x-z* plane

Figure 5.16b) Colormap window

Figure 5.16c) Contours of static temp. and $Z$ velocity in $x$-$z$ plane at 5000 iterations, $Ra = 2491$

Figure 5.16d) Photo of experimental Rayleigh-Benard convection at $Ra = 2490$ with a rigid upper wall, Matsson[7].

**Why do the experiments have a different appearance than the concentric roll cells from ANSYS Fluent simulations?** In the experiments with a rigid upper wall, it is hard to get the perfectly concentric circular ring pattern as shown from simulations. The reason for this is that the experiments are sensitive to the non-flatness and imperfections of the bottom and top surfaces. The upper lid in the experiments is a PVC plate that is not perfectly flat.

17. Open Boundary Conditions under Setup in the Outline View. Double click *cold_wall* under Boundary Conditions. Select the Momentum tab and select Marangoni Stress as Shear Condition. Enter the value -2e-5 as Surface Tension Gradient (n/m-k) for Marangoni Stress. Click OK to exit the window. Uncheck the Gravity box under General in the Setup.

Double click on Initialization under Solution in the Outline View. Select Standard Initialization under Initialization Methods. Enter 0.01 for Z Velocity (m/s), enter 297.395 as Temperature (k) and click on Initialize. Double click Run Calculation under Solution in the Outline View. Set the number of iterations to 5000. Click on the Calculate button. Click on the OK button in the Information window that appears when the calculations are complete. Repeat steps 15 – 16.

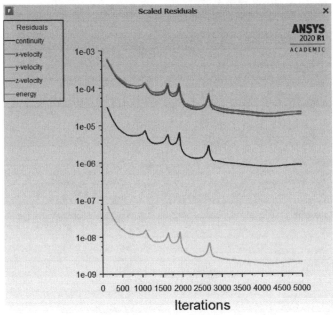

Figure 5.17a) Scaled Residuals for Marangoni convection after 5000 iterations

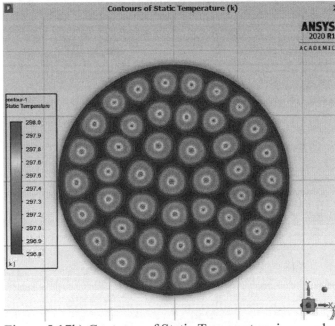

Figure 5.17b) Contours of Static Temperature in x-y plane at 5000 iterations, $M = 895$

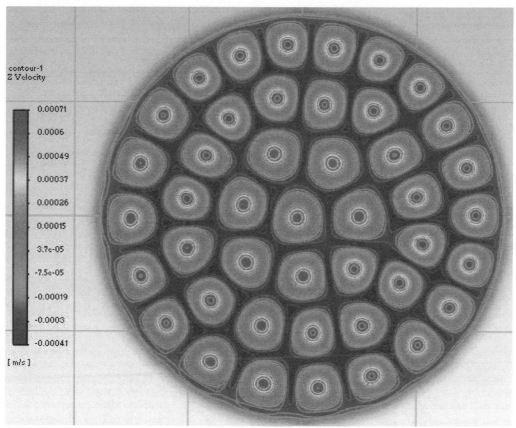

Figure 5.17c) Contours of *Z* Velocity in x-y plane at 5000 iterations, *M* = 895

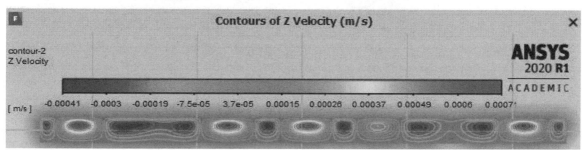

Figure 5.17d) Contours of static temp. and *Z* velocity in *x-z* plane at 5000 iterations, *M* = 895

## H. Theory

### Comparison with Neutral Stability Theory for Rayleigh-Bénard Convection

18. The instability of the fluid layer between two parallel plates heated from below is governed by the Rayleigh number $Ra$.

$$Ra = \frac{g\beta\rho^2 C_p(T_1-T_2)L_c^3}{\mu\,k} \tag{5.1}$$

where $g$ is acceleration due to gravity, $\beta$ is the coefficient of volume expansion, $\rho$ is density of the fluid, $C_p$ is the specific heat, $T_1$ and $T_2$ are the temperatures of the hot and cold surfaces respectively, $L_c$ is the distance between the surfaces (fluid layer thickness), $k$ is thermal conductivity of the fluid, and $\mu$ is the dynamic viscosity of the fluid.

Below the critical $Ra_{crit} = 1708$ for a rigid upper surface, the flow is stable but convective currents will develop above this Rayleigh number. For the case of a free upper surface, the theory predicts a lower critical Rayleigh number at 1101 and for two free boundaries the critical Rayleigh number is 657. The non-dimensional wave number $\alpha$ of this instability is determined by

$$\alpha = \frac{2\pi L_c}{\lambda} \tag{5.2}$$

where $\lambda$ is the wavelength of the instability. The critical wave numbers are $\alpha_{crit} = 3.12, 2.68$ for rigid and free surface boundary conditions, respectively.

From the ANSYS Fluent simulations in this chapter, Figure 5.15c), the wave number can be determined to be

$$\alpha = \frac{2\pi \cdot 0.0048}{0.0103} = 2.927 \tag{5.3}$$

The Rayleigh number in the flow simulation for rigid-rigid boundaries is

$$Ra = \frac{g\beta\rho^2 C_p(T_1-T_2)L_c^3}{\mu\,k} = \frac{9.81*0.000247*997^2*4180*1.5*0.0048\char`\^3}{0.000891*0.607} = 2491 \tag{5.4}$$

The neutral stability curve for Rayleigh-Benard convection with rigid-rigid boundaries can be given to the first approximation, see Figure 5.18a).

$$Ra = \frac{\left(\pi^2+\alpha^2\right)^3}{\alpha^2\left\{1-\dfrac{16\alpha\pi^2\cosh^2\left(\frac{\alpha}{2}\right)}{\left[\left(\pi^2+\alpha^2\right)^2(\sinh\alpha+\alpha)\right]}\right\}} \tag{5.5}$$

The corresponding expression the neutral stability curve to the first approximation for rigid-free boundary conditions is

$$Ra = \frac{\left(\pi^2+\alpha^2\right)^3}{\alpha^2\left\{1-\dfrac{8\alpha\pi^2\sinh^2(\alpha)}{\left[\left(\pi^2+\alpha^2\right)^2(\sinh 2\alpha-2\alpha)\right]}\right\}} \tag{5.6}$$

118

The neutral stability curve for Rayleigh-Benard convection with free-free boundaries is

$$Ra = \frac{(\pi^2 + \alpha^2)^3}{\alpha^2}$$
(5.7)

| Boundaries | $R_{c,\,exact}$ | $R_{c,\,1st\,approx.}$ | $\alpha_c$ |
|---|---|---|---|
| Free-free | 657.5 | ---------- | 2.22 |
| Rigid-free | 1100.7 | 1112.7 | 2.68 |
| Rigid-rigid | 1707.8 | 1715.1 | 3.12 |

Table 5.1 Critical parameters for Rayleigh-Benard convection

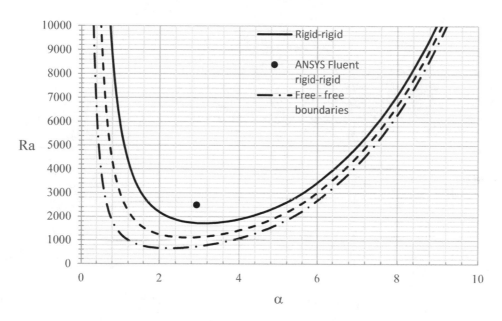

Figure 5.18a) Neutral stability curve for Rayleigh-Bénard convection. The filled circle represents result from ANSYS Fluent simulation.

## Comparison with Neutral Stability Theory for Surface-Tension-Driven Benard Convection (Marangoni Convection)

The instability of the fluid layer heated from below and affected by surface tension gradients is governed by the Marangoni number $M$.

$$M = \frac{\sigma(T_1 - T_2)L_c}{\mu\,\kappa}$$
(5.8)

where $\sigma = -\frac{\partial S}{\partial T}$ is the surface tension $S$ rate of change with temperature $T$, $T_1$ and $T_2$ are the hot and cold temperatures respectively, $L_c$ is the fluid layer thickness, $\kappa$ is thermal diffusivity, and $\mu$ is the dynamic viscosity of the fluid.

Below the critical $M_{crit} = 79.6$, the flow is stable. The non-dimensional wave number $\alpha$ of this instability is determined by

$$\alpha = \frac{2\pi L_c}{\lambda}$$
(5.9)

119

where $\lambda$ is the wavelength of the instability. The critical wave numbers are $\alpha_{crit} = 1.99$. From the ANSYS Fluent simulations in this chapter, Figure 5.17d), the wave number can be determined to be

$$\alpha = \frac{2\pi \cdot 0.0048}{0.01344} = 2.244 \tag{5.10}$$

The Marangoni number in the flow simulation is

$$M = \frac{\sigma(T_1 - T_2)L_c}{\mu \kappa} = \frac{0.00002*1.5*0.0048}{0.000891*1.457E-7} = 895 \tag{5.11}$$

The neutral stability curve for Marangoni convection can be given by

$$M = \frac{8a(a \cosh \alpha + B \sinh \alpha)(\alpha - \sinh \alpha \cosh \alpha)}{a^3 \cosh \alpha - \sinh^3 \alpha} \tag{5.12}$$

where $B = qL_c/k$ is the Biot number and $q = \frac{\partial Q}{\partial T}$ is the heat flux $Q$ rate of change with temperature $T$.

| $B$ | $M_c$ | $\alpha_c$ |
|-----|-------|------------|
| 0   | 79.6  | 1.99       |
| 5   | 250.6 | 2.60       |
| 10  | 413.4 | 2.74       |
| 15  | 575.0 | 2.81       |
| 20  | 736.0 | 2.85       |
| 25  | 896.8 | 2.88       |

Table 5.1 Critical parameters for Marangoni convection

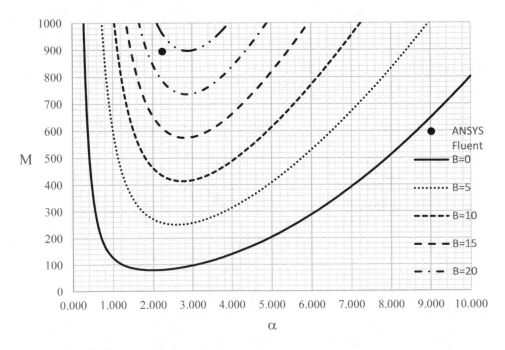

Figure 5.18b) Neutral stability curve for Marangoni convection.

120

# CHAPTER 5. RAYLEIGH BENARD CONVECTION

## I. References

1. Bénard, H. "Les tourbillons cellulaires dans une nappe liquide", *Rev. Gen. Sciences Pure Appl.* **11**, 1261-1271, 1309-1328, 1900
2. Rayleigh, L. "On convection currents in a horizontal layer of fluid when the higher temperature is on the underside.", Phil. Mag. **32**, 529-546, 1916.
3. Chandrasekhar, S. "Hydrodynamic and Hydromagnetic Stability", Dover, 1981.
4. Koschmieder, E.L. "Bénard cells and Taylor vortices", Cambridge University Press, 1993.
5. Koschmieder, E.L. and Pallas, S.G. "Heat transfer through a shallow, horizontal convecting fluid layer.", Int. J. Heat Mass Transfer **17**, 991-1002, 1974.
6. Hoard, C.Q., Robertson, C.R., and Acrivos, A. "Experiments on the cellular structure in Bénard convection", Int. J. Heat Mass Transfer **13**, 849-856, 1970.
7. Matsson J. "A Student Project on Rayleigh-Benard Convection", Annual ASEE Conference & Exposition, June 22-25, Pittsburg, Pa, 2008.
8. Sánchez Torres N.Y., López Sánches E.J., Hernández Zapata S., and Ruiz Chavarría G., 3D Numerical Simulation of Rayleigh-Bénard Convection in a Cylindrical Container. *Selected Topics of Computational and Experimental Fluid Mechanics*, Environmental Science and Engineering, J. Klapp et al.(eds.), Spring International Publishing, Switzerland, 2015.

## J. Exercises

5.1 Run ANSYS Fluent simulations with a rigid upper boundary condition for Rayleigh number $Ra = 3088$ and compare the results with Figure 5.15c) by plotting contours of Z velocity and contours of temperature. Determine the wave number $\alpha$ in the simulations and compare with the neutral stability curve as shown in Figure 5.18a).

5.2 Run ANSYS Fluent simulations with a free upper boundary condition for Rayleigh number $Ra = 2120$ and compare the results with Figure 5.17 by plotting contours of Z velocity and contours of temperature.

Figure 5.18c) Photo of experimental Rayleigh-Benard convection at $Ra = 2120$ with a free surface upper boundary condition (copied from Matsson[7]).

**K. Notes**

## CHAPTER 6. CHANNEL FLOW

## A. Objectives

- Using ANSYS Workbench to Model Geometry and Mesh
- Creating a User Defined Temperature Profile at Inlet
- Inserting Boundary Conditions
- Running Laminar Steady 2D Planar ANSYS Fluent Simulations
- Using Contour Plots for Visualizations of Pressure, Temperature and Velocity Fields
- Using XY Plots for Comparison of Inlet and Outlet Velocity and Temperature Profiles
- Comparing with Theoretical Solution Using Mathematica Code

## B. Problem Description

We will study the development of the laminar flow of aqueous glycerin solution through a channel. The channel has a height of 90 mm and a length of 3,000 mm. The inlet temperature profile is linear where the bottom wall has a temperature of 0 °C and the upper wall is at 100 °C. The inlet velocity profile is laminar with a parabolic velocity profile in between the walls.

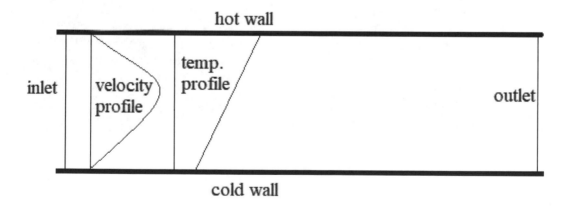

## C. Launching ANSYS Workbench and Selecting Fluent

1. Start by launching the ANSYS Workbench. Double click on Fluid Flow (Fluent).

Figure 6.1 Selecting fluid flow

## D. Launching ANSYS DesignModeler

2. Right click Geometry and select Properties. In Properties of Schematic A2: Geometry, select Analysis Type 2D under Advanced Geometry Options. Right-click on Geometry in the Project Schematic window and select New DesignModeler Geometry. Select Units>>Meter meter as the desired length unit from the menu in DesignModeler.

Figure 6.2a) Launching ANSYS Workbench

124

| 20 | ☐ Advanced Geometry Options | |
|----|----|----|
| 21 | Analysis Type | 3D |
| 22 | Use Associativity | 3D |
| | | 2D |

Figure 6.2b) Advanced geometry options

| ▼ | | A | |
|---|---|---|---|
| 1 | ☼ | Fluid Flow (Fluent) | |
| 2 | 📦 | Geometry | ? |
| 3 | 📦 | Mesh | ? |
| 4 | 📦 | Setup | ? |
| 5 | 📦 | Solution | ? |
| 6 | 📦 | Results | ? |

Fluid Flow (Fluent)

Figure 6.2c) Selecting the geometry

3. Select XY plane in the Tree Outline and select the Sketching tab. Select Look at Sketch .
Draw a rectangle from the origin and set the horizontal length of the rectangle in Details View to
3 m and the vertical height of the rectangle to 0.09 m, see Figure 6.3a). Click on the Modeling tab
in the Tree Outline and highlight Sketch1 under XYPlane. Select Concept>>Surfaces from
Sketches from the menu. Apply Sketch1 as the Base Object in Details View and click on
Generate. Close DesignModeler.

| Details View | ⬍ |
|----|----|
| ☐ Details of Sketch1 | |
| Sketch | Sketch1 |
| Sketch Visibility | Show Sketch |
| Show Constraints? | No |
| ☐ Dimensions: 2 | |
| ☐ H1 | 3 m |
| ☐ V3 | 0.09 m |
| ☐ Edges: 4 | |
| Line | Ln11 |
| Line | Ln12 |
| Line | Ln13 |
| Line | Ln14 |

Figure 6.3a) Surface from a sketch

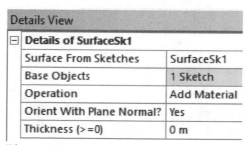

Figure 6.3b) Surface from a sketch

| Details View | |
|----|----|
| ☐ Details of SurfaceSk1 | |
| Surface From Sketches | SurfaceSk1 |
| Base Objects | 1 Sketch |
| Operation | Add Material |
| Orient With Plane Normal? | Yes |
| Thickness (>=0) | 0 m |

Figure 6.3c) Details view

125

## E. Launching ANSYS Meshing

4. Next, we will be creating the mesh for the flow field. Double click on Mesh under Project Schematic in ANSYS Workbench. Right click on Mesh under Outline in the Meshing window and select Generate Mesh. Select Unit Systems>>Metric (mm, kg, N …) from the bottom of the graphics window.

Figure 6.4a) Coarse mesh

Select Mesh>>Controls>>Face Meshing from the menu. Select the mesh region in the graphics window and apply it as Geometry under Scope in Details of "Face Meshing".

Figure 6.4b) Face meshing

Select Mesh>>Controls>>Sizing from the menu. Select Edge ⬚ , control select the four edges of the rectangle and apply them as the Geometry under Scope in Details of "Edge Sizing". Set the element size to 5 mm and the Behavior to Hard. Click on Generate Mesh and select Mesh in the Outline.

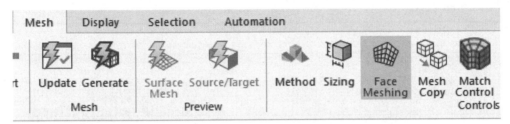

Figure 6.4c) Refined mesh

Select the left vertical edge of the mesh region, right click and select Create Named Selection. Name this edge "inlet". Select the right vertical edge, right click and select Create Named Selection. Name this edge "outlet". Select the horizontal lower edge, right click and select Create Named Selection. Name this edge "cold wall". Finally, select the horizontal upper edge, right click and select Create Named Selection. Name this edge "hot wall".

Figure 6.4d) Named selections

CHAPTER 6. CHANNEL FLOW

Select File>>Save Project from the menu and name the project "Channel Flow". Select File>>Export…>>Mesh>>FLUENT Input File>>Export from the menu in the Meshing window and name the mesh "channel-flow-mesh.msh". Close the meshing window. Right click on Mesh under the Project Schematic in ANSYS Workbench and select Update.

Figure 6.4e) Updating the mesh

## F. Creating a UDF

5. We are now going to create a Used Defined Function for the inlet temperature profile. Start Notepad located in the Windows Accessories folder and include the following text as listed below. Save the file as a text document with the name "udf-inlet-temp-velocity-profiles.txt".

```
#include "udf.h"
DEFINE_PROFILE(inlet_t_temperature, thread, position)
{
real x[ND_ND]; /* this will hold the position vector */
real y;
face_t f;
begin_f_loop(f, thread)
{
F_CENTROID(x,f,thread);
y = x[1];
F_PROFILE(f, thread, position) =273.15+(100*y/0.09);
}
end_f_loop(f, thread)
}
DEFINE_PROFILE(inlet_u_velocity, thread, position)
{
real x[ND_ND]; /* this will hold the position vector */
real y;
face_t f;
begin_f_loop(f, thread)
{
F_CENTROID(x,f,thread);
y = x[1];
F_PROFILE(f, thread, position) =-6*0.03*(y*y-y*0.09)/(0.09*0.09*0.09);
}
end_f_loop(f, thread)
}
```

Figure 6.5 Code for UDF

> **What is a UDF?** A UDF is a user defined function that can be used to define your own boundary conditions, initial conditions or material properties. The C programming language is used for user defined functions and the UDF is saved with the extension .c. All user defined functions start with the first line as #include "udf.h". UDFs are defined using DEFINE macros and can be executed as compiled or interpreted functions. In this chapter we are using the UDF to define the temperature profile at the inlet.

## G. Launching ANSYS Fluent

6. Double click Setup under Project Schematic in ANSYS Workbench. Check the Options box for Double Precision. Select Parallel Processing Options. Set the number of Processes to the number of cores for your computer processor.

   Click on Show More Options, notice the location of the Working Directory and copy the file "udf-inlet-temp-velocity-profiles.txt" to this location. Click on Start to close the Fluent Launcher window.

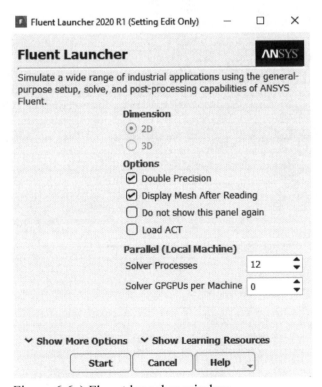

Figure 6.6a) Fluent launcher window

Select the Pressure-Based Solver under General on the Task Page and click on Units… under General, see Figure 6.6b). Scroll down the Quantities and select temperature. Set the Units to $c$ for temperature and do the same for temperature-difference. Close the Set Units window.

Open Models under Setup in the Outline View. Double click Energy-Off under Models and check the box for Energy Equation. Click OK to close the Energy window.

Figure 6.6b) General solution setup

Figure 6.6c) Setting the units

Figure 6.6d) Energy equation

7.  Double click Materials under Setup in the Outline View. Click on Create/Edit… for Fluid on the Task Page and select Fluent Database in the new window. Scroll down in the Fluent Fluid Materials and select glycerin (c3h8o3). Click on Copy and Close the window.

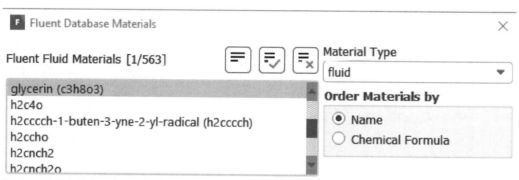

Figure 6.7a) Selection of glycerin as fluid

Select piecewise-linear for Density (kg/m3) under Properties in the Create/Edit Materials window. Increase the number of points to 11 in the Piecewise-Linear Profile window. Set the Temperature (c) for Point 1 to 0 and Value (kg/m3) to 1268.4. Set the values for the remaining points as shown in Table 6.1. Click on the OK button to close the window.

Select piecewise-linear for Viscosity (kg/m-s) under Properties. Increase the number of points to 11. Set the Temperature (c) for Point 1 to 0 and Value (kg/m-s) to 7.2162. Set the values for the remaining points as shown in Table 6.1. Click on the OK button to close the piecewise-linear profile window. Click on Change/Create and Close the Create/Edit Materials window.

Figure 6.7b) Selection of piecewise-linear density for glycerin

Figure 6.7c) Temperature and density for data points

| Point | Temperature (c) | Density (kg/m3) | Viscosity (kg/m-s) |
|-------|-----------------|-----------------|--------------------|
| 1 | 0 | 1268.4 | 7.2162 |
| 2 | 10 | 1262.2 | 2.3857 |
| 3 | 20 | 1256.0 | 0.92181 |
| 4 | 30 | 1249.8 | 0.40505 |
| 5 | 40 | 1243.7 | 0.19801 |
| 6 | 50 | 1237.6 | 0.10591 |
| 7 | 60 | 1231.5 | 0.06113 |
| 8 | 70 | 1225.5 | 0.03767 |
| 9 | 80 | 1219.5 | 0.024552 |
| 10 | 90 | 1213.5 | 0.016809 |
| 11 | 100 | 1207.6 | 0.012009 |

Table 6.1 Properties of glycerin (98 percent weight) at different temperatures

Figure 6.7d) Temperature and viscosity for data points

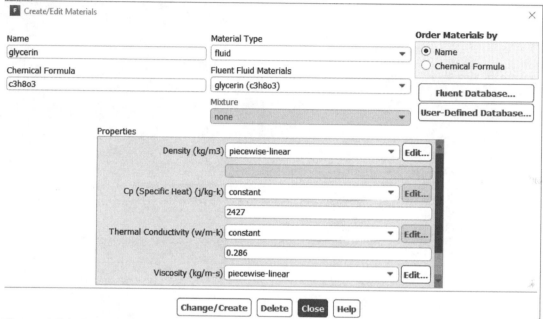

Figure 6.7e) Create/Edit Materials window

8.  Open Cell Zone Conditions under Setup in the Outline View. Double click *surface_body*. Select glycerin as the Material Name and click on OK to close the window.

Figure 6.8a) Selection of glycerin as fluid

Select User-Defined>>Functions>>Interpreted… from the menu. Browse for the source file and Select Files of type: All Files (*). Find the file named "*udf-inlet-temp-velocity-profiles.txt*" in the working directory and click OK. Click on Interpret and Close the Interpreted UDFs window.

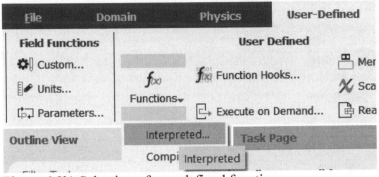

Figure 6.8b) Selection of user defined function

Figure 6.8c) Interpreted UDFs

9.  Open Models under Setup in the Outline View. Double click on the Viscous (SST k-omega) model. Select the Laminar Model and click OK to close the Viscous Model window. Open Boundary Conditions under Setup in the Outline View. Double click on *inlet* under Boundary Conditions. Set the Velocity Specification Method to Components. Select *udf inlet_u_velocity* as X-Velocity (m/s). Click on the Thermal tab and select *udf inlet_t_temperature* from the Temperature drop down menu. Click OK to close the Velocity Inlet window.

Figure 6.9a) Momentum boundary condition for velocity inlet

**F** Velocity Inlet                                                                        ✕

Zone Name

inlet

| Momentum | Thermal | Radiation | Species | DPM | Multiphase | Potential | UDS |
|----------|---------|-----------|---------|-----|------------|-----------|-----|

Temperature  udf inlet_t_temperature                                ▼

Figure 6.9b) Selection of *udf* for velocity inlet as thermal boundary condition

Double click on *cold_wall* under Boundary Conditions in the Outline View. Select the Thermal tab in the Wall window and select Temperature as Thermal Condition. Set the Temperature (c) to 0. Click OK to close the Wall window. Repeat this step for the *hot_wall* and set the temperature to 100 (c).

**F** Wall

Zone Name

cold_wall

Adjacent Cell Zone

surface_body

| Momentum | Thermal | Radiation | Species | DPM | Multiphase |
|----------|---------|-----------|---------|-----|------------|

**Thermal Conditions**

○ Heat Flux                                    Temperature (c) 0

● Temperature                                  Wall Thickness (m) 0

Figure 6.9c) Cold wall thermal boundary condition

**F** Wall

Zone Name

hot_wall

Adjacent Cell Zone

surface_body

| Momentum | Thermal | Radiation | Species | DPM | Multiphase |
|----------|---------|-----------|---------|-----|------------|

**Thermal Conditions**

○ Heat Flux                                    Temperature (c) 100

● Temperature                                  Wall Thickness (m) 0

Figure 6.9d) Hot wall thermal boundary condition

133

10. Open Monitors under Solution in the Outline View and double click on Residual under Monitors. Set Absolute Criteria to 1e-06 for all four Residuals. Click OK to close the Residual Monitors window.

Figure 6.10a) Residual monitors window

Double click on Reference Values under Setup in the Outline View. Select *Compute from inlet* and select *surface_body* as Reference Zone. Double click on Initialization under Solution in the Outline View. Select Standard Initialization on the Task Page as Initialization Method and *Compute from inlet*. Click on *Initialize*. Double click on Run Calculation under Solution in the Outline View. Enter 10000 as *Number of Iterations*. Click on *Calculate*. Click OK when calculation is complete.

Figure 6.10b) Reference values

Figure 6.10c) Solution initialization

Figure 6.10d) Running the calculations

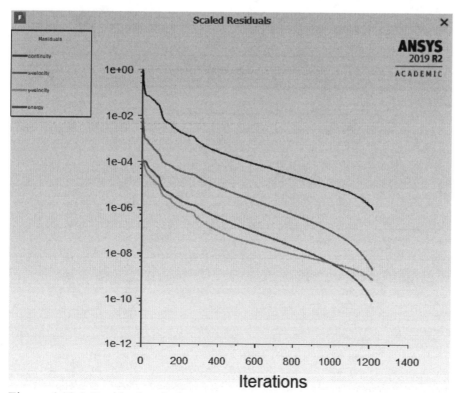

Figure 6.10e) Residuals window

## H. Post-Processing

11. Open Graphics under Results in the Outline View. Double click on Contours under Graphics. Select all Surfaces and click on Colormap Options. Select float as Type and 0 for Precision. Select Top as Colormap Alignment, click on Apply and Close the Colormap window. Click on Save/Display. Display another plot of temperature contours by selecting Contours of Temperature and Static Temperature and click on Save/Display. Finally, select Contours of Velocity and X Velocity and set the Precision to 2 in the Colormap window. Click on Save/Display.

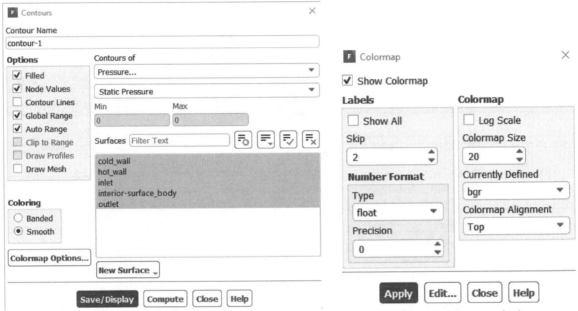

Figure 6.11a) Contours window          Figure 6.11b) Colormap window

Figure 6.11c) Contours of static pressure and static temperature for glycerin flow

Figure 6.11d) Contours of X velocity for glycerin flow

12. Double click on XY Plot under Results and Plots in the Outline View. Uncheck Position on X Axis under Options. Select Mesh and Y-Coordinate as Y Axis Function. Select Velocity and X Velocity as X Axis Function. Click on Load File and load the file with the name *theory channel flow.dat* from the working directory. This file can be downloaded from *sdcpublications.com*. Select inlet and outlet as the Surfaces and click on Curves. Select the first Pattern for Curve # 0 and no Symbol. Click on Apply. Select the next available Pattern for Curve # 1 and no Symbol. Click on Apply. Select the next available Pattern for Curve # 2 and no Symbol. Finally, continue with Curve # 3 in the same way for the Theory. Click on Apply and Close the window.

Click on Axes… and uncheck the box for Auto Range under Options for the X Axis. Set Minimum to 0 and Maximum to 1 under Range. Set Precision to 1 under Number Format. Click on Apply. Check the Y Axis and set the Precision to 2 under Number Format. Click on Apply. Close the window and click on Save/Plot.

Select Temperature and Static Temperature as X Axis Function. Select inlet and outlet as the Surfaces and unselect Theory under File Data. Click on Axes…, select X Axis and check the box for Auto Range under Options. Set Precision to 0 under Number Format, click on Apply and close the window. Click on Save/Plot.

Figure 6.12a) Solution XY Plot window

Figure 6.12b) Solution XY Plot window

Figure 6.12c) Settings for X and Y Axes

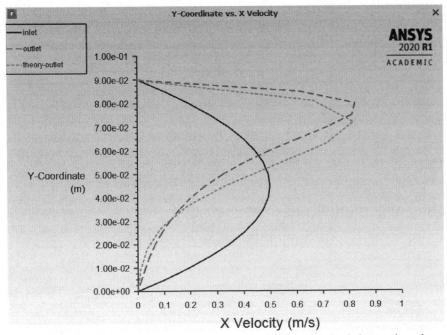

Figure 6.12d) X Velocity profiles for glycerin flow at the inlet and outlet

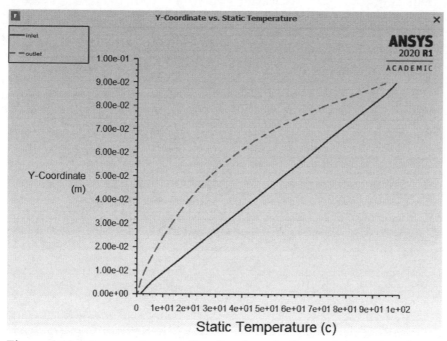

Figure 6.12e) Temperature profiles for glycerin flow at inlet and outlet

## I. Theory

13. The equation of motion for the fluid for fully developed flow is given by the following equation

$$\mu \frac{d^2u}{dy^2} = \frac{dp}{dx} \tag{6.1}$$

where $u$ (m/s) is streamwise velocity, x (m) is streamwise coordinate, $y$ (m) is the wall-normal coordinate, $\mu$ (kg/ms) is dynamic viscosity, and $p$ (Pa) is the pressure. The boundary conditions are $u(0) = u\ (h) = 0$ where $h$ is the height of the channel.

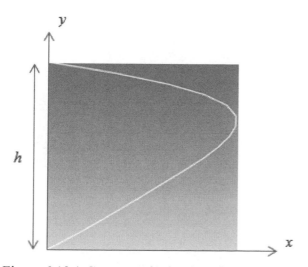

Figure 6.13a) Geometry for laminar flow of glycerin

| Element $i$ | Density (kg/m3) | Viscosity $\mu_i$ (kg/ms) | Pressure gradient $\left(\frac{dp}{dx}\right)_i$ (Pa/m) |
|---|---|---|---|
| 1 | 1265.3 | 4.80095 | -78.9249 |
| 2 | 1259.1 | 1.653755 | -78.9249 |
| 3 | 1252.9 | 0.66343 | -78.9249 |
| 4 | 1246.75 | 0.30153 | -78.9249 |
| 5 | 1240.65 | 0.15196 | -78.9249 |
| 6 | 1234.55 | 0.08352 | -78.9249 |
| 7 | 1228.5 | 0.0494 | -78.9249 |
| 8 | 1222.5 | 0.031111 | -78.9249 |
| 9 | 1216.5 | 0.020681 | -78.9249 |
| 10 | 1210.55 | 0.014409 | -78.9249 |

Table 6.2 Average properties of glycerin (98 percent weight) and pressure gradient for each element

We can now compute the resistance or stiffness matrix for each element, see Moaveni[1]

$$K_i = \frac{10\mu_i}{h}\begin{pmatrix} 1 & -1 \\ -1 & 1 \end{pmatrix} \tag{6.2}$$

, and the forcing vector will be the following for each element

$$F_i = -\frac{h}{20}\left(\frac{dp}{dx}\right)_i\begin{pmatrix} 1 \\ 1 \end{pmatrix} \tag{6.3}$$

Next, we assemble the stiffness matrices into the following matrix

$$K = \frac{10}{h}\begin{pmatrix}
\mu_1 & -\mu_1 & 0 & 0 & 0 & 0 & 0 & 0 & 0 & 0 & 0 \\
-\mu_1 & \mu_1+\mu_2 & -\mu_2 & 0 & 0 & 0 & 0 & 0 & 0 & 0 & 0 \\
0 & -\mu_2 & \mu_2+\mu_3 & -\mu_3 & 0 & 0 & 0 & 0 & 0 & 0 & 0 \\
0 & 0 & -\mu_3 & \mu_3+\mu_4 & -\mu_4 & 0 & 0 & 0 & 0 & 0 & 0 \\
0 & 0 & 0 & -\mu_4 & \mu_4+\mu_5 & -\mu_5 & 0 & 0 & 0 & 0 & 0 \\
0 & 0 & 0 & 0 & -\mu_5 & \mu_5+\mu_6 & -\mu_6 & 0 & 0 & 0 & 0 \\
0 & 0 & 0 & 0 & 0 & -\mu_6 & \mu_6+\mu_7 & -\mu_7 & 0 & 0 & 0 \\
0 & 0 & 0 & 0 & 0 & 0 & -\mu_7 & \mu_7+\mu_8 & -\mu_8 & 0 & 0 \\
0 & 0 & 0 & 0 & 0 & 0 & 0 & -\mu_8 & \mu_8+\mu_9 & -\mu_9 & 0 \\
0 & 0 & 0 & 0 & 0 & 0 & 0 & 0 & -\mu_9 & \mu_9+\mu_{10} & -\mu_{10} \\
0 & 0 & 0 & 0 & 0 & 0 & 0 & 0 & 0 & -\mu_{10} & -\mu_{10}
\end{pmatrix} \tag{6.4}$$

, and we assemble the forcing vector into the following

$$\boldsymbol{F} = 6h \begin{pmatrix} 1 \\ 2 \\ 2 \\ 2 \\ 2 \\ 2 \\ 2 \\ 2 \\ 2 \\ 2 \\ 1 \end{pmatrix} \tag{6.5}$$

After inclusion of boundary conditions, we get the following

$$\begin{pmatrix} 1 & 0 & 0 & 0 & 0 & 0 & 0 & 0 & 0 & 0 & 0 \\ -\mu_1 & \mu_1+\mu_2 & -\mu_2 & 0 & 0 & 0 & 0 & 0 & 0 & 0 & 0 \\ 0 & -\mu_2 & \mu_2+\mu_3 & -\mu_3 & 0 & 0 & 0 & 0 & 0 & 0 & 0 \\ 0 & 0 & -\mu_3 & \mu_3+\mu_4 & -\mu_4 & 0 & 0 & 0 & 0 & 0 & 0 \\ 0 & 0 & 0 & -\mu_4 & \mu_4+\mu_5 & -\mu_5 & 0 & 0 & 0 & 0 & 0 \\ 0 & 0 & 0 & 0 & -\mu_5 & \mu_5+\mu_6 & -\mu_6 & 0 & 0 & 0 & 0 \\ 0 & 0 & 0 & 0 & 0 & -\mu_6 & \mu_6+\mu_7 & -\mu_7 & 0 & 0 & 0 \\ 0 & 0 & 0 & 0 & 0 & 0 & -\mu_7 & \mu_7+\mu_8 & -\mu_8 & 0 & 0 \\ 0 & 0 & 0 & 0 & 0 & 0 & 0 & -\mu_8 & \mu_8+\mu_9 & -\mu_9 & 0 \\ 0 & 0 & 0 & 0 & 0 & 0 & 0 & 0 & -\mu_9 & \mu_9+\mu_{10} & -\mu_{10} \\ 0 & 0 & 0 & 0 & 0 & 0 & 0 & 0 & 0 & 0 & 1 \end{pmatrix} \begin{pmatrix} u_1 \\ u_2 \\ u_3 \\ u_4 \\ u_5 \\ u_6 \\ u_7 \\ u_8 \\ u_9 \\ u_{10} \\ u_{11} \end{pmatrix} = \frac{6h^2}{10} \begin{pmatrix} 0 \\ 2 \\ 2 \\ 2 \\ 2 \\ 2 \\ 2 \\ 2 \\ 2 \\ 2 \\ 0 \end{pmatrix} \tag{6.6}$$

with the following solution

$$\boldsymbol{u} = \begin{pmatrix} 0 \\ 0.0051 \\ 0.0178 \\ 0.0447 \\ 0.0930 \\ 0.1677 \\ 0.2647 \\ 0.3631 \\ 0.4153 \\ 0.3371 \\ 0 \end{pmatrix} \tag{6.7}$$

```
h = 0.09; n = 10; w = 1; dpdx = -78.9249; a = -dpdx * h / n;
μ = {4.80095, 1.653755, 0.66343, 0.30153, 0.15196, 0.08352, 0.0494, 0.031111, 0.020681, 0.014409};
ρ = {1265.3, 1259.1, 1252.9, 1246.75, 1240.65, 1234.55, 1228.5, 1222.5, 1216.5, 1210.55};

{a1, b1, c1} = {Array[-μ[[#]] &, n - 1], Array[μ[[#-2]] + μ[[#-1]] &, n, {2, 11}], Array[-μ[[#-1]] &, n, {2, 11}]};
K = (n / h) * SparseArray[{Band[{1, 2}] → c1, Band[{1, 1}] → b1, Band[{2, 1}] → a1}, 11];
K[[1, 1]] = h / n;
K[[1, 2]] = 0;
K[[n + 1, n + 1]] = h / n;
MatrixForm[Normal[K]];

s = LinearSolve[K, {0, a, a, a, a, a, a, a, a, a, 0}];
```

$$\dot{m} = \sum_{i=1}^{in} \rho[[i]] * w * (h / n) * (s[[i]] + s[[i + 1]]) / 2;$$

```
ListLinePlot[Array[{s[[#]], (# - 1) * h / n} &, n + 1, {1, n + 1}], AxesLabel → {"u (m/s)", "y (m)"}, PlotLabels → {"Theory"}]

mylist = Array[{s[[#]], (# - 1) * h / n} &, n + 1, {1, n + 1}];
TableOfValues1 = Prepend[mylist, {"((xy/key/label \"theory-outlet\")"}];
TableOfValues1 = Prepend[TableOfValues1, {""}];
TableOfValues1 = Prepend[TableOfValues1, {"(labels \"X Velocity\" \"Y-Coordinate\")"}];
TableOfValues1 = Prepend[TableOfValues1, {"(title \"Theory\")"}];
TableOfValues1 = Append[TableOfValues1, {")"}];
Grid[TableOfValues1]
Export["theory.dat", TableOfValues1]
```

Figure 6.13b) Mathematica code for theoretical solution

## J. References

1. S. Moaveni, Finite Element Analysis: Theory and Applications with ANSYS, 3rd Ed., Prentice Hall, 2007.

## K. Exercises

6.1 Replace the fluid with engine oil from the Fluent Database and enter the piecewise-linear values for the four points as listed in the table below. Increase the Gage Total Pressure at the inlet to 500 Pa. Include residuals window, contour plots of Static Pressure, Static Temperature, X Velocity, and the X Velocity profile.

| Point | Temperature (c) | Density (kg/m3) | Viscosity (kg/m-s) |
|-------|-----------------|-----------------|--------------------|
| 1     | 20              | 881.5           | 0.23939            |
| 2     | 30              | 875.4           | 0.12842            |
| 3     | 40              | 869.3           | 0.07455            |
| 4     | 50              | 863             | 0.04643            |

Table 6.3 Properties for engine oil (SAE 30)

6.2 Change the size of the computational domain to 6 m in length and 0.2 m in height and change the mesh size to 0.015 m in horizontal direction and 0.01 m in the vertical direction. Modify the temperature of the cold lower wall to 0 (c) and 100 (c) for the upper hot wall. Rewrite and reinterpret the *udf* file for the new temperatures of the cold and hot wall and modify the *udf* file for the change in height of the computational domain. Replace the fluid with engine oil from the Fluent Database and enter the piecewise-linear values for the 11 points as listed in the table below. Increase the Gage Total Pressure at the inlet to 1000 pascal. Include *udf* code, zoomed in mesh that shows details, residuals window, contour plots of Static Pressure, Static Temperature, X Velocity, and the X Velocity profile.

| Point | Temperature (c) | Density (kg/m3) | Viscosity (kg/m-s) |
|-------|-----------------|-----------------|--------------------|
| 1 | 0 | 867.4 | 0.75352 |
| 2 | 10 | 860.9 | 0.37865 |
| 3 | 20 | 854.5 | 0.20689 |
| 4 | 30 | 848.3 | 0.12190 |
| 5 | 40 | 842.1 | 0.076551 |
| 6 | 50 | 835.8 | 0.050861 |
| 7 | 60 | 829.5 | 0.035409 |
| 8 | 70 | 823.2 | 0.025631 |
| 9 | 80 | 817 | 0.019181 |
| 10 | 90 | 810.6 | 0.014742 |
| 11 | 100 | 804.5 | 0.011619 |

Table 6.4 Properties for engine oil (SAE 5W-40)

**L.  Notes**

# CHAPTER 7. ROTATING FLOW IN A CAVITY

## A. Objectives

- Using ANSYS Fluent to Study Rotating Flow in a Cavity
- Inserting Boundary Conditions and Rotation
- Running Laminar 2D Axi-Symmetric ANSYS Fluent Simulations with Swirl
- Using XY Plots for Profiles of Velocity Components
- Comparing with Results Using Mathematica Code
- Using Contour Plots for Visualizations of Streamlines and Velocity Components
- Using Pathlines to Visualize the Flow Patterns and Compare with Experiments

## B. Problem Description

We will study the rotating flow in a cavity and we will analyze the problem using ANSYS Fluent. The rotating cavity filled with water has a cylindrical geometry with a diameter of 95 mm and a height with the same dimension. The top lid is rotating with a rotational speed of 0.445 rad/s while the remaining walls of the cavity are stationary.

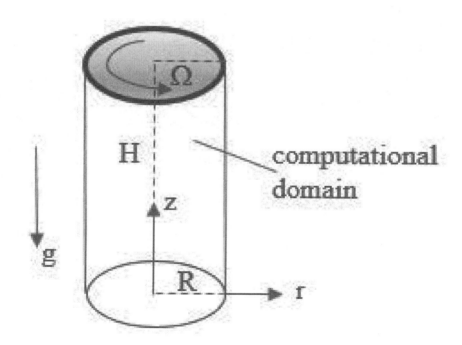

## C. Launching ANSYS Workbench and Selecting Fluent

1. Start by launching ANSYS Workbench. Double click on Fluid Flow (Fluent) under Analysis Systems in Toolbox. Right click on Geometry in the Project Schematic and select Properties. Select 2D Analysis Type in Advanced Geometry Options under Properties of Schematic A2: Geometry.

Figure 7.1a) Selecting Fluid Flow

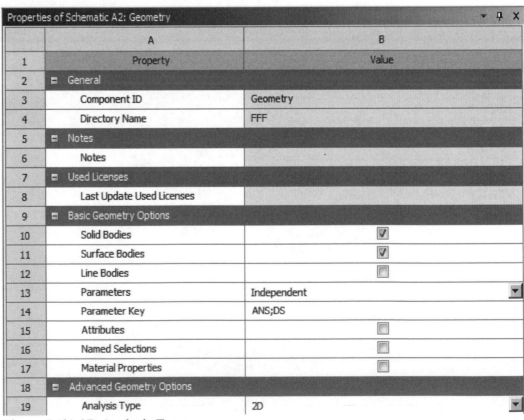

Figure 7.1b) 2D Analysis Type

### D. Launching ANSYS DesignModeler

2.  Right click on Geometry under Project Schematic in ANSYS Workbench and select New DesignModeler Geometry. Select **Units Millimeter** from the menu in DesignModeler.

    Select the XYPlane in Tree Outline. Look At Face/Plane/Sketch . Select the Sketching tab and Rectangle under the Draw tab. Draw a rectangle from the origin in the first quadrant. Select the Dimensions tab. Click on the left vertical edge of the rectangle and the lower horizontal edge. Enter 47.5 mm as the vertical dimension and 95 mm as the horizontal dimension. Select Concept>>Surfaces from Sketches from the menu. Select Sketch 1 under XY Plane in the Tree Outline. Apply the Sketch as Base Object in the Details View. Click on Generate and close DesignModeler.

Figure 7.2 Surface sketch of the rectangle

### E. Launching ANSYS Meshing

3.  Double click on Mesh under Project Schematic in ANSYS Workbench. In the Meshing window, right-click on Mesh under Project and select Update. Select Mesh>>Controls>>Face Meshing from the menu. Select the rectangle in the graphics window and Apply it as Geometry in Details of Face Meshing.

Figure 7.3a) Coarse mesh                    Figure 7.3b) Face meshing

Select Mesh>>Controls>>Sizing from the menu. Select the Edge tool ⬚ , control click on the two vertical edges of the rectangle and Apply them as Geometry in Details of Sizing. Select Number of Divisions as Type and enter 20. Select Hard as Behavior. Select the third Bias type from the drop-down menu and enter 5.0 as Bias Factor. Repeat this step but select the two horizontal edges and 40 as the Number of Divisions. Use the same Bias type and a Bias Factor of 5.0. Right-click on Mesh and select Update.

Figure 7.3c) Details of edge sizing for vertical edges

Figure 7.3d) Details of edge sizing for horizontal edges

4. Control-select the upper horizontal edge and left vertical edge, right-click and select Create Named Selection. Enter the name *wall* and click OK to close the window. Select the right vertical edge, right click and select Create Named Selection. Enter the name *lid*. Finally, name the lower horizontal edge as *symmetry*. Select File>>Save Project from the menu and enter the name "Rotating Lid Flow in Cylinder". Select File>>Export...>>Mesh>>FLUENT Input File>>Export from the menu in ANSYS Mechanical and save the mesh with the name "rotating-lid-cylinder-flow-mesh.msh". Close the Meshing window. Right-click on Mesh in the Project Schematic of ANSYS Workbench and select Update.

Figure 7.4 Named selections

## F. Launching ANSYS Fluent

5.  Double-click on Setup under Project Schematic in ANSYS Workbench. Select Double Precision and select Parallel Processing Options. Set the number of Processes equal to the number of processor cores on your computer. Click on Show More Options and write down the location of the Working Directory as you will need it later. Click on the Start button in the Fluent Launcher window.

Figure 7.5a) Fluent launcher window

Click on Check and Scale… under Mesh in General on the Task Page to verify the Domain Extents. Close the Scale Mesh window. Select Axisymmetric Swirl as 2D Space Solver. Select Relative Velocity Formulation. Check the box for Gravity. Enter -9.81 as Gravitational Acceleration in the X direction.

> **Why did we select Axisymmetric Swirl and Relative Velocity Formulation?** This problem is axisymmetric and has a rotating lid boundary condition that will cause a swirling flow in the container. We choose Relative Velocity Formulation since we are using a small container where the lid is rotating, and this will cause most of the flow in the container to be rotating.

**F** Scale Mesh

**Domain Extents**

| Xmin (m) | 0 | Xmax (m) | 0.095 |
| Ymin (m) | 0 | Ymax (m) | 0.0475 |

**View Length Unit In**

m ▼

Figure 7.5b) Scale mesh window

149

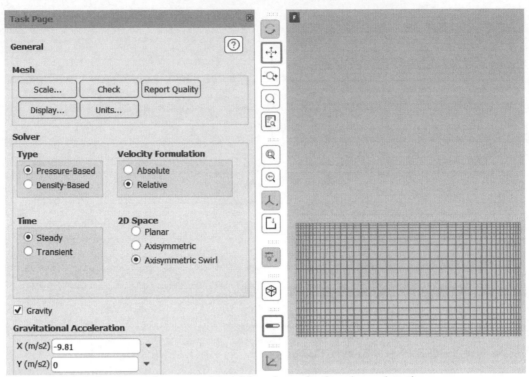

Figure 7.5c) Selecting axisymmetric swirl and gravitational acceleration

6. Next, we double click on Materials under Setup in the Outline View. Select Fluid under Materials on the Task Page and click on Create/Edit…. Click on Fluent Database… in the Create/Edit Materials window. Scroll down in the Fluent Fluid Material section and select water-liquid (h2o<l>). Click on Copy at the bottom of the Fluent Database Materials window. Close the two windows.

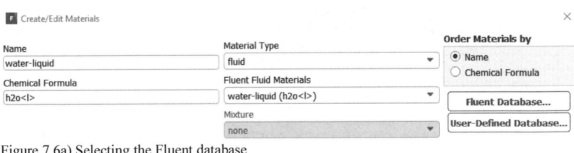

Figure 7.6a) Selecting the Fluent database

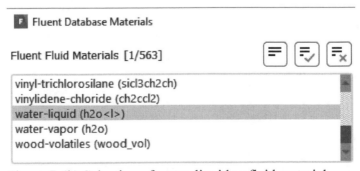

Figure 7.6b) Selection of water-liquid as fluid material

7. Open Cell Zone Conditions and Fluid under Setup in the Outline View. Double click on *surface_body* under Fluid. Select water-liquid as Material Name. Check the box for Frame Motion and enter Speed (rad/s) -0.4449 as Rotational Velocity. Click OK to close the Fluid window.

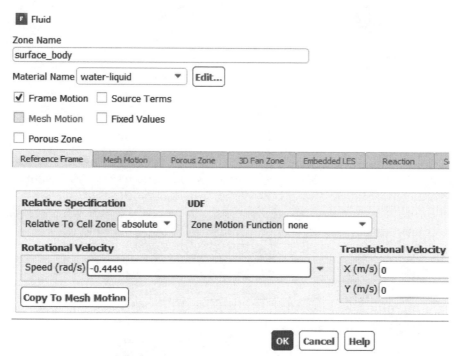

Figure 7.7 Selection of water-liquid and frame motion for the surface body

8. Double click on Boundary Conditions under Setup in the Outline View. Select symmetry under Zone in Boundary Conditions on the Task Page. Choose axis from the Type drop-down menu, rename the Zone Name to *axis* and click OK in the Axis window.

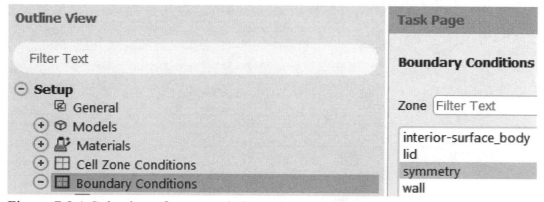

Figure 7.8a) Selection of symmetric boundary condition

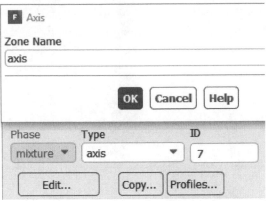

Figure 7.8b) Selection of axis boundary condition

Select *lid* under Zone in Boundary Conditions on the Task Page. Click on the Edit… button for wall Type. Select *Moving Wall* under Wall Motion. Check Absolute and Rotational under Motion and enter 0.4449 as Speed (rad/s). Click OK to close the window. Repeat this step for the *wall* Zone, use Absolute and Rotational Motion and enter 0 as Speed (rad/s), see Figure 7.8d). Click OK to close the window.

Figure 7.8c) Details of wall motion for lid

Figure 7.8d) Details of wall motion for wall

9. Double click on Models and Viscous (SST k-omega) under Setup in the Outline View. Choose Laminar as the Viscous Model and click OK to close the window. Double click on Methods under Solution in the Outline View and choose PRESTO! for Pressure Spatial Discretization on the Task Page. Select SIMPLEC as the Pressure-Velocity Coupling Scheme. Select Green-Gauss Node Based Gradient under Spatial Discretization. Select QUICK for both Momentum and Swirl Velocity under Spatial Discretization. Double click on Controls under Solution in the Tree. Set all Under-Relaxation Factors to 1 except Momentum that is set to 0.7.

> **Why did we choose Green-Gauss Node Based, QUICK, PRESTO! and SIMPLEC Solution Methods?** The reason for using SIMPLEC as Pressure-Velocity Coupling algorithm is that we are studying steady laminar flow and SIMPLEC is used instead of SIMPLE as it provides a faster solution and a higher under-relaxation. PISO is used for transient solutions. Coupled can alternatively give an efficient steady state solution for single phase flows. The PRESTO! pressure scheme is recommended when we have rotating, swirling flows with curvature. QUICK is used with quadrilateral meshes to provide better accuracy for rotating and swirling flows. The Green-Gauss Node Based gradient is more accurate than the cell-based gradient.

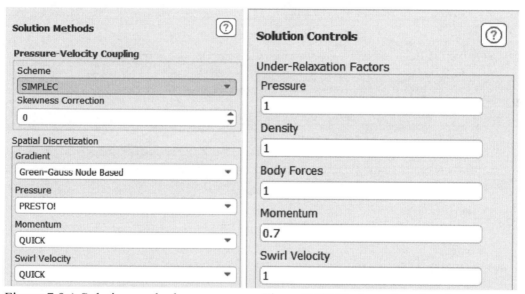

Figure 7.9a) Solution methods          Figure 7.9b) Under-relaxation factors

10. Double click on Monitors and Residual under Solution in the Outline View. Make sure that the box for Plot under Options is checked. Set the Absolute Criteria to 1e-12 for all four residuals and click OK to close the window.

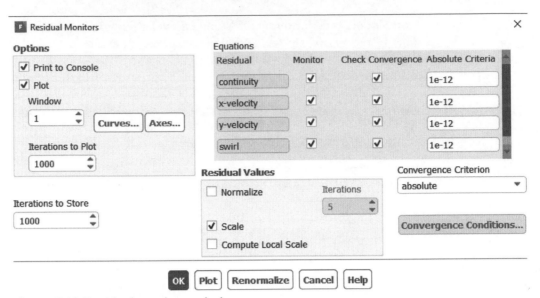

Figure 7.10 Residual monitors window

11. Double click on Initialization under Solution in the Outline View and select Standard Initialization as Initialization Method. Set Swirl Velocity (m/s) to 0.02. This value is approximately the speed of rotation 0.4449 rad/s times the radius 0.0475m. Click on Initialize. Double click on Run Calculation under Solution in the Outline View and set the Number of Iterations to 2000. Click on the *Calculate* button on the Task Page. Click OK in the Information window when the calculation is complete.

Figure 7.11a) Solution initialization

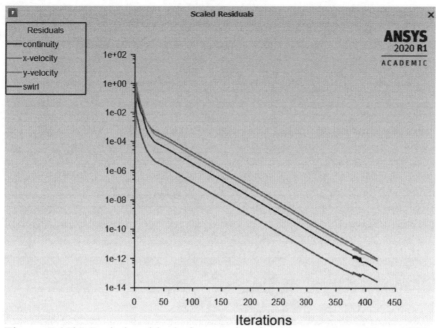

Figure 7.11b) Scaled residuals for rotating flow in a cavity at Re = 1000

## G. Post-Processing

12. Open Graphics under Results in Outline View and double click on Contours under Graphics. Select Contours of Velocity and Stream Function. Select all surfaces including *interior-surface_body*. Click on Save/Display and Close the Contours window.

Figure 7.12a) Contours window

155

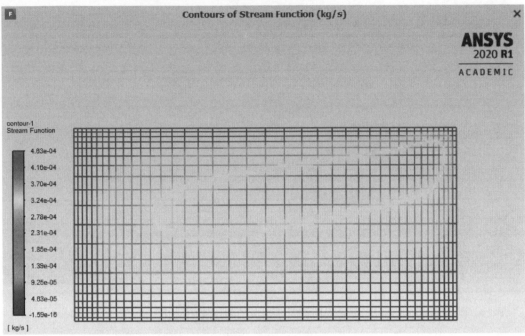

Figure 7.12b) Streamlines for Re = 1,000 and H/R = 2

13. Open Plots and double click on XY Plot under Results in the Outline View. Uncheck Position on X Axis and Position on Y Axis under Options. Select Velocity… and Swirl Velocity as Y Axis Function. Select Mesh… and X-Coordinate as X Axis Function. Select New Surface>>Line/Rake…. Enter x0 (m) 0 and x1 (m) 0.095. Enter y0 (m) 0.0285 and y1 (m) 0.0285. Enter *y=0.0285m* as the New Surface Name and click on Create. Close the Line/Rake Surface window.

    Select *y=0.0285m* under Surfaces in the Solution XY Plot window and click on Axes…. Set Precision to 2 under Number Format for X Axis. Click on Apply. Set Precision to 3 under Number Format for Y Axis. Click on Apply. Close the Axes window. Click on Curves…. Select the first available Line Style Pattern for Curve # 0 and use no symbol. Select the next available Line Style Pattern for Curve # 1 and use no symbol. Click on Apply and Close the Curves – Solution XY Plot window.

    Copy the file $swirl - velocity - y = 0.0285m.dat$ to the Working Directory. This and other files can be downloaded from *sdcpublications.com*. Click on Load File… and read the file $swirl - velocity - y = 0.0285m.dat$ from the working directory. Click on Save/Plot. Repeat this step twice but instead load $radial - velocity - y = 0.0285m.dat$ and $axial - velocity - y = 0.0285m.dat$ and plot the Radial Velocity and the Axial Velocity components, respectively.

    Create another Line/Rake… with x0 (m) 0.0475 and x1 (m) 0.0475. Enter y0 (m) 0 and y1 (m) 0.0475. Enter *x=0.0475m* as the New Surface Name. Plot the three velocity components versus Y-Coordinate and compare with loaded files. Close the Solution XY Plot window.

Figure 7.13a) Line/rake surface window

Figure 7.13b) X Axes settings
Figure 7.13c) Y Axcs settings

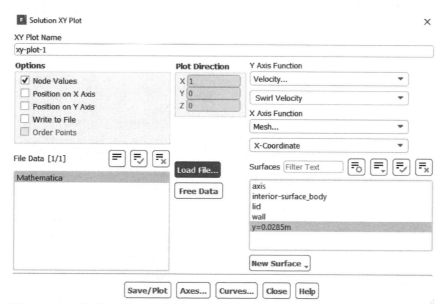

Figure 7.13d) Solution XY Plot window

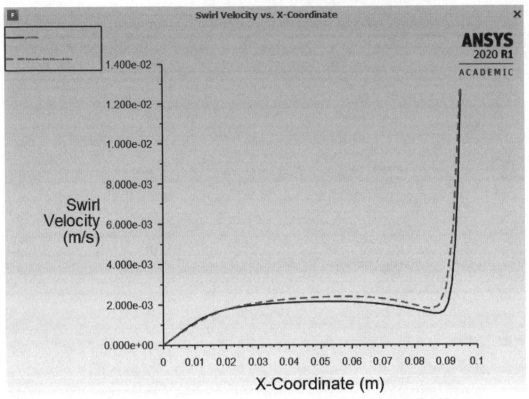

Figure 7.13e) Swirl velocity versus $x$ (Re = 1,000 and H/R = 2) at $y$ = 0.0285 m

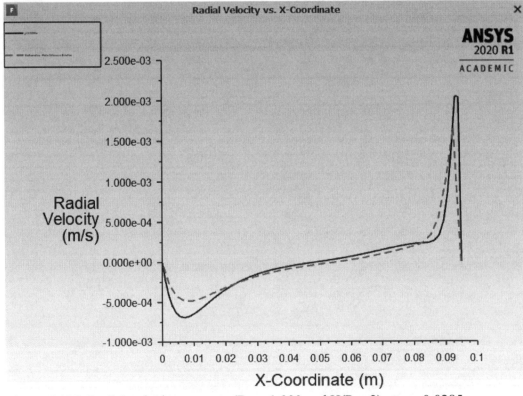

Figure 7.13f) Radial velocity versus $x$ (Re = 1,000 and H/R = 2) at $y$ = 0.0285 m

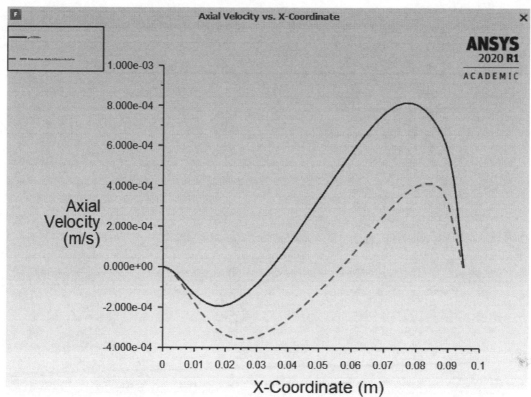

Figure 7.13g) Axial velocity versus *x* (Re = 1,000 and H/R = 2) at *y* = 0.0285m

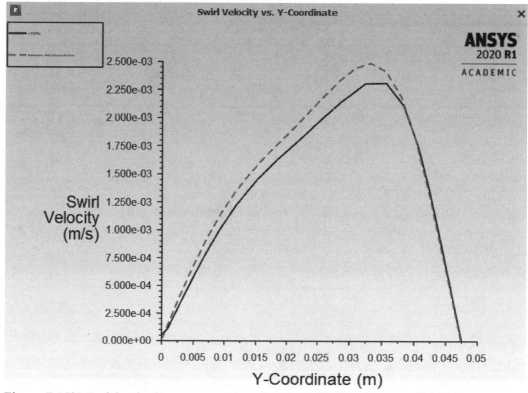

Figure 7.13h) Swirl velocity versus *y* (Re = 1,000 and H/R = 2) at *x* = 0.0475m

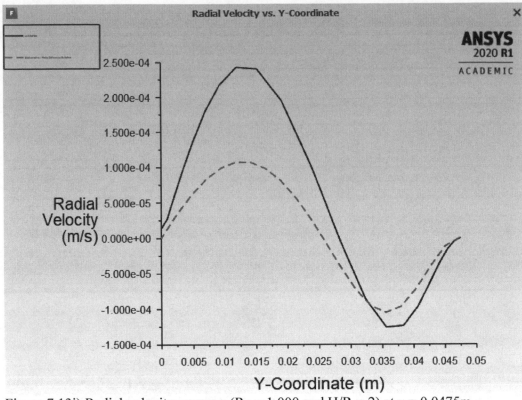

Figure 7.13i) Radial velocity versus $y$ (Re = 1,000 and H/R = 2) at $x$ = 0.0475m

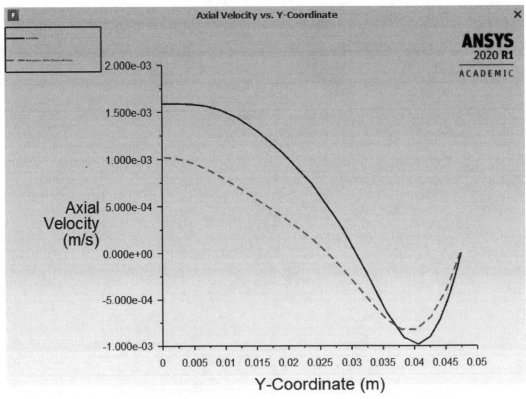

Figure 7.13j) Axial velocity versus $y$ (Re = 1,000 and H/R = 2) at $x$ = 0.0475m

14. Double click on Graphics and Contours under Results in the Outline View. Select Contours of Velocity and Stream Function. Select axis, interior-surface_body, lid and wall under Surfaces. Click on Save/Display.

Select the View tab in the menu and click on Views…. Select *axis* as Mirror Plane and click on Apply. Click on the Camera… button in the Views window. Use your left mouse button to rotate the dial counter-clockwise until the cavity appears upright. Close the Camera Parameters window. Click on the Save button under Actions in the Views window and close the windows.

Figure 7.14a) Views window

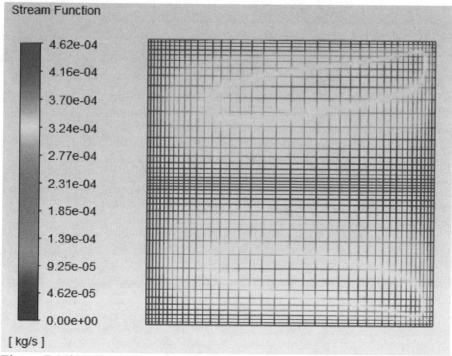

Figure 7.14b) Mirrored streamlines for Re = 1,000 and H/R = 2

Figure 7.14c) Camera parameters

Figure 7.14d) Mirrored and rotated streamlines

Double click on Graphics and Contours under Results in the Outline View. Select Contours of Velocity… and Stream Function. Do not select any surfaces. Click on Save/Display. Select the Viewing tab in the menu and click on Views…. Select *view-0* under Views and axis under Mirror Planes and click on Apply. Close the Views window. Select Contours of Velocity… and Swirl Velocity in the Contours window. Click on Save/Display. Repeat this for Radial Velocity and Axial Velocity. Close the Contours window.

Figure 7.14e) Streamlines and swirl, radial and axial velocities and Re=1000

15. Start another separate standalone session of Fluent 2020 R1 from the Windows Start menu by clicking Start in the bottom-left corner of the Windows desktop screen and choosing Fluent 2020 R1 under ANSYS 2020 R1. In the Fluent Launcher window, select 2D Dimension, Double Precision and Parallel Processing Options. Set the number of Processes equal to the number of processor cores on your computer. Click on the Show More Options and notice the location of the Working Directory. Click on the Start button in the Fluent Launcher window. Copy the file *rotating-flow-mesh-lambda=2.5.msh* to the Working Directory.

Select File>>Import>>Mesh from the Fluent menu. Answer Yes to the question that you get on the screen. Select the file *rotating-flow-mesh-lambda=2.5.msh*. Double click on General under Setup in Outline View. Click on Display… under Mesh and General on the Task Page. Select all Surfaces and click on Display in the Mesh Display window. Close the window. Select Axisymmetric Swirl as 2D Space Solver. Select Relative Velocity Formulation. Check the box for Gravity. Enter -9.81 as Gravitational Acceleration in the X direction. Repeat steps *6* to *11* in this chapter but enter -1 rad/s as Rotational Velocity in step *7*, set the Speed of the Lid in step *8* to 1 rad/s corresponding to *Re* = 2,245 and set the Swirl Velocity (m/s) to 0.0475 in step *11*.

Figure 7.15a) Mesh display window

Figure 7.15b) Settings for rotational velocity of the surface body

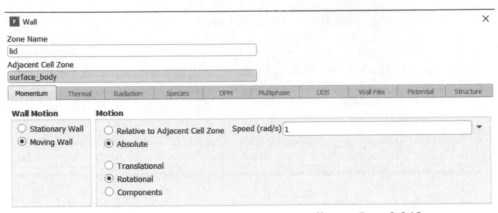

Figure 7.15c) Settings for speed of the lid corresponding to *Re* = 2,245

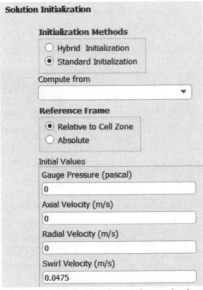

Figure 7.15d) Settings for solution initialization

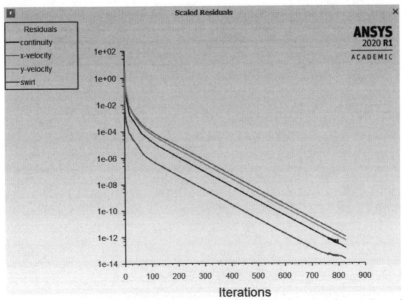

Figure 7.15e) Scaled residuals for rotating flow in a cavity at *Re* = 2245

16. Double click on Graphics and Contours under Results in the Outline View. Select Contours of Velocity and Stream Function. Click on Save/Display. Select the View tab in the menu and click on Views…. Select *axis* as Mirror Plane and click on Apply. Click on the Camera… button in the Views window. Use your left mouse button to rotate the dial counterclockwise until the cavity appears upright. Close the Camera Parameters window. Click on the Save button under Actions in the Views window and close the windows.

Figure 7.16a) Mirrored and rotated streamlines for Re = 2245 and H/R = 2.5

Double click on Graphics and Pathlines under Results in the Outline View. Select Color by Velocity and Velocity Magnitude. Select *interior-surface_body* under Release from Surfaces. Set the Step Size (m) to 0.02, the Number of Steps to 500 and Path Skip to 20. Click on Save/Display.

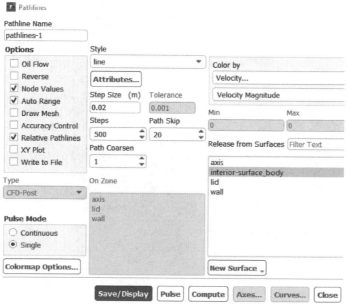

Figure 7.16b) Settings for pathlines

Figure 7.16c) Pathlines at Re = 2245 and H/R = 2.5

Figure 7.16d) Comparison between ANSYS Fluent simulations and experimental visualizations at Re = 2245, H/R = 2.5

## H. Theory

17. We define the Reynolds number as

$$Re = \Omega R^2 / \nu \tag{7.1}$$

where $\Omega$ (rad/s) is the angular velocity of the lid, $R$ (m) is the radius of the cylindrical container and $\nu$ (m$^2$/s) is kinematic viscosity. The aspect ratio of the cylindrical container is defined as

$$\lambda = H/R \tag{7.2}$$

where $H$ (m) is the height of the cylindrical container.

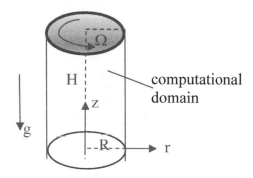

Figure 7.17a) Geometry for cylinder with rotating lid

The incompressible Navier-Stokes equations in cylindrical coordinates $(r, \theta, z)$ with velocity components $\left(u_r(r, \theta, z, t), u_\theta(r, \theta, z, t), u_z(r, \theta, z, t)\right)$ are given by the following equations:

Continuity equation:
$$\frac{1}{r}\frac{\partial(r u_r)}{\partial r} + \frac{1}{r}\frac{\partial u_\theta}{\partial \theta} + \frac{\partial u_z}{\partial z} = 0 \tag{7.3}$$

$r$-component:
$$\rho\left(\frac{\partial u_r}{\partial t} + u_r\frac{\partial u_r}{\partial r} + \frac{u_\theta}{r}\frac{\partial u_r}{\partial \theta} - \frac{u_\theta^2}{r} + u_z\frac{\partial u_r}{\partial z}\right) =$$
$$-\frac{\partial p}{\partial r} + \mu\left[\frac{1}{r}\frac{\partial}{\partial r}\left(r\frac{\partial u_r}{\partial r}\right) - \frac{u_r}{r^2} + \frac{1}{r^2}\frac{\partial^2 u_r}{\partial \theta^2} - \frac{2}{r^2}\frac{\partial u_\theta}{\partial \theta} + \frac{\partial^2 u_r}{\partial z^2}\right] \tag{7.4}$$

$\theta$-component:
$$\rho\left(\frac{\partial u_\theta}{\partial t} + u_r\frac{\partial u_\theta}{\partial r} + \frac{u_\theta}{r}\frac{\partial u_\theta}{\partial \theta} + \frac{u_r u_\theta}{r} + u_z\frac{\partial u_\theta}{\partial z}\right) =$$
$$-\frac{1}{r}\frac{\partial p}{\partial \theta} + \mu\left[\frac{1}{r}\frac{\partial}{\partial r}\left(r\frac{\partial u_\theta}{\partial r}\right) - \frac{u_\theta}{r^2} + \frac{1}{r^2}\frac{\partial^2 u_\theta}{\partial \theta^2} + \frac{2}{r^2}\frac{\partial u_r}{\partial \theta} + \frac{\partial^2 u_\theta}{\partial z^2}\right] \tag{7.5}$$

$z$-component:
$$\rho\left(\frac{\partial u_z}{\partial t} + u_r\frac{\partial u_z}{\partial r} + \frac{u_\theta}{r}\frac{\partial u_z}{\partial \theta} + u_z\frac{\partial u_z}{\partial z}\right) =$$
$$-\frac{\partial p}{\partial z} + \mu\left[\frac{1}{r}\frac{\partial}{\partial r}\left(r\frac{\partial u_z}{\partial r}\right) + \frac{1}{r^2}\frac{\partial^2 u_z}{\partial \theta^2} + \frac{\partial^2 u_z}{\partial z^2}\right] \tag{7.6}$$

where $\rho$ (kg/m$^3$) is density, $g$ (m/s$^2$) is acceleration due to gravity and $\mu$ (kg/m-s) is dynamic viscosity. For axisymmetric flow there is no $\theta$ dependence for the velocity components so they can be expressed as $\left(u_r(r,z), u_\theta(r,z), u_z(r,z)\right)$. This together with a steady flow will reduce the equations above to the following equations:

Continuity equation: $\quad \frac{1}{r}\frac{\partial(ru_r)}{\partial r} + \frac{\partial u_z}{\partial z} = 0$ $\qquad\qquad$ (7.7)

$r$-component: $\quad \rho\left(u_r\frac{\partial u_r}{\partial r} - \frac{u_\theta^2}{r} + u_z\frac{\partial u_r}{\partial z}\right) = -\frac{\partial p}{\partial r} + \mu\left[\frac{1}{r}\frac{\partial}{\partial r}\left(r\frac{\partial u_r}{\partial r}\right) - \frac{u_r}{r^2} + \frac{\partial^2 u_r}{\partial z^2}\right]$ $\quad$ (7.8)

$\theta$-component: $\quad \rho\left(u_r\frac{\partial u_\theta}{\partial r} + \frac{u_r u_\theta}{r} + u_z\frac{\partial u_\theta}{\partial z}\right) = \mu\left[\frac{1}{r}\frac{\partial}{\partial r}\left(r\frac{\partial u_\theta}{\partial r}\right) - \frac{u_\theta}{r^2} + \frac{\partial^2 u_\theta}{\partial z^2}\right]$ $\quad$ (7.9)

$z$-component: $\quad \rho\left(u_r\frac{\partial u_z}{\partial r} + u_z\frac{\partial u_z}{\partial z}\right) = -\frac{\partial p}{\partial z} + \mu\left[\frac{1}{r}\frac{\partial}{\partial r}\left(r\frac{\partial u_z}{\partial r}\right) + \frac{\partial^2 u_z}{\partial z^2}\right]$ $\qquad$ (7.10)

We make the velocity components and pressure non-dimensional using the following relations:

$$u_r^* = u_r/(\Omega R), u_\theta^* = u_\theta/(\Omega R), u_z^* = u_z/\Omega R, p^* = p/(\rho\Omega^2 R^2) \qquad (7.11)$$

and we make the coordinates non-dimensional using the following relations:

$$r^* = r/R, \theta^* = \theta, z^* = z/R \qquad\qquad (7.12)$$

The continuity equation and the different component equations in non-dimensional form after skipping the $*$ superscript symbol:

$$\frac{\partial u_r}{\partial r} + \frac{u_r}{r} + \frac{\partial u_z}{\partial z} = 0 \qquad\qquad (7.13)$$

$$u_r\frac{\partial u_r}{\partial r} - \frac{u_\theta^2}{r} + u_z\frac{\partial u_r}{\partial z} = -\frac{\partial p}{\partial r} + \frac{1}{Re}\left[\frac{\partial^2 u_r}{\partial r^2} + \frac{1}{r}\frac{\partial u_r}{\partial r} - \frac{u_r}{r^2} + \frac{\partial^2 u_r}{\partial z^2}\right] \qquad (7.14)$$

$$u_r\frac{\partial u_\theta}{\partial r} + \frac{u_r u_\theta}{r} + u_z\frac{\partial u_\theta}{\partial z} = \frac{1}{Re}\left[\frac{\partial^2 u_\theta}{\partial r^2} + \frac{1}{r}\frac{\partial u_\theta}{\partial r} - \frac{u_\theta}{r^2} + \frac{\partial^2 u_\theta}{\partial z^2}\right] \qquad (7.15)$$

$$u_r\frac{\partial u_z}{\partial r} + u_z\frac{\partial u_z}{\partial z} = -\frac{\partial p}{\partial z} + \frac{1}{Re}\left[\frac{\partial^2 u_z}{\partial r^2} + \frac{1}{r}\frac{\partial u_z}{\partial r} + \frac{\partial^2 u_z}{\partial z^2}\right] \qquad (7.16)$$

The boundary conditions are the following:

$$u_r(0,z) = u_r(1,z) = u_r(r,0) = u_r(r,2) = 0 \qquad\qquad (7.17)$$

$$u_\theta(0,z) = u_\theta(1,z) = u_\theta(r,0) = 0, \; u_\theta(r,2) = \Omega r \qquad\qquad (7.18)$$

$$\frac{\partial u_z(0,z)}{\partial r} = u_z(1,z) = u_z(r,0) = u_z(r,2) = 0 \qquad\qquad (7.19)$$

```
Remove[XandYGrid,MakeVariables,FDMatrices];
XandYGrid[domain_List,pts_List]:=MapThread[N@Range[Sequence@@#1,Abs[Subtract@@#1]/#2]&,{domain,pts-1}];
BoundaryIndex[rgridlen_,zgridlen_]:=Module[{tmp,left,right,bot,top},tmp=Table[(n-1)zgridlen+Range[1,zgridlen],{n,1,rgridlen}];
  {left,right}=tmp[[{1,-1}]];{bot,top}=Transpose[{First[#],Last[#]}&/@tmp];{top,right[[2;;-2]],bot,left[[2;;-2]]}];
Attributes[MakeVariables]={Listable};MakeVariables[var_,n_]:=Table[Unique[var],{n}];
FDMatrices[deriv_,rzgrid_,difforder_]:=Map[NDSolve`FiniteDifferenceDerivative[#,rzgrid,"DifferenceOrder"->difforder]["Differen
tiationMatrix"]&,deriv];


Options[DrivenCylinderCavitySolver]={"InitialGuess"->1};
DrivenCylinderCavitySolver[Rey_,domain_List,pts_List,difforder_,OptionsPattern[]]:=Module[{rzgrid,rrgrid,rgrid,r2grid,nr,nz,top,r
ight,bot,left,ur,uz,uθ,p,urvar,uzvar,uθvar,pvar,dr,dz,dr2,dz2,eqnur,eqnuz,eqnuθ,eqncont,bcindx,sol,boundaries,deqns,dvars,grid}
,(*Get the grid and differentiation matrices*)rzgrid=XandYGrid[domain,pts];rrgrid=rzgrid[[1]];
  grid=Flatten[Outer[List,Sequence@@rzgrid],1];rgrid=grid[[All,1]];r2grid=rgrid*rrgrid;
  {nr,nz}=Map[Length,rzgrid];{top,right,bot,left}=BoundaryIndex[nr,nz];
  {dr,dz,dr2,dz2}=FDMatrices[{{1,0},{0,1},{2,0},{0,2}},rzgrid,difforder];
  (*Get the discretized axisymmetric Navier Stokes equations*){urvar,uzvar,uθvar,pvar}=MakeVariables[{ur,uz,uθ,p},nr*nz];
  eqnur=r2grid urvar (dr.urvar)-rgrid uθvar uθvar+r2grid uzvar (dz.urvar)+r2grid(dr.pvar)-r2grid (1/Rey) (dr2+dz2).urvar-
rgrid(1/Rey) (dr.urvar)+(1/Rey) urvar;
  eqnuz=rgrid urvar(dr.uzvar)+rgrid uzvar (dz.uzvar)+rgrid(dz.pvar)-rgrid (1/Rey) (dr2+dz2).uzvar-(1/Rey) (dr.uzvar);
  eqnuθ=r2grid urvar (dr.uθvar)+rgrid urvar uθvar+r2grid uzvar (dz.uθvar)-r2grid (1/Rey) (dr2+dz2).uθvar-rgrid(1/Rey)
(dr.uθvar)+(1/Rey) uθvar;
  eqncont=rgrid (dr.urvar)+urvar+rgrid(dz.uzvar);
  (*Apply the boundary conditions and solve the
system*)boundaries=Join[top,right,bot,left];eqnur[[boundaries]]=urvar[[boundaries]];
  eqnuz[[boundaries]]=uzvar[[boundaries]];eqnuz[[left]]=(dr[[left]].uzvar);
  eqnuθ[[boundaries]]=uθvar[[boundaries]];eqnuθ[[top]]=uθvar[[top]]-(rrgrid-1);
  eqncont[[top[[1]]]]=pvar[[top[[1]]]];
  {deqns,dvars}={Join[eqnur,eqnuz,eqnuθ,eqncont],Join[urvar,uzvar,uθvar,pvar]};
  sol=dvars/.Quiet@FindRoot[deqns,Thread[{dvars,OptionValue["InitialGuess"]}]];
  (*Get Interpolating
functions*)grid=Flatten[Outer[List,Sequence@@rzgrid],1];Map[Interpolation@Join[grid,Transpose@List@#,2]&,Partition[sol,Len
gth[grid]]]];


(* Calculate Solution *)
Timing[res={ur,uz,uθ,p}=DrivenCylinderCavitySolver[1000,{{1,2},{0,2}},{30,60},4]]
StreamDensityPlot[{ur[r,z],uz[r,z]},{r,1,2},{z,0,2},AspectRatio->2,PlotLabel->Style[Text["Streamfunction at Re = 1000"]]]


(* Plot Results and Save Velocity Profiles for uθ *)
SetDirectory["C:\\Users\\johne"];r1=1;omega=0.4449;radius=0.0475;
Plot[uθ[0.6+r1,z]*omega*radius,{z,0,2},PlotRange->{{0,2},{0,0.014}},AxesLabel->{z,Uθ[m/s]},PlotLabel->Style[Text["r=1.6,
Re=1000"]]]
mylist=Table[{uθ[0.6+r1,z]*omega*radius,z*radius},{z,0,2,0.05}];
Plotex[mylist];Export["swirl-velocity-y=0.0285m.dat",TableOfValues1];


Plot[uθ[r,1]*omega*radius,{r,0+r1,1+r1},AxesLabel->{r+1,Uθ[m/s]},PlotLabel->Style[Text["z=1, Re=1000"]]]
mylist=Table[{uθ[r,1]*omega*radius,(r-r1)*radius},{r,0+r1,1+r1,0.05}];Plotex[mylist];Export["swirl-velocity-
x=0.0475m.dat",TableOfValues1];


Plotex[n_]:=(mylist[[All,{1,2}]]=n[[All,{2,1}]];TableOfValues1=Prepend[mylist,{""}];
  TableOfValues1=Prepend[TableOfValues1,{"((xy/key/label \"Mathematica - Finite Difference Solution\")"}];
  TableOfValues1=Prepend[TableOfValues1,{""}];
  TableOfValues1=Prepend[TableOfValues1,{"(labels \"Swirl Velocity (m/s)\" \"Position (m)\")"}];
  TableOfValues1=Prepend[TableOfValues1,{"(title
\"Mathematica\")"}];TableOfValues1=Append[TableOfValues1,{")"}];Grid[TableOfValues1];)


(* Plot Results and Save Velocity Profiles for ur *)
SetDirectory["C:\\Users\\johne"];r1=1;omega=0.4449;radius=0.0475;
Plot[ur[0.6+r1,z]*omega*radius,{z,0,2},PlotRange->{{0,2},{-0.001,0.0025}},AxesLabel->{z,Ur[m/s]},PlotLabel->Style[Text["r=1.6,
Re=1000"]]]
mylist=Table[{ur[0.6+r1,z]*omega*radius,z*radius},{z,0,2,0.05}];
Plotex[mylist];Export["radial-velocity-y=0.0285m.dat",TableOfValues1];


Plot[ur[r,1]*omega*radius,{r,0+r1,1+r1},AxesLabel->{r+1,Ur[m/s]},PlotLabel->Style[Text["z=1, Re=1000"]]]
mylist=Table[{ur[r,1]*omega*radius,(r-r1)*radius},{r,0+r1,1+r1,0.05}];Plotex[mylist];Export["radial-velocity-
x=0.0475m.dat",TableOfValues1];
```

```
Plotex[n_]:=(mylist[[All,{1,2}]]=n[[All,{2,1}]]);TableOfValues1=Prepend[mylist,{""}];
 TableOfValues1=Prepend[TableOfValues1,{"((xy/key/label \"Mathematica - Finite Difference Solution\")"}];
 TableOfValues1=Prepend[TableOfValues1,{""}];
 TableOfValues1=Prepend[TableOfValues1,{"(labels \"Radial Velocity (m/s)\" \"Position (m)\")"}];
 TableOfValues1=Prepend[TableOfValues1,{"(title
\"Mathematica\")"}];TableOfValues1=Append[TableOfValues1,{")"}];Grid[TableOfValues1];)

(* Plot Results and Save Velocity Profiles for uz *)
SetDirectory["C:\\Users\\johne"];r1=1;omega=0.4449;radius=0.0475;
Plot[uz[0.6+r1,z]*omega*radius,{z,0,2},PlotRange→{{0,2},{-0.0004,0.0010}},AxesLabel→{z,Uz[m/s]},PlotLabel→Style[Text["r=1.6,
Re=1000"]]]
mylist=Table[{uz[0.6+r1,z]*omega*radius,z*radius},{z,0,2,0.05}];
Plotex[mylist];Export["axial-velocity-y=0.0285m.dat",TableOfValues1];

Plot[uz[r,1]*omega*radius,{r,0+r1,1+r1},AxesLabel→{r+1,Uz[m/s]},PlotLabel→Style[Text["z=1, Re=1000"]]]
mylist=Table[{uz[r,1]*omega*radius,(r-r1)*radius},{r,0+r1,1+r1,0.05}];Plotex[mylist];Export["axial-velocity-
x=0.0475m.dat",TableOfValues1];

Plotex[n_]:=(mylist[[All,{1,2}]]=n[[All,{2,1}]]);TableOfValues1=Prepend[mylist,{""}];
 TableOfValues1=Prepend[TableOfValues1,{"((xy/key/label \"Mathematica - Finite Difference Solution\")"}];
 TableOfValues1=Prepend[TableOfValues1,{""}];
 TableOfValues1=Prepend[TableOfValues1,{"(labels \"Axial Velocity (m/s)\" \"Position (m)\")"}];
 TableOfValues1=Prepend[TableOfValues1,{"(title
\"Mathematica\")"}];TableOfValues1=Append[TableOfValues1,{")"}];Grid[TableOfValues1];)
```

Figure 7.17b) Mathematica 8.0 code for cylinder with rotating lid

## I. References

1. ANSYS Fluid Dynamics Verification Manual, Release 15.0, November 2013.
2. Granger, R.A., Experiments in Fluid Mechanics, Dryden Press, 1988.
3. Michelsen, J.A., Modeling of Laminar Incompressible Rotating Fluid Flow, AFM 86-05, Ph.D. thesis, Department of Fluid Mechanics, Technical University of Denmark, 1986.
4. Mokhasi, Paritosh, Using Mathematica to Simulate and Visualize Fluid Flow in a Box, 2013.
5. Sorensen, J.N. and Loc,T.P., Higher-Order Axisymmetric Navier-Stokes Code: Description and Evolution of Boundary Conditions, *International Journal For Numerical Methods in Fluids*, 9:1517-1537, 1989.
6. Sorensen, J.N. and Christensen, E.A., Direct Numerical Simulation of Rotating Fluid Flow in a Closed Cylinder, *Physics of Fluids* 7:764, 1995.

## J. Exercises

7.1 Use ANSYS Fluent to study the rotating cavity filled with water that has a cylindrical geometry with a radius of 100 mm and a height 300 mm. The top lid is rotating with a Reynolds number $Re = \frac{\Omega R^2}{\nu} = 2,800$ while the remaining walls of the cavity are stationary. Visualize pathlines, streamlines, swirl velocity, radial velocity and axial velocity for this flow case.

CHAPTER 7. ROTATING FLOW IN A CAVITY

7.2 Use ANSYS Fluent to study the rotating cavity filled with water that has a cylindrical geometry with a radius of 100 mm and a height 150 mm. The top lid is rotating with a Reynolds number $Re = \frac{\Omega R^2}{\nu} = 1,400$ while the remaining walls of the cavity are stationary. Visualize pathlines, streamlines, swirl velocity, radial velocity and axial velocity for this flow case.

7.3 Use ANSYS Fluent to study a rotating cavity filled with water that has a frustum geometry with a bottom radius of 50 mm, top radius of 100 mm and a height 150 mm. The top lid is rotating with a Reynolds number $Re = \frac{\Omega Rt^2}{\nu} = 2,000$ while the remaining walls of the cavity are stationary. Visualize pathlines, streamlines, swirl velocity, radial velocity and axial velocity for this flow case.

7.4 Use ANSYS Fluent to study a rotating cavity filled with water that has a frustum geometry with a bottom radius of 50 mm, top radius of 100 mm and a height 150 mm. The top lid is rotating with a Reynolds number $Ret = \frac{\Omega t Rt^2}{\nu} = 2,000$ and the bottom is rotating with the same Reynolds number $Reb = \frac{\Omega b Rb^2}{\nu} = 2,000$ while the remaining walls of the cavity are stationary. Visualize pathlines, streamlines, swirl velocity, radial velocity and axial velocity for this flow case.

**K. Notes**

**K. Notes**

# CHAPTER 8. SPINNING CYLINDER

## A. Objectives

- Using ANSYS Fluent to Study the Fluid in an Open Cylinder with a Free Surface and Solid Body Rotation
- Inserting Boundary Conditions and System Rotation
- Using Volume of Fluid Model for Multiphase Flow with Surface Tension
- Running Laminar 2D Axisymmetric ANSYS Fluent Simulations with Swirl
- Using Contour Plots for Visualizations of Volume Fraction and Swirl Velocity
- Using Excel for Free Surface Plots

## B. Problem Description

We will study the startup flow in a partially filled spinning open cylindrical container where the fluid has a free surface. We will analyze the problem using ANSYS Fluent. The cylindrical container has a diameter of 304.8 mm and the same height. The rotational speed of the cylinder is 12 rad/s.

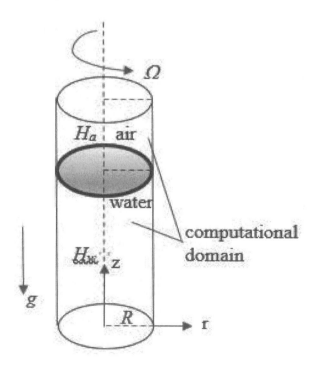

## C. Launching ANSYS Workbench and Selecting Fluent

1. Start by launching ANSYS Workbench. Launch Fluid Flow (Fluent) that is available under Analysis Systems in ANSYS Workbench. Select Geometry under Project Schematic, right click and select Properties. Select 2D Analysis Type under Advanced Geometry Options. Right click on Geometry in Project Schematic and select New DesignModeler Geometry to start DesignModeler.

Figure 8.1 Launching ANSYS Fluent and selecting 2D analysis type

## D. Launching ANSYS DesignModeler

2. Select Units>>Millimeter from the menu in DesignModeler. Select the XYPlane in the Tree Outline. Select Look At Face/Plane/Sketch. Select the Sketching tab and Rectangle. Draw a rectangle from the origin in the first quadrant of the graphics window.

   Select Dimensions and click on the left vertical edge of the rectangle and the lower horizontal edge. Enter 304.8 mm as the horizontal dimension and 152.4 mm as the vertical dimension. Right click in the graphics window and select Zoom to Fit.

   Select Concept>>Surfaces from Sketches from the menu. Select Sketch 1 under XY Plane in the Tree Outline. Apply the sketch as a Base Object in Details View. Click on Generate and close DesignModeler.

Figure 8.2a) Rectangle with dimensions

Figure 8.2b) Surface sketch for the rectangle

## E. Launching ANSYS Meshing

3. Double click on Mesh under Project Schematic in ANSYS Workbench. Right-click on Mesh under Project and Model (A3) in the Meshing window and select Update. Select Mesh>>Controls>Face Meshing from the menu. Click on the rectangle in the graphics window and Apply it as Geometry in Details of Face Meshing.

Figure 8.3a) Launching meshing window

Figure 8.3b) Coarse mesh

Figure 8.3c) Selecting face meshing

Figure 8.3d) Details of face meshing

Select Mesh>>Controls>>Sizing from the menu. Select the Edge tool 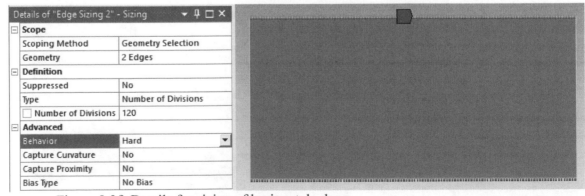, control click on the two vertical edges and Apply them as Geometry in Details of Sizing. Select Number of Divisions as Type and enter 60. Select Hard as Behavior. Repeat this step but select the two horizontal edges and 120 as the Number of Divisions and Hard as Behavior. Right click on Mesh and select Update.

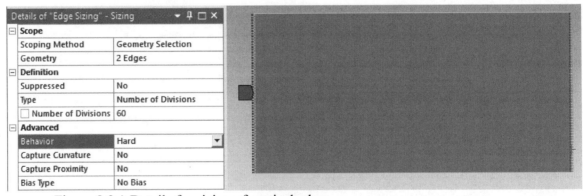

Figure 8.3e) Details for sizing of vertical edges

Figure 8.3f) Details for sizing of horizontal edges

Figure 8.3g) Final mesh used in this chapter

Select the lower horizontal edge, right click and select Create Named Selection. Enter the name *symmetry-2* and click OK to close the window. Control-select the right vertical edge and the upper horizontal edge, right click and select Create Named Selection. Enter the name *wall-1*. Name the left vertical edge as *pressure-inlet-4*. Finally, select the face tool , select the interior of the mesh, right click and name it *mesh-3*.

Figure 8.3h) Named selections

Select File>>Export...>>Mesh>>FLUENT Input File>>Export from the menu. Save the mesh with the name *spinning-cylinder.msh*. Select File>>Save Project from the menu and save the project with the name *Spinning Cylinder.wbpj*. Close the meshing window. Right click on Mesh in the Project Schematic and select Update.

**F. Launching ANSYS Fluent**

4. Double click on Setup under Project Schematic in ANSYS Workbench. Check the box for Double Precision and uncheck the box for Display Mesh After Reading. Click on Show More Options and write down the location of your *Working Directory*. You will need this information later. Select Parallel Processing Options and set the number of processes equal to the number of processor cores for your computer. Click on the Start button.

   Click on Display under General in Mesh on the Task Page in ANSYS Fluent. Select all Surfaces and click on Display in the Mesh Display window and close the same window.

Figure 8.4a) Fluent launcher

Figure 8.4b) Mesh display window

Figure 8.4c) Cylinder with mesh in ANSYS Fluent

5. Select Axisymmetric Swirl for 2D Space in the General Solver settings on the Task Page in ANSYS Fluent. Select Transient for Time in the General Solver settings.

Open Models under Setup in the Outline View and double click on Viscous (SST k-omega). Select Laminar Model and click on OK to close the Viscous Model window. Double click on Multiphase. Select the Volume of Fluid Model and check the box for Implicit Body Force under Body Force Formulation. Click on Apply and Close the Multiphase Model window.

> **Why did we select Axisymmetric Swirl and Transient for Time?** This problem is axisymmetric and has rotation. We choose Transient since we are interested in studying the shape of the free surface and how it deforms over time.

> **Why did we select Volume of Fluid as Multiphase model and Implicit Body Force?** The Volume of Fluid model is used when we have two or more immiscible fluids where the position of the interface between the fluids is of interest. The applications of the VOF Model includes free-surface flows, stratified flows and the tracking of liquid-gas interfaces in general. The VOF model is limited to the pressure-based solver and doesn't allow for void regions without a fluid. Implicit Body Force is used when we have large body forces such as is the case when we have gravity, surface tension and rotation in multiphase flows. Checking the box for Implicit Body Force will make the solution more robust with better convergence.

Figure 8.5a) General settings

Figure 8.5b) Multiphase model

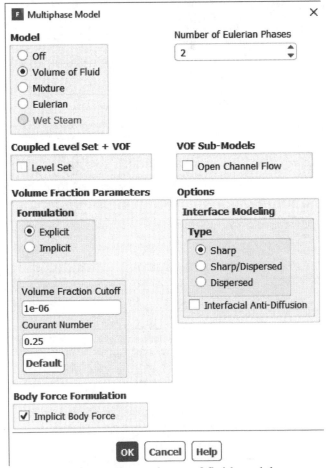

Figure 8.5c) Selecting volume of fluid model

6. Next, we double click on Materials under Setup in the Outline View. Select Fluid under Materials on the Task Page and click on Create/Edit…. Click on Fluent Database… in the Create/Edit Materials window. Scroll down in the Fluent Fluid Material section and select *water-liquid (h2o<l>)*. Click Copy at the bottom of the Fluent Database Materials window. Close the two windows.

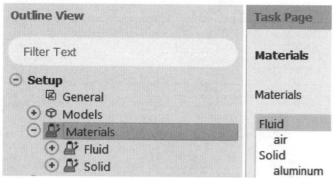

Figure 8.6a) Selecting fluid materials

Figure 8.6b) Selecting Fluent database

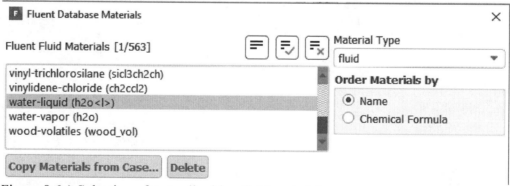

Figure 8.6c) Selection of water-liquid as fluid material

7. Select the Physics tab in the menu and select Models>>Multiphase Model. Select the Phases tab at the top of the Multiphase Model window. Select phase-1-Primary Phase and enter *air* as name for the Primary Phase. Select phase-2-Secondary Phase and select *water-liquid* as the Phase Material and enter *water* as the Name for the Secondary Phase. Click on Apply in the Multiphase Model window. Click on the Phase Interaction tab at the top of the Multiphase Model window. Select constant for Surface Tension Coefficients (n/m) and enter 0.07286 as the value. Click on Apply and Close the Multiphase Model window.

Figure 8.7a) Setting up the physics

Figure 8.7b) Editing phase-1-Primary Phase

Figure 8.7c) Name for phase-1          Figure 8.7d) Name for phase-2

Figure 8.7e) Entering value for surface tension between water and air

8. Select the Physics tab in the menu and select Operating Conditions… under Solver. Check the box for Gravity and enter 9.81 m/s2 for Gravitational Acceleration in the X direction. Select user-input as Operating Density Method. Enter 1.225 as Operating Density (kg/m3). Click on the OK button to close the window.

Figure 8.8a) Selecting operating conditions

Figure 8.8b) Including gravity and specified operating density

9. Double click on Boundary Conditions under Setup in the Outline View. Select *symmetry-2* under Zone in Boundary Conditions on the Task Page. Choose *axis* from the Type drop-down menu, change the zone name to *axis-2* and click OK in the Axis window. Select *pressure-inlet-4* under Zone in Boundary Conditions on the Task Page. Click on the Edit… button. Leave the Gauge Total Pressure at 0 and click OK to close the window.

Figure 8.9a) Axis boundary

Figure 8.9b) Pressure-inlet boundary

10. For *pressure-inlet-4*, select water from the Phase drop-down menu under Boundary Conditions on the Task Page. Click on the Edit... button and make sure that the value for the Volume Fraction is 0 and click OK to close the window.

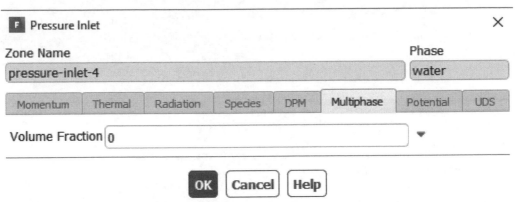

Figure 8.10 Details for pressure-inlet boundary condition

11. For *wall-1*, select mixture from the Phase drop-down menu under Boundary Conditions on the Task Page. Click on the Edit... button and select Moving Wall for Wall Motion. Choose Rotational Motion and set the Speed (rad/s) to 12. Click OK to exit the Wall window.

Figure 8.11 Selection of moving wall and rotational speed

12. Double click on Methods under Solution in the Outline View and choose Body Force Weighted for Pressure and First Order Upwind for Momentum under Spatial Discretization. Select SIMPLE as the Pressure-Velocity Coupling Scheme.

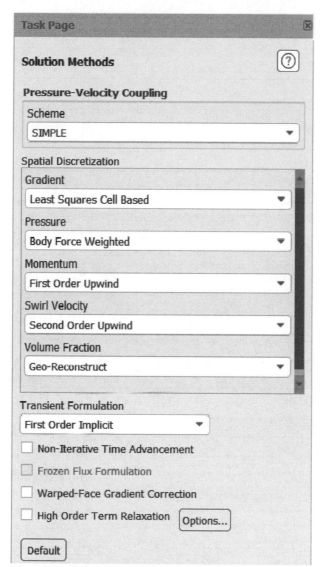

Figure 8.12 Solution methods

13. We are going to define a point close to the outer edge of the cylinder to enable the plotting of the swirl velocity over time. Select the Results tab from the menu and Create Point. Set the x0 (m) and y0 (m) coordinates to 0.2339 and 0.1372, respectively. Click Create and Close the window.

Figure 8.13a) Creating a point surface

Figure 8.13b) Point surface window

14. Open Monitors and double click on Report Plots under Solution in the Outline View. Click on New… in the Report Plot Definitions window. Select New>>Surface Report>>Vertex Average… in the New Report Plot window. Check the Report File, Report Plot and Print to Console boxes under Create in the Surface Report Definition window. Select Vertex Average as Report Type. Select Velocity and Swirl Velocity as Field Variable. Select *point-4* in the Surfaces list. Enter *swirl-velocity.out* as Name. Click OK to exit the Surface Report Definition window. Click OK to close the New Report Plot window. Close the Report Plot Definitions window. Double click on Initialization under Solution in the Tree and select Compute from *pressure-inlet-4* on the Task Page. Click on Initialize.

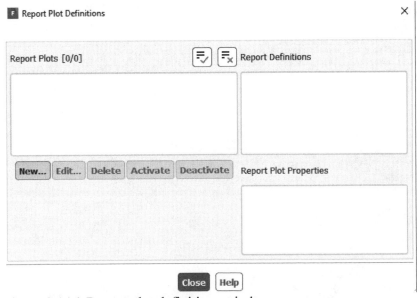

Figure 8.14a) Report plot definitions window

Figure 8.14b) New report plot window

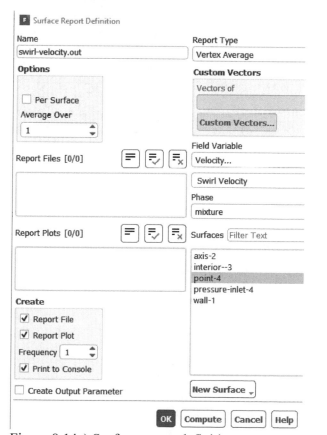

Figure 8.14c) Surface report definition

Figure 8.14d) Initialization

187

15. Select the *Domain* tab in the menu and select Adapt>>Refine/Coarsen…. Select Cell Registers>>New>>Region from the Adaption Controls window. Set X Min (m) to 0.2058, X Max (m) to 0.3048, and Y Max (m) to 0.1524. Click on Display Options…. Select red as Color and no Symbol. Check the box for Filled and uncheck the boxes for Wireframe and Marker under Options. Click on OK. Click on Save/Display in the Region Register window. Close the windows.

Figure 8.15a) Domain adaption

Figure 8.15b) Adaption controls

Figure 8.15c) Settings for region register

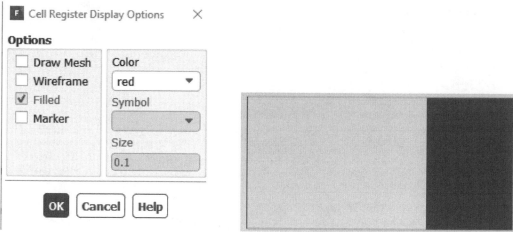

Figure 8.15d) Cell register display      Figure 8.15e) Bottom 33% of cylinder

16. Click on the Patch button on the Solution Initialization Task Page. Select *water* as Phase in the Patch window and select Volume Fraction as Variable. Select region_0 as Registers to Patch and set the Value to 1. Click on the Patch button. You have now defined the lower third of the cylinder to be filled with water. Select Mixture as Phase and choose Swirl Velocity as Variable. Set the Value (m/s) to 0 and click on the Patch button. Close the Patch window.

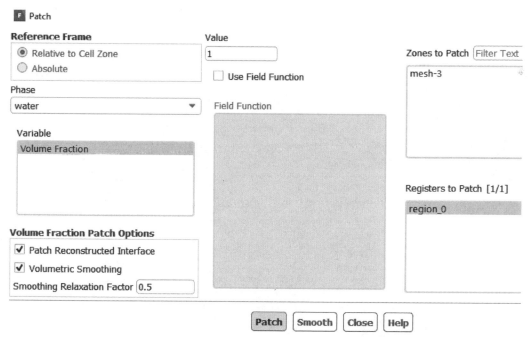

Figure 8.16a) Patching settings for water

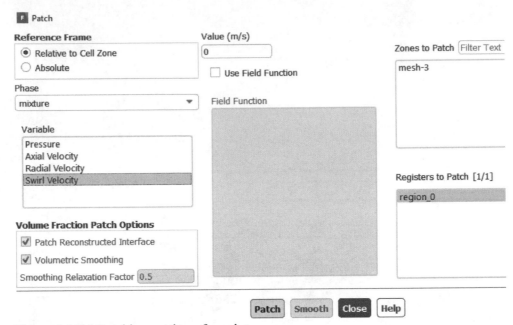

Figure 8.16b) Patching settings for mixture

17. Double click on Graphics and Contours under Results in the Outline View. Select Contours of Velocity and Swirl Velocity. Select Colormap Options… and set the Colormap Size to 30. Click on Apply and Close the Colormap window. Unselect all Surfaces and click on Save/Display. Close the Contours window.

Figure 8.17a) Contours window

Select the View tab in the menu and click on Views.... Select *axis-2* as Mirror Plane and click on Apply. Zoom out and translate the view if needed so that the entire cylinder is visible in the graphics window. Click on the Camera... button in the Views window. Use your left mouse button to rotate the dial clockwise until the bowl rotates 90 degrees clockwise and appears upright. Close the Camera Parameters window. Click on the Save button under Actions in the Views window and Close the Views window.

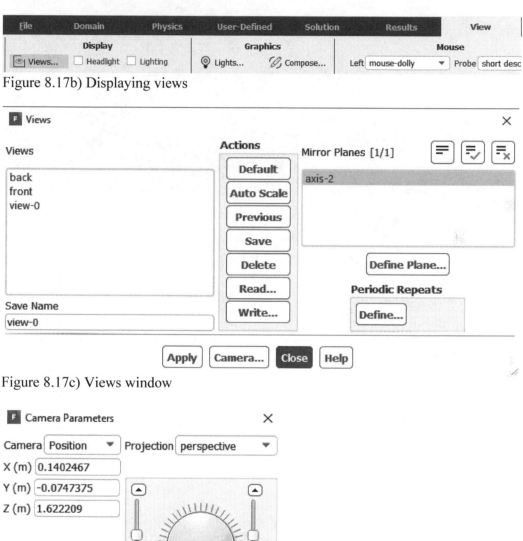

Figure 8.17b) Displaying views

Figure 8.17c) Views window

Figure 8.17d) Camera parameters window

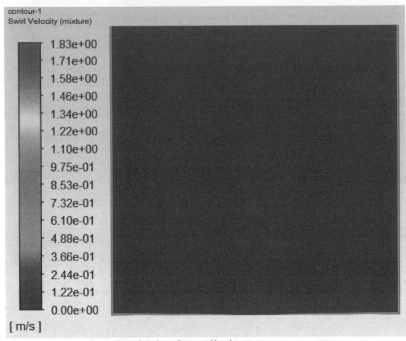

Figure 8.17e) Swirl velocity for cylinder

18. Double click on Contours under Results and Graphics in the Outline View. Select
Contours of Phases… and Volume Fraction. Select *water* as the Phase. Unselect all
Surfaces. Click on Save/Display and Close the Contours window. Double click on Run
Calculation under Solution in the Outline View and set the Time Step Size to 0.01 s. Set
the Number of Time Steps to 10000. Click on the Calculate button on the Task Page.
Click OK in the Information window when the calculation is complete.

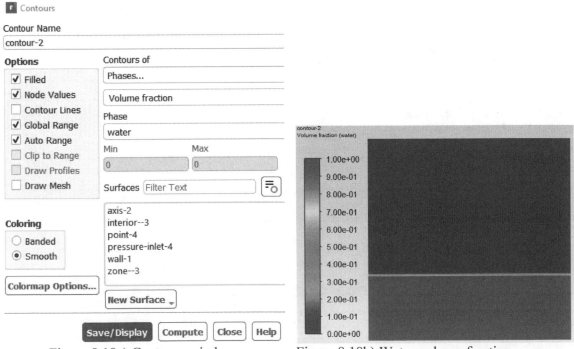

Figure 8.18a) Contours window          Figure 8.18b) Water volume fraction

Figure 8.18c) Calculation settings

Figure 8.18d) Scaled residuals

## G. Post-Processing

19. Select File>>Export>>Data… from the menu. Save the data file in the *Working Directory* folder with the name *t=100s.dat.* Select the View tab in the menu and click on Views. Select *view-0*, click on Apply and Close the window.

Select the Results tab from the menu and select Surface>>Create>>Iso-Surface…. Select Surface of Constant Phases… and Volume Fraction. Select *air* as the Phase and set Iso-Values to 0.5. Select mesh-3 under From Zones and mesh-3 under From Surface. Click on Create.

Select *water* as the Phase and set Iso-Values to 0.5. Select mesh-3 under From Zones and mesh-3 under From Surface. Enter *free-surface* as New Surface Name and click on Create. Close the window.

Select File>>Export>>Solution Data… from the menu. Select ASCII as File Type, Node under Location and Space as Delimeter. Select mesh-3 under Cell Zones and free-surface under Surfaces. Select Volume fraction (water) under Quantities. Click on Write and save the ASCII File in the working directory with the name "free-surface-coordinates-t100s". Close the Export window.

Open the saved file in Excel and answer Yes to the question that you get. Click on Next in the Text Import Wizard – Step 1 of 3. Click on Next in Text Import Wizard – Step 2 of 3. Click on Finish in Text Import Wizard – Step 3 of 3. Plot the free surface in comparison with the final parabolic shape for the free surface, see Figures 7.19d), 7.19e) and the theory section for the definition of the two coordinate systems $(x, y)$ and $(r, z)$:

$$z = H_w + H_a - x = 0.3048 - x, \; r = y \tag{8.1}$$

$$H(r, t) = Z(r, t) - H_w = z - H_w \tag{8.2}$$

Double click on contour-2 under Contours that is located under Results and Graphics in the Outline View. Click on Save/Display in the Contours window to display the volume fraction (water) at $t = 100$ s, see Figure 8.19f). Close the Contours window. Select the View tab in the menu and click on Views. Select *view-0*, click on Apply and Close the window. Repeat this step but instead double click on contour-1 to display swirl velocity, see Figure 8.19g). Continue to run the calculations to $t = 200$ s and $t = 300$ s and plot the free surface evaluations, volume fraction of water and swirl velocity.

Figure 8.19a) Iso-surface settings for air phase

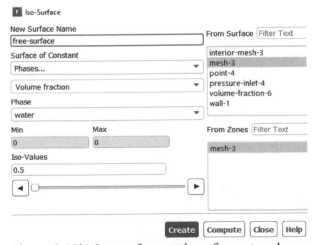

Figure 8.19b) Iso-surface settings for water phase

Figure 8.19c) Export settings

Figure 8.19d) Dimensional free surface elevation at different times.

Figure 8.19e) Non-dimensional free surface elevation at different times.

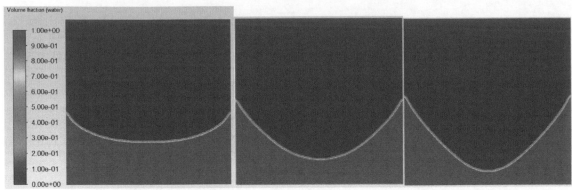

Figure 8.19f) Contours of water volume fraction at $t = 100$, $200$, and $300$ s

Figure 8.19g) Contours of swirl velocity at $t = 100$, $200$, and $300$ s

## H. Theory

20. We start by defining the Reynolds number for this flow case as

$$Re = \frac{\Omega R^2}{\nu} = \frac{12*0.1524^2}{1.0038*10^{-6}} = 277,650 \tag{8.3}$$

where $\Omega$ (rad/s) is the angular velocity of the cylinder, $R$ (m) is the inside radius of the cylindrical container and $\nu$ (m²/s) is kinematic viscosity. Another non-dimensional number that is commonly used in the Ekman number that is the inverse of the Reynolds number. The initial height of water is $H_w = 0.099$ m and the initial height of air in the cylinder is $H_a = 0.2058$ m. The initial condition for the location of the free surface without rotation can be described as $Z(r,0) = H_w$. Next, we assume that the cylinder has been rotating long enough with constant angular velocity so that the fluid has attained solid-body rotation. We can then describe the shape of the surface as a parabola with the following function for the elevation of the free surface

$$Z(r, \infty) = H_w + \frac{\Omega^2}{2g}\left(r^2 - \frac{R^2}{2}\right) \tag{8.4}$$

We can now define the deviation for the height of the free surface from the initial height $H_w$ as

$$H(r, \infty) = Z(r, \infty) - H_w = \frac{\Omega^2}{2g}\left(r^2 - \frac{R^2}{2}\right) \tag{8.5}$$

Then, we can modify equation (8.3) and define a non-dimensional variable related to the deviation of the free surface from the initial height, see Figure 8.19f).

$$\frac{gH(r,\infty)}{\Omega^2 R^2} = \frac{1}{2}\left[\left(\frac{r}{R}\right)^2 - \frac{1}{2}\right] \tag{8.6}$$

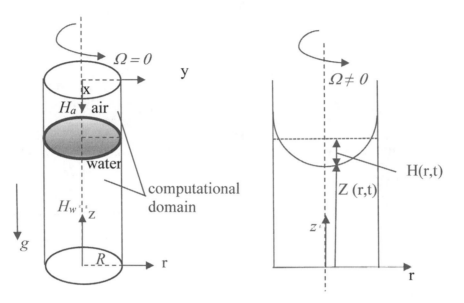

Figure 8.20 Geometry and shape of free surface for cylinder without and with solid body rotation

Generally, the incompressible Navier-Stokes equations in cylindrical coordinates $(r, \theta, z)$ with velocity components $\big(u_r(r, \theta, z, t), u_\theta(r, \theta, z, t), u_z(r, \theta, z, t)\big)$ are given by the following equations:

Continuity equation: $\quad \frac{1}{r}\frac{\partial(ru_r)}{\partial r} + \frac{1}{r}\frac{\partial u_\theta}{\partial \theta} + \frac{\partial u_z}{\partial z} = 0 \tag{8.7}$

$r$-component: $\quad \rho\left(\frac{\partial u_r}{\partial t} + u_r\frac{\partial u_r}{\partial r} + \frac{u_\theta}{r}\frac{\partial u_r}{\partial \theta} - \frac{u_\theta^2}{r} + u_z\frac{\partial u_r}{\partial z}\right) =$

$-\frac{\partial p}{\partial r} + \mu\left[\frac{1}{r}\frac{\partial}{\partial r}\left(r\frac{\partial u_r}{\partial r}\right) - \frac{u_r}{r^2} + \frac{1}{r^2}\frac{\partial^2 u_r}{\partial \theta^2} - \frac{2}{r^2}\frac{\partial u_\theta}{\partial \theta} + \frac{\partial^2 u_r}{\partial z^2}\right] \tag{8.8}$

$\theta$-component: $\quad \rho\left(\frac{\partial u_\theta}{\partial t} + u_r\frac{\partial u_\theta}{\partial r} + \frac{u_\theta}{r}\frac{\partial u_\theta}{\partial \theta} + \frac{u_r u_\theta}{r} + u_z\frac{\partial u_\theta}{\partial z}\right) =$

$-\frac{1}{r}\frac{\partial p}{\partial \theta} + \mu\left[\frac{1}{r}\frac{\partial}{\partial r}\left(r\frac{\partial u_\theta}{\partial r}\right) - \frac{u_\theta}{r^2} + \frac{1}{r^2}\frac{\partial^2 u_\theta}{\partial \theta^2} + \frac{2}{r^2}\frac{\partial u_r}{\partial \theta} + \frac{\partial^2 u_\theta}{\partial z^2}\right] \tag{8.9}$

$z$-component: $\quad \rho\left(\frac{\partial u_z}{\partial t} + u_r\frac{\partial u_z}{\partial r} + \frac{u_\theta}{r}\frac{\partial u_z}{\partial \theta} + u_z\frac{\partial u_z}{\partial z}\right) =$

$-\frac{\partial p}{\partial z} + \mu\left[\frac{1}{r}\frac{\partial}{\partial r}\left(r\frac{\partial u_z}{\partial r}\right) + \frac{1}{r^2}\frac{\partial^2 u_z}{\partial \theta^2} + \frac{\partial^2 u_z}{\partial z^2}\right] \tag{8.10}$

where $\rho$ (kg/m$^3$) is density, $g$ (m/s$^2$) is acceleration due to gravity and $\mu$ (kg/m-s) is dynamic viscosity. For axisymmetric flow there is no $\theta$ dependence for the velocity components so they can be expressed as $(u_r(r, z, t), u_\theta(r, z, t), u_z(r, z, t))$. This will reduce the equations above to the following equations:

Continuity equation: $\quad \frac{1}{r}\frac{\partial(r u_r)}{\partial r} + \frac{\partial u_z}{\partial z} = 0$ \hfill (8.11)

r-component: $\quad \rho\left(\frac{\partial u_r}{\partial t} + u_r\frac{\partial u_r}{\partial r} - \frac{u_\theta^2}{r} + u_z\frac{\partial u_r}{\partial z}\right) =$
$$-\frac{\partial p}{\partial r} + \mu\left[\frac{1}{r}\frac{\partial}{\partial r}\left(r\frac{\partial u_r}{\partial r}\right) - \frac{u_r}{r^2} + \frac{\partial^2 u_r}{\partial z^2}\right]$$
\hfill (8.12)

$\theta$-component: $\quad \rho\left(\frac{\partial u_\theta}{\partial t} + u_r\frac{\partial u_\theta}{\partial r} + \frac{u_r u_\theta}{r} + u_z\frac{\partial u_\theta}{\partial z}\right) =$
$$\mu\left[\frac{1}{r}\frac{\partial}{\partial r}\left(r\frac{\partial u_\theta}{\partial r}\right) - \frac{u_\theta}{r^2} + \frac{\partial^2 u_\theta}{\partial z^2}\right]$$
\hfill (8.13)

z-component: $\quad \rho\left(\frac{\partial u_z}{\partial t} + u_r\frac{\partial u_z}{\partial r} + u_z\frac{\partial u_z}{\partial z}\right) = -\frac{\partial p}{\partial z} + \mu\left[\frac{1}{r}\frac{\partial}{\partial r}\left(r\frac{\partial u_z}{\partial r}\right) + \frac{\partial^2 u_z}{\partial z^2}\right]$ \hfill (8.14)

We make the velocity components and pressure non-dimensional using the following relations:

$$u_r^* = u_r/\Omega R,\ u_\theta^* = u_\theta/\Omega R,\ u_z^* = u_z/\Omega R,\ p^* = p/\rho\Omega^2 R^2 \tag{8.15}$$

and we make the coordinates non-dimensional using the following relations:

$$r^* = \frac{r}{R},\ \theta^* = \theta,\ z^* = \frac{z}{R},\ t^* = t\,\Omega \tag{8.16}$$

The continuity equation and the different component equations in non-dimensional form after skipping the $*$ superscript symbol:

$$\frac{\partial u_r}{\partial r} + \frac{u_r}{r} + \frac{\partial u_z}{\partial z} = 0 \tag{8.17}$$

$$\frac{\partial u_r}{\partial t} + u_r\frac{\partial u_r}{\partial r} - \frac{u_\theta^2}{r} + u_z\frac{\partial u_r}{\partial z} = -\frac{\partial p}{\partial r} + \frac{1}{Re}\left[\frac{\partial^2 u_r}{\partial r^2} + \frac{1}{r}\frac{\partial u_r}{\partial r} - \frac{u_r}{r^2} + \frac{\partial^2 u_r}{\partial z^2}\right] \tag{8.18}$$

$$\frac{\partial u_\theta}{\partial t} + u_r\frac{\partial u_\theta}{\partial r} + \frac{u_r u_\theta}{r} + u_z\frac{\partial u_\theta}{\partial z} = \frac{1}{Re}\left[\frac{\partial^2 u_\theta}{\partial r^2} + \frac{1}{r}\frac{\partial u_\theta}{\partial r} - \frac{u_\theta}{r^2} + \frac{\partial^2 u_\theta}{\partial z^2}\right] \tag{8.19}$$

$$\frac{\partial u_z}{\partial t} + u_r\frac{\partial u_z}{\partial r} + u_z\frac{\partial u_z}{\partial z} = -\frac{\partial p}{\partial z} + \frac{1}{Re}\left[\frac{\partial^2 u_z}{\partial r^2} + \frac{1}{r}\frac{\partial u_z}{\partial r} + \frac{\partial^2 u_z}{\partial z^2}\right] \tag{8.20}$$

The boundary conditions excluding surface tension are the following:

$$u_r(0, z, t) = u_\theta(0, z, t) = \frac{\partial u_z(0, z, t)}{\partial r} = 0,\ ,\ 0 \le z \le h(0, t) \tag{8.21}$$

$$u_r(1, z, t) = u_z(1, z, t) = 0,\ u_\theta(1, z, t) = 1,\ 0 \le z \le h(1, t) \tag{8.22}$$

$$p = \frac{\partial h}{\partial t} + u_r\frac{\partial h}{\partial r} - u_z = 0,\ z = h(r, t) \tag{8.23}$$

and the initial conditions are
$$u_r(r, z, 0) = u_\theta(r, z, 0) = u_z(r, z, 0) = 0,\ 0 \le r \le 1, 0 \le z \le H_w/R \tag{8.24}$$

# CHAPTER 8. SPINNING CYLINDER

## I. References

1. Greenspan, H.P. and Howard, L.N., "On a Time-Dependent Motion of a Rotating Fluid", *Journal of Fluid Mechanics,* **17**, 3, 385-404, (1963).
2. Kim, K.Y. and Hyun, J.M., "Solution for Spin-Up from Rest of Liquid with a Free Surface", *AIAA Journal*, **34**, 7, 1441-1446, (1996).
3. Van de Konijnenberg, J.A, van Heijst, G.J.F., "Nonlinear spin-up in a circular cylinder", *Phys. Fluids,* **7** (12), (1995).

## J. Exercises

8.1 Use ANSYS Fluent to continue running the simulations in this chapter and include free surface elevation plots at $t = 150$ s and $t = 200$ s as shown in Figures 8.19f) and 8.19g). Include contours of water volume fraction and swirl velocity at $t = 150$ and 200 s.

8.2 Use ANSYS Fluent to rerun the calculations shown in this chapter but change the rotational speed to 8 rad/s. Include free surface elevation plots at $t = 100$, 150 and 200 s as shown in Figures 8.19f) and 8.19g). Include contours of water volume fraction and swirl velocity at $t = 100$, 150 and 200 s. Determine the Reynolds number.

8.3 Use ANSYS Fluent to rerun the calculations shown in this chapter but change the rotational speed to 16 rad/s. Include free surface elevation plots at $t = 100$, 150 and 200 s as shown in Figures 8.19f) and 8.19g). Include contours of water volume fraction and swirl velocity at $t = 100$, 150 and 200 s. Determine the Reynolds number.

8.4 Use ANSYS Fluent to rerun the calculations shown in this chapter but change the rotational speed to 10 rad/s. Also, change the radius of the cylinder to R = 0.2 m with everything else being the same. Include free surface elevation plots at $t = 100$, 150 and 200 s as shown in Figures 8.19f) and 8.19g). Include contours of water volume fraction and swirl velocity at $t = 100$, 150 and 200 s. Determine the Reynolds number.

8.5 Use ANSYS Fluent to rerun the calculations shown in this chapter but change the rotational speed to 10 rad/s. Also, change the geometry to a frustum shape with bottom radius of the cylinder $R_{bottom} = 0.1$ m and top radius $R_{top} = 0.2$ m with everything else being the same. Include free surface elevation plots at $t = 100$, 150 and 200 s as shown in Figures 8.19f) and 8.19g). Include contours of water volume fraction and swirl velocity at $t = 100$, 150 and 200 s. Determine the Reynolds number based on the average radius.

**K. Notes**

## CHAPTER 9. KELVIN-HELMHOLTZ INSTABILITY

## A. Objectives

- Using ANSYS Workbench to Create Geometry and Mesh for Kelvin-Helmholtz Instability
- Inserting Wall Boundary Conditions and an Acceleration Due to Gravity Vector Corresponding to a Tilt Angle of 4 degrees for the Tube
- Using Volume of Fluid Model for Multiphase Flow with Surface Tension
- Running Laminar Transient 2D Planar ANSYS Fluent Simulations
- Using Contour Plots of Volume Fraction and a Movie for Visualizations

## B. Problem Description

The Kelvin-Helmholtz instability is a classical problem originally studied by Helmholtz[1] and Kelvin[2]. The mechanism causing the instability has been studied in detail by Lamb[3], Bachelor[4], Drazin and Reid[5], Chandrasekahr[6], Craik[7], and many others. The Kelvin-Helmholtz instability can appear at the interface of two fluid layers flowing with different velocities and with different densities. For a complete review of this instability, please see Thorpe[8]. Thorpe[9-12] found that the Kelvin-Helmholtz instability can be generated and visualized by tilting a tube that contains two fluids at different densities.

We will study the Kelvin-Helmholtz instability and analyze the problem using ANSYS Fluent. The length of the tube is 2,400 mm and the diameter 200 mm.

| (fresh water) $\rho_1 = 998.2 \text{ kg/m}^3$, $\mu_1 = 0.001002 \text{ kg/ms}$, $\gamma_1 = 0.07274 \text{ N/m}$ |
| --- |
| (salt water) $\rho_2 = 1074.9 \text{ kg/m}^3$, $\mu_2 = 0.001259 \text{ kg/ms}$, $\gamma_2 = 0.07422 \text{ N/m}$ |

## C. Launching ANSYS Workbench and Selecting Fluent

1. Start by launching the ANSYS Workbench. Double click on Fluid Flow (Fluent) under Analysis Systems in the Toolbox.

Figure 9.1 Fluid Flow (Fluent)

## D. Launching ANSYS DesignModeler

2. Right click on Geometry in the Project Schematic and select Properties. Select 2D Analysis Type under Advanced Geometry Options in Properties of Schematic A2: Geometry. Right click on Geometry and select New DesignModeler Geometry. Select Units>>Millimeter from the menu as the length unit in DesignModeler.

Figure 9.2a) Selecting Geometry          Figure 9.2b) Selecting 2D Analysis Type

3. Next, we will be creating the mesh for the simulation. Select XYPlane from the Tree Outline. Select Look at Sketch . Click on the Sketching tab on the left-hand side. Select Draw and sketch a Rectangle from the origin. Select the Dimensions tab in the Sketching Toolboxes. Select one of the vertical edges of the rectangle and enter a length of 200 mm. Select one of the horizontal edges of the rectangle and enter a length of 2400 mm.

Figure 9.3a) Selection of XYPlane

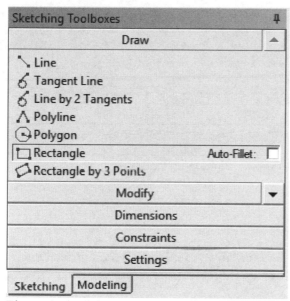

Figure 9.3b) Selection of Sketching Toolboxes and Rectangle

Figure 9.3c) Dimensions for rectangle in Details View

4.  Click on the Modeling tab. Select Concept>>Surfaces from Sketches from the menu. Select Sketch1 under XYPlane in the Tree Outline on the left and select Apply as Base Objects in Details View. Click on Generate in the toolbar. The rectangle turns gray. Right click in the graphics window and select Zoom to Fit. Close the DesignModeler window.

Figure 9.4a) Selecting Surfaces from Sketches

Figure 9.4b) Base Object and completed rectangle in DesignModeler

## E. Launching ANSYS Meshing

5.  We are now going to double click on Mesh in ANSYS Workbench to open the Meshing window. Select Mesh in the Outline. Click on Update under Mesh in the menu. A coarse mesh is created.

    Select Mesh>>Controls>>Face Meshing from the menu. Click on the rectangle in the graphics window. Select the yellow region next to Geometry that is labeled No Selection and click on the Apply button for Geometry in Details of "Face Meshing".

    Select Mesh>>Controls>>Sizing from the menu and select the Edge ⬚ selection filter. Click on the upper horizontal edge of the rectangle and control select the lower horizontal edge. Click on Apply for the Geometry in "Details of Edge Sizing". Under Definition in "Details of Edge Sizing", select Number of Divisions as Type, 480 as Number of Divisions, and Hard as Behavior.

    Repeat the selection of Mesh>>Controls>>Sizing from the menu and control-select the two vertical edges of the rectangle. Enter 40 for Number of Divisions and Hard Behavior. Choose the Bias Type ―― ― - ― ―― and enter 3.0 as Bias Factor. Select Mesh>>Update in the menu and select Mesh in the Outline. The finished mesh is shown in the graphics window.

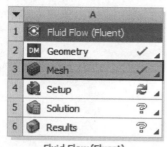

Fluid Flow (Fluent)

Figure 9.5a) Starting Mesh

Figure 9.5b) Selection of Mesh in Outline

Figure 9.5c) Coarse mesh

Figure 9.5d) Face Meshing

Figure 9.5e) Applied Geometry in Details

Figure 9.5f) Mesh Control Sizing

Figure 9.5g) Details of edge sizing for horizontal edges

Figure 9.5h) Details of edge sizing for vertical edges

Figure 9.5i) Details of finished mesh

6.  We are now going to rename the edges for the rectangle. Select the Edge filter  and control-select the four edges of the rectangle, right click and select Create Named Selection. Enter *wall* as the name for the selection group and click on the OK button.

    Select File>>Export…>>Mesh>>FLUENT Input File>>Export from the menu and save the mesh with the name "*khi-mesh.msh*" in the working directory. Select File>>Save Project from the menu and save the project with the name "Kelvin-Helmholtz Instability". Close the Meshing window. Right click on Mesh in ANSYS Workbench in the Project Schematic and select Update.

Figure 9.6a) Selection of a name for the four edges of the rectangle

Figure 9.6b) Named selections

## F. Launching ANSYS Fluent

7. Double-click on Setup under Project Schematic in ANSYS Workbench. Select Double Precision and select Parallel Processing Options. Set the number of Processes equal to the number of processor cores for your computer. Click on the plus sign next to Show More Options and take a note of the location of the Working Directory. Click on the Start button in the Fluent Launcher window.

Figure 9.7a) Starting Setup

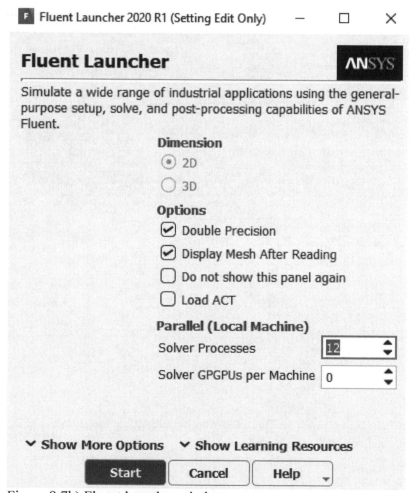

Figure 9.7b) Fluent launcher window

8. Check the mesh by selecting the Check button under Mesh in General on Task Page. Check the scale of the mesh by selecting the Scale button. Make sure that the Domain Extent is correct and close the Scale Mesh window.

Figure 9.8a) Mesh Check

Figure 9.8b) Scale Mesh window

9. Select Transient Time for the Solver in General on the Task Page. Check the Gravity box and enter -9.71453 m/s2 as the Gravitational Acceleration in the Y direction. Enter -1.365288 m/s2 as the Gravitational Acceleration in the X direction. These components correspond to a tilt angle of 8 degrees for the tube.

Open Models under Setup in the Outline View and double click on Viscous (SST k-omega). Select the Laminar Model and select OK to close the Viscous Model window. Double click on Multiphase (Off). Select the Volume of Fluid Model. Click on Apply and Close the Multiphase Model window.

Figure 9.9a) General Setup

Figure 9.9b) Models Problem Setup

Figure 9.9c) Multiphase model

10. Double click on Materials under Setup in the Outline View. Click on the Create/Edit button for Fluid on the Task Page to open the Create/Edit Materials window. Click on Fluent Database. Scroll down in the Fluent Fluid Materials window and select *water-liquid (h2o<l>)*. Click on the Copy button and Close the Fluent Database Materials window. Click on the Change/Create button and the Close button in the Create/Edit Materials window.

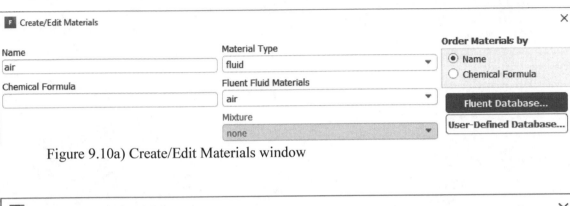

Figure 9.10a) Create/Edit Materials window

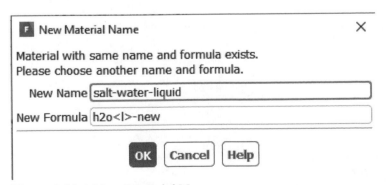

Figure 9.10b) Selecting water-liquid as FLUENT Fluid Material

Repeat these steps above and select *water-liquid*. You will get a New Material Name window when you click on the Copy button in the Fluent Database Materials window. Enter *salt-water-liquid* as the New Name and click OK. Close the Fluent Database Materials window. Click on the Change/Create button and the Close button in the Create/Edit Materials window.

Figure 9.10c) New Material Name

11. Open Models under Setup in the Outline View, double click on Multiphase (On) and select the Phases tab in the Multiphase Model window. Select phase-1-Primary Phase. Select *water-liquid* from Phase Materials and enter *fresh-water* as the name of the Primary Phase. Click on the Apply button.

Figure 9.11a) Multiphase

Figure 9.11b) Primary Phase Setup

Repeat these steps for the Secondary Phase to select *salt-water-liquid* and enter the name *salt-water*. Click on the Apply button.

Select the Phase Interactions tab at the top of the Multiphase Model window. Click on the Surface Tension tab, check the Surface Tension Force Modeling box, select constant from the Surface Tension Coefficients drop down menu, enter the value 0.00148 n/m and click on the Apply button.

Select salt-water-liquid under Materials and Fluid on the Task Page and click on Create/Edit. Enter 1074.9 as Density (kg/m3) and 0.001259 as Viscosity (kg/m-s). Click on Change/Create and Close the window. For a reference of the dynamic viscosity value used for salt-water, see Sharqawy, Lienhard, and Zubair[13].

Figure 9.11c) Secondary Phase Setup

Figure 9.11d) Phase interaction tab

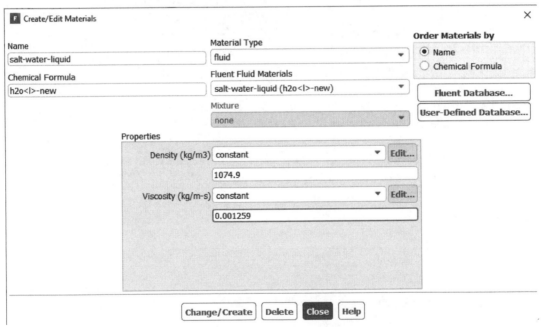

Figure 9.11e) Values of density and viscosity for salt-water

12. Double click on Methods under Solution in the Tree. Select Default settings except for First Order Upwind for Momentum. Double click on Initialization under Solution in the Outline View, select Standard Initialization and click on Initialize.

Figure 9.12a) Solution Methods

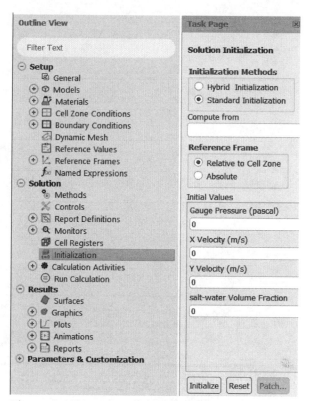

Figure 9.12b) Solution Initialization

13. Select the Domain tab in the menu and select Adapt>>Refine/Coarsen…. Select Cell Registers>>New>>Region in the Adaption Controls window. Enter 2.4 for X Max, and 0.1 for Y Max. Click on the Save button and Close the window. Click OK to close the Adaption Controls window.

Figure 9.13a) Adapting a Region

Figure 9.13b) Region Adaption Settings

Click on the Patch… button on the Task Page for Solution Initialization and select *salt-water* as the phase. Select Volume Fraction as the Variable and region_0 as Registers to Patch. Set the value to 1 and click on the Patch button.

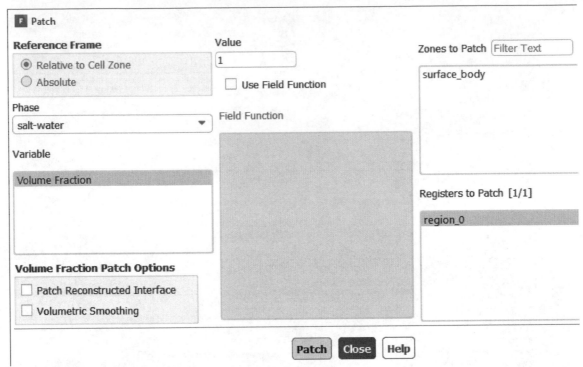

Figure 9.13c) Patch Settings for Volume Fraction

Select mixture for the phase. Select X Velocity as the Variable and region_0 as Registers to Patch. Set the value to 0 and click on the Patch button and Close the window.

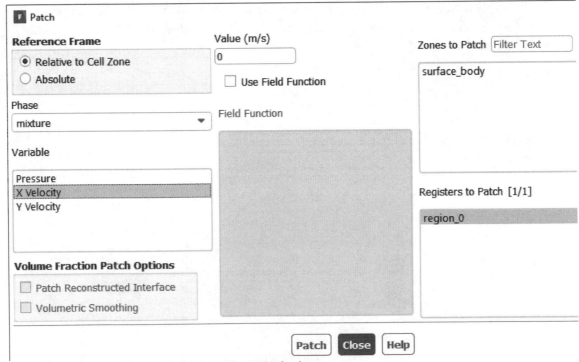

Figure 9.13d) Patch Settings for X Velocity

214

14. Open Graphics and double click on Contours under Results in the Outline View. Select Phases and Volume fraction under Contours of and select *fresh-water* as the Phase. Click on Colormap Options and select Top as Colormap Alignment. Set Type to float and Precision to 1 as Number Format. Click on Apply and Close the Colormap window. Click on the Save/Display button and Close the window.

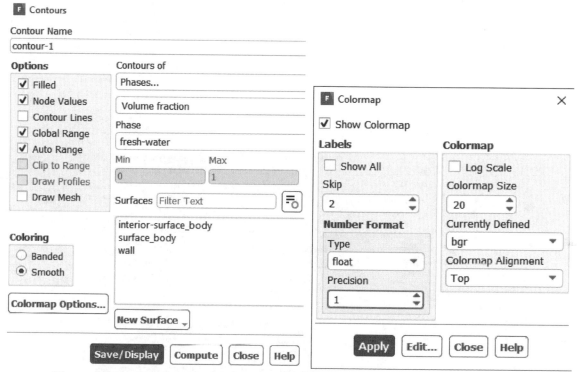

Figure 9.14a) Contours and colormap settings

Figure 9.14b) Contours of Volume Fraction (fresh-water)

15. Open Calculation Activities and double click on Solution Animations under Solution in the Outline View. Enter *khi-animation* as the name and select *contour-1* as Animation Object. Set Record after every 10 time-step. Click on the OK button to close the Animation Definition window.

Double click on Run Calculation under Solution, enter 0.01 as Time Step Size, and 200 for Number of Time Steps. Click on the Calculate button. Click OK when the calculation is complete. Open Graphics and double click on *contour-1* under Contours that is under Results in the Outline View. Click on the Save/Display button and Close the window.

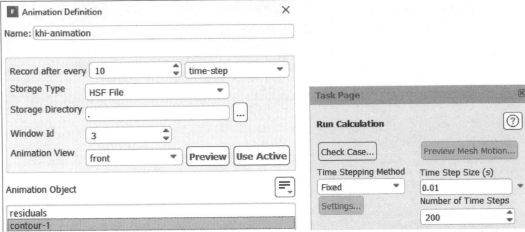

Figure 9.15a) Animation definition window     Figure 9.15b) Running calculations

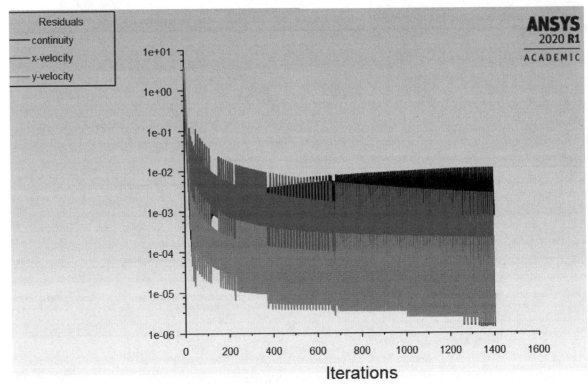

Figure 9.15c) Scaled residuals for the first two seconds.

Figure 9.15d) Contour of Volume Fraction for fresh-water after 2 s

## G. Post-Processing

16. Enter 100 for Number of Time Steps and continue running the calculations twice followed by entering 50 for the Number of Time Steps. Next, continue running the calculations six more times for a total of 7 seconds. ANSYS Fluent simulations can be compared with experiments of this instability, see Matsson and Boiselle[14].

Figure 9.16a) Contour of Volume Fraction for fresh-water after 3, 4, 4.5, 5, 5.5, 6, 6.5, 7 s

Figure 9.16b) Experiments of Kelvin-Helmholtz instability at $t = 5.0$ s (8° tilt angle), from Matsson and Boisselle[1]

Select File>>Export>Case & Data… from the menu. Save the file with the name *khi-computation.cas*.

Double click on Animations and Playback under Results in the Outline View. Set the Replay Speed to low and select Play Once as Playback Mode. Select MPEG as Write/Record Format. Click on the Write button. This will create the mpeg movie in your working directory. Close the Playback window. The movie can be viewed using for example VLC Media Player.

In VLC Media Player select Media>>Open File… from the menu. Open the movie from the working directory. Select Playback>>Speed>>Slower several times from the menu in the VLC Media Player until you have a suitable speed for the movie.

## H. Theory

17. We will look at the inviscid theory for the Kelvin-Helmholtz instability in terms of a sinusoidal disturbance between two fluids with velocities $U_1$, $U_2$ and densities $\rho_1$, $\rho_2$.

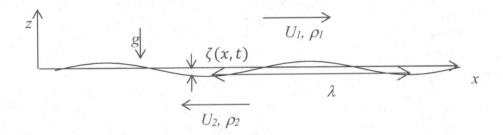

Figure 9.17 Development of Kelvin Helmholtz instability from a perturbation

The velocity vector in a Cartesian coordinate system can be described as

$$\bar{U} = u_x \bar{e}_x + u_y \bar{e}_y + u_z \bar{e}_z \tag{9.1}$$

where $u_x$, $u_y = 0$ and $u_z$ are the velocity components in the streamwise, spanwise and normal directions, respectively. Euler equations of motion can be written as

$$\frac{\partial u_x}{\partial t} + u_x \frac{\partial u_x}{\partial x} + u_z \frac{\partial u_x}{\partial z} = -\frac{1}{\rho} \frac{\partial P}{\partial x} \tag{9.2}$$

$$\frac{\partial u_z}{\partial t} + u_x \frac{\partial u_z}{\partial x} + u_z \frac{\partial u_z}{\partial z} = -\frac{1}{\rho} \frac{\partial P}{\partial z} - g \tag{9.3}$$

$$\frac{\partial u_x}{\partial x} + \frac{\partial u_z}{\partial z} = 0 \tag{9.4}$$

The velocity components can be divided into mean flow components in the main streamwise direction plus a perturbation

$$\bar{U} = (U(z) + u)\bar{e}_x + w\bar{e}_z \tag{9.5}$$

and the pressure is $\qquad P = P_0 - \rho g z + p \tag{9.6}$

A perturbation is introduced in the form

$$u, w, p = [u_n(z), w_n(z), p_n(z)]e^{i(kx-\omega t)} \tag{9.7}$$

where $k$ is the streamwise wave number, $\omega$ is the frequency and $u_n(z), w_n(z), p_n(z)$ are eigenfunctions. The linearized Euler equations can be written as

$$i(kU - \omega)u_n + \frac{ik}{\rho}p_n = 0 \tag{9.8}$$

$$i(kU - \omega)w_n + \frac{1}{\rho}p_n' = 0 \tag{9.9}$$

$$iku_n + w_n' = 0 \tag{9.10}$$

From equations (9.8) – (9.10) we can find the equation for $w_n$

$$w_n'' - k^2 w_n = 0 \tag{9.11}$$

with the general solution

$$w_n = c_1 e^{-kz} + c_2 e^{kz} \tag{9.12}$$

To get exponentially decaying solutions far from the interface, we set $c_1$ and $c_2$ equal to zero in the lower and upper layers, respectively. The interface location is defined by

$$z = \zeta(x, t) = ae^{i(kx-\omega t)} \tag{9.13}$$

The normal velocity $w$ at the interface is given by the material derivative of $\zeta(x, t)$

$$w = w_n(z)e^{i(kx-\omega t)} = \frac{D\zeta}{Dt} = \frac{\partial \zeta}{\partial t} + U\frac{\partial \zeta}{\partial x} =$$
$$i(kU - \omega)\zeta = i(kU - \omega)ae^{i(kx-\omega t)} \tag{9.14}$$

, we find that $c_1 = i(kU_1 - \omega)a$ , $c_2 = -i(kU_2 + \omega)a$

$$w_{n,1} = i(kU_1 - \omega)ae^{-kz}$$
$$w_{n,2} = -i(kU_2 + \omega)ae^{kz} \tag{9.15}$$

We can now find the pressure eigenfunctions in the upper and lower layers from equation (9.9).

$$p_{n,1} = -\rho_1(kU_1 - \omega)^2 ae^{-kz}/k$$
$$p_{n,2} = \rho_2(kU_2 + \omega)^2 ae^{kz}/k \tag{9.16}$$

Next, we use equation (9.6) and set the pressures identical at the interface to get the dispersion relation

$$P_0 - \rho_1 g\zeta + p_{n,1}e^{i(kx-\omega t)} = P_0 - \rho_2 g\zeta + p_{n,2}e^{i(kx-\omega t)} \tag{9.17}$$

$$(\rho_2 - \rho_1)gk = \rho_2(kU_2 + \omega)^2 + \rho_1(kU_1 - \omega)^2 \tag{9.18}$$

and we find the following equation for the frequency

219

$$\omega = \frac{k}{\rho_1+\rho_2}[(\rho_1 U_1 - \rho_2 U_2) \pm \sqrt{\frac{2(\rho_2^2-\rho_1^2)g}{k} - \rho_1\rho_2(U_1 + U_2)^2}] \qquad (9.19)$$

The frequency is complex with the associated growth of Kelvin-Helmholtz instability waves when the expression under the square root is negative

$$\frac{2(\rho_2^2-\rho_1^2)g}{k} < \rho_1\rho_2(U_1 + U_2)^2 \qquad (9.20)$$

Using the definition of wave number as inversely proportional to the wave-length

$$k = \frac{2\pi}{\lambda} \qquad (9.21)$$

We find that waves are amplified and develop when their wave-lengths fulfill the following condition as shown in equation (9.22). A boundary below or above the interface can destabilize the flow as shown by Hazel[15].

$$\lambda < \frac{\pi\rho_1\rho_2(U_1+U_2)^2}{g(\rho_2^2-\rho_1^2)} \qquad (9.22)$$

## I. References

1. Helmholtz H. "On discontinuous movement of fluids", *Phil. Mag.* (4) **36**, 337, (1868).
2. Kelvin L. "Hydrokinetic solutions and observations", *Phil. Mag.* (4) **42**, 362, (1871).
3. Lamb H. "Hydrodynamics", *Cambridge University Press*, (1932).
4. Batchelor G.K. "An introduction to fluid dynamics", *Cambridge University Press*, (1967).
5. Drazin P.G. and Reid W.H. "Introduction to hydrodynamic instability", *Cambridge University Press*, (1981).
6. Chandrasekhar S. "Hydrodynamic and Hydromagnetic Stability", *Dover Publications, Inc.*, New York (1961).
7. Craik A.D.D. "Wave interactions and fluid flows", *Cambridge University Press*, (1985).
8. Thorpe S.A. "Transitional phenomena and the development of turbulence in stratified fluids: a review", *J. Geophys. Res.*, **92**, 5231 (1987).
9. Thorpe S.A. "A method of producing a shear flow in a stratified fluid", *J. Fluid Mech.*, **32**, 693 (1968).
10. Thorpe S.A. "Experiments on the instability of stratified shear flows: miscible fluids", *J. Fluid Mech.*, **46**, 299 (1971).
11. Thorpe S.A. "Turbulence in stably stratified fluids: a review of laboratory experiments", *Boundary-Layer Meteorol.*, **5**, 95 (1973).
12. Thorpe S.A. "Experiments on the instability and turbulence in a stratified shear flow", *J. Fluid Mech.*, **61**, 731 (1973).
13. Sharqawy M.H, Lienhard J.H., and Zubair S.M. "Thermophysical Properties of Sea Water: A Review of existing Correlations and Data, Desalination, and Water Treatment", *Desalination and Water Treatment*, **16**, 354 (2010).
14. Matsson J. and Boisselle J. "A Senior Design Project on the Kelvin-Helmholtz Instability", 122nd ASEE Annual Conference and Exposition, June 14-17, 2015, Seattle, WA.
15. Hazel P. "Numerical Studies of the stability of inviscid stratified shear flows", *J. Fluid Mech.*, **51**, 39 (1972).

## J. Exercises

9.1 Run the ANSYS Fluent simulations for a tube tilt angle of 4 degrees and show the development of the instability using contours of volume fraction for fresh water for the same fluids as used in this chapter.

9.2. Run the ANSYS Fluent simulations for a tube tilt angle of 12 degrees and show the development of the instability using contours of volume fraction for fresh water for the same fluids as used in this chapter.

9.2 Run the ANSYS Fluent simulations shown in this chapter but instead use a transient 3D geometry and mesh for the model. Use a tube tilt angle of 4 degrees and use contours of volume fraction for fresh water to visualize the flow for the same fluids as used in this chapter.

9.3 Run the ANSYS Fluent simulations shown in this chapter but instead use a transient 3D geometry and mesh for the model. Use a tube tilt angle of 8 degrees and use contours of volume fraction for fresh water to visualize the flow for the same fluids as used in this chapter.

9.4 Run the ANSYS Fluent simulations shown in this chapter but instead use a transient 3D geometry and mesh for the model. Use a tube tilt angle of 12 degrees and use contours of volume fraction for fresh water to visualize the flow for the same fluids as used in this chapter.

**K. Notes**

# CHAPTER 10. RAYLEIGH-TAYLOR INSTABILITY

## A. Objectives

- Using ANSYS Workbench to Create Geometry and Mesh for Rayleigh-Taylor Instability
- Inserting Symmetry and Wall Boundary Conditions
- Using Volume of Fluid Model for Multiphase Flow
- Using a User Defined Function to Trigger the Rayleigh-Taylor Instability
- Running Laminar Transient 2D Planar ANSYS Fluent Simulations
- Using Contour Plots of Volume Fractions and a Movie for Visualizations

## B. Problem Description

We will study the Rayleigh-Taylor instability and will analyze the problem using ANSYS. The Geometry for Rayleigh-Taylor instability (total height 1 m, width 0.25 m) is shown below. The heavier fluid is initially on top of the lighter fluid.

Salt-water
$\rho_1 = 1075$ kg/m$^3$
$\mu_1 = 0.00126$ kg/m-s

$H = 1$ m

Fresh-water
$\rho_2 = 998.2$ kg/m$^3$
$\mu_2 = 0.001$ kg/m-s

$D = 0.25$ m

## C. Launching ANSYS Workbench and Selecting Fluent

1. Start by launching ANSYS Workbench. Double click on Fluid Flow (Fluent).

Figure 10.1 Selecting Fluent

## D. Launching ANSYS DesignModeler

2. Right click on Geometry under Project Schematic in ANSYS Workbench and select Properties. Select 2D Analysis Type under Advanced Geometry Options in Properties of Schematic A2: Geometry. Right click on Geometry and select New DesignModeler Geometry to open ANSYS DesignModeler. **Select Units>>Millimeter from the menu as the length unit in DesignModeler.**

Fluid Flow (FLUENT)

Figure 10.2a) Selecting Geometry     Figure 10.2b) Selecting 2D Analysis Type

3. Next, we will be creating the mesh for the simulation. Select XYPlane in the Tree Outline. Select Look at Sketch  . Click on the Sketching tab and Draw a Rectangle from the origin. Select the Dimensions tab in the Sketching Toolboxes. Click on one of the vertical edges of the rectangle and enter a vertical length of 1,000 mm. Click on one of the horizontal edges and a horizontal length of 250 mm.

Figure 10.3a) Selection of XYPlane in the Tree Outline

Figure 10.3b) Selection of Sketching Toolboxes and Rectangle

Figure 10.3c) Dimensions in Details View

4. Click on the Modeling tab and select Concept>>Surfaces from Sketches in the menu. Open XYPlane in the Tree Outline, select Sketch1 as Base Objects and select Apply in Details View. Click on  ⚡ Generate in the toolbar. The rectangle turns gray. Right click in the graphics window, select Zoom to Fit and close DesignModeler.

Figure 10.4 Completed rectangle in DesignModeler

## E. Launching ANSYS Meshing

5. We are now going to double click on Mesh in ANSYS Workbench to open the Meshing window. Select Mesh in the Outline. Click on Update. A coarse mesh is created. Select Mesh>>Controls>>Face Meshing from the menu. Click on the rectangle in the graphics window. Apply the Geometry in Details of "Face Meshing".

Figure 10.5a) Starting Mesh

Figure 10.5b) Selection of Mesh in Outline

Figure 10.5c) Generation of Face Meshing

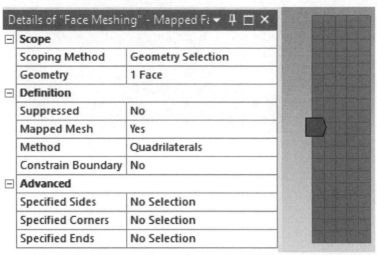

Figure 10.5d) Applying Geometry in Details of "Face Meshing"

6. Select Mesh>>Controls>>Sizing from the menu and select Edge 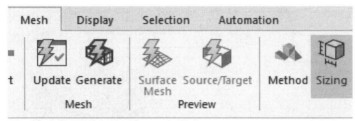. Control-select the four edges of the rectangle. Click on Apply for the Geometry in "Details of Edge Sizing". Under Definition in "Details of Edge Sizing", select Element Size as Type, 2.0 mm as Element Size, and Hard as Behavior. Click on Update and select Mesh in the Outline. The finished mesh is shown below.

Figure 10.6a) Mesh Control Sizing

Figure 10.6b) Details of "Edge Sizing"

Figure 10.6c) Details of finished mesh

7.  We are now going to rename the edges for the rectangle. Use the Edge tool , control-select the left and right edges of the rectangle, right click and select Create Named Selection. Enter *symmetry* as the name and click on the OK button.

    Repeat this step for the upper and lower horizontal edges (control select both edges) of the rectangle and name them *wall*. Select File>>Export…>>Mesh>>FLUENT Input File>>Export from the menu and save the mesh with the name "*rt-mesh.msh*". Select File>>Save Project from the menu. Save the project with the name "Rayleigh-Taylor-Instability". Select File>>Close Meshing. Right click on Mesh under Project Schematic in ANSYS Workbench and select Update.

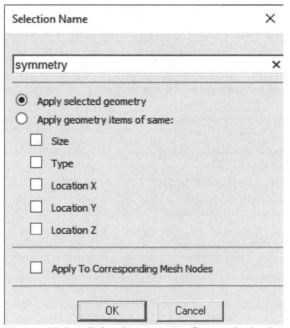

Figure 10.7a) Selecting a name for vertical edges

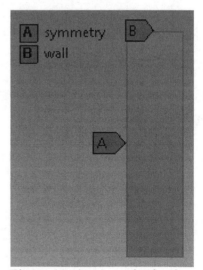

Figure 10.7b) Named selections

## F. Launching ANSYS Fluent

8.  Double click on Setup under Project Schematic in ANSYS Workbench. Select the Double Precision Option in Fluent Launcher. Click on the plus sign next to Show More Options and note the location for your *Working Directory*. In this case the location of the *Working Directory* is *C:\Users\jmatsson*. Set Dimension to 2D, and set the number of Processes equal to the number of processor cores for your computer. Click Start to launch Fluent.

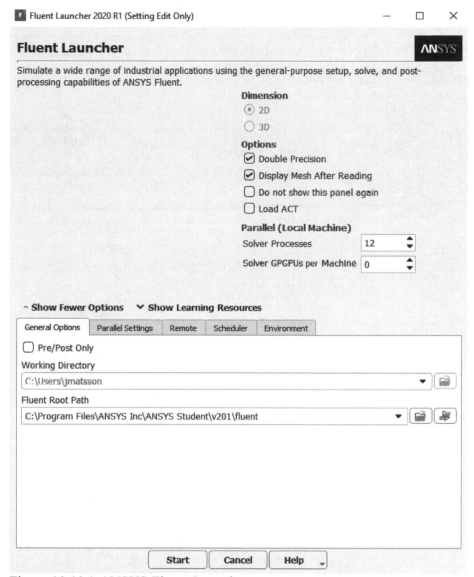

Figure 10.10a) ANSYS Fluent Launcher

Figure 10.10b) A part of the mesh in ANSYS Fluent

9.  Check the mesh in ANSYS Fluent by selecting the Check button under Mesh in General Problem Setup. Check the scale of the mesh by selecting the Scale button. Make sure that the Domain Extent is correct and close the Scale Mesh window.

Figure 10.11a) Mesh check

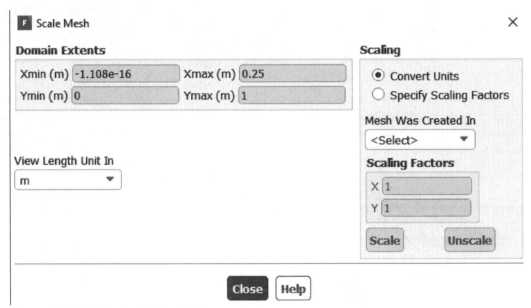

Figure 10.11b) Scale Mesh window

10. Select Transient Time for the Solver in General Problem Setup. Check the Gravity box and enter -9.81 as the Gravitational Acceleration in the Y direction.

    Open Models and double click on Viscous (SST k-omega) under Setup in the Outline View. Select Laminar Model and click OK to close the Viscous Model window. Double click on Multiphase (Off) under Setup in the Outline View. Select the Volume of Fluid Model. Check the box for Implicit Body Force. Click Apply and Close the Multiphase Model window.

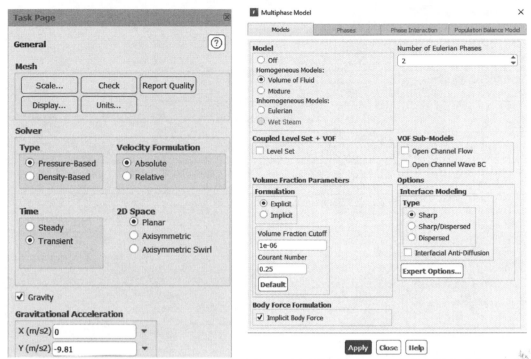

Figure 10.12a) General Setup        Figure 10.12b) Volume of Fluid Model

11. Double click on Materials, Fluid and air under Setup in the Outline View. Change the Name from *air* to *light-fluid*. Change the Density (kg/m3) to 998.2 and the Viscosity (kg/m-s) to 0.001002. Click on the Change/Create button and answer *Yes* to the question that appears and Close the window.

   Click on Create/Edit for Fluid under Materials on the Task Page. Click on Fluent Database. Scroll down in the Fluent Fluid Materials window and select *water-liquid (h2o<l>)*. Click on the Copy button and Close the Fluent Database Materials window. Change the Name from *water-liquid* to *heavy-fluid*. Change the Density (kg/m3) to 1074.9 and the Viscosity (kg/m-s) to 0.001259. Erase the Chemical Formula. Click on the Change/Create button, answer *Yes* to the question that appears and Close the window.

Figure 10.13a) Settings for light-fluid

231

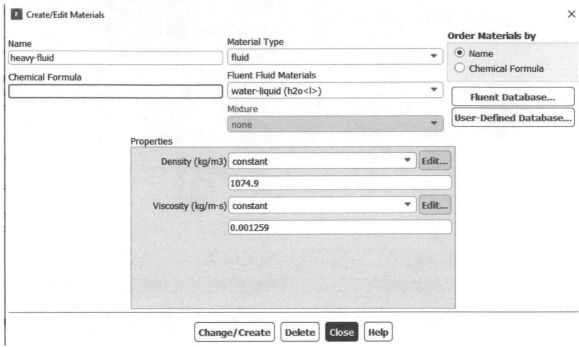

Figure 10.13b) Settings for heavy-fluid

12. Double click on Models and Multiphase under Setup in the Outline View. Select the Phases tab at the top of the Multiphase Model window. Select *light-fluid* as Phase Materials and enter *light-fluid* as the name of the Primary Phase. Click on Apply. Repeat this step to select and name *heavy-fluid* as the Secondary Phase.

Select the Phase Interaction tab at the top of the Multiphase Model window, check the Surface Tension Force Modeling box, select constant from the Surface Tension Coefficients drop down menu, enter the value 0.00148 and click on the Apply button and Close the Multiphase Model window.

Figure 10.14a) Primary Phase Setup

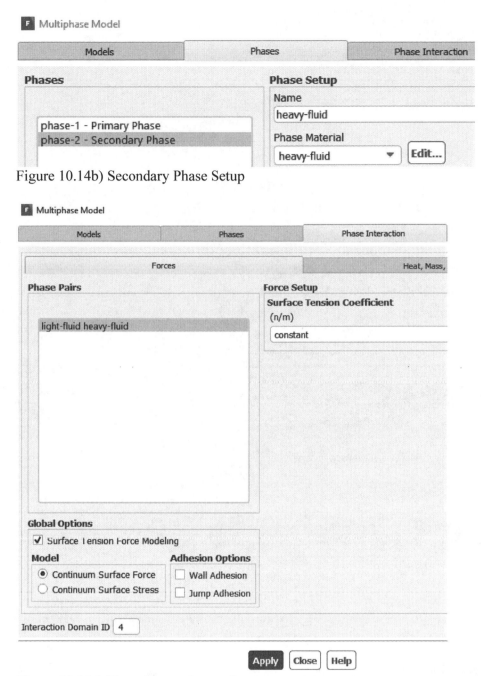

Figure 10.14b) Secondary Phase Setup

Figure 10.14c) Phase interaction toolbox

13. Copy the files *rayleigh-taylor.c* and *udfconfig.h* to your *Working Directory*. These files are available for download at *sdcpublications.com*. Select User-Defined>>Functions>>Interpreted… from the menu. Browse for the file *rayleigh-taylor.c,* select the file and click OK. Click on the Interpret button. Close the window.

```
#include "udf.h"
DEFINE_INIT(init_cos, domain)
{
cell_t c;
Thread*thread;
```

```
real xc[ND_ND];
thread_loop_c(thread,domain)
{
begin_c_loop_all(c,thread)
{
C_CENTROID(xc,c,thread);
if(xc[1] <= 0.5+0.05*cos(2*3.141592654/0.25*xc[0]))
{
C_V(c,thread)=0;
}
else
{
C_V(c,thread)=-0.1;
}
}
end_c_loop_all (c,thread)
}
}
```

Figure 10.15a) Code for the *rayleigh-taylor.c* file

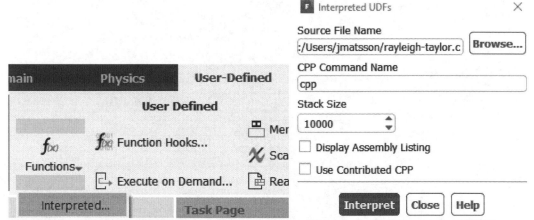

Figure 10.15b) Used defined interpreted function   Figure 10.15c) Interpreted UDFs

Select User-Defined>>Functions Hook from the menu. Click on the Edit button next to Initialization. Select *init_cos* from Available Initialization Functions and click on the Add button to move it over to the Selected Initialization Functions. Click on OK buttons to close windows.

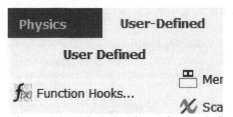

Figure 10.15d) Selection of user defined function hooks

Figure 10.15e) User defined function hooks window

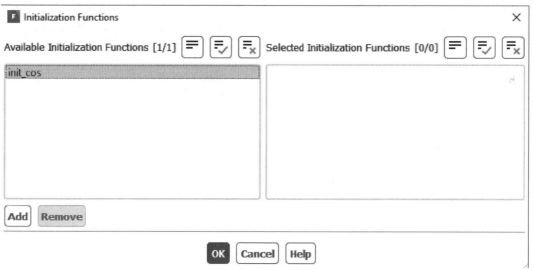

Figure 10.15f) Initializations functions window

14. Double click on Boundary Conditions under Setup in the Outline View. Click on the Operating Conditions on the Task Page in the Boundary Conditions section. Select user-input as Operating Density Method and enter the value 998.2 for Operating Density (this is the value for the less dense fluid). Click OK to close the Operating Conditions window.

Figure 10.16a) Settings for operating conditions

Double click on Methods under Solution in the Outline View. Select Default settings except for First Order Upwind for Momentum and Body Force Weighted for Pressure.

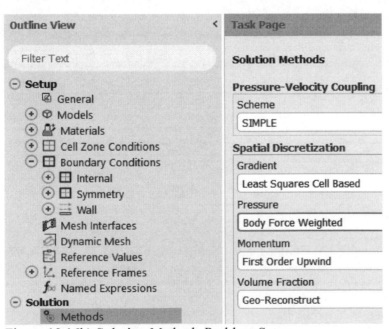

Figure 10.16b) Solution Methods Problem Setup

15. Double click on Initialization under Solution in the Tree, select Standard Initialization, set the Y Velocity to -0.1 and click on the Initialize button.

Figure 10.17 Solution initialization settings

16. Select the *Domain* tab in the menu and choose Adapt>>Refine/Coarsen. Select Cell Registers>>New>>Region… in the Adaption Controls window. Enter 0.25 for X Max, 0.5 for Y Min, and 1 for Y Max. Click on the Save button and close the windows.

Figure 10.18a) Adaption          Figure 10.18b) Region Adaption Settings

17. Click on the Patch button on the Task Page and select *heavy-fluid* as the phase. Select Volume Fraction as the Variable and region_0 as Registers to Patch. Set the value to 1, click on the Patch button and close the window.

Click on the Patch button on the Task Page and select *mixture* for the phase. Select Y Velocity as the Variable and region_0 as Registers to Patch. Set the value to -0.1 and click on the Patch button and Close the window.

Figure 10.19a) Patch Settings for Volume Fraction

Figure 10.19b) Patch Settings for Y Velocity

18. Double click on Graphics and Contours under Results in the Outline View. Select Phases… and Volume fraction under Contours of and select *heavy-fluid* as the Phase. Uncheck the Boundary Values box under Options. Click on Colormap Options…, set Type to float and Precision to 1 under Number Format, click on Apply and Close the Colormap window. Click on the Save/Display button and Close the Contours window.

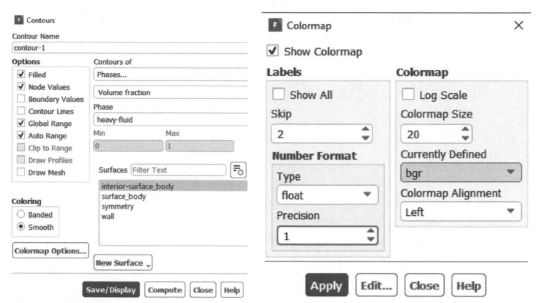

Figure 10.20a) Contours window     Figure 10.20b) Colormap window

Figure 10.20c) Contours of Volume Fraction (heavy-fluid)

19. Double click on Calculation Activities and Solution Animations under Solution in the Outline View. Enter *rayleigh-taylor-instability* as the Name, enter Record after every 10 and select time-step. Set the Window ID to 2 and select contour-1 under Animation Object. Click OK to close the Animation Definition window.

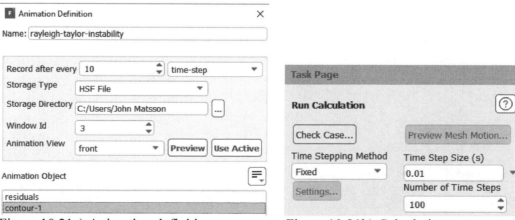

Figure 10.21a) Animation definition     Figure 10.21b) Calculations

Double click on Run Calculation under Solution, enter 0.01 as Time Step Size, and 100 for Number of Time Steps. Click on the Calculate button. Continue running the calculations with 20 as Number of Time Steps 14 more times for a total of 3.8 seconds. Select File>>Write>Case & Data… from the menu. Save the file with the name *rt-computation.cas*.

## G. Post-Processing

20. Double click on Animations and Solution Animation Playback under Results in the Outline View. Set the Replay Speed to low and select Play Once as Playback Mode. Select MPEG as Write/Record Format. Click on the Write button. This will create the mpeg movie in your working directory. Close the Playback window. The movie can be viewed using for example VLC Media Player.

    In VLC Media Player select Media>>Open File… from the menu. Open the movie from the working directory. Select Playback>>Speed>>Slower several times from the menu in the VLC Media Player until you have a suitable speed for the movie.

Figure 10.22a) Playback settings      Figure 10.22b) Movie playing

Figure 10.22c) Volume Fraction Contours after 1, 1.2, 1.4, 1.6 and 1.8 s

Figure 10.22d) Volume Fraction Contours after 2, 2.2, 2.4, 2.6, 2.8, 3, 3.2, 3.4, 3.6 and 3.8 s

## H. Theory

21. We will look at the inviscid theory for the Rayleigh-Taylor instability in the same way as we did for the Kelvin-Helmholz instability in terms of a sinusoidal disturbance between two fluids with densities $\rho_1$, $\rho_2$.

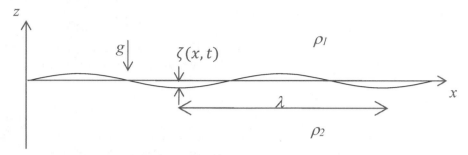

Figure 10.23 Development of Rayleigh-Taylor instability from a perturbation

The velocity vector in a Cartesian coordinate system can be described as

$$\bar{U} = u_x \bar{e}_x + u_y \bar{e}_y + u_z \bar{e}_z \tag{10.1}$$

where $u_x$, $u_y = 0$, $u_z$ are the velocity components in the streamwise, spanwise and normal directions, respectively. Euler equations of motion can be written as

$$\frac{\partial u_x}{\partial t} + u_x \frac{\partial u_x}{\partial x} + u_z \frac{\partial u_x}{\partial z} = -\frac{1}{\rho}\frac{\partial P}{\partial x} \tag{10.2}$$

$$\frac{\partial u_z}{\partial t} + u_x \frac{\partial u_z}{\partial x} + u_z \frac{\partial u_z}{\partial z} = -\frac{1}{\rho}\frac{\partial P}{\partial z} - g \tag{10.3}$$

$$\frac{\partial u_x}{\partial x} + \frac{\partial u_z}{\partial z} = 0 \tag{10.4}$$

The velocity components can be divided into mean flow components in the main streamwise direction plus a perturbation (no mean flow components in this case)

$$\bar{U} = u\bar{e}_x + w\bar{e}_z \tag{10.5}$$

and the pressure is $\qquad P = P_0 - \rho g z + p \tag{10.6}$

A perturbation is introduced in the form

$$u, w, p = [u_n(z), w_n(z), p_n(z)]e^{i(kx-\omega t)} \tag{10.7}$$

where $k = 2\pi/\lambda$ is the wave number, $\lambda$ is the wave length, $\omega$ is the frequency and $u_n(z), w_n(z), p_n(z)$ are eigenfunctions. The linearized Euler equations can be written as

$$-i\omega u_n + \frac{ik}{\rho}p_n = 0 \tag{10.8}$$

$$-i\omega w_n + \frac{1}{\rho}p_n' = 0 \tag{10.9}$$

$$iku_n + w_n' = 0 \tag{10.10}$$

243

From equations (10.8) – (10.10) we can find the equation for $w_n$

$$w_n'' - k^2 w_n = 0 \qquad (10.11)$$

with the general solution

$$w_n = c_1 e^{-kz} + c_2 e^{kz} \qquad (10.12)$$

To get exponentially decaying solutions far from the interface, we set $c_1$ and $c_2$ equal to zero in the lower and upper layers, respectively. The interface location is defined by

$$z = \zeta(x,t) = \mathcal{R}\{a e^{i(kx - \omega t)}\} \qquad (10.13)$$

where $\mathcal{R}$ stands for the real part and $a$ is the amplitude of the initial disturbance. The normal velocity $w$ at the interface is given by the material derivative of $\zeta(x,t)$

$$w = w_n(z) e^{i(kx - \omega t)} = \frac{D\zeta}{Dt} = \frac{\partial \zeta}{\partial t} = -i\omega\, \zeta = -i\omega a e^{i(kx - \omega t)} \qquad (10.14)$$

We find the following results: $c_1 = -i\omega a$, $c_2 = -i\omega a$

$$w_{n,1} = -i\omega a e^{-kz}, \quad w_{n,2} = -i\omega a e^{kz} \qquad (10.15)$$

We can now find the pressure eigenfunctions in the upper and lower layers from equation (10.9)

$$p_{n,1} = -\rho_1 \omega^2 a e^{-kz}/k \qquad (10.16)$$
$$p_{n,2} = \rho_2 \omega^2 a e^{kz}/k \qquad (10.17)$$

Next, we use equation (10.6) and set the pressures identical at the interface to get the dispersion relation

$$P_0 - \rho_1 g\zeta + p_{n,1} e^{i(kx - \omega t)} = P_0 - \rho_2 g\zeta + p_{n,2} e^{i(kx - \omega t)} - \sigma k^2 \zeta \qquad (10.18)$$

$$(\rho_2 - \rho_1) gk = (\rho_2 + \rho_1)\omega^2 - \sigma k^3 \qquad (10.19)$$

where $\sigma$ is surface tension. We find the following equation for the frequency without surface tension

$$\omega = \sqrt{\frac{(\rho_2 - \rho_1)gk}{\rho_1 + \rho_2}} = i\sqrt{\frac{(\rho_1 - \rho_2)gk}{\rho_1 + \rho_2}} = i\sqrt{gkAt} \qquad (10.20)$$

and including surface tension

$$\omega = \sqrt{\frac{(\rho_2 - \rho_1)gk + \sigma k^3}{\rho_1 + \rho_2}} = i\sqrt{\frac{(\rho_1 - \rho_2)gk - \sigma k^3}{\rho_1 + \rho_2}} = i\sqrt{gkAt\left(1 - \frac{4\pi^2}{Bo}\right)} \qquad (10.21)$$

where $At = (\rho_1 - \rho_2)/\rho_1 + \rho_2$ is non-dimensional Atwood number and $Bo = (\rho_1 - \rho_2)gD^2/\sigma$ is non-dimensional Bond number. The frequency is complex with the associated growth of waves when the expression under the square root without surface tension is negative for

$$\rho_2 - \rho_1 < 0 \qquad \text{or} \qquad \rho_2 < \rho_1 \tag{10.22}$$

and including surface tension we get

$$(\rho_2 - \rho_1)gk + \sigma k^3 < 0 \qquad \text{or} \qquad \lambda > 2\pi\sqrt{\frac{\sigma}{(\rho_1 - \rho_2)g}} \tag{10.23}$$

The Bond number $Bo > 4\pi^2$ will give growth of waves when $\lambda = D$. The interface location can now be written as

$$z = \zeta(x,t) = \mathcal{R}\left\{ae^{\sqrt{gkAt(1-\frac{4\pi^2}{Bo})}\,t}e^{ikx}\right\} = ae^{\sqrt{gkAt(1-\frac{4\pi^2}{Bo})}\,t}\cos(kx) \tag{10.24}$$

and we see that surface tension has a very small but stabilizing effect. In ANSYS Fluent simulations we used $a = 0.05$ m, $k = 8\pi$ m$^{-1}$, $g = 9.81$ m/s$^2$, $\lambda = D = 0.25$ m, $\sigma = 0.00148$ N/m, $\rho_1 = 1074.9\frac{kg}{m^3}$, $\rho_2 = 998.2\frac{kg}{m^3}$. The Atwood and Bond numbers used in ANSYS Fluent are

$$At = \frac{1074.9 - 998.2}{1074.9 + 998.2} = 0.037 \tag{10.25}$$

$$Bo = \frac{(1074.9 - 998.2)*9.81*0.25^2}{0.00148} = 31,775 \tag{10.26}$$

There are a few more non-dimensional parameters in this problem that we can define such as the aspect ratio for the rectangular computational domain $/D = 4$, the density ratio $\rho_1/\rho_2 = 1.077$, the dynamic viscosity ratio $\mu_1/\mu_2 = 1.256$ and non-dimensional time $\tau = t\sqrt{gkAt(1 - \frac{4\pi^2}{Bo})}$. The interface location is

$$z = \zeta(x,t) \approx \frac{e^{3t}}{20}\cos(8\pi x) \tag{10.27}$$

Using the inviscid theory, we find that the wave-length with surface tension included according to equation (10.23) must be $\lambda > 0.0088\,m$ to get growth of waves.

## I. References

1. Andrews, M.J. and Dalziel, S.B. "Small Atwood number Rayleigh-Taylor Experiments", *Phil. Trans. R. Soc. A*, **368**, 1663-1679, (2010).
2. Chandrasekhar S. "Hydrodynamic and Hydromagnetic Stability", *Dover Publications, Inc.*, New York (1961).
3. Drazin P.G. and Reid W.H. "Introduction to hydrodynamic instability", *Cambridge University Press*, (1981).
4. Sharqawy M.H, Lienhard J.H., and Zubair S.M. "Thermophysical Properties of Sea Water: A Review of existing Correlations and Data, Desalination, and Water Treatment", *Desalination and Water Treatment*, **16**, 354 (2010).

5.  Strubelj, L., and Tiselj, I., "Numerical Simulations of Basic Interfacial Instabilities with Improved Two-Fluid Model", *International Conference Nuclear Energy for New Europe*, September 14–17, Bled, Slovenia, (2009).
6.  Strubelj, L., and Tiselj, I., "Numerical Simulations of Rayleigh-Taylor Instability with Two-Fluid Model and Interface Sharpening", *Proceedings of ASME Fluids Engineering Division Summer Conference*, August 10-14, Jacksonville, FL, (2008).
7.  Tryggvason, G., "Numerical Simulations of the Rayleigh-Taylor Instability", *Journal of Computational Physics*, **75**, 253-282, (1988).

## J. Exercises

10.1 Use ANSYS Fluent to study the same problem as we completed in this chapter but instead complete transient 2D axisymmetric simulations. Visualize the instability using contours of volume fraction for the heavy fluid.

10.2 Use ANSYS Fluent to study the same problem as we completed in this chapter but instead use the following dimensions $H = 2$ m, $D = 0.25$ m. Visualize the instability using contours of volume fraction for the heavy fluid.

10.3 Use ANSYS Fluent to study the same problem as we completed in this chapter but instead use a frustum shaped geometry with the following dimensions $H = 1$ m, $D_{bottom} = 0.25$ m and $D_{top} = 0.5$ m. Visualize the instability using contours of volume fraction for the heavy fluid.

## CHAPTER 11. FLOW UNDER A DAM

### A. Objectives

- Using ANSYS Workbench to Model Seepage Flow of Water under a Concrete Dam
- Inserting Boundary Conditions and a Porous Medium Zone with Viscous and Inertial Resistance
- Running Laminar Steady 2D Planar ANSYS Fluent Simulations
- Using Contour Plots for Static Pressure and Velocity Magnitude
- Using XY Plots for Visualizations of Velocity and Pressure
- Comparing ANSYS Fluent Results with Results Using Mathematica

### B. Problem Description

We will study the seepage flow of water under a concrete dam using ANSYS Fluent. The dimensions and water levels are shown below.

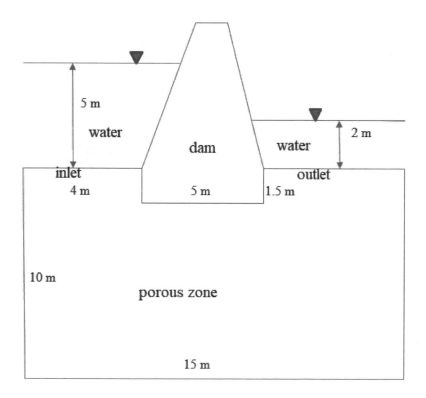

## C. Launching ANSYS Workbench and Selecting Fluent

1. Start by launching ANSYS Workbench. Double click on Fluid Flow (Fluent) under Analysis Systems in the Toolbox.

Figure 11.1 Selecting Fluid Flow (Fluent)

## D. Launching ANSYS DesignModeler

2. Right click Geometry under Project Schematic in ANSYS Workbench and select Properties. In Properties of Schematic A2: Geometry, select Analysis Type 2D under Advanced Geometry Options. Right click on Geometry in the Project Schematic window and select New DesignModeler Geometry.

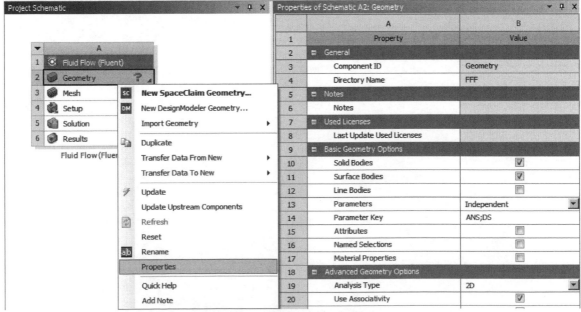

Figure 11.2a) Selecting properties and 2D analysis type

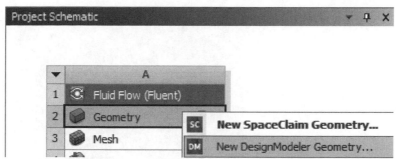

Figure 11.2b) Selecting new DesignModeler geometry

3. Select the Sketching tab in the Tree Outline and select Line under Draw. Click on Look at Face/Plane/Sketch [icon]. Draw a horizontal line to the right from the origin of the coordinate system in the graphics window. Make sure you have the letters *P* at the origin, *H* along the line and *C* when you end the line.

   Click on the Dimensions tab under Sketching Toolboxes and click on the new line. Enter 15 m for the length of the line. Continue adding lines with lengths as shown in Fig. 11.3a).

   Select Concepts>>Surfaces from Sketches from the menu. Click on Sketch 1 under XYPlane in the Tree Outline and select Apply for Base Objects in Details View. Click on Generate. Close DesignModeler.

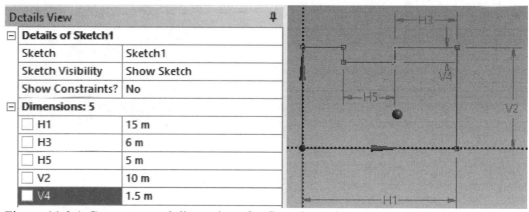

Figure 11.3a) Geometry and dimensions for flow through a porous medium

Figure 11.3b) Creating surfaces from Sketches

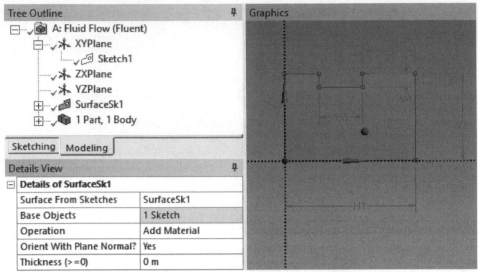

Figure 11.3c) Finished model for seepage flow under a dam

## E. Launching ANSYS Meshing

4. Double click on Mesh under the Project Schematic in ANSYS Workbench. Select Mesh under Model (A3) and Project in the Outline. Right click on Mesh and select Update.

Figure 11.4a) Mesh in ANSYS

Figure 11.4b) Coarse mesh

Select Mesh>>Controls>>Face Meshing from the menu. Select the face of the mesh region. Apply the Geometry under Details of "Face Meshing".

Figure 11.4c) Face meshing

Select Mesh>>Controls>>Sizing from the menu and select the face of the mesh region. Apply the Geometry under Details of "Face Sizing". Set the Element Size to 50 mm and set the Behavior to Hard. Right click on Mesh in the tree outline and select Generate Mesh.

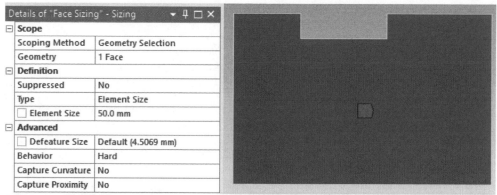

Figure 11.4d) Details of face sizing for the mesh

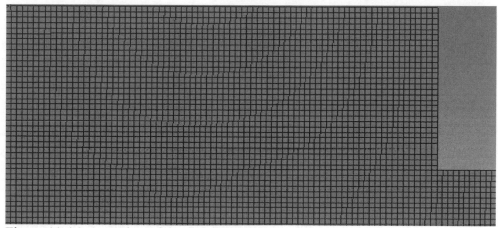

Figure 11.4e) A portion of the finished mesh

Select Geometry under Project and Model (A3) in the Outline. Select the Edge Selection Filter 🔲. Select the upper left horizontal edge, right click and select Create Named Selection. Name the edge "pressure-inlet" and click OK. Name the upper horizontal edge to the right "pressure-outlet" and control-select all the remaining six edges and enter the name "wall".

Select File>>Export…>>Mesh>>FLUENT Input File>>Export from the menu and save the mesh with the name *seepage-flow.msh*. Select File>>Save Project from the menu and save the project with the name *Dam-Seepage-Flow.wbpj*. Close the meshing window. Right click on Mesh and select Update under Project Schematic in ANSYS Workbench.

Figure 11.4f) Selection of Geometry

Figure 11.4g) Named selections

**F. Launching ANSYS Fluent**

5. Double click on Setup under Project Schematic in ANSYS Workbench. Check the Options box Double Precision. Select Parallel Processing Options. Move the cursor to the bottom of the computer monitor, right click and select Task Manager and click on the Performance tab. Click on Open Resource Monitor and select the number of Processes equal to the total number of CPUs. Click Start to launch Fluent.

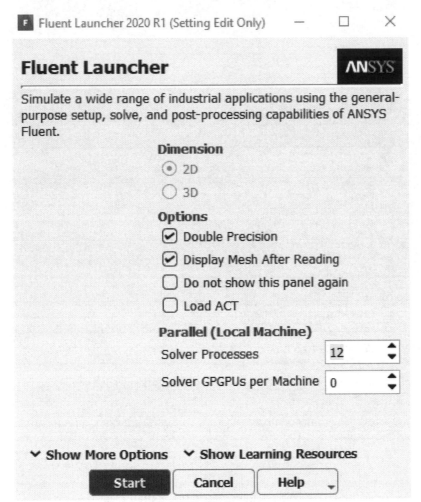

Figure 11.5 Launching ANSYS Fluent

6. Double click on Models and Viscous (SST k-omega) under Setup in the Outline View. Select Laminar Model and select OK to close the Viscous Model window. Double click on Materials under Setup in the Outline View. Click on Create/Edit for Fluid under Materials on the Task Page. Click on Fluent Database in the Create/Edit Materials window. Select *water-liquid (h2o<l>)* as the Fluent Fluid Material. Click on Copy and Close. Set the Density to 992.2 (kg/m3) and the Viscosity to 0.00065 (kg/m-s). Click Change/Create and Close the window.

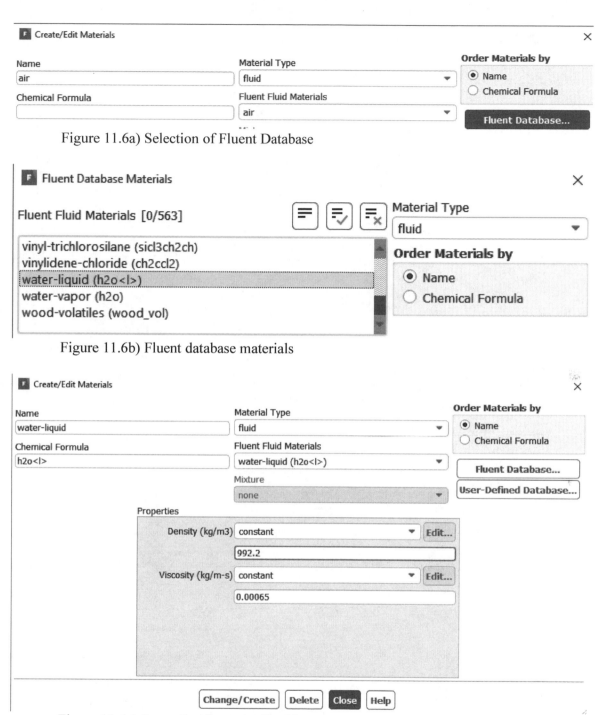

Figure 11.6a) Selection of Fluent Database

Figure 11.6b) Fluent database materials

Figure 11.6c) Properties for water-liquid

7. Double click on Cell Zone Conditions and *surface_body* under Setup in the Outline View. Select *water-liquid* from the Material Name drop-down menu. Check the box for Porous Zone. Click on the Porous Zone tab and enter 1.98807e+06 (1/m2) for Viscous Resistance in both Direction-1 and Direction-2. Enter 1719.4 (1/m) for Inertial Resistance in both Direction-1 and Direction-2. Set the Fluid Porosity to 0.5. Click on the OK button to close the Fluid window.

F Fluid

Zone Name

surface_body

Material Name  water-liquid  ▼   Edit...

☐ Frame Motion   ☐ Source Terms

☐ Mesh Motion   ☐ Fixed Values

☑ Porous Zone

| Reference Frame | Mesh Motion | Porous Zone | 3D Fan Zone | E... |

**Update From Line Tool**

**Direction-1 Vector**

X 1 ▼

Y 0 ▼

☑ Relative Velocity Resistance Formulation

**Viscous Resistance (Inverse Absolute Permeability)**

Direction-1 (1/m2) 1988070 ▼

Direction-2 (1/m2) 1988070 ▼

**Inertial Resistance**

☐ Alternative Formulation

Direction-1 (1/m) 1719.4 ▼

Direction-2 (1/m) 1719.4 ▼

**Power Law Model**

C0 0 ▼

C1 0 ▼

**Fluid Porosity**

Porosity 0.5 ▼

**Relative Viscosity**

constant ▼  Edit...

1

Figure 11.7 Fluid window

8. Double click on Boundary Conditions under Setup in the Outline View. Select the *pressure-inlet* Zone on the Task Page. Click on Edit. Enter 49050 (pascal) as the Gauge Total Pressure. Click on OK to close the window. Select the *pressure-outlet* Zone on the Task Page. Click on Edit. Enter 19620 (Pa) as the Gauge Pressure. Click OK to close the window.

Figure 11.8a) Selection of pressure-inlet boundary condition

Figure 11.8b) Pressure inlet window

Figure 11.8c) Pressure outlet window

9. Double click on Initialization under Solution in the Outlet View. Check Standard Initialization as Initialization Method on the Task Page. Select Compute from *pressure-inlet* from the drop-down menu and click on Initialize.

Figure 11.9 Solution initialization

10. Double click on Monitors and Residual under Solution in the Outline View. Set the Absolute Criteria to 1e-12 for all Residuals and click on OK to exit the window.

Double click on Run Calculation under Solution in the Outline View, enter 1000 for Number of Iterations on the Task Page and click on Calculate.

Figure 11.10a) Residual monitors window

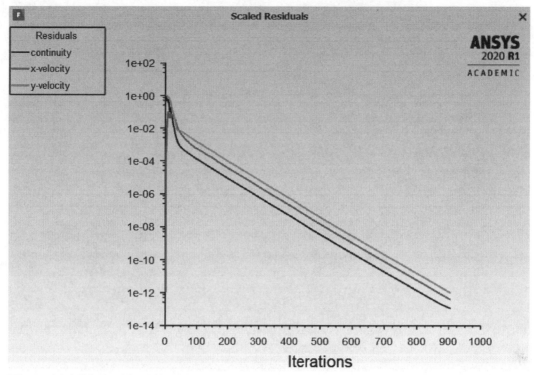

Figure 11.10b) Residual iterations

## G. Post-Processing

11. Double click on Graphics and Contours under Results in the Outline View. Select Contours of Velocity and Velocity Magnitude from the drop-down menu. Deselect all Surfaces and click on Save/Display. Select Contours of Pressure and Static Pressure and click on Save/Display. Close the window.

Figure 11.11a) Contours window

257

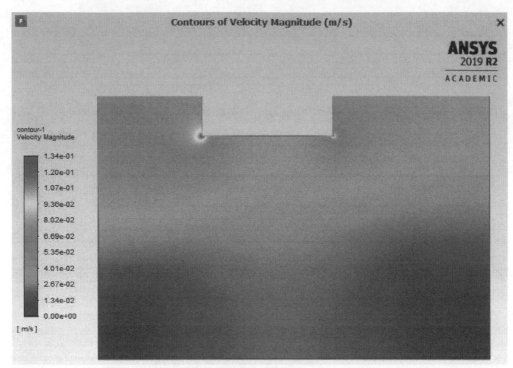

Figure 11.11b) Contours for velocity magnitude

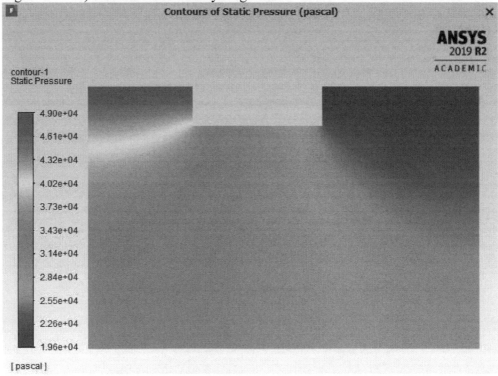

Figure 11.11c) Contours for static pressure

12. Double click on Plots and XY Plot under Results in the Outline View. Select Velocity and Velocity Magnitude for Y Axis Function and Direction Vector for X Axis Function. Select New Surface >> Line/Rake from the drop–down menu. Enter the following end points: x0 (m) = 9, y0 (m) = 10 and x1 (m) = 15, y1 (m) = 10. Click on Create and Close

the window. Click on Load File… and load the file with the name "*theory-flow-under-dam.dat*". This and other files are available for download at *sdcpublications.com*. Select *line-5* in the Surfaces section, select *Theory* under File Data. Click on Curves…, select Curve # 1, select the second available pattern and no symbol as shown in Figure 11.12c). Click on Apply and Close the Curves-Solution XY Plot window. Click on Axes… in the Solution XY Plot window. Select X Axis, set Type to float, set Precision under Number Format to 0 and click on Apply. Select Y Axis, set Type to General, set Precision under Number Format to 2 and click on Apply. Close the Axes – Solution XY Plot window. Click on Save/Plot in the Solution XY Plot window.

Select New Surface >> Line/Rake from the drop–down menu. Enter the following end points: x0 (m) = 9, y0 (m) = 0 and x1 (m) = 9, y1 (m) = 8.5. Click on Create and Close the window. Select *line-6* in the Surfaces section, uncheck Position on X Axis under Options and select Mesh and Y-Coordinate as Y Axis Function. Select Pressure and Static Pressure as X Axis Function. Click on Axes… and uncheck Auto Range under Options for the X Axis. Set Minimum under Range to 25000 and Maximum to 30000. Set Precision under Number Format to 0. Select Y Axis and set the Precision to 0. Click on Apply and Close the Axes window. Click on Curves…, select Curve # 0, select the first available pattern and no symbol. Click on Save/Plot.

Figure 11.12a) Line/Rake Surface window

Figure 11.12b) Solution XY Plot

Figure 11.12c) Curves window          Figure 11.12d) Axes window

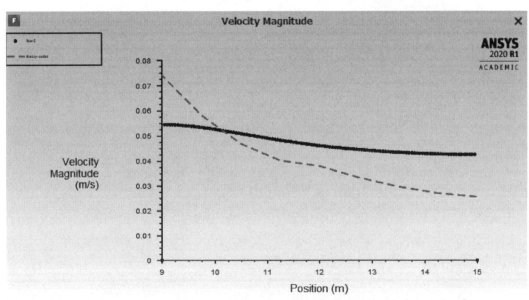

Figure 11.12e) Comparison of the variation for seepage velocity at the outlet from ANSYS Fluent simulations (full line) and finite element calculations (dashed line).

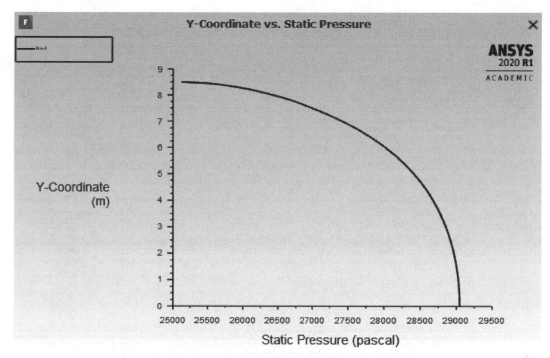

Figure 11.12f) Static pressure distribution along a vertical line under the dam

## H. Theory

13. Groundwater seepage can frequently occur in soils and has many engineering applications. We can relate the mean fluid velocity $v$ (m/s) through the porous medium to the pressure gradient $dP/dx$ (Pa) using Darcy's law

$$v = -\frac{\kappa}{\mu}\frac{dP}{dx}$$

(11.1)

where $\kappa$ (m$^2$) is permeability of the porous medium and $\mu$ (kg/m-s) is the dynamic viscosity of the fluid. Furthermore, we define the hydraulic conductivity or coefficient of permeability $k$ (m/s) as

$$k = \kappa\frac{\rho g}{\mu}$$

(11.2)

Where $g$ (m/s$^2$) is acceleration due to gravity and $\rho$ (kg/m$^3$) is the density of the fluid. We will also use the following equation from the ANSYS Fluent user manual

$$\frac{dP}{dx} = -(\frac{\mu v}{\alpha} + \frac{C_2\rho v^2}{2})$$

(11.3)

where $1/\alpha$ (1/m$^2$) is viscous resistance or inverse absolute permeability for the porous medium and $C_2$(1/m) is inertial resistance of the porous medium. When we combine the equations we get the following expression for the permeability coefficient

$$k = \frac{g}{\frac{vC_2}{2} + \frac{\mu}{\alpha\rho}}$$ (11.4)

The following values were used in or determined from the ANSYS Fluent simulations.

| | |
|---|---|
| $C_2$ (1/m) | 1719.4 |
| $1/\alpha$ (1/m$^2$) | $1.98807 \cdot 10^6$ |
| $\rho$ (kg/m$^3$) | 992.2 |
| $\mu$ (kg/m-s) | 0.00065 |
| $v$ (m/s) | 0.05 |
| $g$ (m/s$^2$) | 9.81 |
| $k$ (m/s) | 0.221508 |
| $p_1$ (Pa) | 29046.9 |
| $p_2$ (Pa) | 25124.4 |

Table 11.1 Parameters & coefficients used or determined by ANSYS Fluent simulations

The 2D flow through a porous medium is governed by

$$k_x \frac{\partial^2 \phi}{\partial x^2} + k_y \frac{\partial^2 \phi}{\partial y^2} = 0$$ (11.5)

where $\phi$ is the hydraulic head and $k_x = k_y = k$ are coefficients of permeability in the $x$ and $y$-directions. The seepage velocity components are related to the hydraulic head through

$$v_x = -k_x \frac{\partial \phi}{\partial x} \quad \text{and} \quad v_y = -k_y \frac{\partial \phi}{\partial y}$$ (11.6)

We follow the approach by Bhatti[3] using second order ($n = 2$) p-formulation. The equations for element **1**:

$$
\begin{pmatrix}
+0.2424 & -0.2021 & -0.1212 & +0.0809 & -0.0164 & +0.1320 & +0.0164 & -0.1320 \\
-0.2021 & +0.2424 & +0.0809 & -0.1212 & -0.0164 & -0.1320 & +0.0164 & +0.1320 \\
-0.1212 & +0.0809 & +0.2424 & -0.2021 & +0.0164 & -0.1320 & -0.0164 & +0.1320 \\
+0.0809 & -0.1212 & -0.2021 & +0.2424 & +0.0164 & +0.1320 & -0.0164 & -0.1320 \\
-0.0164 & -0.0164 & +0.0164 & +0.0164 & +0.4445 & 0 & +0.2021 & 0 \\
+0.1320 & -0.1320 & -0.1320 & +0.1320 & 0 & +0.1615 & 0 & -0.0809 \\
+0.0164 & +0.0164 & -0.0164 & -0.0164 & +0.2021 & 0 & +0.4445 & 0 \\
-0.1320 & +0.1320 & +0.1320 & -0.1320 & 0 & -0.0809 & 0 & +0.1615
\end{pmatrix}
\begin{pmatrix}
\phi_1 \\ \phi_4 \\ \phi_5 \\ \phi_2 \\ \delta_1^{(1,4)} \\ \delta_1^{(4,5)} \\ \delta_1^{(2,5)} \\ \delta_1^{(1,2)}
\end{pmatrix}
=
\begin{pmatrix}
0 \\ 0 \\ 0 \\ 0 \\ 0 \\ 0 \\ 0 \\ 0
\end{pmatrix}
$$

Equations for element **2**:

$$
\begin{pmatrix}
+0.1902 & +0.0380 & -0.0951 & -0.1331 & -0.0932 & +0.0233 & +0.0932 & -0.0233 \\
+0.0380 & +0.1902 & -0.1331 & -0.0951 & -0.0932 & -0.0233 & +0.0932 & +0.0233 \\
-0.0951 & -0.1331 & +0.1902 & +0.0380 & +0.0932 & -0.0233 & -0.0932 & +0.0233 \\
-0.1331 & -0.0951 & +0.0380 & +0.1902 & +0.0932 & +0.0233 & -0.0932 & -0.0233 \\
-0.0932 & -0.0932 & +0.0932 & +0.0932 & +0.1521 & 0 & -0.0380 & 0 \\
+0.0233 & -0.0233 & -0.0233 & +0.0233 & 0 & +0.3233 & 0 & +0.1331 \\
+0.0932 & +0.0932 & -0.0932 & -0.0932 & -0.0380 & 0 & +0.1521 & 0 \\
-0.0233 & +0.0233 & +0.0233 & -0.0233 & 0 & +0.1331 & 0 & +0.3233
\end{pmatrix}
\begin{pmatrix}
\phi_2 \\ \phi_5 \\ \phi_6 \\ \phi_3 \\ \delta_1^{(2,5)} \\ \delta_1^{(5,6)} \\ \delta_1^{(3,6)} \\ \delta_1^{(2,3)}
\end{pmatrix}
=
\begin{pmatrix}
0 \\ 0 \\ 0 \\ 0 \\ 0 \\ 0 \\ 0 \\ 0
\end{pmatrix}
$$

Equations for element **3**:

$$
\begin{pmatrix}
+0.2424 & -0.2021 & -0.1212 & +0.0809 & -0.0164 & +0.1320 & +0.0164 & -0.1320 \\
-0.2021 & +0.2424 & +0.0809 & -0.1212 & -0.0164 & -0.1320 & +0.0164 & +0.1320 \\
-0.1212 & +0.0809 & +0.2424 & -0.2021 & +0.0164 & -0.1320 & -0.0164 & +0.1320 \\
+0.0809 & -0.1212 & -0.2021 & +0.2424 & +0.0164 & +0.1320 & -0.0164 & -0.1320 \\
-0.0164 & -0.0164 & +0.0164 & +0.0164 & +0.4445 & 0 & +0.2021 & 0 \\
+0.1320 & -0.1320 & -0.1320 & +0.1320 & 0 & +0.1615 & 0 & -0.0809 \\
+0.0164 & +0.0164 & -0.0164 & -0.0164 & +0.2021 & 0 & +0.4445 & 0 \\
-0.1320 & +0.1320 & +0.1320 & -0.1320 & 0 & -0.0809 & 0 & +0.1615
\end{pmatrix}
\begin{pmatrix}
\phi_4 \\ \phi_7 \\ \phi_8 \\ \phi_5 \\ \delta_1^{(4,7)} \\ \delta_1^{(7,8)} \\ \delta_1^{(5,8)} \\ \delta_1^{(4,5)}
\end{pmatrix}
=
\begin{pmatrix}
0 \\ 0 \\ 0 \\ 0 \\ 0 \\ 0 \\ 0 \\ 0
\end{pmatrix}
$$

Equations for element **4**:

$$
\begin{pmatrix}
+0.1902 & +0.0380 & -0.0951 & -0.1331 & -0.0932 & +0.0233 & +0.0932 & -0.0233 \\
+0.0380 & +0.1902 & -0.1331 & -0.0951 & -0.0932 & -0.0233 & +0.0932 & +0.0233 \\
-0.0951 & -0.1331 & +0.1902 & +0.0380 & +0.0932 & -0.0233 & -0.0932 & +0.0233 \\
-0.1331 & -0.0951 & +0.0380 & +0.1902 & +0.0932 & +0.0233 & -0.0932 & -0.0233 \\
-0.0932 & -0.0932 & +0.0932 & +0.0932 & +0.1521 & 0 & -0.0380 & 0 \\
+0.0233 & -0.0233 & -0.0233 & +0.0233 & 0 & +0.3233 & 0 & +0.1331 \\
+0.0932 & +0.0932 & -0.0932 & -0.0932 & -0.0380 & 0 & +0.1521 & 0 \\
-0.0233 & +0.0233 & +0.0233 & -0.0233 & 0 & +0.1331 & 0 & +0.3233
\end{pmatrix}
\begin{pmatrix}
\phi_5 \\ \phi_8 \\ \phi_9 \\ \phi_6 \\ \delta_1^{(5,8)} \\ \delta_1^{(8,9)} \\ \delta_1^{(6,9)} \\ \delta_1^{(5,6)}
\end{pmatrix}
=
\begin{pmatrix}
0 \\ 0 \\ 0 \\ 0 \\ 0 \\ 0 \\ 0 \\ 0
\end{pmatrix}
$$

where $\phi_1...,\phi_9$ are hydraulic heads at the node points for the four elements and $\delta$ are the *p*-mode parameters, subscripts indicate mode number for the side modes and superscripts indicate node numbers on the corresponding line segments for an element. The boundary conditions are the following:

$$(\phi_1,\phi_2,\phi_3,\phi_6,\phi_9,\delta_1^{(1,2)},\delta_1^{(3,6)},\delta_1^{(6,9)}) =(2.98422, 2.58123, 2, 2, 2, 0, 0, 0) \tag{11.7}$$

The hydraulic head boundary conditions $\phi_1,\phi_2$ were determined from the static pressures

$$p_1, p_2 = \rho g \phi_1, \rho g \phi_2 = 29046.9, 25124.4 \; Pa \tag{11.8}$$

at nodes and 1 and 2, respectively. We can now assemble the global stiffness matrix.

Figure 11.13a) Four element model for seepage flow

CHAPTER 11. FLOW UNDER A DAM

$$
\begin{pmatrix}
+0.485 & +0.162 & -0.202 & -0.121 & -0.016 & 0 & +0.016 & -0.264 & -0.016 & 0 & +0.016 & +0.132 & 0 \\
+0.162 & +0.865 & -0.121 & -0.164 & +0.016 & +0.023 & -0.110 & -0.264 & +0.016 & -0.047 & -0.110 & +0.132 & +0.023 \\
-0.202 & -0.121 & +0.242 & +0.081 & 0 & 0 & 0 & +0.132 & -0.016 & 0 & +0.016 & -0.132 & 0 \\
-0.121 & -0.164 & +0.081 & +0.433 & 0 & 0 & 0 & +0.132 & +0.016 & +0.023 & -0.110 & -0.132 & -0.023 \\
-0.016 & +0.016 & 0 & 0 & +0.445 & 0 & +0.202 & 0 & 0 & 0 & 0 & 0 & 0 \\
0 & +0.023 & 0 & 0 & 0 & +0.323 & 0 & 0 & 0 & +0.133 & 0 & 0 & 0 \\
+0.016 & -0.110 & 0 & 0 & +0.202 & 0 & +0.597 & 0 & 0 & 0 & 0 & 0 & 0 \\
-0.264 & -0.264 & +0.132 & +0.132 & 0 & 0 & 0 & +0.323 & 0 & 0 & 0 & -0.081 & 0 \\
-0.016 & +0.016 & -0.016 & +0.016 & 0 & 0 & 0 & 0 & +0.445 & 0 & +0.202 & 0 & 0 \\
0 & -0.047 & 0 & +0.023 & 0 & +0.133 & 0 & 0 & 0 & +0.647 & 0 & 0 & +0.133 \\
+0.016 & -0.110 & +0.016 & -0.110 & 0 & 0 & 0 & 0 & +0.202 & 0 & +0.597 & 0 & 0 \\
+0.132 & +0.132 & -0.132 & -0.132 & 0 & 0 & 0 & -0.081 & 0 & 0 & 0 & +0.161 & 0 \\
0 & +0.023 & 0 & -0.023 & 0 & 0 & 0 & 0 & 0 & +0.133 & 0 & 0 & +0.323
\end{pmatrix}
\begin{pmatrix}
\phi_4 \\ \phi_5 \\ \phi_7 \\ \phi_8 \\ \delta_1^{(1,4)} \\ \delta_1^{(2,3)} \\ \delta_1^{(2,5)} \\ \delta_1^{(4,5)} \\ \delta_1^{(4,7)} \\ \delta_1^{(5,6)} \\ \delta_1^{(5,8)} \\ \delta_1^{(7,8)} \\ \delta_1^{(8,9)}
\end{pmatrix} =
$$

$$
\begin{pmatrix}
+0.916 \\ +1.698 \\ 0 \\ +0.456 \\ +0.007 \\ +0.060 \\ -0.139 \\ -0.735 \\ 0 \\ -0.060 \\ -0.373 \\ 0 \\ 0
\end{pmatrix}
\text{, with the solution }
\begin{pmatrix}
\phi_4 \\ \phi_5 \\ \phi_7 \\ \phi_8 \\ \delta_1^{(1,4)} \\ \delta_1^{(2,3)} \\ \delta_1^{(2,5)} \\ \delta_1^{(4,5)} \\ \delta_1^{(4,7)} \\ \delta_1^{(5,6)} \\ \delta_1^{(5,8)} \\ \delta_1^{(7,8)} \\ \delta_1^{(8,9)}
\end{pmatrix} =
\begin{pmatrix}
+2.699 \\ +2.192 \\ +2.703 \\ +2.193 \\ -0.012 \\ +0.038 \\ +0.100 \\ -0.316 \\ +0.027 \\ -0.024 \\ +0.023 \\ -0.155 \\ +0.010
\end{pmatrix}
\qquad (11.9)
$$

We can summarize the solution at the outflow for elements 2 and 4 with the following table where $v_y$ velocity component is compared with ANSYS Fluent in Figure 11.12e).

| | x | y | φ | ∂φ/∂x | ∂φ/∂y | $v_y$ |
|---|---|---|---|---|---|---|
| 2 | 0 | 10 | 2. | 0. | −0.32565825428980166 | 0.07432144875149277 |
| 2 | 0.75 | 10 | 2. | 0. | −0.2555161785079309 | 0.05831368410289106 |
| 2 | 1.5 | 10 | 2. | 0. | −0.2057152107246451 | 0.04694814975476898 |
| 2 | 2.25 | 10 | 2. | 0. | −0.1762553509399443 | 0.04022484570712651 |
| 4 | 3 | 10 | 2. | 0. | −0.16713659915382845 | 0.03814377195996365 |
| 4 | 3.75 | 10 | 2. | 0. | −0.14647549864168652 | 0.03342851324124527 |
| 4 | 4.5 | 10 | 2. | 0. | −0.13050473334316898 | 0.029783678820436723 |
| 4 | 5.25 | 10 | 2. | 0. | −0.1192243032582763 | 0.027209268697538133 |
| 4 | 6 | 10 | 2. | 0. | −0.11263420838700836 | 0.025705282872549466 |

Table 11.2 Solution summary at the outflow region

```
(*Seepage through soil, p=q=0,
2nd order p-formulation (n=2), wi = wj = 1, kx = ky = 0.2282191462137928` *)
Clear["Global`*"]; wi = 1; wj = 1; kx = 0.2282191462137928`; ky = 0.2282191462137928`;
NT = {(1 - s) * (1 - t) / 4, (1 + s) * (1 - t) / 4, (1 + s) * (1 + t) / 4, (1 - s) * (1 + t) / 4,
      (3 * s^2 / 2 - 3 / 2) * (1 - t) / (2 * Sqrt[6]), (3 * t^2 / 2 - 3 / 2) * (1 + s) / (2 * Sqrt[6]),
      (3 * s^2 / 2 - 3 / 2) * (1 + t) / (2 * Sqrt[6]), (3 * t^2 / 2 - 3 / 2) * (1 - s) / (2 * Sqrt[6])};
gcd[x0_, y0_] := Module[{x = x0, y = y0}, {J = {{D[x, s], D[x, t]}, {D[y, s], D[y, t]}};
     BT = Inverse[J] . {D[NT, s], D[NT, t]}; k = wi*wj*Transpose[BT] . {{kx, 0}, {0, ky}} . BT*Det[J];
     k1 = k //. {s -> -0.57735, t -> -0.57735}; k2 = k //. {s -> -0.57735, t -> 0.57735};
     k3 = k //. {s -> 0.57735, t -> -0.57735}; k4 = k //. {s -> 0.57735, t -> 0.57735}; kk = k1 + k2 + k3 + k4;}]


(*Element 1: 0<x<3, 0<y<8.5, -1<s<1, -1<t<1, Element 2: 0<x<3, 8.5<y<10, -1<s<1, -1<t<1,
Element 3: 3<x<6, 0<y<8.5, -1<s<1, -1<t<1, Element 4: 3<x<6, 8.5<y<10, -1<s<1, -1<t<1 *)
gcd[3*s/2 + 3/2, 8.5*t/2 + 8.5/2]; kk1 = kk; kk1 // MatrixForm;
gcd[3*s/2 + 3/2, 3*t/4 + 37/4]; kk2 = kk; kk2 // MatrixForm;
gcd[3*s/2 + 9/2, 8.5*t/2 + 8.5/2]; kk3 = kk; kk3 // MatrixForm;
gcd[3*s/2 + 9/2, y = 3*t/4 + 37/4]; kk4 = kk; kk4 // MatrixForm;


(*Global stiffness matrix and Boundary conditions *)
kG = SparseArray[{}, {21, 21}]; r1 = {1, 4, 5, 2, 11, 15, 13, 10}; kG[[r1, r1]] = kG[[r1, r1]] + kk1;
r2 = {2, 5, 6, 3, 13, 17, 14, 12};
kG[[r2, r2]] = kG[[r2, r2]] + kk2; r3 = {4, 7, 8, 5, 16, 20, 18, 15};
kG[[r3, r3]] = kG[[r3, r3]] + kk3; r4 = {5, 8, 9, 6, 18, 21, 19, 17}; kG[[r4, r4]] = kG[[r4, r4]] + kk4;
kG[[1]] = UnitVector[21, 1]; kG[[2]] = UnitVector[21, 2]; kG[[3]] = UnitVector[21, 3];
kG[[6]] = UnitVector[21, 6]; kG[[9]] = UnitVector[21, 9]; kG[[10]] = UnitVector[21, 10];
kG[[14]] = UnitVector[21, 14]; kG[[19]] = UnitVector[21, 19];


(*Global solution and element solutions) *)
RHS = {2.984224966974819`, 2.581234546896989`, 2, 0, 0, 2, 0, 0, 2, 0, 0, 0, 0, 0, 0, 0, 0, 0, 0, 0, 0};
φ = LinearSolve[kG, RHS]
gce[x0_, y0_, s0_, t0_] :=
  Module[{x = x0, y = y0}, {J = {{D[x, s], D[x, t]}, {D[y, s], D[y, t]}}; NT1 = NT //. {s → s0, t → t0};
     dNTds = D[NT, s] //. {s → s0, t → t0}; dNTdt = D[NT, t] //. {s → s0, t → t0};
     dNTdsodNTdt = {dNTds, dNTdt} //. {s → s0, t → t0}; BT = Inverse[J] . dNTdsodNTdt;
     B = Transpose[BT]; BTx = BT[[1]]; BTy = BT[[2]]; φxy = NT1.dT; dφdx = BTx.dT; dφdy = BTy.dT;}]


(*Solution for element 2 at location (x,y) = (0,10), (0.75,10), (1.5,10), (2.25,10) *)
dT = {φ[[2]], φ[[5]], φ[[6]], φ[[3]], φ[[13]], φ[[17]], φ[[14]], φ[[12]]};
gce[3*s/2 + 3/2, 3*t/4 + 37/4, -1, 1]; mxy1 = {0, 10, φxy, dφdx, dφdy, -ky*dφdy};
gce[3*s/2 + 3/2, 3*t/4 + 37/4, -0.5, 1]; mxy2 = {0.75, 10, φxy, dφdx, dφdy, -ky*dφdy};
gce[3*s/2 + 3/2, 3*t/4 + 37/4, 0, 1]; mxy3 = {1.5, 10, φxy, dφdx, dφdy, -ky*dφdy};
gce[3*s/2 + 3/2, 3*t/4 + 37/4, 0.5, 1]; mxy4 = {2.25, 10, φxy, dφdx, dφdy, -ky*dφdy};


(*Solution for element 4 at location (x,y) = (3,10), (3.75,10), (4.5,10), (5.25,10), (6,10) *)
dT = {φ[[5]], φ[[8]], φ[[9]], φ[[6]], φ[[18]], φ[[21]], φ[[19]], φ[[17]]};
gce[3*s/2 + 9/2, 3*t/4 + 37/4, -1, 1]; mxy5 = {3, 10, φxy, dφdx, dφdy, -ky*dφdy};
gce[3*s/2 + 9/2, 3*t/4 + 37/4, -0.5, 1]; mxy6 = {3.75, 10, φxy, dφdx, dφdy, -ky*dφdy};
gce[3*s/2 + 9/2, 3*t/4 + 37/4, 0, 1]; mxy7 = {4.5, 10, φxy, dφdx, dφdy, -ky*dφdy};
gce[3*s/2 + 9/2, 3*t/4 + 37/4, 0.5, 1]; mxy8 = {5.25, 10, φxy, dφdx, dφdy, -ky*dφdy};
gce[3*s/2 + 9/2, 3*t/4 + 37/4, 1, 1]; mxy9 = {6, 10, φxy, dφdx, dφdy, -ky*dφdy};
```

```
(* Nodal solution summary and write to file*)
mm = {mxy1, mxy2, mxy3, mxy4, mxy5, mxy6, mxy7, mxy8, mxy9}; MatrixForm[mm,
  TableHeadings → {{"2", "2", "2", "2", "4", "4", "4", "4", "4"}, {"x", "y", "ϕ", "∂ϕ/∂x", "∂ϕ/∂y", "vy"}}]
SetDirectory["C:\\Users\\jmatsson"]; mylist = Table[
    {{9, mxy1[[6]]}, {9.75, mxy2[[6]]}, {10.5, mxy3[[6]]}, {11.25, mxy4[[6]]}, {12, mxy5[[6]]},
      {12.75, mxy6[[6]]}, {13.5, mxy7[[6]]}, {14.25, mxy8[[6]]}, {15, mxy9[[6]]}}];
TableOfValues1 = Prepend[mylist, {"((xy/key/label \"theory-outlet\")"}];
TableOfValues1 = Prepend[TableOfValues1, {""}];
TableOfValues1 = Prepend[TableOfValues1, {"(labels \"X-Coordinate\" \"Velocity\")"}];
TableOfValues1 = Prepend[TableOfValues1, {"(title \"Theory\")"}];
TableOfValues1 = Append[TableOfValues1, {")"}]; Grid[TableOfValues1]
Export["theory.dat", TableOfValues1]
```

Figure 11.13b) Mathematica code for seepage flow under a dam

## I. References

1. Ochs et al., "Soil-Water Pit Heat Store with Direct Charging System", Ecostock 2005 Conference Proceedings.
2. Moaveni S., "Finite Element Analysis: Theory and Applications with ANSYS", 3rd Ed., Prentice Hall, 2007.
3. Bhatti, M.A., "Fundamental Finite Element Analysis and Applications", John Wiley & Sons, Inc., 2005.

## J. Exercise

11.1 Use ANSYS Fluent to study the seepage flow of water through the porous medium under the dam as shown in Figure 11.14. Include contour plots for velocity magnitude and static pressure together with an XY Plot of the velocity magnitude at the outlet. Use the same values for viscous and inertial resistance and mesh size as was used in this chapter.

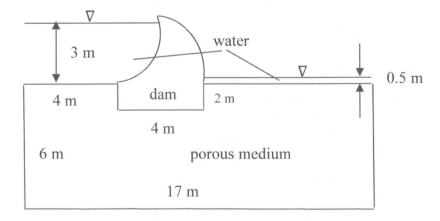

Figure 11.14 Geometry for Exercise 10.1

## CHAPTER 12. WATER FILTER FLOW

### A. Objectives

- Using ANSYS Workbench to Model Flow Through Water Filter
- Inserting Boundary Conditions and Porous Medium Zone for Filter with Viscous and Inertial Resistance
- Using Volume of Fluid Model for Multiphase Flow with Surface Tension
- Running Laminar Transient 2D Axisymmetric ANSYS Fluent Simulations
- Using Volume Fraction Contour Plots for Visualizations and Movie
- Comparing ANSYS Fluent Results with Theory

### B. Problem Description

We will study the flow through a ceramic gravity driven clay pot water filter using ANSYS Fluent. The dimensions and initial water levels are shown below. The thickness of the filter is $d = 20$ mm and the radius $R - 100$ mm while the initial height of water $h_0 = 200$ mm. The height $h(t)$ of the water in the filter will vary over time as the fluid seeps through the filter.

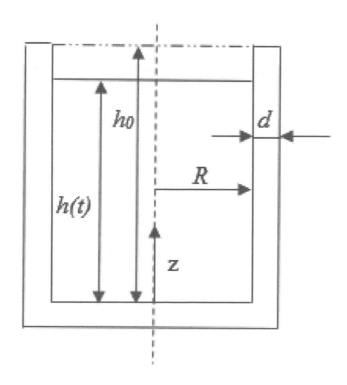

## C. Launching ANSYS Workbench and Selecting Fluent

1. Start by launching ANSYS Workbench. Double click on Fluid Flow (Fluent) under Analysis Systems in the Toolbox.

Figure 12.1 Selecting Fluent

## D. Launching ANSYS DesignModeler

2. Right click Geometry under Project Schematic in ANSYS Workbench and select Properties. In Properties of Schematic A2: Geometry, select Analysis Type 2D under Advanced Geometry Options. Right click on Geometry in the Project Schematic window and select New DesignModeler Geometry.

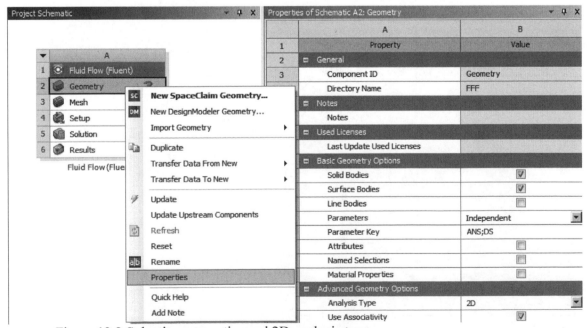

Figure 12.2 Selecting properties and 2D analysis type

3. Select Units>>Millimeter from the menu in DesignModeler. Select XY Plane in the Tree Outline and click on Look at Face/Plane/Sketch 🔲. Select Sketching tab and Draw>>Polyline from Sketching Toolboxes. Start at origin and draw the Sketch with Dimensions as shown in Figure 12.3c).

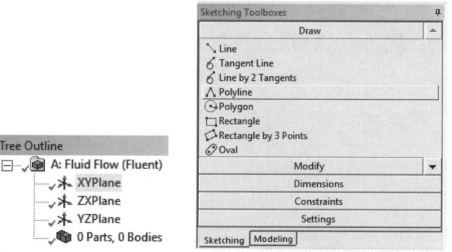

Figure 12.3a) Tree outline          Figure 12.3b) Sketching toolboxes

Figure 12.3c) Sketch of cylindrical water filter with dimensions

4. Select the Modeling tab and select Concepts>>Surfaces from Sketches from the menu. Select Sketch1 under XYPlane in the Tree Outline and Apply the sketch in Details View. Click on Generate.

Select the XYPlane once again in the Tree Outline and click on New Sketch 🔲. Select the new sketch (Sketch2) under XYPlane and click on the Sketching tab. Select Rectangle under Draw in Sketching Toolboxes and draw a rectangle inside the filter from the origin, see Figure 12.4. Select Concepts>>Surfaces from Sketches from the menu and Apply the new sketch in Details View. Select Add Frozen as Operation in Details View. Click on Generate and Close DesignModeler.

Figure 12.4 Finished model for cylindrical water filter

269

## E. Launching ANSYS Meshing

5. Double click on Mesh under Project Schematic in ANSYS Workbench. Select Mesh in the Outline. Set the Element Size to 2.0 mm under Defaults in Details of "Mesh". Select Yes for Capture Curvature under Sizing and set Smoothing to High under Quality. Right click on Mesh in the Outline and select Generate Mesh.

Figure 12.5a) ANSYS Meshing

Figure 12.5b) Finished mesh for cylindrical water filter

6. Select Edge  selection filter and control select the two edges on the right side of the computational domain. Right click on the edges and select Create Named Selection. Name the edges *outlet*.

Figure 12.6a) Named selections for outlet

Control-select the upper horizontal edge and the left outer vertical edge, right click and select Create Named Selection. Name the edges *outlet-filter*.

Figure 12.6b) Named selections for outlet-filter

Select Body  and select the outer L-shaped filter region, right click and select Hide

Body. Select Edge and control-select the upper horizontal edge and the left vertical edge, right click and select Create Named Selection. Name the edges *interface1*. Right click in the graphics window and select Show All Bodies.

Figure 12.6c) Named selections for interface1

Select Body , left click on the inner fluid region, right click and select Hide Body.

Select Edge and control-select the middle horizontal edge and the middle vertical edge, right click and select Create Named Selection. Name the edges *interface2*. Right click in the graphics window and select Show All Bodies.

Figure 12.6d) Named selections for interface2

Control select the two lower horizontal edges and name them *symmetry*.

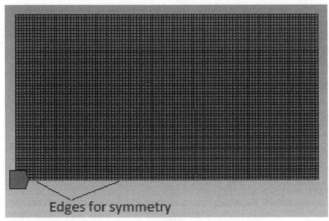

Figure 12.6e) Named selections for symmetry

Figure 12.6f) Named selections for cylindrical water filter

272

Open Geometry in the Outline, select the first Surface Body, right click and select Rename. Name this body *Porous zone*. Rename the next Surface Body and call it *Inlet zone*.

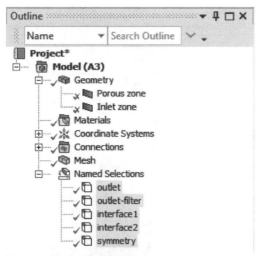

Figure 12.6g) Outline

Select File>>Export...>>Mesh>>FLUENT Input File>>Export from the menu and save the mesh with the name *cylindrical-water-filter.msh.* Select File>>Save Project from the menu and enter the name *Cylindrical Water Filter*. Close the ANSYS Meshing window. Right click on Mesh under Project Schematic in ANSYS Workbench and select Update.

## F. Launching ANSYS Fluent

7.  Double click on Setup under Project Schematic in ANSYS Workbench. Select Double Precision and Parallel Processing Options. Set the number of Processes equal to the number of processor cores. Select Show More Options and take a note of the location for the *Working Directory*. Click on Start to run Fluent Launcher.

Select Transient Time and Axisymmetric 2D Space for the Solver on the Task Page. Check the box for Gravity and enter -9.81 as Gravitational Acceleration in the X direction. Double click on Models and Viscous (SST k-omega) and select Laminar Model. Click on OK to close the Viscous Model window. Double click on Models and Multiphase (Off) under Setup in the Outline View. Select Volume of Fluid model and check the box for Implicit Body Force. Click on Apply and Close the window.

Figure 12.7 Volume of Fluid Multiphase Model

273

8. Double click on Materials under Setup in the Tree. Select Create/Edit for Fluid under Materials on the Task Page. Select Fluent Database and scroll down to *water-liquid (h2o<l>)* and select this as Fluent Fluid Materials. Click on Copy and Close the window. Close the Create/Edit Materials window.

Figure 12.8 Fluent Fluid Materials

9. Double click on Models and Multiphase (On) under Setup in the Outline View. Select the Phases tab at the top of the Multiphase Model window. Select phase-1 – Primary Phase under Phases. Select *water-liquid* as the Primary Phase Material and enter *water* as the name under Phase Setup. Click on Apply. Select phase-2 – Secondary Phase under Phases and select *air* as the Secondary Phase Material and enter *air* as the name under Phase Setup. Click OK to close the Secondary Phase window. Click on Apply and Close the Multiphase Model window.

Figure 12.9a) Primary phase

Figure 12.9b) Secondary phase

Select the Phase Interaction tab at the top of the Multiphase Model window. Check the box for Surface Tension Force Modeling. Select constant for the Surface Tension Coefficients (n/m) and enter 0.07286 as the value. Click on Apply and Close the Phase Interaction window.

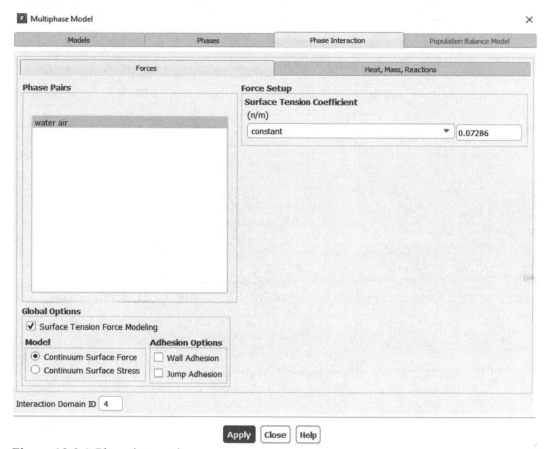

Figure 12.9c) Phase interaction

10. Double click on Cell Zone Conditions under Setup in the Outline View. Select the *porous_zone* under Cell Zone Conditions on the Task Page. Select *fluid* as Type and *mixture* as Phase and click on the Edit button on the Task Page. Check the Porous Zone box. Select the Porous Zone tab and make sure that Porosity is set to 0.5. Click OK to close the Fluid window.

Select water as the Phase for the *porous_zone* and click on Edit. Enter 9.76305e+08 as the Viscous Resistance in both directions. Click OK to close the Fluid window. Click on Operating Conditions on the Task Page under Cell Zone Conditions. Select user-input as Operating Density Method and enter the value 1.225 Operating Density (kg/m3). Enter Y (m) 0.2 as Reference Pressure Location. Click OK to close the Operating Conditions window.

Figure 12.10a) Porous zone mixture phase

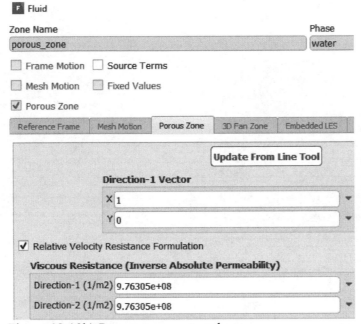

Figure 12.10b) Porous zone water phase

Figure 12.10c) Operating conditions

11. Double click on Boundary Conditions under Setup in the Outline View. Select the *outlet-inlet_zone* Boundary Condition on the Task Page and make sure that Type is set to pressure-outlet. Select *mixture* as Phase and click on Edit. Make sure that Gauge Pressure (pascal) is set to 0 and Backflow Pressure Specification as Total Pressure. Click OK to close the window. Select *air* as Phase and click on the Edit button on the Task Page under Boundary Conditions. Set the Backflow Volume Fraction to 1 and click OK to close the window. Repeat this step for the *outlet-porous_zone* Boundary Condition.

Furthermore, continue with the *outlet-filter* Boundary Condition. Make sure that Type is set to pressure-outlet on the Task Page and select *mixture* as Phase and click on Edit. Gauge Pressure (pascal) is set to 0 and Backflow Pressure Specification as Total Pressure. Click OK to close the window. Select *air* as Phase and click on the Edit button. Select *From Neighboring Cell* as Volume Fraction Specification Method and click OK to close the window.

Figure 12.11a) Outlet-inlet_zone boundary condition for mixture phase

Figure 12.11b) Outlet-inlet_zone boundary condition for air phase

Figure 12.11c) Outlet-porous_zone boundary condition for mixture phase

Figure 12.11d) Outlet-porous_zone boundary condition for air phase

Figure 12.11e) Outlet-filter boundary condition for mixture phase

Figure 12.11f) Outlet-filter boundary condition for air phase

Select *symmetry-inlet_zone* under Zone in Boundary Conditions on the Task Page. Select *mixture* as Phase and choose *axis* from the Type drop-down menu, change the zone name to *axis-inlet_zone* and click OK in the Axis window. Repeat this step for the *symmetry-porous_zone* in order to rename it to *axis-porous_zone*.

Figure 12.11g) Axis inlet zone for mixture phase

Figure 12.11h) Axis porous zonc for mixture phase

12. Double click on Initialization under Solution in the Outline View. Select Hybrid Initialization Method on the Task Page and click on Initialize. Click on Patch on the Task Page under Solution Initialization. Select *air* as the Phase, select Volume Fraction as Variable, select *inlet_zone* and *porous_zone* as Zones to Patch, set the Value to 0 and click on Patch. Close the window.

Figure 12.12a) Initialization of solution

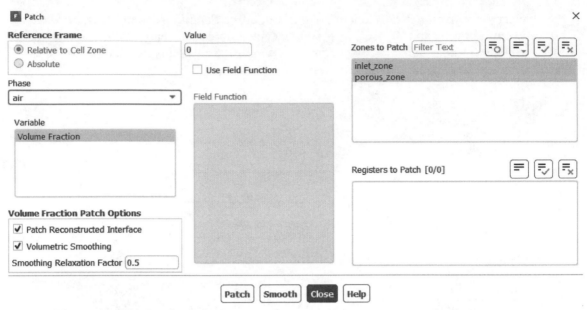

Figure 12.12b) Patch settings

13. Double click on Graphics and Contours under Results in the Outline View. Select Contours of Phases and Volume fraction for *water* as the Phase. Scroll down and deselect all Surfaces and uncheck Auto Range Options. Set Min to 0 and Max to 1. Click on Save/Display and Close the Contours window.

Figure 12.13a) Contours settings

Select the View tab in the menu and click on Views.... Select *axis-porous_zone* and *axis-inlet_zone* as Mirror Planes and click on Apply. Click on the Camera... button in the Views window. Use your left mouse button to rotate the dial counterclockwise 90 degrees until the bowl is upright. Close the Camera Parameters window. Click on the Save button under Actions in the Views window and Close the window.

Figure 12.13b) Water volume fraction before and after rotation and mirroring

Double click on Calculation Activities and Solution Animations under Solution in the Outline View. Enter *water-filter* as the Name, enter Record after every 10 and select time-step. Set the Window ID to 2 and select *contour-1* as Animation Object. Click OK to close the Animation Definition window.

**F** Animation Definition ✕

Name: water-filter

Record after every | 10 | time-step

Storage Type | HSF File

Storage Directory | . | ...

Window Id | 2

Animation View | front | Preview | Use Active

Animation Object

residuals
contour-1

Figure 12.13c) Animation definition

281

14. Double click on Report Definitions under Solution in the Outline View. Select New>>Surface Report>>Volume Flow Rate. Enter *volume-flow-rate* as the name. Select *water* as the Phase and select *outlet-filter* under Surfaces. Check the boxes for Report File, Report Plot and Print to Console under Create. Click OK to close the window.

Select New>>Expression in the Report Definitions window. Select Functions>>Mathematical>>abs and select *volume-flow-rate* as Report Definition, see Figure 12.14b). Enter *absolute-volume-flow-rate* as Name and check the boxes for Report File, Report Plot and Print to Console under Create. Click on OK to close the window. Close the Report Definitions window.

Figure 12.14a) Surface report definition for volume flow rate

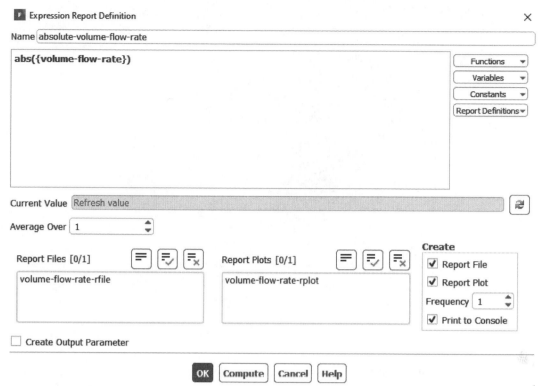

Figure 12.14b) Expression report definition for absolute flow rate

15. Double click on Run Calculation under Solution in the Outline View and set the Time Step Size (s) to 0.005. Set the Number of Time Steps to 50 and Max Iterations/Time Step to 30. Click on the Calculate button on the Task Page. Click OK in the window that appears. Click OK in the Information window when the calculation is complete.

Figure 12.15a) Calculation settings

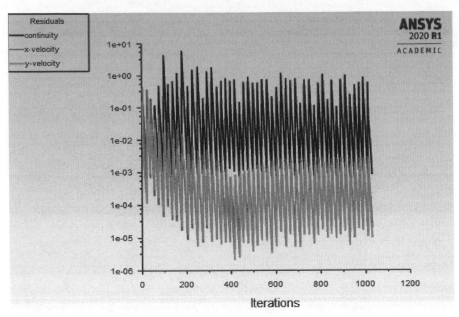

Figure 12.15b) Residuals during the first 0.25 s

## G. Post-Processing and Continued Simulations

16. Select the tab Contours of Volume fraction (water) in the graphics window. Select the View tab in the menu and click on Views…. Select *view-0* in Views, click on Apply in the Views window and Close the window.

   Select the Results tab from the menu and select Surface>>Create>>Iso-Surface…. Select Surface of Constant Phases… and Volume Fraction. Select water as the Phase and set Iso-Values to 0.5. Select *inlet_zone* under From Zones. Enter *free-surface -t=0.25s* as New Surface Name and click on Create. (If you get a message that surface creation failed, do the following: select *air* and click on Create. Next, select *water* and click on Create). Close the window.

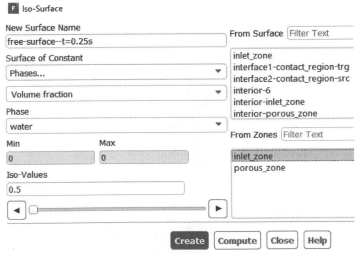

Figure 12.16a) Iso-surface settings

Select File>>Export>>Solution Data… from the menu. Select ASCII as File Type, Node under Location and Space as Delimiter. Select *inlet_zone* and *porous_zone* under Cell Zones and *Iso-surface>> free-surface-time-t=0.25s* under Surfaces. Select *Volume fraction (water)* under Quantities. Click on Write and save the ASCII File in the working directory with the name "free-surface-coordinates-t=0.25s". Close the Export window.

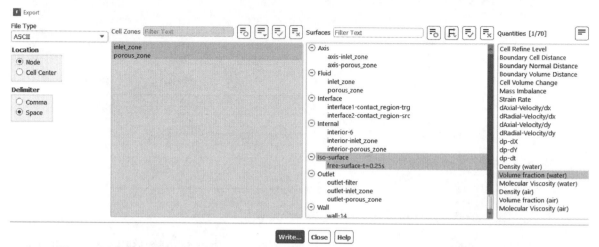

Figure 12.16b) Export settings

Open the saved file in Excel. Click on Next twice in the Text Import Wizard and click on Finish. Plot the free surface and take the average free surface height for the first 50 points. Repeat steps 15 – 16 seven more times for a total of 2 seconds.

Figure 12.16c) Free surface height *h* (m) versus radius *r* (m) at *t* = 0.5 s

| *t* (s) | Average *h* (m), ANSYS Fluent | *h* (m), Theory |
|---|---|---|
| 0 | 0.2 | 0.2 |
| 0.25 | 0.139 | 0.1429 |
| 0.5 | 0.0988 | 0.1080 |
| 0.75 | 0.0730 | 0.08457 |
| 1 | 0.0550 | 0.06788 |
| 1.25 | 0.0417 | 0.05548 |
| 1.5 | 0.0319 | 0.04597 |
| 1.75 | 0.0243 | 0.03849 |
| 2 | 0.0178 | 0.03249 |

Table 12.1 Data for average free surface height over time

Figure 12.16d) Average free surface height $h$ (m) versus time

Figure 12.16e) Water volume fraction at t = 0 – 2 s with an increment of 0.25 s

Double click on Animations and Solution Animation Playback under Results in the Tree. Uncheck the box for Use Stored View, set the Replay Speed to low and select Play Once as Playback Mode. Select MPEG as Write/Record Format. Click on the Write button for your chosen Animation Sequence. This will create the MPEG movie in your working directory. Close the Playback window. The movie can be viewed using, for example, VLC Media Player. In VLC Media Player select Media>>Open File… from the menu and open the movie. Select Playback>>Speed>>Slower from the menu in the VLC Media Player until you have a suitable speed for the movie.

Figure 12.16f) Playback settings

Double click on Data Sources under Results and Plots in the Outline View. Click on Load File… under Data Sources and load the file "absolute-volume-flow-rate-rfile.out". Select *flow-time* as X Axis Variable and *absolute-volume-flow-rate* as Y Axis Variable.

Next, load the file "volume-flow-rate.dat". This and other files are available for download at *sdcpublications.com*. Select *Time(s)* as X Axis Variable and *Volume Flow Rate (m3/s)* as Y Axis Variable. Click on Axes… at the bottom of the Plot Data Sources window. Uncheck Auto Range under Options for X Axis. Set Minimum to 0 and Maximum to 2 under Range. Click on Apply and select Y Axis. Select float as Type under Number Format and set Precision to 3. Click on Apply and Close the Axes – Plot Data Sources window. Change the X Axis Label under Plot to "*t* " and the Y Axis Label to "*dV/dt* (m3/s)". Delete the Title and Legend Label under Plot.

Click on Curves… and select the first available Pattern under Line Style for Curve # 0. Set the Color under Line Style to dark blue. Select no (blank) Symbol under Marker Style and click on Apply. Select Curve # 1, select the second available Pattern under Line Style and select dark blue Color. Select no (blank) Symbol under Marker Style and click on Apply. Close the Curves – Plot Data Sources window. Click on Plot at the bottom of the Plot Data Sources window.

287

Open the saved file "*absolute-volume-flow-rate-rfile*" in Excel. Select Delimited instead of Fixed width in Text Import Wizard – Step 1 of 3. Click on Next. Uncheck Tab as Delimiters and check Space as Delimiters in Text Import Wizard – Step 2 of 3. Click on Next. Click on Finish in Text Import Wizard – Step 3 of 3. Use the trapezoidal rule to find the area under the volume flow rate curve (2$^{nd}$ column in Excel file) for each time interval (3$^{rd}$ column) and sum these areas in order to show the volume produced by the filter as seen in Figure 12.16i). Select File>>Export>>Data… from the menu in Fluent. Save the data file in the *working directory* folder with the name *water-filter-t=2s.dat*.

Figure 12.16g) File XY Plot settings

Figure 12.16h) Comparing ANSYS Fluent and theory-dashed curve for volume flow rate

288

Figure 12.16i) Comparison ANSYS Fluent and theory for volume produced

## H. Theory

17. We can relate the mean fluid velocity $v$ (m/s) through the porous medium to the pressure gradient $dP/dx$ (Pa) using Darcy's law in the same way as we did in the former chapter

$$v = -\frac{\kappa}{\mu}\frac{dP}{dx}$$ (12.1)

where $\kappa$ (m$^2$) is permeability of the porous medium and $\mu$ (kg/m-s) is the dynamic viscosity of the fluid. Furthermore, we define the hydraulic conductivity or coefficient of permeability $k$ (m/s) as

$$k = \kappa\frac{\rho g}{\mu}$$ (12.2)

Where $g$ (m/s$^2$) is acceleration due to gravity and $\rho$ (kg/m$^3$) is the density of the fluid. We will also use the following equation from the ANSYS Fluent user manual

$$\frac{dP}{dx} = -\left(\frac{\mu v}{\alpha} + \frac{C_2\rho v^2}{2}\right)$$ (12.3)

where $1/\alpha$ (1/m$^2$) is viscous resistance or inverse absolute permeability for the porous medium and $C_2$(1/m) is inertial resistance of the porous medium. When we combine these equations we get this expression for the permeability coefficient

$$k = \frac{g}{\frac{vC_2}{2} + \frac{\mu}{\alpha\rho}}$$ (12.4)

The following values were used in the ANSYS Fluent simulations in this chapter.

| Parameter | Value |
|---|---|
| $C_2$ (1/m) | 0 |
| $1/\alpha$ (1/m$^2$) | $9.76305 \cdot 10^8$ |
| $\rho$ (kg/m$^3$) | 998.2 |
| $\mu$ (kg/m-s) | 0.001003 |
| $g$ (m/s$^2$) | 9.81 |
| $k$ (m/s) | 0.01 |
| $R$ (m) | 0.1 |
| $h_0$ (m) | 0.2 |
| $d$ (m) | 0.02 |
| $\gamma$ | 2 |

Table 12.2 Parameters used in ANSYS Fluent simulations

For a cylindrical filter with a constant thickness $d$ and constant radius $R$ we have the schematic diagram as shown in Figure 12.17a).

Figure 12.17a) Geometry for cylindrical ceramic water filter

The height of the free surface $h(t)$ will decrease over time as water is filtered through the filter. The volumetric flow rate through the filter can be described by

$$\dot{V}(t) = \frac{k}{d}\left[\pi R^2 h + R\int_0^{2\pi}\int_0^h (h-z)dzd\theta\right] = \frac{k\pi Rh}{d}(R+h) \tag{12.5}$$

We can alternatively describe the volumetric flow rate as

$$\dot{V}(t) = -\pi R^2 \frac{dh}{dt} \tag{12.6}$$

Combining these two equations we get the following first order ordinary differential equation

$$\frac{dh}{dt} + \frac{kh}{d}\left(1 + \frac{h}{R}\right) = 0 \tag{12.7}$$

with the following solution where we have used the initial condition $h(0) = h_0$

$$h(t) = \frac{h_0 R}{e^{kt/d}(R+h_0) - h_0} \tag{12.8}$$

The volume flow rate using equation (12.6) will be

$$\dot{V}(t) = \frac{(R+h_0)\pi R^3 k h_0 e^{kt/d}}{d(e^{kt/d}(R+h_0)-h_0)^2} \tag{12.9}$$

The total water volume produced can be expressed as

$$V(t) = \pi R^2(h_0 - h(t)) \tag{12.10}$$

and with the use of equation (12.8) we get

$$V(t) = \pi R^2 h_0 (1 - \frac{R}{e^{kt/d}(R+h_0)-h_0}) \tag{12.11}$$

We can alternatively make equation (12.7) non-dimensional using non-dimensional variables $h^* = \frac{h}{h_0}$ and $t^* = \frac{kt}{d}$ where $h_0$ is the initial height of fluid in the cylinder. This will transform equation (12.7) to the following equation after skipping[*]

$$\frac{dh}{dt} + h(1 + \gamma h) = 0 \tag{12.12}$$

where $\gamma = \frac{h_0}{R} = 2$ is the aspect-ratio.

Using initial condition $h(0) = 1$ we get the following solution

$$h(t) = \frac{1}{e^t(1+\gamma)-\gamma} = \frac{1}{3e^t-2} \tag{12.13}$$

Now we can express the volumetric flow rate in non-dimensional form as (after introducing $V^* = \frac{V}{\pi R^2 h_0}$ and skipping[*])

$$\dot{V}(t) = -\frac{dh}{dt} = \frac{e^t(1+\gamma)}{[\gamma-e^t(1+\gamma)]^2} = \frac{3e^t}{(2-3e^t)^2} \tag{12.14}$$

The total water volume produced can be expressed as

$$V(t) = \pi R^2(h_0 - h(t)) \tag{12.15}$$

and in non-dimensional form this expression will be the following after skipping[*]

$$V(t) = 1 - h(t) = 1 - \frac{1}{e^t(1+\gamma)-\gamma} = \frac{3e^t-3}{3e^t-2} \tag{12.16}$$

For a frustum filter with a constant thickness $d$ and varying radius $r$ we have the schematic diagram as shown in Figure 12.17b).

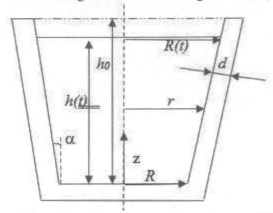

Figure 12.17b) Geometry for frustum water filter

The volumetric flow rate in this case can be described as

$$\dot{V}(t) = \frac{k}{d}\left[\pi R^2 h + \int_0^{2\pi}\int_0^h (h-z)rdzd\theta\right] \tag{12.17}$$

Using $r = R + z\,tan\alpha$, we can express equation (12.13) as

$$\dot{V}(t) = \frac{k\pi h}{d}(R^2 + hR + \frac{h^2 tan\alpha}{3}) \tag{12.18}$$

and equation (12.6) for a frustum shaped filter will be modified to

$$\dot{V}(t) = -\pi R(t)^2 \frac{dh}{dt} \tag{12.19}$$

where $R(t) = R + h(t)\,tan\alpha$. The differential equation for $h(t)$ will then be

$$\frac{dh}{dt} + \frac{kh}{d}\frac{(R^2 + hR + \frac{h^2 tan\alpha}{3})}{(R + h tan\alpha)^2} = 0 \tag{12.20}$$

and in non-dimensional form after skipping* we have

$$\frac{dh}{dt} + \frac{h}{(1+\delta h)^2}\left(1 + \gamma h + \frac{1}{3}\delta\gamma h^2\right) = 0 \tag{12.21}$$

where $\delta = \gamma tan\alpha$. There is no analytical solution available except in the case $\delta = 0$ corresponding to the cylindrical geometry. Equation (11.17) can be solved numerically in the general case $\delta \neq 0$ using the initial condition $h(0) = 1$.

We express the volumetric flow rate in non-dimensional form after skipping*

$$\dot{V}(t) = -(1 + \delta h)^2\frac{dh}{dt} \tag{12.22}$$

The total water volume produced can be expressed as

$$V(t) = \pi \left[ R^2 + R(h_0 + h)\tan\alpha + \left(h_0^2 + h_0 h + h^2\right)\frac{\tan^2\alpha}{3} \right] (h_0 - h) \qquad (12.23)$$

and in non-dimensional form this expression will be the following after skipping*

$$V(t) = (1 - h) + \delta(1 - h^2) + \frac{\delta^2}{3}(1 - h^3) \qquad (12.24)$$

## I. References

1. Kelly, A.C., "Finite Element Modeling of Flow Through Ceramic Pot Filters.", *Master's Thesis in Civil and Environmental Engineering*, MIT, (2013).
2. Schweitzer, R.W., Cunningham, J.A., Mihelcic, J.R., "Hydraulic Modeling of Clay Ceramic Water Filters for Point-of-Use Water Treatment.", *Environ. Sci. Technol.*, **47**, 429-435, (2013).
3. Wald, I., "Modeling Flow Rate to Estimate Hydraulic Conductivity in a Parabolic Ceramic Water Filter.", *Undergraduate Journal of Mathematical Modeling*, **4**, 2, (2012).

## J. Exercise

12.1 Complete ANSYS Fluent simulation of the flow through a frustum-shaped filter using the values listed in Table 12.3. Include graphs of your results showing a comparison between ANSYS Fluent and Theory for free surface height, volume flow rate and volume produced by the filter. Use a time step size of 0.005 s and a total of 200 time-steps with 50 time steps for each run. Include contours of volume fraction for water at t = 0, 0.25, 0.5, 0.75 and 1 second.

| Parameter | Value |
|---|---|
| $C_2$ (1/m) | 0 |
| $1/\alpha$ (1/m$^2$) | $9.76305 \cdot 10^8$ |
| $\rho$ (kg/m$^3$) | 998.2 |
| $\mu$ (kg/m-s) | 0.001003 |
| $g$ (m/s$^2$) | 9.81 |
| $k$ (m/s) | 0.01 |
| $R$ (m) | 0.1 |
| $h_0$ (m) | 0.3 |
| $d$ (m) | 0.01 |
| $\gamma$ | 3 |
| $\alpha$ (degrees) | 10 |

Table 12.3 Parameter values for frustum shaped filter

**K. Notes**

# CHAPTER 13.  MODEL ROCKET FLOW

## A. Objectives

- Model Geometry and Mesh
- Run Simulations for Turbulent Steady 3D Flow Past a Model Rocket in ANSYS Fluent
- Determine Drag Coefficient for Model Rocket
- Visualize Flow Around Model Rocket

## B. Problem Description

We will study the flow past the model rocket Estes Firestreak SST with a free stream velocity of 30 m/s.

## C. Launching ANSYS Workbench and Importing the Geometry

1. Start by launching ANSYS Workbench. Select File>>Import from the menu. Select Geometry File as format and open the file *Estes Model Rocket.IGS*. This and other files can be downloaded from *sdcpublications.com*.

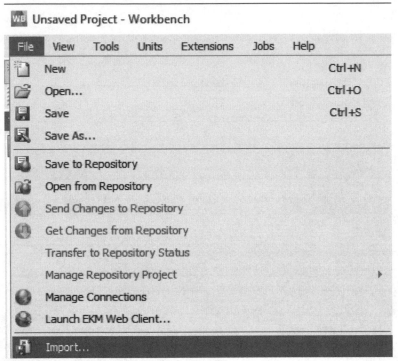

Figure 13.1 Import of geometry file

## D. Launching ANSYS DesignModeler

2. Right click on the imported Geometry in ANSYS Workbench and select Edit Geometry in DesignModeler. Click on Generate in DesignModeler.

   Select Tools>>Enclosure from the menu. Set the Number of Planes to 2 in Details View. Select ZXPlane from the Tree Outline as Symmetry Plane 1 and Apply the plane in Details View. Select YZPlane from the Tree Outline as Symmetry Plane 2 and Apply it in Details View. Click on Generate.

Figure 13.2a) Editing geometry

Figure 13.2b) Computational domain around the model rocket

3. Select Create>>Boolean from the menu. Select Subtract as Operation. Click on the plus sign next to 2 Parts, 2 Bodies in the Tree Outline. Select the second Solid and Apply it as Target Body in Details of Boolean1. Select the first Solid and Apply it as Tool Body in Details of Boolean1. Click on Generate. Right click on the Solid in the Tree Outline and Rename it to *Air*. Select File>>Save Project and name it "Model Rocket Flow Study" and close DesignModeler.

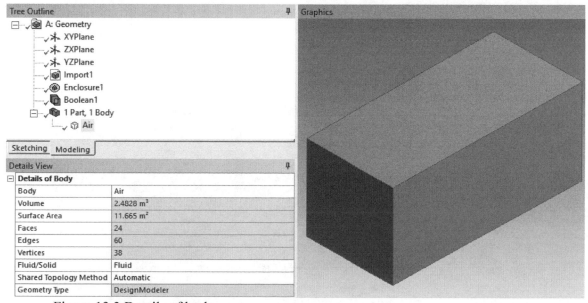

Figure 13.3 Details of body

**E. Launching ANSYS Meshing**

4.  Double click on Fluid Flow (Fluent) under Analysis Systems in the Toolbox in ANSYS Workbench. Drag the Geometry to the Geometry under Fluid Flow (Fluent).

    Double click on Mesh under Fluid Flow (Fluent). In the Meshing window, right click on Mesh in the Outline and select Update. Click on the plus sign next to Sizing under Details of Mesh. Change Capture Proximity and Capture Curvature both to Yes. Click on the plus sign next to Quality under Details of Mesh. Set Smoothing to High. Update the mesh once again. Rotate the Mesh to see the details of the mesh around the model rocket.

Figure 13.4a) Shared geometry with Fluent

Figure 13.4b) Refined mesh around model rocket

5. Right click on Mesh in the Outline, select Insert>> Sizing. Select Face 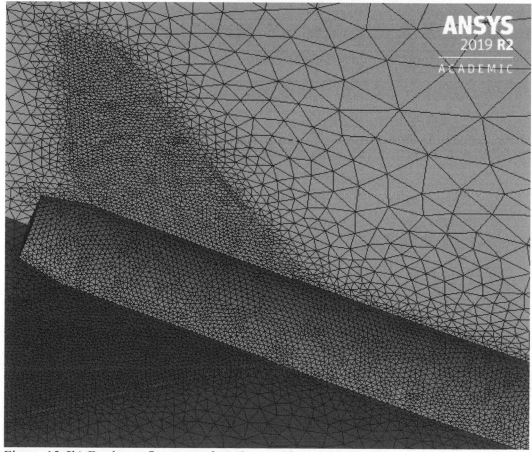 and control select the 5 faces of the model rocket as shown in figure 13.5a). Apply the faces as the Geometry under Scope in Details of "Face Sizing". Set the Element Size to 0.84347 mm. Update the mesh once again.

Figure 13.5a) Face sizing for the five faces of the model rocket

Figure 13.5b) Further refinement of mesh around model rocket

299

6. Click on the plus sign next to Inflation in Details of "Mesh". Set Use Automatic Inflation to Program Controlled. Update the mesh once again. Select Box Select from the menu of the graphics window, see Figure 13.6a). Select Face  and make a Box Select around the model rocket. This will select all surfaces, see Figure 13.6b).

Figure 13.6a) Box Select        Figure 13.6b) Selection of surfaces

Right click in the graphics window and select Create Named Selection. Enter the name "model rocket' and click OK. Select *model rocket* under Named Selections and select *Include* from the drop-down menu for Program Controlled Inflation under Definition in Details of "model rocket". Update the mesh once again.

| Details of "model rocket" | |
|---|---|
| **Scope** | |
| Scoping Method | Geometry Selection |
| Geometry | 18 Faces |
| **Definition** | |
| Send to Solver | Yes |
| Protected | Program Controlled |
| Visible | Yes |
| Program Controlled Inflation | Include |
| **Statistics** | |
| Type | Manual |
| ☐ Total Selection | 18 Faces |
| ☐ Surface Area | 5864.7 mm² |
| Suppressed | 0 |
| Used by Mesh Worksheet | No |

Figure 13.6c) Details for model rocket named selection

Select Isometric View, select Single Select, see Figure 13.6a), and select the velocity-inlet face for the computational domain, see Figure 13.6d). Right click in the graphics window and select Create Named Selection. Enter the name "velocity-inlet' and click OK.

Select Face  and select the opposite side of the computational domain. Right click in the graphics window and select Create Named Selection. Enter the name "pressure-outlet and click OK.

Select one of the plane side surfaces (the one on the side) of the computational domain containing the model rocket and name it "symmetry1". Name the other face containing the model rocket (the bottom face) to "symmetry2". Name the remaining two surfaces "symmetry-top" and "symmetry-side". Update the mesh.

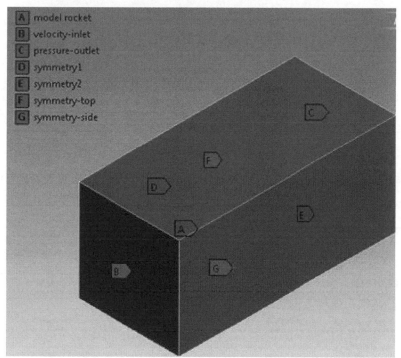

Figure 13.6d) Named selections for the model rocket

7. Go back to DesignModeler by double clicking on the first Geometry A under Project Schematic in ANSYS Workbench. Select Bottom view and select YZ Plane under Tree Outline in DesignModeler. Right click on YZ Plane and select Look At. Create a new sketch . Zoom in on the model rocket.

Click on the Sketching tab in the Tree Outline and select Rectangle. Draw a rectangle around the model rocket. Make sure you start drawing the rectangle on the vertical axis and that you get a *C* when you move the cursor on the vertical axis. This means that one of the sides will be positioned on the same vertical axis. Select Dimensions and click on the horizontal and vertical sides of the new rectangle. Enter 0.6375 m as the vertical height of the rectangle and 0.1275 m as the width. Select the Vertical dimensioning tool, click on the horizontal coordinate axis and the lower side of the rectangle and enter 0.275 m as this vertical dimension.

Select the Modeling tab in the Tree Outline and select  Extrude . Select Sketch1 under YZ plane in the Tree Outline and Apply it as Geometry in Details of Extrude. Enter 0.1275 m as the FD1, Depth (>0) of the Extrusion. Click on Generate. Go to 2 Parts, 2 Bodies in the Tree Outline, right click on Solid and select Rename. Rename it to *ModelRocketBox*.

Go back to ANSYS Workbench, double click on Mesh and answer *Yes* to the question whether you would like to read upstream data.

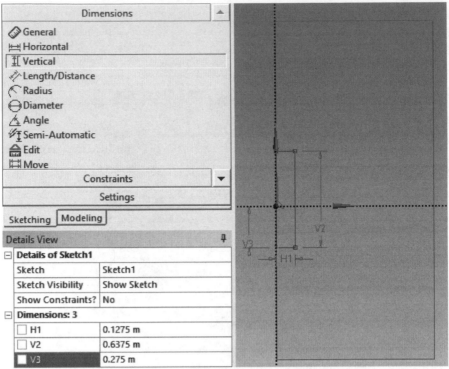

Figure 13.7a) Dimensions and location for rectangle around the model rocket

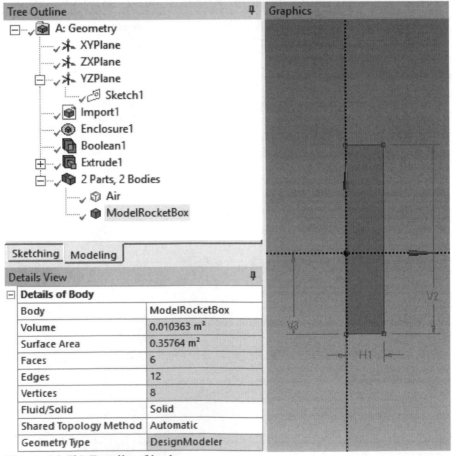

Figure 13.7b) Details of body

8.   Right click Mesh under Project in Outline and select Update. Right click Mesh under Project in Outline, select Insert>>Sizing. Select Body  and select the larger computational domain in the graphics window. Apply the computational domain in Geometry under Scope for Details of Body Sizing. Select *Body of Influence* as Type under Definition.

Select Bottom view in the graphics window, zoom in on the model rocket, select the *ModelRocketBox* in the graphics window and Apply it as the Body of Influence. You will need to select the second blue small rectangle in the lower left corner of the graphics window in Figure 13.8 before you can select the *ModelRocketBox* that turns from green to red when you apply it as the *Body of Influence*. Update the Mesh.

Right click on *ModelRocketBox* under Geometry in Project Outline and select Hide Body. Select Mesh in the Outline and click on the plus sign next to Quality in Details of "Mesh". Select Skewness as Mesh Metric. The max skewness should not be above 0.9.

Delete any contact regions that you may have in the Outline and update the mesh. Select File>>Save Project. Select File>>Export…>>Mesh>>FLUENT Input File>>Export and save the mesh with the name "model-rocket-flow-mesh.msh". Close the Meshing window.

Figure 13.8 Selection of ModelRocketBox as Body of Influence

## F. Launching ANSYS Fluent

9. Double click on Setup in ANSYS Workbench. Check Double Precision under Options and check Parallel under Processing Options. Select the number of Processes equal to the number of computer cores. Click on Show More Options and take a note of the location of the *Working Directory*. Click Start to launch ANSYS Fluent.

   Double click on Models and Viscous (SST k-omega) under Setup in the Outline View. Set the k-omega Model to Standard and click Ok to close the Viscous Model window.

**F** Viscous Model

**Model**

- ○ Inviscid
- ○ Laminar
- ○ Spalart-Allmaras (1 eqn)
- ○ k-epsilon (2 eqn)
- ● k-omega (2 eqn)
- ○ Transition k-kl-omega (3 eqn)
- ○ Transition SST (4 eqn)
- ○ Reynolds Stress (7 eqn)
- ○ Scale-Adaptive Simulation (SAS)
- ○ Detached Eddy Simulation (DES)
- ○ Large Eddy Simulation (LES)

**Model Constants**

Alpha*_inf
`1`

Alpha_inf
`0.52`

Beta*_inf
`0.09`

Beta_i
`0.072`

TKE Prandtl Number
`2`

SDR Prandtl Number

**k-omega Model**

- ● Standard
- ○ GEKO
- ○ BSL
- ○ SST

**User-Defined Functions**

Turbulent Viscosity
`none`

Prandtl Numbers

TKE Prandtl Number
`none`

SDR Prandtl Number
`none`

**k-omega Options**

- ☐ Low-Re Corrections
- ☑ Shear Flow Corrections

**Options**

- ☐ Curvature Correction
- ☐ Production Kato-Launder
- ☑ Production Limiter

[ OK ] [ Cancel ] [ Help ]

Figure 13.9 Details for the viscous model

10. Double click on Boundary Conditions under Setup in the Tree and select velocity-inlet under Zone for Boundary Conditions on the Task Page. Click on the Edit button. Select Components as Velocity Specification Method. Enter -30 as Z-Velocity (m/s). Set the Turbulent Intensity to 1%. Click OK to close the Velocity Inlet window.

Figure 13.10 Velocity inlet boundary condition

11. Double click Projected Areas under Results and Reports in the Outline View. Select *model_rocket* as the Surface, enter 0.0001 as Min Feature Size (m), select Z as Projection Direction and click on Compute. The computed frontal Area (m2) is 0.00010233. Close the window.

Figure 13.11a) Projected surface areas

Double click on Reference Values under Setup in the Outline View and change the Area (m2) to 0.00010233 and the Velocity (m/s) to 30. Select Compute from velocity-inlet and set Reference Zone to air.

Double click on Methods under Solution in the Outline View and set the Pressure-Velocity Coupling scheme to Coupled. Set the Spatial Discretization Gradient to Least Squares Cell Based, and Pressure to Standard. Set the remaining three (Momentum, Turbulent Kinetic Energy and Specific Dissipation Rate) to First Order Upwind.

Figure 13.11b) Reference values

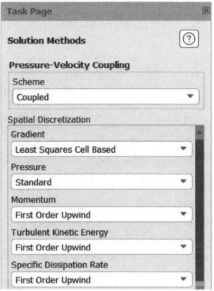

Figure 13.11c) Solution Methods

12. Double click on Controls under Solution in the Outline View and set the Pressure and Momentum Pseudo Transient Explicit Relaxation Factors to 0.25 and set the Turbulent Viscosity Explicit Relaxation Factor to 0.8. Click on Limits… and set the Maximum Turb. Viscosity Ratio to 10000000. Click on the OK button to close the Solution Limits window.

Figure 13.12a) Solution controls          Figure 13.12b) Solution limits

13. Double click on Monitors and Residual under Solution. Check the box for Show Advanced Options. Set the Convergence Criterion to none. Click on OK to close Residual Monitors.

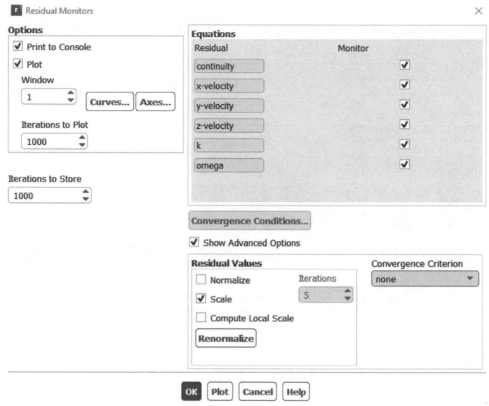

Figure 13.13 Settings for Residual Monitors

14. Double-click on Report Definitions under Solution in the Outline View. Select New>>Force Report>>Drag… from the drop-down menu. Select *model_rocket* as Wall Zone. Check the boxes for Report File, Report Plot and Print to Console under Create. Set the Force Vector to X = 0, Y = 0, and Z = -1. Click on the OK button to close the Drag Report Definition window. Close the Report Definitions window.

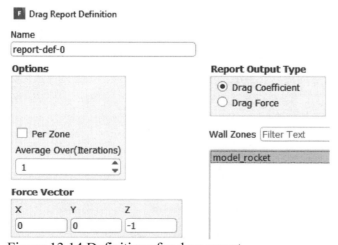

Figure 13.14 Definitions for drag report

307

15. Double click on Initialization under Solution in the Outline View and select *Hybrid Initializa*tion. Click on the Initialize button. Double click on Calculation Activities under Solution in the Outline View and click on Edit... for Autosave Every (Iterations). Set Save Data File Every (Iterations) to 100. Click OK to close the Autosave window.

Figure 13.15a) Solution initialization          Figure 13.15b) Autosave window

Double click on Run Calculation under Solution in the Outline View. Set the Number of Iterations to 100. Click on Calculate.

Figure 13.15c) Scaled residuals

Figure 13.15d) Drag coefficient

## G. Post-Processing

16. Double click on Methods under Solution in the Outline View and replace First Order Upwind with Second Order Upwind for Momentum, Turbulent Kinetic Energy and Specific Dissipation Rate.

    Double click on Controls under Solution and set the Turbulent Viscosity value to 0.95. Double click on Run Calculation under Solution and set Number of Iterations to 300. Click on Calculate and Click OK in the window that appears.

    Double-click on Reports under Results in the Outline View and double-click on Forces under Reports. Set Direction Vector for X to 0, Y to 0, and Z to -1. Check the *model_rocket* Wall Zone and click on the Print button. The total drag coefficient is 0.437. Close the Force Reports window.

Figure 13.16a) Scaled residuals

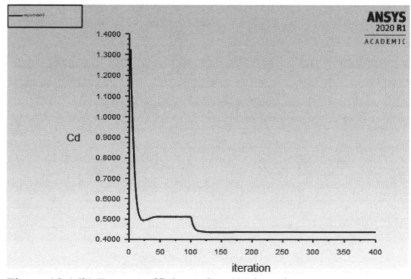

Figure 13.16b) Drag coefficient after 400 iterations

17. Double click on Graphics and Contours under Results. Select the settings as shown in Figure 13.17a) and Apply the Colormap settings as shown in Figure 13.17b). Click on Save/Display. Select the Y-Z plane view in the graphics window. Zoom in on the rocket. Close the Contours window.

Figure 13.17a) Contours settings          Figure 13.17b) Colormap settings

Figure 13.17c) Velocity magnitude for the flow around the model rocket

Double click on Pathlines under Results and Graphics in the Outline View. Select the settings and Apply the same Colormap Options and settings as shown in Figures 13.17b) and 13.17d). Click on Save/Display. Close the Pathlines window.

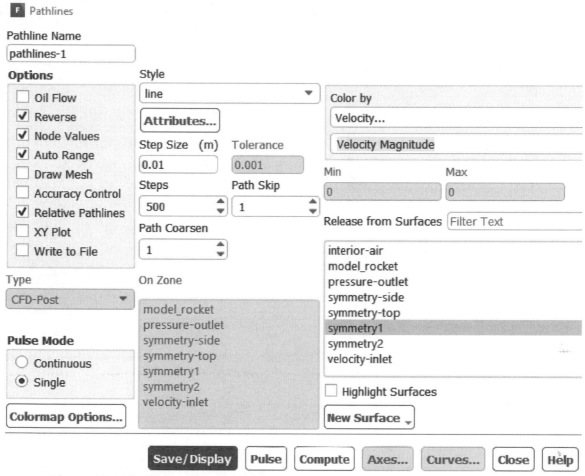

Figure 13.17d) Settings for pathlines

Figure 13.17e) Pathlines around model rocket fin

Double click on Contours under Results and Graphics in the Outline View. Select the settings as shown in Figure 13.17f) for static pressure. Apply the same Colormap settings as shown in Figures 13.17b). Click on Save/Display. Close the Contours window.

Figure 13.17f) Settings for static pressure

Figure 13.17g) Static pressure for the flow past the model rocket

## H. Theory

18. The total drag coefficient for a model rocket[1,2] can be expressed using equation (13.1).

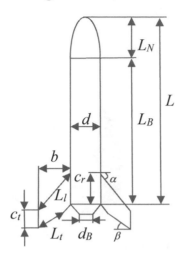

Figure 13.18 Geometry for model rocket

$$C_{D,T} = C_{D,NT} + C_{D,B} + C_{D,F} + C_{D,I} + C_{D,L} \tag{13.1}$$

, where

$$C_{D,NT} = 1.02 \frac{C_{f,turb}A_{w,NT}}{A_c}\left(1 + \frac{3}{2}\left(\frac{L}{d}\right)^{-3/2}\right) \tag{13.2}$$

$$C_{D,B} = \frac{0.029}{\sqrt{C_{D,NT}}}\left(\frac{d_b}{d}\right)^3 \tag{13.3}$$

$$C_{D,F} = \frac{2C_{f,lam}A_{w,F}}{A_c}\left(1 + 2\frac{t}{c_r}\right) \tag{13.4}$$

$$C_{D,I} = \frac{C_{f,lam}ndc_r}{A_c}\left(1 + 2\frac{t}{c_r}\right) \tag{13.5}$$

The different drag coefficients and parameters are explained in Table 13.1. We define the Reynolds number for the nose cone and body tube as

$$Re_{NT} = \frac{UL\rho}{\mu} = \frac{30*0.2365*1.225}{0.000017894} = 485,714 \tag{13.6}$$

, and the Reynolds number for the fin as

$$Re_F = \frac{Uc_{ave}\rho}{\mu} = \frac{30*0.0271525*1.225}{0.000017894} = 55,765 \tag{13.7}$$

, where $c_{ave} = S/b$. The surface area for the fin can be determined from the geometry in Figure 13.19.

$$S = (c_t + L_l \sin\alpha)L_l \cos\alpha - \frac{1}{2}\{L_l^2 \sin\alpha \cos\alpha + L_t^2 \sin\beta \cos\beta + (L_l \cos\alpha - L_t \cos\beta)[(c_t - c_r + L_l \sin\alpha - L_t \sin\beta) + 2L_t \sin\beta]\} \tag{13.8}$$

The skin friction coefficient can be approximated assuming fully turbulent flow on nose cone and body tube

$$C_{f,turb} = \frac{0.0315}{Re_{NT}^{1/7}} = \frac{0.0315}{485,714^{1/7}} = 0.00485255 \tag{13.9}$$

, and for a laminar boundary layer on the fin as

$$C_{f,lam} = \frac{1.328}{Re_F^{1/2}} = \frac{1.328}{55,765^{1/2}} = 0.00562365 \tag{13.10}$$

For an ogive nose cone we have the following relation

$$\frac{A_{w,NT}}{A_c} = \frac{8L_N + 12L_B}{3d} = 39.2012 \tag{13.11}$$

The different drag coefficient and the total value becomes

$$C_{D,NT} = 1.02 * 0.00485255 * 39.2012 \left(1 + \frac{3}{2}(10.8986)^{-\frac{3}{2}}\right) = 0.2021 \tag{13.12}$$

$$C_{D,B} = \frac{0.029}{\sqrt{0.202}} \left(\frac{0.0164}{0.0217}\right)^3 = 0.0278 \tag{13.13}$$

$$C_{D,F} = \frac{2*0.00562*0.00419}{0.00037} \left(1 + 2\frac{0.0007}{0.0038}\right) = 0.1321 \tag{13.14}$$

$$C_{D,I} = \frac{0.00562*0.038*4*0.0217}{0.00037} \left(1 + 2\frac{0.0007}{0.0038}\right) = 0.0520 \tag{13.15}$$

$$C_{D,T} = 0.2021 + 0.0278 + 0.1321 + 0.0520 = 0.414 \tag{13.16}$$

The value for the total drag coefficient 0.437 according to the theory can be compared with the value 0.4 from ANSYS Fluent simulations, a difference of 5.6 %.

| |
|---|
| $A_c$ $(m^2)$: cross sectional area for body tube 0.000369836 m$^2$ |
| $A_{w,F}$ $(m^2)$: total wetted surface area for all fins 0.00418879 m$^2$ |
| $A_{w,NT}$ $(m^2)$: wetted surface area for nose and body tube 0.014498 m$^2$ |
| $\alpha$ : fin leading edge sweep angle 50° |
| $\beta$ : fin trailing edge angle 15° |
| $b$ $(m)$: span for the fin 0.0385673 m |
| $c_{ave}$ $(m)$: average fin chord length 0.0271525 m |
| $c_r$ $(m)$: root fin chord length 0.038 m |
| $c_t$ $(m)$: tip fin chord length 0.010 m |
| $C_{D,NT}$: nose and body tube drag coefficient 0.2021 |
| $C_{D,B}$: base drag coefficient 0.0278 |
| $C_{D,F}$: fin drag coefficient 0.1321 |
| $C_{D,I}$: interference drag coefficient 0.0520 |
| $C_{D,T}$: total drag coefficient 0.414 |
| $C_{f,lam}$: skin friction coefficient for laminar boundary layer 0.00562365 |
| $C_{f,turb}$: skin friction coefficient for turbulent boundary layer 0.00485255 |
| $d$ $(m)$: body tube diameter 0.0217 m |
| $d_b$ $(m)$: base diameter 0.0164 m |

| |
|---|
| $L\ (m)$: length of nose and body 0.2365 m |
| $L_B\ (m)$: length of body tube 0.165 m |
| $L_l\ (m)$: length of leading edge of fin 0.060 m |
| $L_N\ (m)$: length of nose 0.0715 m |
| $L_t\ (m)$: length of trailing edge of fin 0.033 m |
| $n$: number of fins 4 |
| $Re_F$: Reynolds number for the fin 55,765 |
| $Re_{NT}$: Reynolds number for nose cone and body tube 485,714 |
| $S\ (m^2)$: area for fin 0.0010472 m$^2$ |
| $t\ (m)$: thickness of fin 0.0007 m |
| $U(m/s)$: free stream velocity 30 m/s |
| $\rho(kg/m^3)$: density of air 1.225 kg/m$^3$ |
| $\mu(kg/ms)$: dynamic viscosity of air 0.000017894kg/m$^3$ |

Table 13.1 Drag coefficients and parameters

## I. References

1. DeMar, J.S.,"Model Rocket Drag Analysis Using a Computerized Wind Tunnel", NARAM-37, 1995.
2. Gregorek, G.M., "Aerodynamic Drag of Model Rockets.", Estes Industries, Penrose, CO, 1970.
3. Cannon, B.,"Model Rocket Simulation with Drag Analysis", BYU, 2004.
4. Milligan, T.V, "Determining the Drag Coefficient of a Model Rocket Using Accelerometer Based Payloads", NARAM-54, 2012.

## J. Exercise

13.1 Rerun ANSYS Fluent simulations in this chapter at 10, 20, 40 and 50 m/s and compare the drag coefficient with values using the theory section. Include a plot of total drag coefficient versus Reynolds number Re$_{NT}$ corresponding to free stream velocities 10, 20, 30, 40 and 50 m/s and fill out Table 12.2 below.

| $U$ (m/s) | $Re_{NT}$ | $Re_F$ | $C_{D,NT}$ | $C_{D,B}$ | $C_{D,F}$ | $C_{D,I}$ | $C_{D,T}$ | $C_{D,Fluent}$ | % Diff. |
|---|---|---|---|---|---|---|---|---|---|
| 10 | | | | | | | | | |
| 20 | | | | | | | | | |
| 30 | 485714 | 55765 | 0.2021 | 0.0278 | 0.1321 | 0.0520 | 0.414 | 0.437 | 5.6 |
| 40 | | | | | | | | | |
| 50 | | | | | | | | | |

Table 13.2 Drag coefficients at different Reynolds numbers

**K. Notes**

# CHAPTER 14. AHMED BODY

## A. Objectives

- Model the Flow Past an Ahmed Body
- Run Simulations for Turbulent Steady 3D Flow Past the Ahmed Body
- Determine the Drag Coefficient for the Ahmed Body
- Visualize the Flow Around Ahmed Body using Pathlines, Pressure and Velocity

## B. Problem Description

Studying the flow around the Ahmed body is a standard flow test case for wind tunnel experiments and CFD codes[1-6]. The geometry in *mm* that is being used for the Ahmed body in this chapter is shown below.

**C. 3D Ahmed Body Design**

1.  Start by launching ANSYS Workbench. Double click on Fluid Flow (Fluent) under Analysis Systems in the Toolbox.

    Right-click on Geometry in the Project Schematic window and select New DesignModeler Geometry. Select Units>>Millimeter from the menu as the desired length unit, see step 2.

    Select Look At Face ![icon]. Select XY Plane in the Tree Outline and New Sketch ![icon]. Select the Sketching tab, click on Draw and select Rectangle. Draw a rectangle from the origin in the first quadrant. Select Dimensions and set the height of the rectangle to 288 mm and the length to 1044 mm. Right click in the graphics window and select Zoom to Fit.

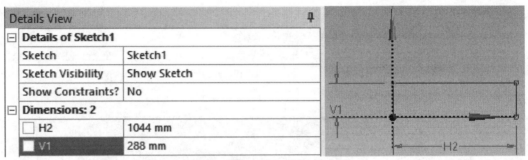

Figure 14.1 First step in the creation of the 3D Ahmed body

2.  Select Modify and Fillet under Sketching Toolboxes. Set the Radius of the Fillet to 100 mm. Click on the two left hand side corners of the rectangle.

    Click on Chamfer under Modify. Set the Length of the Chamfer to 201.2 mm. Click on the upper right corner of the rectangle. The rear slant angle is 25 degrees. Select Dimensions and set the Angle to 25 degrees. You may need to right-click and select alternate angle when you define the angle. Select General under Dimensions and select the chamfer to set the length to 201.2 mm, see Figure 14.2a).

Figure 14.2a) 2D shape for Ahmed body

Click on ![Extrude icon] and select Sketch 1 in the Tree Outline under XYPlane. Apply the sketch in Details View next to Geometry. Set the Direction for the Extrude to Both -

Symmetric in Details View and set the depth of the extrusion to 194.5 mm. Click on Generate.

Select Blend>>Fixed Radius ┊ Blend ▾  ◈ Chamfer / ◈ Fixed Radius ┊ from under menu. Set the Radius to 100 mm. Control select the two vertical edges at the front of the Ahmed body and Apply the edges next to Geometry in Details View. Click on Generate.

Figure 14.2b) Extruded Ahmed body

Figure 14.2c) Extruded and blended Ahmed body

3.  Select ZXPlane in the Tree Outline. Right click in the graphics window and select View>>Bottom View. Select the Sketching tab in Tree Outline and select Circle. Draw a circle and use General under Dimensions to define a 30 mm diameter circle that you position 202 mm from the front of the Ahmed body and 163.5 mm from the center plane.

Create three more circles with the same diameter and position them according to Figure 14.3a).

Click on ▎ 🔲 Extrude ▎ and select Sketch 2 in the Tree Outline under ZXPlane. Apply the sketch in Details View next to Geometry. Set the Direction under Details View to Reversed and set the depth of the extrusion to 50 mm. Click on Generate.

Select Create>> New Plane from the menu. Select in Details View From Plane as Type, ZXPlane as the Base Plane and Offset Z as Transform 1 (RMB). Set the Offset Z value to – 50 mm. Click on Generate.

Select Tools>>Enclosure from the menu. Select Box as the Shape in Details View and set the Number of Planes to 2. Select XYPlane as Symmetry Plane 1, Plane4 as Symmetry Plane 2 and Apply them in Details View. Set the Model Type to Full Model and the Cushion to Non-Uniform. Set the different Cushion values FD1 – FD4 as listed in Figure 14.3c). Click on Generate.

Figure 14.3a) Locations for the four cylindrical supports

Figure 14.3b) Details view for extrusion and finished Ahmed model

| Details of Enclosure1 | |
|---|---|
| Enclosure | Enclosure1 |
| Shape | Box |
| Number of Planes | 2 |
| Symmetry Plane 1 | XYPlane |
| Symmetry Plane 2 | Plane4 |
| Model Type | Full Model |
| Cushion | Non-Uniform |
| ☐ FD1, Cushion +X value (>0) | 5000 mm |
| ☐ FD2, Cushion +Y value (>0) | 2000 mm |
| ☐ FD3, Cushion +Z value (>0) | 1000 mm |
| ☐ FD4, Cushion -X value (>0) | 2000 mm |
| ☐ FD5, Cushion -Y value (>0) | 30 mm |
| ☐ FD6, Cushion -Z value (>0) | 30 mm |
| Target Bodies | All Bodies |
| Export Enclosure | Yes |

Figure 14.3c) Details for enclosure

4. Select Create>>Boolean from the menu. Select Subtract as Operation. Click on the plus sign next to 2 Parts, 2 Bodies in the Tree Outline. Select the second Solid and Apply it as Target Body in Details of Boolean1. Select the first Solid and Apply it as Tool Body in Details of Boolean1. Click on Generate. Right click on the Solid in the Tree Outline and Rename it to Air. Select File>>Save Project and name it "3D Ahmed Body Study" and close DesignModeler.

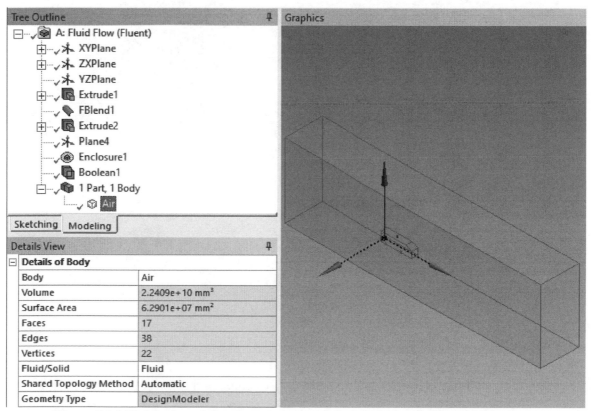

| Details of Body | |
|---|---|
| Body | Air |
| Volume | 2.2409e+10 mm³ |
| Surface Area | 6.2901e+07 mm² |
| Faces | 17 |
| Edges | 38 |
| Vertices | 22 |
| Fluid/Solid | Fluid |
| Shared Topology Method | Automatic |
| Geometry Type | DesignModeler |

Figure 14.4 Finished model and computational domain around Ahmed body

## D. 3D Ahmed Body Mesh

5.  Double click on Mesh under Project Schematic in ANSYS Workbench. In the Meshing window, right click on Mesh in the Outline and select Update. Select the Home tab in the menu. Select Layout>>Reset Layout under the Home tab.

    Click on the plus sign next to Sizing under Details of "Mesh". Change Capture Proximity and Capture Curvature both to Yes. Click on the plus sign next to Quality under Details of "Mesh". Set Smoothing to High. Update the mesh once again. Right click in the graphics window and select View>>Back.

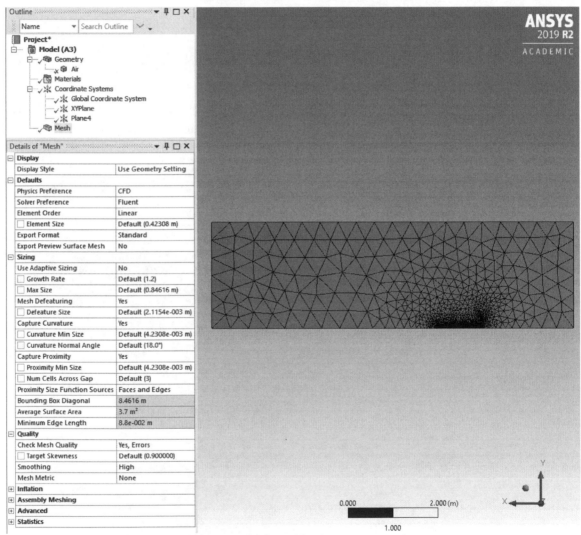

Figure 14.5 Refined mesh around Ahmed body

6.  Right click on Mesh in the Outline, select Insert>> Sizing. Right click in the graphics window and select Cursor Mode>>Face. Select all 11 faces of the Ahmed body as shown in figure 14.6a). You will need to rotate and zoom in on the model in order to select all faces. Apply the faces as the Geometry under Scope in Details of "Face Sizing". Set the Element Size to 7.5 mm. Update the mesh once again.

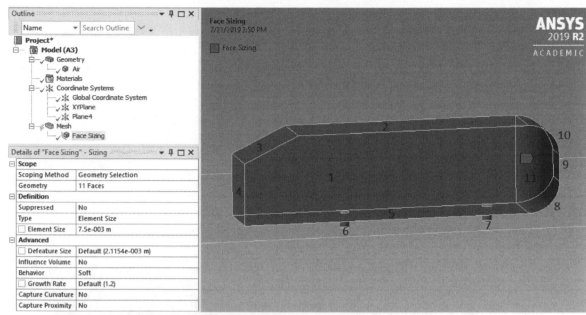

Figure 14.6a) Face sizing for the eleven faces of the Ahmed body

Figure 14.6b) Refined mesh after face sizing

7. Click on the plus sign next to Inflation in Details of Mesh. Set Use Automatic Inflation to Program Controlled. Right click in the graphics window and select Cursor Mode>>Vertex. Control select the 14 vertices as shown in Figure 14.7a).

Figure 14.7a) Program controlled inflation and selected vertices for Ahmed body

Right click in the graphics window and select Create Named Selection. Enter the name "ahmed body" and click OK. Select *ahmed body* under Named Selections and select Include from the drop-down menu for Program Controlled Inflation under Definition in Details of "ahmed body", see Figure 14.7b).

Figure 14.7b) Program controlled inflation set to include for Ahmed body

8. Right click in the graphics window and select View>>Left. Right click in the graphics window and select Cursor Mode>>Face. Select the face for the computational domain that is available from the Left View. Right click in the graphics window and select Create Named Selection. Enter the name "velocity-inlet" and click OK.

Right click in the graphics window and select View>>Right. Select the face for the computational domain that is available from the Right View. Right click in the graphics window and select Create Named Selection. Enter the name "pressure-outlet" and click OK.

Right click in the graphics window and select View>>Back. Select the face for the computational domain that is available from the Back View. Right click in the graphics window and select Create Named Selection. Enter the name "symmetry1" and click OK.

Right click in the graphics window and select View>>Bottom. Select the face for the computational domain that is available from the Bottom View. Right click in the graphics window and select Create Named Selection. Enter the name "street" and click OK.

Right click in the graphics window and select View>>Top. Select the face for the computational domain that is available from the Top View. Right click in the graphics window and select Create Named Selection. Enter the name "symmetry-top" and click OK.

Right click in the graphics window and select View>>Front. Select the face for the computational domain that is available from the Front View. Right click in the graphics window and select Create Named Selection. Enter the name "symmetry-side" and click OK. Update the mesh.

Figure 14.8 Named selections for the Ahmed body

9. Go back to DesignModeler by double clicking on Geometry under Project Schematic in ANSYS Workbench. Select Back View. Select XYPlane in the Tree Outline and create a new Sketch .

Click on the Sketching tab in the Tree Outline and select Rectangle. Draw a rectangle around the Ahmed body from the bottom of the computational domain. Select Dimensions and click on the vertical and horizontal sides of the new rectangle. Enter 900 mm as the vertical height of the rectangle and 2700 mm as the width. Set the horizontal distance from the front of the Ahmed body to the right-hand side vertical edge of the rectangle to 552 mm. Set the vertical distance between the lower horizontal edge of the rectangle and the bottom of the Ahmed body to 50 mm.

Select the Modeling tab in the Tree Outline and select Extrude. Select the new Sketch3 under XYPlane in the Tree Outline and Apply it as Geometry in Details of Extrude3. Enter 450 mm as the FD1, Depth (>0) of the Extrusion. Click on Generate. Click on plus sign next to 2 Parts, 2 Bodies in the Tree Outline, right click on Solid and select Rename. Rename Solid to "AhmedBodyBox". Close the DesignModeler window.

Go back to ANSYS Workbench, double click on Mesh and answer *Yes* to the question whether you would like to read upstream data.

Figure 14.9a) Dimensions for rectangle surrounding the Ahmed body

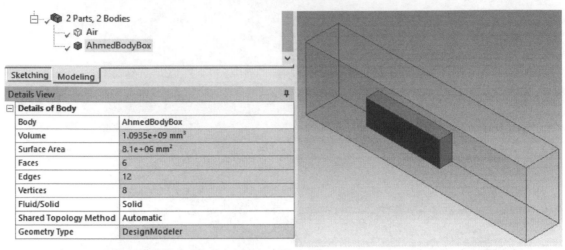

Figure 14.9b) Details of body

10. Right click Mesh under Project in Outline, select Insert>>Sizing. Right click in the graphics window and select Cursor Mode>>Body. Select the computational domain in the graphics window. Apply the computational domain in Geometry under Scope in Details of "Sizing". Select Body of Influence as Type under Definition.

Select Back view in the graphics window, zoom in on the Ahmed body, select the AhmedBodyBox and Apply it as the Body of Influence. You will need to select the second small rectangle in the lower left corner of Figure 14.10a) before you can select the AhmedRocketBox that turns from green to red when you apply it as the body of influence. Update the Mesh. If you click on the plus sign next to Statistics in Details of Mesh you will find that the number of Elements for the mesh is 482268 and the number of Nodes is 139186.

Right click on AhmedBodyBox under Geometry in Outline and select Hide Body. Select Mesh in the Outline and click on the plus sign next to Quality in Details of Mesh. Select Skewness as Mesh Metric. The max skewness should not be above 0.9. Select File>>Save Project. Select File>>Export>>Mesh>>FLUENT Input File>>Export and save the mesh with the name "ahmed-body-flow-mesh.msh". Close the Meshing window.

Figure 14.10a) Selection of AhmedBodyBox as Body of Influence

Figure 14.10b) Finished mesh for Ahmed body

## E. Launching ANSYS Fluent for 3D Ahmed Body

11. Double click on Setup in ANSYS Workbench. Check Double Precision under Options and set the number of Processes equal to the number of cores for the computer. Click Start to launch Fluent.

Double click on Models under Setup in the Outline View and double click on Viscous – SST k-omega under Models on the Task Page. Select the k-epsilon (2 eqn) turbulence model. Select Realizable as the k-epsilon model and check Non-Equilibrium Wall Functions as Near-Wall Treatment. Click OK to exit the Viscous Model window.

Double click on Boundary Conditions under Setup in the Outline View and select *velocity-inlet* under Zone for Boundary Conditions on the Task Page. Click on the Edit… button. Select Components as Velocity Specification Method. Enter 30 as X-Velocity (m/s). Click OK to close the Velocity Inlet window.

Figure 14.11 Velocity inlet specifications for X-Velocity

12. Double click Projected Areas under Results and Reports in the Outline View. Select *wall-air* as the Surface, enter 0.030 as Min Feature Size (m), select X as Projection Direction and click on Compute. The computed frontal area is 0.06175669 m2. Close the window.

Figure 14.12a) Projected surface area

Double click on Reference Values under Setup in the Outline View and change the Area (m2) to 0.06175669 and the Velocity (m/s) to 30. Select Compute from velocity-inlet and set Reference Zone to air.

Double click on Methods under Solution in the Outline View and set the Pressure-Velocity Coupling scheme to Coupled. Set the Spatial Discretization Gradient to Least Squares Cell Based, and Pressure to Standard. Set the remaining three for Momentum, Turbulent Kinetic Energy and Turbulent Dissipation Rate to First Order Upwind. Uncheck the box for Pseudo Transient.

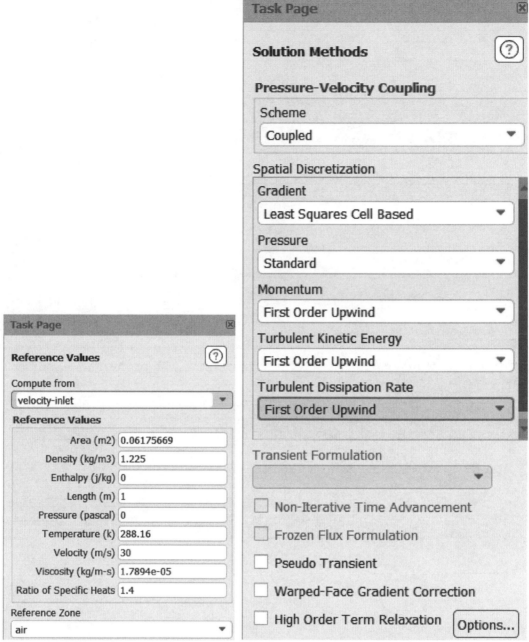

Figure 14.12b) Reference values      Figure 14.12c) Solution methods

13. Double click on Controls under Solution in the Outline View, set the Flow Courant Number to 50, set the Momentum and Pressure Explicit Relaxation Factors to 0.25 and set the Turbulent Viscosity Under-Relaxation Factor to 0.8. Click on Limits… and set the Maximum Turb. Viscosity Ratio to 10000000. Click on the OK button to close the window.

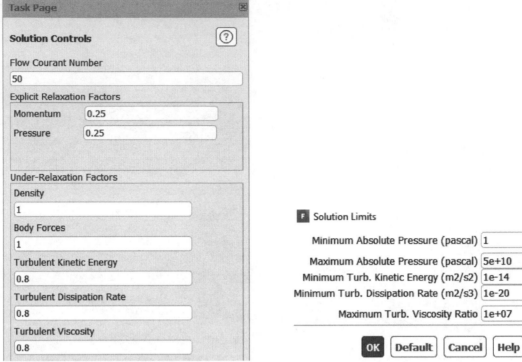

Figure 14.13a) Solution controls          Figure 14.13b) Solution limits

Double click on Monitors and Residual under Solution in the Outline View. Check the box for Show Advanced Options and set the Convergence Criterion to none. Click on OK to close Residual Monitors.

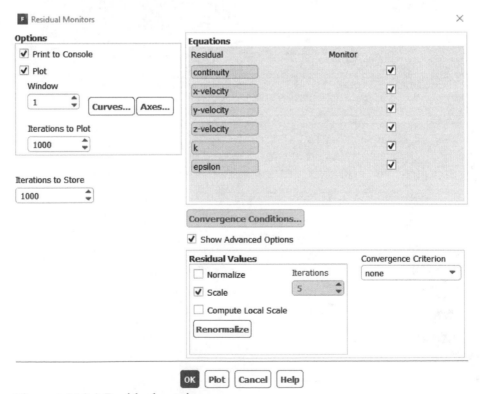

Figure 14.13c) Residual monitors

Double-click on Report Definitions on the left-hand side under Solution in the Tree. Select New>>Force Report>>Drag… from the drop-down menu. Select *wall-air* as Wall Zone. Check the boxes for Report File, Report Plot and Print to Console under Create. Set the Force Vector to X = 1, Y = 0, and Z = 0. Click on the OK button to close the window. Close the Report Definitions window.

Figure 14.13d) Drag report definition

14. Double click on Initialization under Solution in the Outline View and select *Hybrid Initializa*tion. Click on the Initialize button. Double click on Calculation Activities under Solution in the Outline View and click on Edit… for Autosave Every (Iterations). Set Save Data File Every (Iterations) to 100. Click OK to close the Autosave window.

Double click on Run Calculation under Solution in the Outline View. Set the Number of Iterations to 200. Click on Calculate.

Double click on Methods under Solution in the Outline View and replace First Order Upwind with Second Order Upwind for Momentum, Turbulent Kinetic Energy and Turbulent Dissipation Rate. Double click on Controls under Solution and set the Turbulent Viscosity value to 0.95. Double click on Run Calculation under Solution and set Number of Iterations to 500. Click on Calculate and Click OK in the window that appears.

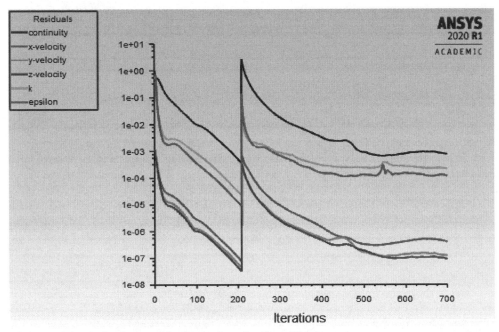

Figure 14.14a) Scaled residuals during the first 700 iterations

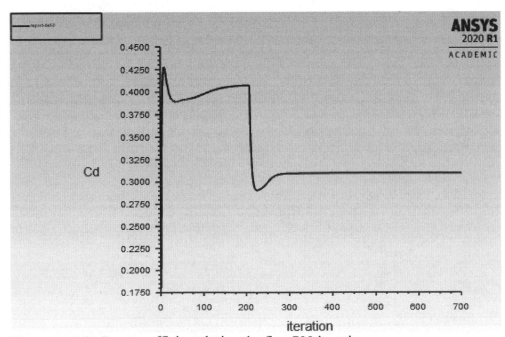

Figure 14.14b) Drag coefficient during the first 700 iterations

## F. Post-Processing for 3D Ahmed Body

15. Double-click on Reports under Results in the Outline View and double-click on Forces under Reports. Set Direction Vector for X to 1, Y to 0, and Z to 0. Select the *wall-air* Wall Zone, deselect *street* Wall Zone and click on the Print button. The total drag coefficient is 0.30981. Close the Force Reports window.

    Double-click on Graphics and Contours under Results in the Outline View. Select Contours of Pressure... and Static Pressure. Select *symmetry1* as Surfaces and click on Save/Display.

Figure 14.15a) Static pressure for Ahmed body at 30 m/s.

    Double-click on Graphics and Contours under Results in the Outline View. Select Contours of Velocity... and Velocity Magnitude. Select *symmetry1* as the Surface and click on Save/Display.

Figure 14.15b) Velocity magnitude around Ahmed body at 30 m/s.

    Double-click on Graphics and Pathlines under Results in the Outline View. Select the settings as shown in Figure 14.15c). Select *symmetry1* as the Surface and click on Save/Display.

Figure 14.15c) Settings for pathlines

Figure 14.15d) Pathlines around Ahmed body at 30 m/s.

16. Set the inlet velocity in the boundary condition to 40 m/s. Double click on Methods under Solution in the Outline View and replace Second Order Upwind with First Order Upwind for Momentum, Turbulent Kinetic Energy and Turbulent Dissipation Rate. Double click on Controls under Solution and set the Turbulent Viscosity value to 0.8. Double click on Reference Values under Setup in the Outline View and set the Velocity (m/s) to 40. Repeat steps 14-15.

| U (m/s) | Re | Cd, Fluent | Cd, Meile et al. | Percent difference |
|---------|-----------|------------|------------------|--------------------|
| 3 | 214,413 | 0.39436 | 0.36001 | 9.5 |
| 4 | 285,884 | 0.36780 | 0.35684 | 3.1 |
| 5 | 357,354 | 0.35126 | 0.35380 | 0.7 |
| 6 | 428,825 | 0.33785 | 0.35088 | 3.7 |
| 7.5 | 536,032 | 0.32895 | 0.34670 | 5.1 |
| 10 | 714,709 | 0.32216 | 0.34027 | 5.3 |
| 15 | 1,072,063 | 0.31652 | 0.32919 | 3.8 |
| 20 | 1,429,418 | 0.31307 | 0.32010 | 2.2 |
| 30 | 2,144,127 | 0.30981 | 0.30655 | 1.1 |
| 40 | 2,858835 | 0.31136 | 0.29744 | 4.7 |
| 50 | 3,573,544 | 0.31150 | 0.29133 | 6.9 |
| 60 | 4,288,253 | 0.31134 | 0.28722 | 8.4 |
| 70 | 5,002,962 | 0.31186 | 0.28445 | 9.6 |

Table 14.1 Comparison between ANSYS Fluent and established data

Repeat step 16 for all inlet velocities as listed in Table 14.1.

Figure 14.16 Drag coefficient versus Reynolds number for Ahmed body

## G. Theory

We start by defining the Reynolds number for the 3D case outlined in this chapter

$$Re = \frac{UL\rho}{\mu}$$ (14.1)

where $U$ (m/s) is inlet velocity, $L$ (m) is the length of the Ahmed body, $\rho$ (kg/m$^3$) is the density of the fluid and $\mu$ (m$^2$/s) is dynamic viscosity of the fluid.

Next, we define the drag coefficient $C_d$ as

$$C_d = \frac{F_d}{\frac{1}{2}\rho U^2 A} \tag{14.2}$$

where $F_d$(N) is the drag force and $A$ (m$^2$) is the frontal area of the Ahmed body. Meile *et al.*[6] determined the following relationship between the drag coefficient and the Reynolds number for the Ahmed body.

$$C_d = 0.2788 + 0.0915e^{-Re/1797100} \tag{14.3}$$

## H. References

1. Ahmed, S.R., Ramm, G.,"Some Salient Features of the Time-Averaged Ground Vehicle Wake", *SAE-Paper 840300*, 1984.

2. Dogan, T., Conger, M., Kim, D-H., Mousaviraad, M., Xing, T., Stern, F.,"Simulation of Turbulent Flow over the Ahmed Body", *ME: 5160 Intermediate Mechanics of Fluids CFD Lab 4*, (2016).

3. Kalyan, D.K., Paul, A.R., "Computational Study of Flow around a Simplified 2D Ahmed Body", *International Journal of Engineering Science and Innovative Technology (IJESIT)*, **2**, 3, (2013).

4. Khan, R.S, Umale, S.,"CFD Aerodynamic Analysis of Ahmed Body", *International Journal of Engineering Trends and Technology (IJETT)*, **18**, 7, (2014).

5. Lienhart, H., Stoots, C. and Becker, S.,"Flow and Turbulence Structures in the Wake of a Simplified Car Model (Ahmed Model), *Notes on Numerical Fluid Mechanics*, **77**, 6, (2002).

6. Meile, W., Brenn, G., Reppenhagen, A., Lechner, B., Fuchs, A.,"Experiments and numerical simulations on the aerodynamics of the Ahmed body", *CFD Letters*, **3**, 1, (2011).

## I. Exercise

14.1    Model the 3D flow past the Ahmed body with the dimensions as shown and units in mm from Figure 14.17. Follow the same steps as shown in this chapter. Find the drag curve corresponding to Figure 14.16 and compare the two rear slant angles 25 and 35 degrees in the same graph.

Figure 14.17 Dimensions of Ahmed body

**J. Notes**

# CHAPTER 15. HOURGLASS

## A. Objectives

- Using ANSYS Workbench to Create Geometry and Mesh for the Hourglass
- Inserting Boundary Conditions
- Running the Calculations
- Using Contour Plots for Volume Fractions and a Movie for Visualizations

## B. Problem Description

We will study the flow in the hourglass and will analyze the problem using ANSYS Fluent.

## C. Launching ANSYS Workbench and Selecting Fluent

1. Start by launching ANSYS Workbench. Double click on Fluid Flow (Fluent) under Analysis Systems in the Toolbox.

Figure 15.1 Selecting Fluent

**D. Launching ANSYS DesignModeler**

2. Right click Geometry under Project Schematic in ANSYS Workbench and select Properties. In Properties of Schematic A2: Geometry, select Analysis Type 2D under Advanced Geometry Options. Right click on Geometry in the Project Schematic window and select New DesignModeler Geometry.

Figure 15.2 Selecting properties and 2D analysis type

3. Select Units>>Millimeter from the menu in DesignModeler. Select the XY Plane in the Tree Outline and click on Look at Face/Plane/Sketch ▮◨. Select the Sketching tab and select Line under Draw from Sketching Toolboxes. Start at the origin and draw the sketch with the dimensions as shown in Figure 15.3a).

Figure 15.3a) Dimensions for hourglass

Select Concept>>Surfaces from Sketches from the menu. Select Sketch1 under XYPlane in Tree Outline and apply the sketch as the Base Object in Details View. Click on Generate and close DesignModeler.

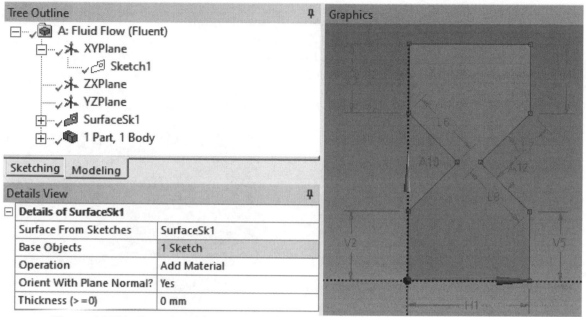

Figure 15.3b) Completed hourglass in DesignModeler

## E. Launching ANSYS Meshing

4. Double click on Mesh under Project Schematic in ANSYS Workbench. Set the Element Size under Defaults in Details of Mesh to 0.5 mm. Right click on Mesh under Project in Outline and select Generate Mesh.

Figure 15.4a) Completed mesh for the hourglass

Right click in the graphics window and select Cursor Mode>> Edge 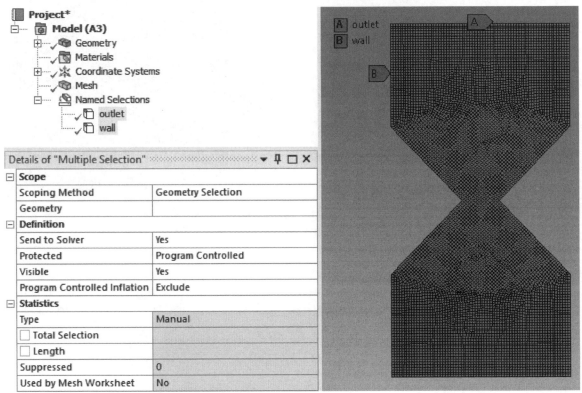 and select the upper horizontal edge for the mesh. The edge turns green. Right click on the edge and select Create Named Selection. Enter *outlet* as the name and click OK to close the Selection Name window. Control select the remaining nine edge of the mesh, right click and select Create Named Selection. Name these edges *wall*.

Select File>>Export>>Mesh>>FLUENT Input File>>Export from the menu and save the mesh with the name *hourglass-mesh.msh*. Select File>>Save Project from the menu and save the project with the name *Hour-Glass.wbpj*. Close the Meshing window and right-click on Mesh under Project Schematic in ANSYS Workbench and select Update.

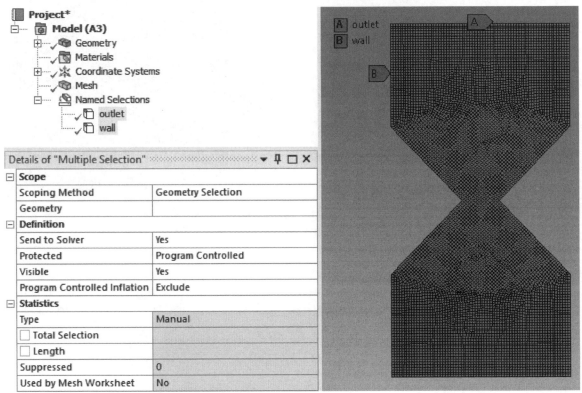

Figure 15.4b) Named selections for the hourglass

## F. Launching ANSYS Fluent

5. Double click on Setup under Project Schematic in ANSYS Workbench. Check the box for Double Precision under Options in the ANSYS Fluent Launcher and set the number of Processes equal to the number of core processors for your computer. Click on Start to launch Fluent.

Figure 15.5a) Launching ANSYS Fluent

Select Transient under Time on the Task Page. Check the box for Gravity and enter -9.81 as the value for Y (m/s2).

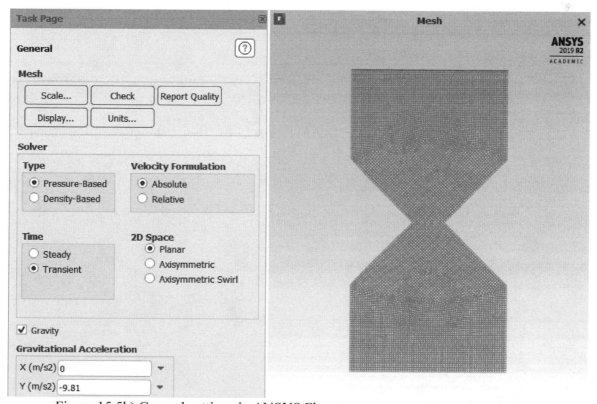

Figure 15.5b) General settings in ANSYS Fluent

6. Double click on Models and Multiphase under Setup in the Outline View. Select Eulerian Inhomogeneous Model. Set the Number of Eulerian Phases to 2 and Implicit Formulation for Volume Fraction Parameters. Click Apply and Close the Multiphase Model window. Double click on Models and Viscous under Setup in the Outline View. Select Laminar Model and click OK to close the Viscous Model window.

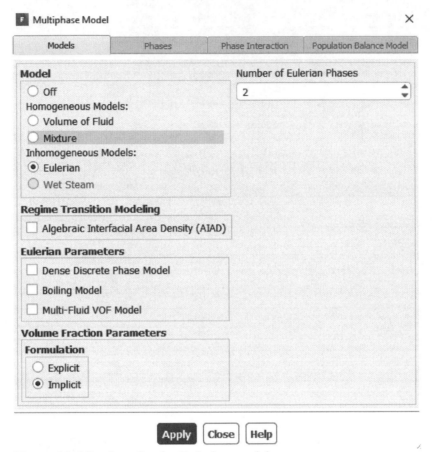

Figure 15.6 Settings for the Eulerian model

7. Open Materials and Fluid under Setup in the Outline View and select *air*. Right click on *air* and select copy. Enter the name *wood* and set the Density (kg/m3) to 850. Click on Change/Create and answer Yes to the question that appears. Close the Create/Edit Materials window.

Figure 15.7 Settings for wood

8. Double click on Multiphase under Models in the Setup and select the Phases tab at the top of the Multiphase Model window. Select phase- 1 – Primary Phase under Phases. Select *air* as Phase Material and enter *air* as the Name for the Primary Phase. Click on Apply.

Figure 15.8a) Primary phase

Select phase- 2 – Secondary Phase under Phases. Select *wood* as Phase Material and enter *wood* as the Name for the Secondary Phase. Check the box for Granular and enter 0.0002 as Diameter (m). Set the Granular Properties as shown in Table 15.1. Click on Apply.

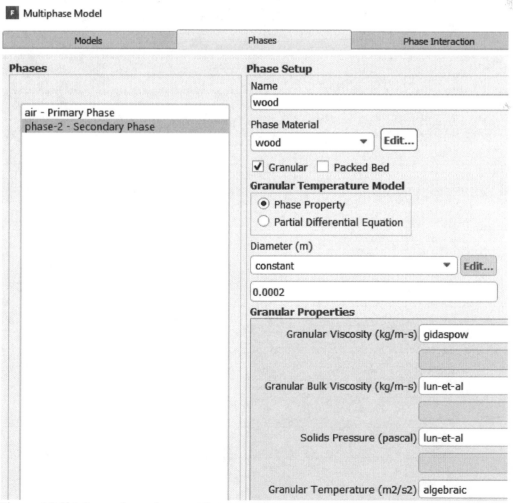

Figure 15.8b) Secondary phase settings

| Diameter (m) | 0.0002 |
|---|---|
| Granular Viscosity (kg/m-s) | gidaspow |
| Granular Bulk Viscosity (kg/m-s) | lun-et-al |
| Frictional Viscosity (kg/m-s) | schaeffer |
| Angle Of Internal Friction (deg) | 45 |
| Frictional Pressure (pascal) | based-ktgf |
| Frictional Modulus (pascal) | derived |
| Friction Packing Limit | 0.45 |
| Granular Temperature (m2/s2) | algebraic |
| Solids Pressure (pascal) | lun-et-al |
| Radial Distribution | lun-et-al |
| Elasticity Modulus (pascal) | derived |
| Packing Limit | 0.63 |

Table 15.1 Settings for secondary phase

9. Select the Phase Interaction tab at the top of the Multiphase Model window. Select *air wood* under Phase Pairs and set Virtual Mass Coefficient, Drag Coefficient and Lift Coefficient to *none*. Select *wood wood* under Phase Pairs and set the Restitutions Coefficient to 0.001. Click Apply and Close the Phase Interactions window.

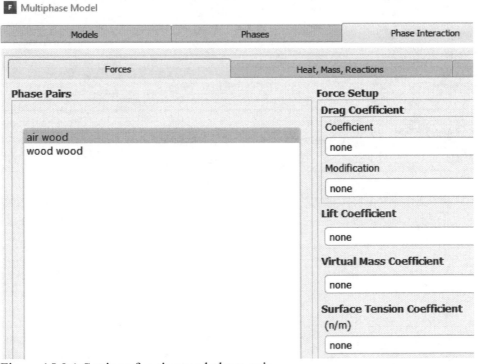

Figure 15.9a) Settings for air-wood phase pair

Figure 15.9b) Settings for wood-wood phase pair

10. Double-click on Boundary Conditions under Setup and click on Operating Conditions under Boundary Conditions on the Task Page. Select user-input as Operating Density Method. Enter Reference Pressure Location X (m) 0.0175 and Y (m) 0.06828427. Click OK to close the Operating Conditions window.

Figure 15.10 Settings for operating conditions

11. Double-click on Methods under Solution and set the Spatial Discretization for Momentum to Second Order Upwind. Double-click on Controls under Solution and set the Under-Relaxation Factor for Momentum to 0.3. Double click on Residual under Monitors and Solution. Set all Absolute Criteria for continuity, u-air and v-air to 1e-05. Set the other Absolute Criteria to 0.001 and click OK to close the Residual Monitors window.

Figure 15.11a) Solution methods

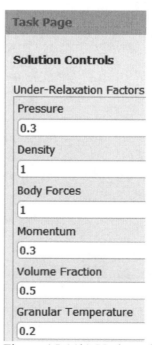

Figure 15.11b) Under-relaxation factors

347

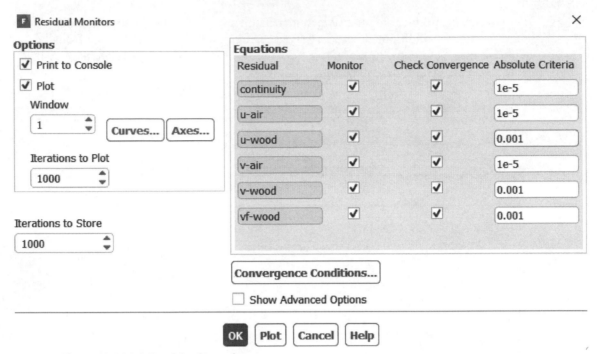

Figure 15.11c) Residual monitors

12. Double-click on Initialization under Solution and set Initializations Method to Hybrid Initialization. Click on Initialize.

Figure 15.12a) Hybrid initialization

Select Adapt>>Refine / Coarsen… from the Domain tab in the menu. Select Cell Registers>>New>>Field Variable… in the Adaption Controls window.

Select Gradient as Derivative Option, *wood* as Phase and Gradients of Phases… and Volume Fraction. Select Cells in Range as Type and set the Gradient-Min to 0.001 and Gradient-Max to 0.01. Click on Save and Close the Field Variable Register window. Check Dynamic Adaption in the Adaption Controls window and set the Frequency (time-step) to 1.

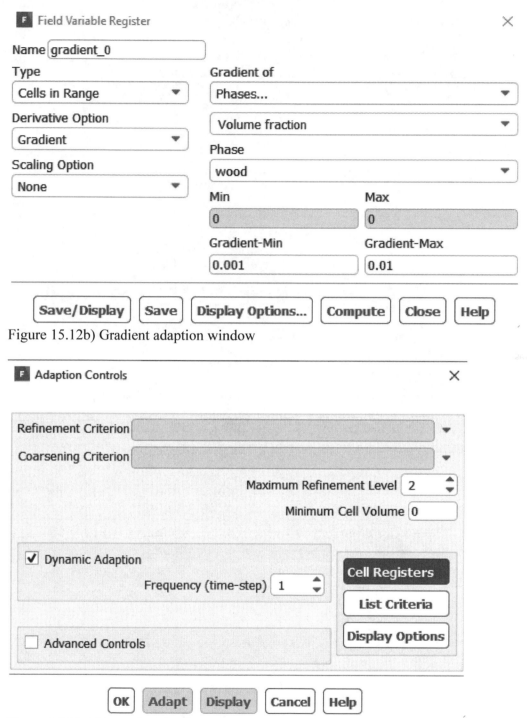

Figure 15.12b) Gradient adaption window

Figure 15.12c) Dynamic adaption

Select Cell Registers>>New>>Region… in the Adaption Controls window.

Set the X Max (m) value to 0.035 and Y Min (m) value to 0.034 and Y Max (m) value to 0.04. Click on Save and Close the Region Register window. Click OK to close the Adaption Controls window.

349

Figure 15.12d) Region register settings

Click on Patch... under Solution Initialization on the Task Page. Select wood as the Phase, select Volume Fraction as Variable, region_0 as Registers to Patch and Value to 0.63. Click on Patch and Close the Patch window.

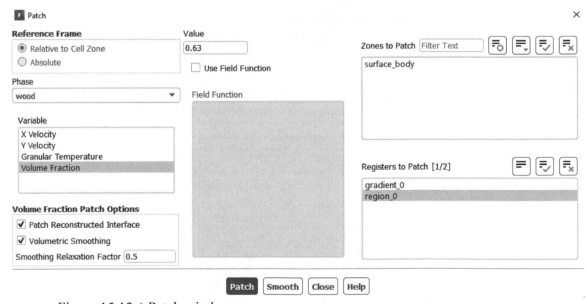

Figure 15.12e) Patch window

13. Double-click on Contours under Graphics and Results in the Outline View. Select wood as Phase and select Contours of Phases… and Volume fraction. Select the surface_body under Surfaces. Click on Save/Display and Close the Contours window.

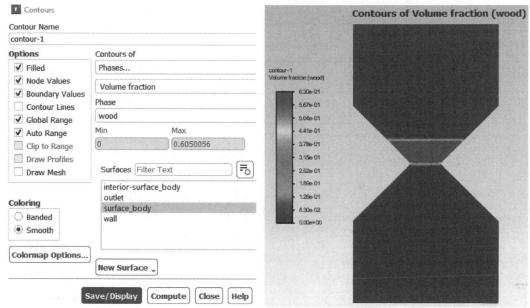

Figure 15.13a) Contours window

Figure 15.13b) Volume fraction (wood)

14. Double-click on Solution Animations under Solution and Calculation Activities in the Outline View. Select Record after every 1 time-step. Select HSF File as Storage Type. Set Window Id to 2 and select contour-1 as Animation Object. Enter *hour-glass* as Name and click OK to close the Animation Definition window.

Figure 15.14 Contours window

15. Double-click on Run Calculation under Solution in the Outline View. Enter 0.001 as Time Step Size (s). Enter 40 as Number of Time Steps, set Max Iterations/Time Step to 30, see Figure 15.15a). Select File>>Export>>Case & Data... from the menu and save the Case/Data File with the name *hour-glass.cas*. Click on Calculate under Run Calculation on the Task Page. After the first calculations are complete, continue running the calculations two more times with the same settings, see Figure 15.15b).

Figure 15.15a) Run calculations window

## G. Post-Processing

t = 0 s            t = 0.04 s            t = 0.08 s            t = 0.12s

Figure 15.15b) Volume fraction (wood) at different times

## H. Theory

16. We start with continuity, momentum and energy equations.

$$\frac{\partial}{\partial t}(\alpha_s \rho_s) + \nabla \cdot (\alpha_s \rho_s \bar{u}_s) = \dot{m}_{fs} \tag{15.1}$$

$$\frac{\partial}{\partial t}(\alpha_s \rho_s \bar{u}_s) + \nabla \cdot (\alpha_s \rho_s \bar{u}_s \bar{u}_s) = -\alpha_s \nabla p_f + \nabla \cdot \tau_s + \sum_{s=1}^{n}(\bar{R}_{fs} + \dot{m}_{fs} \bar{u}_{fs}) + \bar{F}_s \tag{15.2}$$

$$\frac{3}{2}\left[\frac{\partial}{\partial t}(\alpha_s \rho_s \theta_s) + \nabla \cdot (\alpha_s \rho_s \bar{u}_s \theta_s)\right] = \tau_s : \nabla \bar{u}_s + \nabla \cdot (\kappa_\theta \nabla \theta_s) - \gamma_s + \phi_{lm} + \phi_{fs} \tag{15.3}$$

where
$$\tau_s = -P_s \bar{I} + 2\alpha_s \mu_s \bar{S} + \alpha_s (\lambda_s - \frac{2}{3}\mu_s)\nabla \cdot \bar{u}_s \bar{I} \tag{15.4}$$

$$\bar{S} = \frac{1}{2}[\nabla \cdot \bar{u}_s + (\nabla \cdot \bar{u}_s)^T] \tag{15.5}$$

The total granular solids phase pressure is the sum of kinetic and frictional pressures

$$P_s = P_{s,friction} + P_{s,kinetic} \tag{15.6}$$

The Frictional Pressure (pascal) in ANSYS Fluent is the frictional part of equation (15.6). The following expression was given by Johnson and Jackson[4].

$$P_{s,friction} = \frac{\alpha_s}{10} \frac{(\alpha_s - \alpha_{s,min})^2}{(\alpha_{s,max} - \alpha_s)^5} \tag{15.7}$$

353

Alternatively, we have the expression by Syamlal et al[7].

$$P_{s,friction} = 2\alpha_s^2 \rho_s g_0 \theta_s (1 + e_s) \qquad (15.8)$$

where the radial distribution function

$$g_0 = \frac{1}{1 - (\frac{\alpha_s}{\alpha_{s,max}})^{1/3}} \qquad (15.9)$$

The Solids Pressure (pascal) in ANSYS Fluent is the kinetic portion of granular solids phase pressure and can be described using the following relation by Lun et al[5].

$$P_{s,kinetic} = \alpha_s \rho_s \theta_s [1 + 2\alpha_s g_0 (1 + e_s)] \qquad (15.10)$$

The granular phase shear viscosity can be described as the sum of the collisional, kinetic and frictional parts.

$$\mu_s = \mu_{s,collision} + \mu_{s,kinetic} + \mu_{s,friction} \qquad (15.11)$$

The collisional part of the solids phase shear viscosity was modeled by Gidaspow et al.[1] and Syamlal et al[7].

$$\mu_{s,collision} = \frac{4}{5} \alpha_s^2 \rho_s d_s g_0 (1 + e_s) \sqrt{\frac{\theta_s}{\pi}} \qquad (15.12)$$

The Granular Viscosity (kg/m-s) in ANSYS Fluent is the kinetic part of equation (15.11). The following expression was given by Gidaspow et al[1].

$$\mu_{s,kinetic} = \frac{10\sqrt{\pi\theta_s}\rho_s d_s}{96(1+e_s)g_0} \left[1 + \frac{4}{5}(1 + e_s)g_0\alpha_s\right]^2 \qquad (15.13)$$

Alternatively, we have the expression by Syamlal et al[7].

$$\mu_{s,kinetic} = \frac{\alpha_s\sqrt{\pi\theta_s}\rho_s d_s}{6(3-e_s)} \left[1 + \frac{2}{5}(1 + e_s)(3e_s - 1)g_0\alpha_s\right] \qquad (15.14)$$

The Frictional Viscosity (kg/m-s) in ANSYS Fluent is the frictional part of equation (15.11). The equation is given by Schaeffer[6]

$$\mu_{s,friction} = \frac{P_{s,friction}\sin\varphi}{2\sqrt{I_2}} \qquad (15.15)$$

The Granular Bulk Viscosity (kg/m-s) in ANSYS Fluent accounts for resistance of the granular material to compression and expansion. The equation is given by Lun et al[5].

$$\lambda_s = \frac{4}{3} \alpha_s^2 \rho_s d_s g_0 (1 + e_s) \sqrt{\frac{\theta_s}{\pi}} \qquad (15.16)$$

| | |
|---|---|
| $\alpha_s$ | volume fraction for granular material |
| $\alpha_{s,min}$ | friction packing limit |
| $\alpha_{s,max}$ | packing limit |
| $\varphi$ | internal angle of friction |
| $\gamma_s$ | energy dissipation |
| $\kappa_\theta$ | granular temperature conductivity |
| $\lambda_s$ | bulk viscosity |
| $\mu_s$ | granular shear viscosity |
| $\mu_{s,collision}$ | collisional viscosity |
| $\mu_{s,friction}$ | frictional viscosity |
| $\mu_{s,kinetic}$ | kinetic viscosity |
| $\phi_{fs}$ | energy exchange between fluid and granular phase |
| $\phi_{lm}$ | energy exchange between granular phases |
| $\rho_s$ | density |
| $\theta_s$ | temperature |
| $\tau_s$ | stress tensor |
| $d_s$ | particle diameter |
| $e_s$ | coefficient of restitution |
| $g_0$ | radial distribution function |
| $I_2$ | second invariant of the deviatoric stress tensor |
| $m_{fs}$ | unidirectional mass transfer |
| $p_f$ | fluid pressure |
| $P_s$ | granular pressure |
| $P_{s,friction}$ | frictional pressure |
| $P_{s,kinetic}$ | kinetic pressure |
| $\bar{S}$ | strain rate |
| $t$ | time |
| $\bar{u}_s$ | granular velocity vector |

Table 15.2 Parameters used in theory section

# I. References

1. Gidaspow, D., Bezburuah, R., Ding, J. "Hydrodynamics of Circulating Fluidized Beds: Kinetic Theory Approach", *7th Fluidization Conference*, May 3, (1992).
2. Hirt, C.W.," A Flow-3D Continuum Model for Granular Media.", Flow Science Report 02-13, (2013).
3. Jansson, M., "CFD Simulations of Silos Content, An Investigation of Flow Patterns and Segregation Mechanisms.", *Master's Thesis within the Innovative and Sustainable Chemical Engineering Programme*, Chalmers, (2014).
4. Johnson, P.C., Jackson. R.," Frictional-Collisional Constitutive Relations for Granular Materials, with Application to Plane Shearing". *J. Fluid Mech*. **176**. (1987).
5. Lun, C.K.K., Savage, S.B., Jeffrey, D.J., Chepurniy, N., "Kinetic Theories for Granular Flow: Inelastic Particles in Couette Flow and Slightly Inelastic Particles in a General Flow Field". *J. Fluid Mech*. **140**, (1984).
6. Schaeffer, D.G., "Instability in the Evolution Equations Describing Incompressible Granular Flow.", *Journal of Differential Equations*, **66**, (1987).
7. Syamlal, M., Rogers, W., O'Brien, T.J. "MFIX Documentation Theory Guide", DOE/METC-94/1004 (1993).

## J. Exercises

15.1 Use ANSYS Fluent to simulate an axisymmetric cylindrical heap of sand that deforms due to gravity into a conical pile. Use an initial 100 mm in diameter and 100 mm high heap of sand resting on a horizontal surface with a volume fraction packing limit of 0.63, see Hirt[2]. Use the density 1638 kg/m3 for the sand, a grain diameter of 0.45 mm and an internal angle of friction of 34 degrees. Determine the angle of repose for the conical pile of sand and show contours for the volume fraction of sand over time as it slumps.

15.2 Use ANSYS Fluent to simulate a 2-D hourglass. The shape of the hourglass is 200 mm wide at the top and the bottom, a total height of 500 mm and sides with a slope of 40.5 degrees. The opening at the waist of the hourglass is 10 mm. Start the simulation with sand (1638 kg/m3) and a grain diameter of 0.45 mm in the upper half of the hourglass with a packing limit of 0.63 for the volume fraction of sand. Use an internal angle of friction of 34 degrees. Determine the angle of repose for the final conical pile of sand in the bottom half of the hourglass and show contours for the volume fraction of sand over time as it moves due to gravity from the upper half to the lower half of the hourglass. See Hirt[2] for a similar simulation using Flow-3D.

15.3 Use ANSYS Fluent to simulate the flow of wood when filling a 2-D axisymmetric silo, see Jansson[3]. The shape of the silo is shown in Figure 15.16 with the following dimensions: $v1$ = 9 m, $h1$ = 10 m, $v2$ = 17 m, $h2$ = 0.5 m, $v3$ = 0.5 m, $v4$ = 1.5 m, $h3$ = 0.5 m. Use an inlet volume fraction for wood of 0.4 and other values as listed in Table 15.2.

Figure 15.16 Geometry for silo

| | |
|---|---|
| $\alpha_{s,min}$ = 0.45 | friction packing limit |
| $\alpha_{s,max}$ =0.63 | packing limit |
| $\varphi$ = 45° | internal angle of friction |
| $\rho_s$ = 850 $kg/m3$ | wood density |
| $d_s$ = 0.02 $m$ | particle diameter |
| $e_s$ = 0.001 | coefficient of restitution |

Table 15.3 Parameters used in Exercise 15.3

## CHAPTER 16. BOUNCING SPHERES

### A. Objectives

- Use the Macroscopic Particle Model
- Create a Movie of the Resulting Motion of the Spheres

### B. Problem Description

In this tutorial we will be simulating a number of spheres falling through an hourglass shaped geometry. We will let the balls bounce with each other and they will bounce with the walls.

### C. Launching ANSYS Workbench and Selecting Fluent

1. Start by launching ANSYS Workbench. Double click on Fluid Flow (Fluent) under Analysis Systems in the Toolbox.

Figure 16.1 Selecting Fluent

### D. Launching ANSYS DesignModeler

2. Right click on Geometry in the Project Schematic window in ANSYS Workbench and select New DesignModeler Geometry. Select Units>>Millimeter from the menu in DesignModeler. Select the XY Plane in the Tree Outline and click on Look at Face/Plane/Sketch ⌨. Select the Sketching tab and select Polyline under Draw from Sketching Toolboxes. Start at the origin and draw the sketch, right click and select *closed end* and enter the dimensions as shown in Figure 16.2a). Select 🔄 Revolve and apply

Sketch1 as Geometry in Details View. Select the left vertical side of the sketch and apply it as the Axis in Details View. Click on Generate and close DesignModeler.

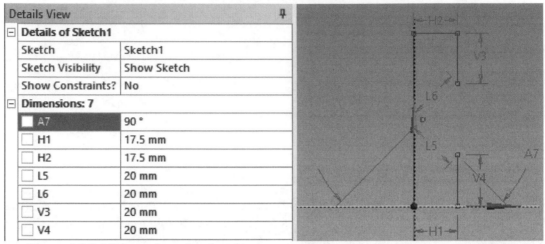

Figure 16.2a) Dimensions for sketch

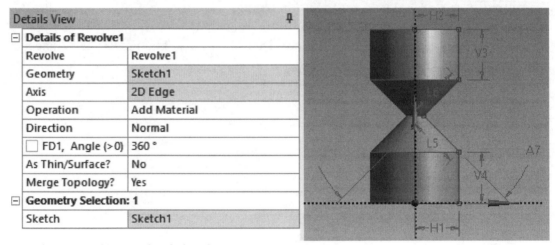

Figure 16.2b) Revolved sketch

## E. Launching ANSYS Meshing

3.  Double click on Mesh under Project Schematic in ANSYS Workbench. Set the Element Size under Defaults in Details of Mesh to 1.0 mm. Right click on Mesh under Project in Outline and select Generate Mesh. Under Statistics in Details of Mesh we can see that this mesh has 111,860 Nodes and 107,352 Elements. Right click in the graphics window and select Cursor Mode>>Face. Control select the 6 faces of the mesh, right click and select Create Named Selection. Enter the name *wall* and click on OK to close the Selection Name window.

    Select File>>Export...>>Mesh>>FLUENT Input File>>Export from the menu and save the mesh with the name *3d-enclosure-mesh.msh*. Select File>>Save Project from the menu and save the project with the name *3D-Enclosure.wbpj*. Close the Meshing window, right-click on Mesh under Project Schematic in ANSYS Workbench and select Update.

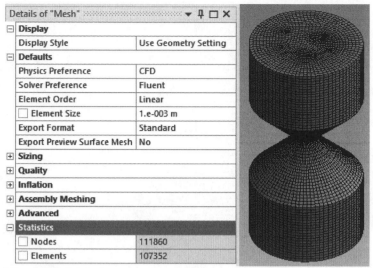

Figure 16.3 Mesh

## F. Launching ANSYS Fluent

4.  Double click on Setup under Project Schematic in ANSYS Workbench. Check the box for Double Precision under Options in the ANSYS Fluent Launcher and set the number of Processes equal to the number of core processors for your computer. Click on the plus sign next to Show More Options and take a note of the location of your *Working Directory* under the General Options tab as you will need this information later in step 9. Click on Start to launch Fluent.

Figure 16.4a) Launching ANSYS Fluent

Enter the following commands on the Console to load the Macroscopic Particle Model (MPM).

> **define**
/define> **models**
/define/models/> **addon**
Enter Module Number: [0] **10**

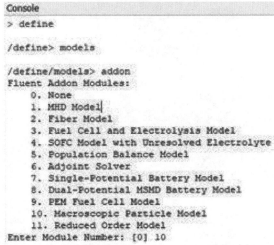

Figure 16.4b) Console commands to load MPM module

5. Double click on General under Setup in the Outline View and select Transient under Time on the Task Page. Check the box for Gravity and enter -9.81 as the value for Y (m/s2). Click on Scale… under Mesh in General on the Task Page.

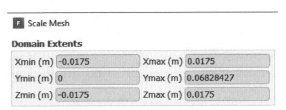

Figure 16.5a) General settings          Figure 16.5b) Scale mesh

6. Double click on Models and Macroscopic Particles under Setup in the Outline View and check the box to Enable Macroscopic Particle Model. Select the Drag tab and select Disable Drag Calculations under Drag Law Options. Select the Injections tab and click on Create. Select plane as Injection Type. Set the Diameter (m) to 0.003. Set the Plane Shape to Circular and select Y as Axis Direction. Enter Y (m) 0.06828427 and Radius (m) 0.0175 under Center Location/Radius of Circular Plane. Click on Create/Modify.

Figure 16.6a) Drag law options

Figure 16.6b) Injection options

Select the Initialize MPM tab in the MPM window. Check the box for ASCII File under Write Particle Data and save the file with the name *bouncing-spheres*. Check the box for Print Warning Messages and click on Initialize MPM Functions. Click on Initialize Particles.

Select ⬡ at the bottom of the graphics window. Select *wall* under Surfaces. Uncheck the box for Faces under Options and select Outline as Edge Type, see Figure 16.6d). Click on Display and Close the window.

Click on Display Injections. Select Particle ID under Display Particles Colored by, click on Display and Close the Display Particles window. Click on Apply in the MPM window and Close the same window.

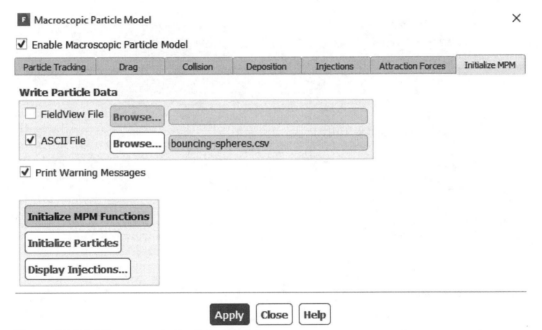

Figure 16.6c) Macroscopic Particle Model

Figure 16.6d) Mesh display

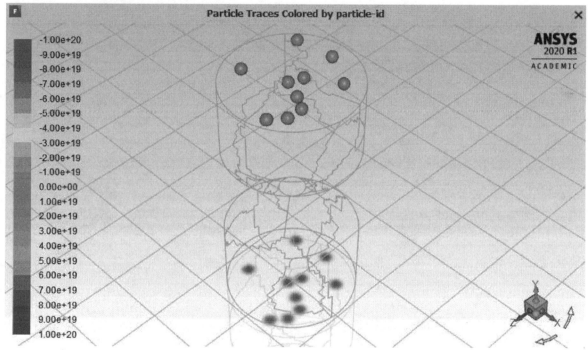

Figure 16.6e) Display particles settings

Figure 16.6f) Ten spheres randomly distributed on top of the mesh domain

7. Double click on Methods under Solution in the Outline View and select Second Order Implicit as Transient Formulation under Solution Methods on the Task Page.

Figure 16.7a) Solution methods settings

Double click on Cell Zone Conditions and Fluid>>solid (fluid, id=2) under Setup in the Outline View and uncheck the box for Source Terms in the Fluid window. Click on OK to close the Fluid window.

Double click on Monitors and Residual under Setup in the Outline View and uncheck the box for Plot under Options. Check the box for Show Advanced Options, select none as Convergence Criterion and click on OK to close the Residual Monitors window.

Figure 16.7b) Fluid window

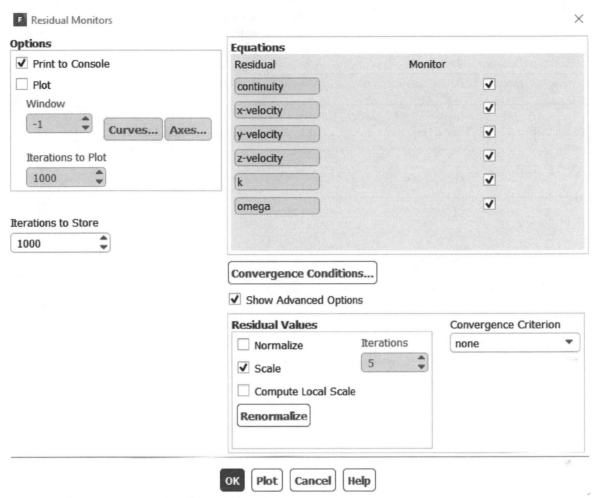

Figure 16.7c) Residual monitors window

8. Double click on Initialization under Solution in the Outline View and select Hybrid Initialization. Click on Initialize. Answer OK if you get a question.

Figure 16.8 Solution initialization

9. Create a new folder in your *working directory* called *jpg-files*. Double click on Calculation Activities and Execute Commands under Solution in the Outline View. Enter the commands listed below and as shown with settings in Figure 16.9. You will need to change the second command so that it is in line with the name and location of your *Working Directory*. Click OK to close the window.

(display-mpm-injections 'particle-id 0 10)
dis hard C:/Users/jmatsson/jpg-files/mpm-%t.jpg

**F** Execute Commands

Defined Commands  2

| Active | Name | Every | When | Command |
|--------|------|-------|------|---------|
| ✔ | mpm1 | 1 | Time Step ▾ | (display-mpm-injections 'particle-id 0 10) |
| ✔ | mpm3 | 1 | Time Step ▾ | dis hard C:/Users/jmatsson/jpg-files/mpm-%t.jpg |

Figure 16.9 Executive commands

10. Select  at the bottom of the graphics window and select Post Processing as shown in Figure 16.10a). Double click on Run Calculation under Solution in the Outline View and set the Time Step Size (s) to 0.01 and Number of Time Steps to 5. Set Max Iterations/Time Step to 1 and click on Calculate.

Meshing
Solution
✓ Post Processing

Figure 16.10a) Post processing appearance in the graphics window

Figure 16.10b) Running the calculations

## G. Post-Processing

11. Select the *YZ* plane by clicking on the red *X* axis of the coordinate system in the lower right corner of the graphics window as shown in Figure 16.11a). Continue running the calculations two more times. Next, change the Number of Time Steps to 10 and run the calculations once again. Answer OK to the question that you may get. Next, change the Number of Time Steps to 25 and run the calculations once again. Answer OK to the question that you may get. Next, change the Number of Time Steps to 50 and run the calculations once again. Answer OK to the question that you may get. Next, change the Number of Time Steps to 100 and run the calculations. Next, change the Number of Time Steps to 300 and run the calculations. Answer OK to the question that you may get.

Figure 16.11a) Coordinate system in the graphics window

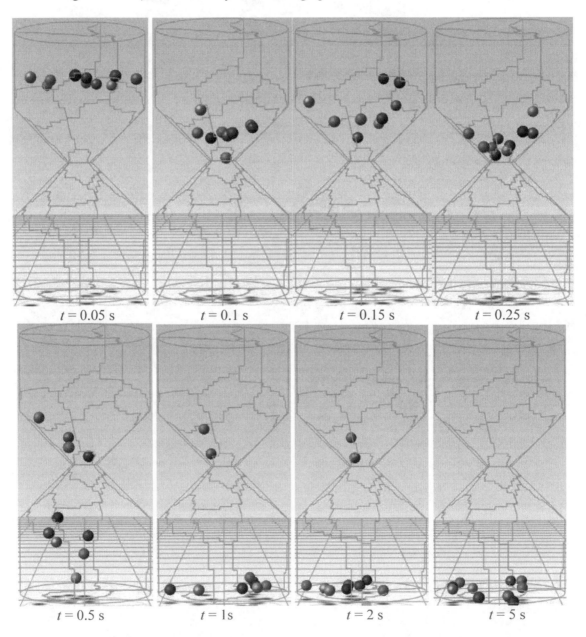

Figure 16.11b) Distribution of spheres at different times

## H. Reference

1. Agrawal, M., Bakker, A., Prinkey, M.T. "Macroscopic Particle Model Tracking Big Particles in CFD", *AIChE Annual Meeting, Particle Technology Forum, Paper 268b, November 7-12, Austin, TX*, (2004).

## I. Exercise

16.1     Use ANSYS Fluent and the macroscopic particle model to perform a billiard table simulation of the first shot to break the balls including the collision of the cue ball with the 15 object balls initially racked together in a triangular pattern on a 50 inch x 100 inch billiard table. The diameter of the billiard balls is 57 mm.

**J. Notes**

# CHAPTER 17. FALLING SPHERE

## A. Objectives

- Using the Macroscopic Particle Model Module
- Determine the Terminal Velocity for a Falling Sphere

## B. Problem Description

A 2 mm diameter sphere with a density of 1695 kg/m³ is falling in a tube with a diameter of 20 mm and a length of 60 mm.

## C. Launching ANSYS Workbench and Selecting Fluent

1. Start by launching ANSYS Workbench. Double click on Fluid Flow (Fluent) under Analysis Systems in the Toolbox. Select Units>>Metric (tonne, mm, s, …) from the menu.

Figure 17.1 Selecting Fluent

## D. Launching ANSYS DesignModeler

2. Right click on Geometry in the Project Schematic window in ANSYS Workbench and select New DesignModeler Geometry. Select Units>>Millimeter from the menu in DesignModeler. Select the XY Plane in the Tree Outline and click on Look at Face/Plane/Sketch ⬛. Select the Sketching tab and select Rectangle under Draw from

Sketching Toolboxes. Start at the origin (make sure you see a P when the cursor is at the origin and you are about to start drawing) and draw the rectangle in the first quadrant. Click on Dimensions and click on the lower horizontal edge of the rectangle. Enter a length of 10 mm for the horizontal edge. Click on the right vertical edge of the rectangle. Enter a length of 60 mm for the vertical edge.

Select 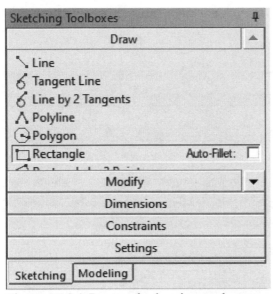 Revolve and apply Sketch1 under XYPlane as Geometry in Details View. Select the left vertical side of the rectangle sketch and apply it as the Axis in Details View. Click on Generate and close DesignModeler.

Figure 17.2a) Rectangle drawing tool

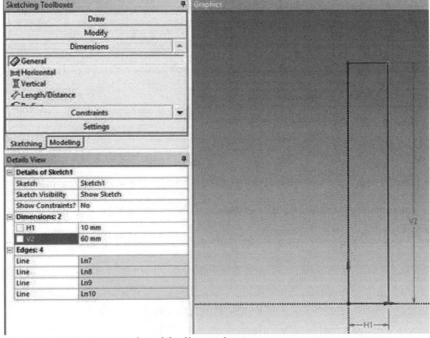

Figure 17.2b) Rectangle with dimensions

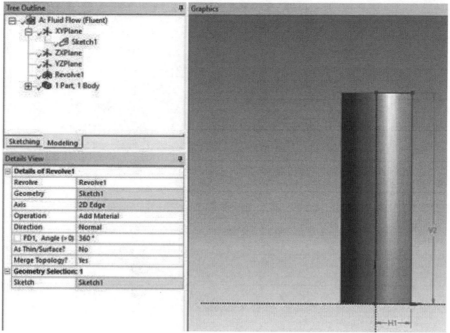

Figure 17.2c) Finished cylinder

## E. Launching ANSYS Meshing

3. Double click on Mesh under Project Schematic in ANSYS Workbench. Click on Mesh in the Outline under Project. Select Home>>Tools>>Units>>Metric (mm, kg, N, …) from the menu. Right click on Mesh under Project in Outline and select Generate Mesh. A coarse mesh is generated.

   Set the Element Size under Defaults in Details of Mesh to 0.4 mm. Right click on Mesh under Project in Outline and select Generate Mesh. Under Statistics in Details of Mesh we can see that this mesh has 524423 Nodes and 510300 Elements.

   Right click in the graphics window and select Cursor Mode>>Face. Control select the three faces of the mesh, right click and select Create Named Selection. Enter the name *wall* and click on OK to close the Selection Name window.

Figure 17.3a) Starting ANSYS Meshing

373

Figure 17.3b) Mesh for cylinder

Select File>>Export…>>Mesh>>FLUENT Input File>>Export from the menu and save the mesh in the *Working Directory* with the name *cylinder-mesh-lambda-0.1.msh*. Select File>>Save Project from the menu and save the project with the name *Cylinder Mesh Falling Sphere Lambda = 0.1.wbpj*. Close the Meshing window and right-click on Mesh under Project Schematic in ANSYS Workbench and select Update.

## F. Launching ANSYS Fluent

4.  Double click on Setup under Project Schematic in ANSYS Workbench. Check the box for Double Precision under Options in the ANSYS Fluent Launcher and set the number of Processes equal to the number of cores of your computer. Take a note of the location of your *Working Directory* under Show More Options as you will need this information later in this chapter. Click on Start to launch Fluent.

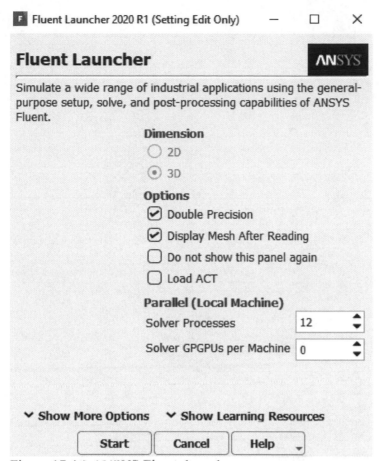

Figure 17.4a) ANSYS Fluent launcher

Enter the following commands in the Console to load the Macroscopic Particle Model (MPM).

>**define**
/define> **models**
/define/models/> **addon**
Enter Module Number: [0] **10**

```
Console
> define

/define> models

/define/models> addon
Fluent Addon Modules:
    0. None
    1. MHD Model
    2. Fiber Model
    3. Fuel Cell and Electrolysis Model
    4. SOFC Model with Unresolved Electrolyte
    5. Population Balance Model
    6. Adjoint Solver
    7. Single-Potential Battery Model
    8. Dual-Potential MSMD Battery Model
    9. PEM Fuel Cell Model
    10. Macroscopic Particle Model
    11. Reduced Order Model
Enter Module Number: [0] 10
```

Figure 17.4b) Console commands to load MPM module

5. Double click on General under Setup in the Outline View and select Transient under Time on the Task Page. Check the box for Gravity and enter -9.8 as the value for Y (m/s2). Click on Scale... under Mesh in General on the Task Page.

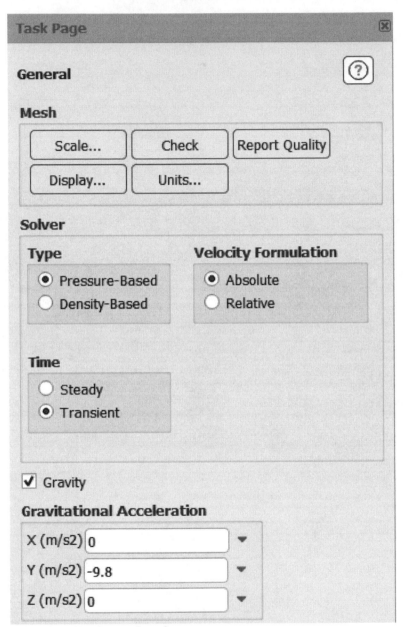

Figure 17.5a) General settings

**Scale Mesh**

**Domain Extents**

| | |
|---|---|
| Xmin (m) -0.01 | Xmax (m) 0.01 |
| Ymin (m) -2.91611e-18 | Ymax (m) 0.06 |
| Zmin (m) -0.009998023 | Zmax (m) 0.009998023 |

Figure 17.5b) Scale mesh

6. Double click on Models and Viscous (SST k-omega) under Setup in the Outline View. Select Laminar Model and click OK to close the Viscous Model window. Double click on Materials under Setup in the Outline View. Click on Create/Edit for Fluid under Materials on the Task Page. Click on Fluent Database in the Create/Edit Materials window. Scroll down and select *water-liquid (h2o<l>)* as the Fluent Fluid Material. Click on Copy and Close the Fluent Database Materials window. Set the Density (kg/m3) to 1020 and Viscosity (kg/m-s) to 0.49. Click on Change/Create and Close the Create/Edit Materials window.

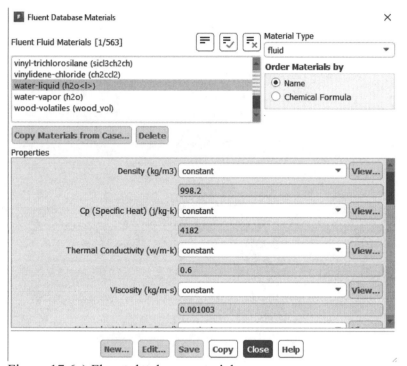

Figure 17.6a) Fluent database materials

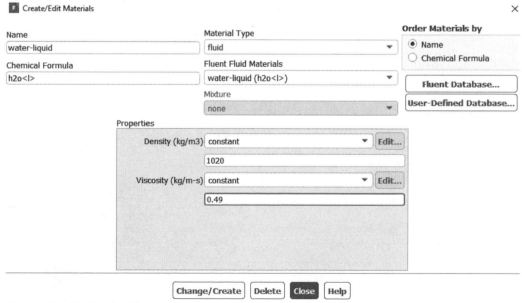

Figure 17.6b) Setting the density and viscosity for the fluid

Open Cell Zone Conditions and Fluid under Setup in the Outline View. Double click on *solid (fluid, id=3)* under Cell Zone Conditions and Fluid in the Outline View. Select *water-liquid* as Material Name and enter *water-liquid* as Zone Name. Check the box for Source Terms and click on the Source Terms tab. Click on Edit for X Momentum. Set Number of X Momentum Sources to 1, select *udf x_mom::mpm* and click OK. Repeat this for Y Momentum, Z Momentum and Mass. Click OK to close the Fluid window.

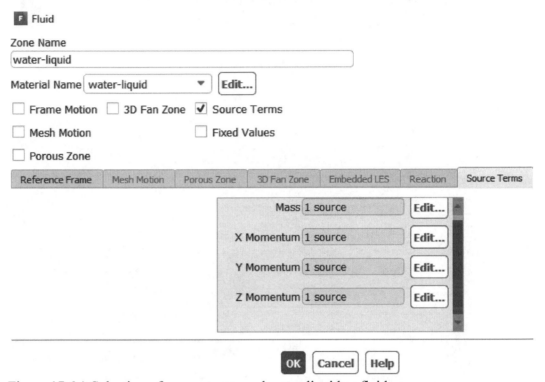

Figure 17.6c) Selection of source terms and water-liquid as fluid

Double click on Models and Macroscopic Particles under Setup in the Outline View and check the box to Enable Macroscopic Particle Model. Select the Particle Tracking tab and check the box for Enable Interaction with Continuous Phase. Set the Particle Sub-Timesteps within each Flow Timestep to 10 and Under-Relaxation Factor to Velocities in Touched Cells to 1. Click on Apply.

Figure 17.6d) Particle tracking

Select the Drag tab and select Momentum Deficit Rate (MDR) under Drag Law Options. Click on Apply.

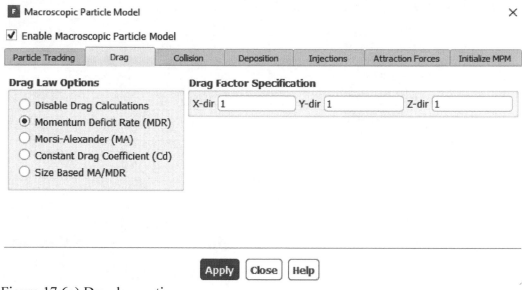

Figure 17.6e) Drag law options

Select the Collision tab and uncheck Enable Particle-Particle Collision and uncheck Enable Particle-Wall Collision. Click on Apply.

Figure 17.6f) Collision options

Select the Injections tab and click on Create. Select *point* as Injection Type. Set the Diameter (m) to 0.002 and set the Density (kg/m3) to 1695. Check the box for Cylindrical Coordinates and select Y as Axis Direction. Enter Axial (m) 0.03 under Initial Location. Click on Create/Modify. Click on Apply.

Figure 17.6g) Injection options

Select the Initialize MPM tab and check the box for ASCII File under Write Particle Data. Click on Browse, enter the file name *sphere-falling-lambda-0p1.csv*, save the file in the *Working Directory* and click on OK. Check the box for Print Warning Messages. Click on Initialize MPM Functions. Click on Initialize Particles. Click on Apply.

Select at the bottom of the graphics window. Select *wall* under Surfaces. Only have the box for Edges checked under Options and select Outline as Edge Type, see Figure 17.6i). Click on Display and Close the Mesh Display window. Click on Apply.

Click on Display Injections. Select Display Particles Colored by Particle Diameter. Click on Display and Close the Display Particles window. Click on Apply and close the Macroscopic Particle Model window.

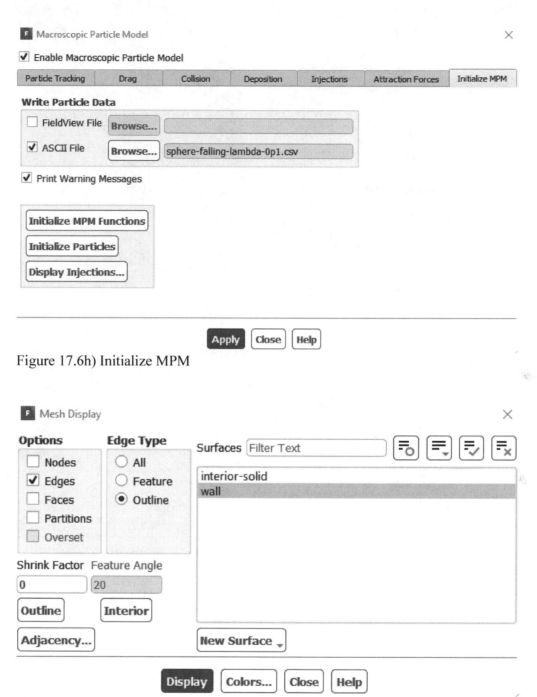

Figure 17.6h) Initialize MPM

Figure 17.6i) Mesh display

Figure 17.6j) Display particles

Figure 17.6k) Sphere in the cylinder

7. Double click on Methods under Solution in the Outline View and select Second Order Implicit as Transient Formulation under Solution Methods on the Task Page. Click on Options. Select Flow Variables Only and set the Relaxation Factor to 0.75. Click OK to close the window.

Figure 17.7a) Solution methods settings

Figure 17.7b) Relaxations

Double click on Monitors and Residual under Setup in the Outline View and check the boxes for Print to Console and Plot under Options. Click on OK to close the Residual Monitors window.

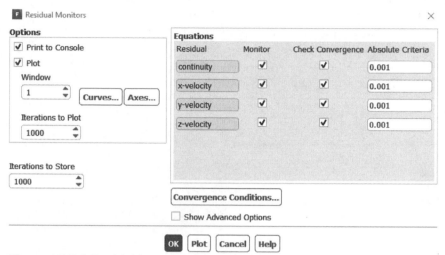

Figure 17.7c) Residual monitors window

8. Double click on Initialization under Solution in the Tree and select Hybrid Initialization. Click on Initialize. Answer OK to the question that you may get.

Figure 17.8 Solution initialization

9. Create a folder in your working directory called *falling-sphere-lambda-0.1-jpg-files*. Double click on Calculation Activities and Execute Commands under Solution in the Outline View. Enter the commands listed below and as shown with settings in Figure 17.9a). You will need to change the second command so that it is in line with the name and location of your *Working Directory*. Click OK to close the window.

(display-mpm-injections 'particle-id 0 20)
dis hard C:/Users/jmatsson/falling-sphere-lambda-0.1-jpg-files/mpm-%t.jpg

Figure 17.9a) Executive commands

Double click on Results>>Graphics>>Particle Tracks in the Outline View. Set the Track Style to *sphere* and Color by Particle Variables… and Particle Diameter. Select *injection-0* under Release from Injections. Click on Attributes under Track Style. Check the Constant box under Options and set the Diameter to 0.002. Click on Apply and Close the window. Check the box for Draw Mesh under Options. Select *wall –solid* as Surfaces. Click on Display and Close the Mesh Display window. Click on Save/Display and Close the Particle Tracks window.

Figure 17.9b) Particle sphere style attributes

Figure 17.9c) Mesh display

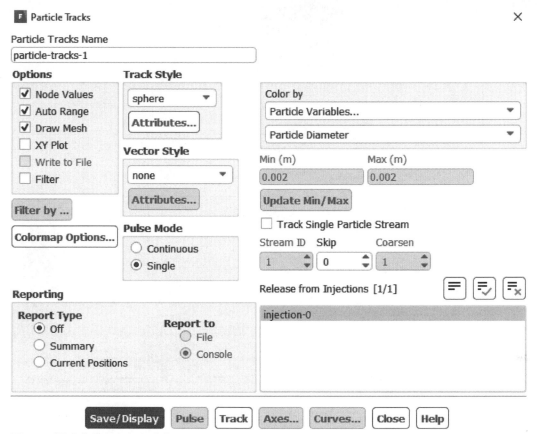

Figure 17.9d) Particle tracks

10. Select  at the bottom of the graphics window and select Post Processing as shown in Figure 17.10a). Select File>>Save Project from the menu. Select File>>Export>>Case & Data from the menu. Save the Case/Data File in the *Working Directory* with the name *falling-sphere-lambda-0.1.cas.gz*.

Double click on Run Calculation under Solution in the Outline View and set the Time Step Size (s) to 2e-5 and Number of Time Steps to 2000. Set Max Iterations/Time Step to 20 and click on Calculate.

Figure 17.10a) Post processing appearance in the graphics window

Figure 17.10b) Running the calculations

## G. Post-Processing

11. Open Excel and open the file *sphere-falling-lambda-0.1.csv*. Copy the first column *A* to column *O*. In position P3, enter "=ABS(G3)" and drag the column downwards to get the absolute *y*-velocity component. Select the data values in columns *O* and *P*. Select from the Excel menu Insert>>Charts>>Scatter with Smooth Lines, see Figures 17.11a) – c).

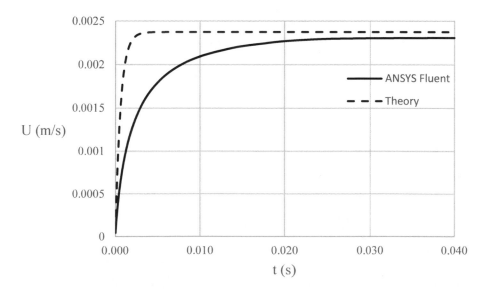

Figure 17.11a) Sphere velocity versus time for $\lambda = 0.1$

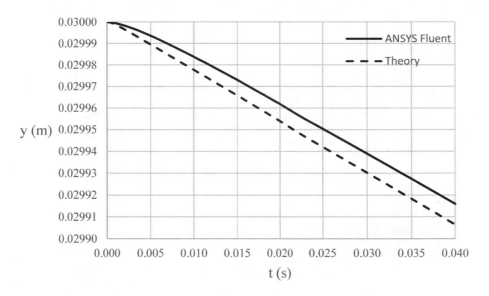

Figure 17.11b) Sphere position versus time for $\lambda = 0.1$

Figure 17.11c) Drag force versus time for $\lambda = 0.1$

| diameter of sphere | $d$ (m) | 0.002 |
|---|---|---|
| diameter of mesh | $D$ (m) | 0.02 |
| diameter ratio | $\lambda = d / D$ | 0.1 |
| height of mesh | $H$ (m) | 0.06 |
| wall factor | $f$ | 0.791576 |
| density of sphere | $\rho_s$ (kg/m3) | 1695 |
| density of fluid | $\rho_f$ (kg/m3) | 1020 |
| dynamic viscosity of fluid | $\mu$ (Pa-s) | 0.49 |
| terminal velocity | $U_\infty$ (m/s) | 0.003 |
| modified terminal velocity | $U = f U_\infty$ (m/s) | 0.002375 |
| terminal drag force | $F_d$ (N) | 0.000277 |
| Reynolds number | $Re$ | 0.009887 |
| upper limit for Reynolds number | $Re_{max}$ | 0.027 |
| terminal dragcoefficient | | 3067 |
| relaxation time | $\tau_\infty$ (s) | 0.001 |
| upper limit for time step size | $\Delta t$ (s) | 0.00002 |
| element size used to create mesh | Element Size (mm) | 0.4 |
| number of nodes for mesh | #Nodes | 524,423 |
| number of elements for mesh | #Elements | 510,300 |
| mesh count | $N$ | 510,300 |
| volume of sphere | $V_s$ (m³) | 4.1888E-09 |
| total volume of mesh | $V_{mesh}$ (m³) | 1.8850E-05 |
| number of cells per particle volume | $N_{CPV}$ (m⁻³) | 113.4 |
| number of cells per particle diameter | $N_{CPD}$ (m⁻¹) | 6.0 |
| modified terminal velocity from ANSYS Fluent | $f U_\infty$ (m/s), Fluent | 0.002309 |
| percent different between ANSYS Fluent and Theory | % Difference | 2.8 |
| wall factor from ANSYS Fluent | $f$, Fluent | 0.77 |
| terminal drag force on sphere ANSYS Fluent | $F_d$ (N) | 2.20E-05 |
| terminal drag coefficient for sphere ANSYS Fluent | $C_d$ | 2576 |

Table 17.1 Parameter values for ANSYS Fluent simulation.

## H. Theory

12. For Stokes flow or creeping flow with Reynolds number $\ll 1$ we can define the terminal velocity $U_\infty$ for a sphere falling in an infinite quiescent Newtonian fluid under the influence of gravity as

$$U_\infty = \frac{(\rho_s - \rho_f) d^2 g}{18 \mu} \qquad (17.1)$$

, where $d\,(m)$ is the diameter of the sphere, $\rho_s$ (kg/m³) is the density of the sphere, $\rho_f$ (kg/m³) is the density of the fluid, $\mu$ (kg/m-s) is the dynamic viscosity of the fluid, and

$g$ (m/s$^2$) is acceleration due to gravity. The relaxation time for an infinite fluid is defined by

$$\tau_\infty = \frac{\left(\rho_s + \frac{\rho_f}{2}\right)d^2}{18\mu} \tag{17.2}$$

The terminal velocity will be reduced by a factor $f$ by the presence of a surrounding cylindrical wall, see Figure 7.12a). Using Newton's second law we get

$$W - F_d - F_b = m\frac{d^2Y}{dt^2} = m\frac{dU}{dt} \tag{17.3}$$

, where $m$ is the mass of the sphere, $W$ is the weight of the sphere, $F_d$ is the drag force on the sphere and $F_b$ is the buoyancy force. Using Stokes law in combination with the wall effect factor, we replace the drag force with $F_d = 3\pi\mu dU/f$. We also use the buoyancy force on the sphere $F_b = \rho_f g V_s$ and the weight of the sphere $W = \rho_s g V_s$ to get

$$\rho_s g V_s - 3\pi\mu dU/f - \rho_f g V_s = m\frac{dU}{dt} \tag{17.4}$$

After expressing the volume of the sphere in terms of the diameter of the sphere we get the following

$$\rho_s g \frac{\pi d^3}{6} - 3\pi\mu dU/f - \rho_f g \frac{\pi d^3}{6} = \rho_s \frac{\pi d^3}{6}\frac{dU}{dt} \tag{17.5}$$

This equation can be rewritten as an ordinary first order differential equation for the velocity of a falling sphere in a cylinder

$$\frac{dU}{dt} + bU/f - a = 0 \tag{17.6}$$

, where $a = g(1 - \rho_f/\rho_s)$ and $b = \frac{18\mu}{\rho_s d^2}$. The solution to equation 17.6 is of the form

$$U = \frac{fa}{b}\left(1 - e^{-bt/f}\right) \tag{17.7}$$

When $t \to \infty$, $U \to fU_\infty = fa/b$, equation 17.7 gives equation 17.1. The location of the sphere can be expressed as

$$y = y_0 + \frac{fa}{b^2}\left[f\left(1 - e^{-bt/f}\right) - bt\right] \tag{17.8}$$

The drag force can now be expressed as

$$F_d = \frac{3\pi\mu dU}{f} = 3\pi\mu d\frac{a}{b}\left(1 - e^{-bt/f}\right) \tag{17.9}$$

When $t \to \infty$, $F_d = \frac{3\pi\mu da}{b} = 3\pi\mu dU_\infty$. The terminal drag coefficient can be expressed as

$$C_d = \frac{F_d}{\frac{1}{2}\rho_f U^2 A} = \frac{3\pi\mu dU}{f\frac{1}{2}\rho_f U^2 \pi d^2/4} = \frac{24\mu}{f\rho_f Ud} = \frac{24}{f Re} \tag{17.10}$$

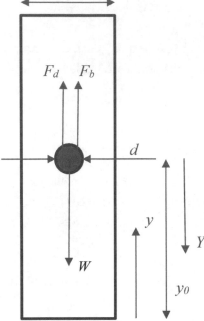

Figure 7.12a) Geometry for falling sphere

The wall factor for very low Reynolds numbers is, according to Haberman and Sayre, (1958)

$$f = \frac{1-2.105\lambda+2.0865\lambda^3-1.7068\lambda^5+0.72603\lambda^6}{1-0.75857\lambda^5} \tag{17.11}$$

, where $\lambda = d/D$ and D is the mesh diameter or inner diameter of the clear glass graduated cylinder. The modified terminal velocity is defined as $U = fU_\infty$. The upper level of the Reynolds number for the Stokes regime and the wall factor is shown versus $\lambda$ in Table 17.2 and Figure 17.12, see Chhabra *et al.* (2003).

| $\lambda$ | $f$ | $Re_{max}$ |
|------|-------|-------|
| 0.1 | 0.792 | 0.027 |
| 0.2 | 0.595 | 0.040 |
| 0.3 | 0.422 | 0.050 |
| 0.4 | 0.279 | 0.083 |
| 0.5 | 0.170 | 0.18 |
| 0.6 | 0.094 | 0.52 |
| 0.7 | 0.047 | 2.10 |
| 0.8 | 0.020 | 8.40 |
| 0.9 | 0.008 | 25.17 |

Table 17.2 Values of wall factor and max Re for different $\lambda$

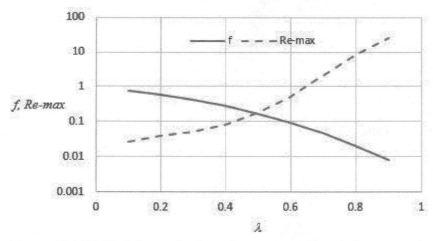

Figure 17.12b) Wall factor $f$ and maximum Reynolds number versus $\lambda$

The Reynolds number is defined as

$$Re = \frac{Ud\rho_f}{\mu} = \frac{fU_\infty d\rho_f}{\mu} \tag{17.12}$$

The time step size used in ANSYS Fluent simulations is described by the following

$$\Delta t = \frac{2\tau_\infty}{100} \tag{17.13}$$

The volume for the spherical particle is given by

$$V_s = \frac{\pi d^3}{6} \tag{17.14}$$

The total volume of the mesh including the volume of the sphere used in ANSYS Fluent simulations

$$V_{mesh} = \frac{\pi H D^2}{4} \tag{17.15}$$

, where $H$ is the height of the mesh. This height needs to be a minimum of $H = 3D$ in the ANSYS Fluent simulations. We can now determine the number of cells per particle volume

$$N_{CPV} = \frac{NV_s}{V_{mesh}} \tag{17.16}$$

, where $N$ is the mesh count or number of elements for the mesh. The number of cells per particle diameter is defined as

$$N_{CPD} = \left(\frac{6N_{CPV}}{\pi}\right)^{\frac{1}{3}} = \left(\frac{6NV_s}{\pi V_{mesh}}\right)^{\frac{1}{3}} \tag{17.17}$$

, and was chosen to be at least 5 in the ANSYS Fluent simulations. The modified terminal velocity will depend on this parameter in simulations.

## I. References

1. Agrawal M., Bakker A. and Prinkey M.T. "Macroscopic particle model – tracking big particles in CFD", *Proceedings of AIChE 2004 Annual Meeting, Austin, TX.*
2. Chhabra R.P., Agarwal S. and Chaudhary K. "A note on wall effect on the terminal falling velocity of a sphere in quiescent Newtonian media in cylindrical tubes", *Powder Technology*, **129**, 53 - 58, (2003).
3. Haberman W.L and Sayre R.M. "David Taylor Model Basin Report No. 1143", *Department of Navy, Washington, DC* (1958).

## J. Exercises

17.1 Run ANSYS Fluent Simulations for $\lambda = 0.1 - 0.9$ as shown in Table 17.3. Fill out the missing results in the table based on your simulations. Use the element size as listed in the table when you create the mesh for each $\lambda$. Change the #Nodes, #Elements and Mesh Count in the table to the values that you get when creating the mesh for each $\lambda$. The value for Mesh Count is equal to the value for #Elements. #Cells/Particle Volume and #Cells/Particle Diameter will need to be recalculated based on your actual values. Plot the modified terminal velocity versus $\lambda$ from ANSYS Fluent simulations and compare with Haberman and Sayre (1958).

| d (m) | 0.002 | 0.004 | 0.006 | 0.008 | 0.01 | 0.012 | 0.014 | 0.016 | 0.018 |
|---|---|---|---|---|---|---|---|---|---|
| D (m) | 0.02 | 0.02 | 0.02 | 0.02 | 0.02 | 0.02 | 0.02 | 0.02 | 0.02 |
| $\lambda = d / D$ | 0.1 | 0.2 | 0.3 | 0.4 | 0.5 | 0.6 | 0.7 | 0.8 | 0.9 |
| H (m) | 0.06 | 0.06 | 0.06 | 0.06 | 0.06 | 0.06 | 0.06 | 0.06 | 0.06 |
| f | 0.79157616 | 0.595336803 | 0.421995126 | 0.279200952 | 0.170357599 | 0.09440553 | 0.046675065 | 0.020398637 | 0.008245803 |
| $\rho_s$(kg/m3) | 1695 | 1695 | 1695 | 1695 | 1695 | 1695 | 1695 | 1695 | 1695 |
| $\rho_f$(kg/m3) | 1020 | 1020 | 1020 | 1020 | 1020 | 1020 | 1020 | 1020 | 1020 |
| $\mu$(Pa-s) | 0.49 | 1.96 | 4.41 | 7.84 | 12.25 | 17.64 | 24.01 | 31.36 | 39.69 |
| $U_\infty$(m/s) | 0.003 | 0.003 | 0.003 | 0.003 | 0.003 | 0.003 | 0.003 | 0.003 | 0.003 |
| $fU_\infty$(m/s) | 0.00237473 | 0.00178601 | 0.001265985 | 0.000837603 | 0.000511073 | 0.000283217 | 0.000140025 | 6.11959E-05 | 2.47374E-05 |
| Re | 0.00988662 | 0.003717818 | 0.001756878 | 0.000871791 | 0.000425546 | 0.000196518 | 8.32803E-05 | 3.18469E-05 | 1.14432E-05 |
| $Re_{max}$ | 0.027 | 0.04 | 0.05 | 0.083 | 0.18 | 0.52 | 2.1 | 8.4 | 25.17 |
| $\tau_\infty$ (s) | 0.001 | 0.001 | 0.001 | 0.001 | 0.001 | 0.001 | 0.001 | 0.001 | 0.001 |
| Time Step Size (s) | 0.00002 | 0.00002 | 0.00002 | 0.00002 | 0.00002 | 0.00002 | 0.00002 | 0.00002 | 0.00002 |
| #Nodes | 346,060 | 47,141 | 13,720 | 6,450 | 3,059 | 1,890 | 1,092 | 980 | 624 |
| #Elements | 335,787 | 44,776 | 12,753 | 5,829 | 2,684 | 1,600 | 840 | 741 | 465 |
| Element Size(mm) | 0.465 | 1.045 | 1.555 | 2.065 | 2.705 | 3.16 | 317 | 320 | 420 |
| Mesh Count | 335,787 | 44,776 | 12,753 | 5,829 | 2,684 | 1,600 | 840 | 741 | 465 |
| Particle Volume (m^3) | 4.1888E-09 | 3.3510E-08 | 1.1310E-07 | 2.6808E-07 | 5.2360E-07 | 9.0478E-07 | 1.4368E-06 | 2.1447E-06 | 3.0536E-06 |
| Total Volume (m^3) | 1.8850E-05 | 1.8850E-05 | 1.8850E-05 | 1.8850E-05 | 1.8850E-05 | 1.8850E-05 | 1.8850E-05 | 1.8850E-05 | 1.8850E-05 |
| #Cells/Particle Volume | 74.62 | 79.60 | 76.52 | 82.90 | 74.56 | 76.80 | 64.03 | 84.31 | 75.33 |
| #Cells/Particle Diameter | 5.2 | 5.3 | 5.3 | 5.4 | 5.2 | 5.3 | 5.0 | 5.4 | 5.2 |
| $fU_\infty$ (m/s), Fluent | | | | | | | | | |
| % Diff | | | | | | | | | |
| f, Fluent | | | | | | | | | |

Table 17.3 Data for $\lambda = 0.1 - 0.9$

17.2 Run ANSYS Fluent Simulations for $\lambda = 0.1$ as shown in Table 17.3 for different values of #Cells/Particle Diameter from 2 – 10. Include a plot of f versus #Cells/Particle Diameter.

# CHAPTER 18. FLOW PAST A SPHERE

## A. Objectives

- Using ANSYS DesignModeler to Model the Sphere
- Inserting Boundary Conditions and Free Stream Velocity
- Running the Calculations
- Using Velocity and Pressure Plots for Visualizations
- Determining the Drag Coefficient

## B. Problem Description

We will study the axisymmetric flow past a sphere, and we will analyze the problem using ANSYS Fluent. A 50 mm diameter sphere will be used and the Reynolds number will be set to $Re = 100$.

## C. Launching ANSYS Workbench and Selecting Fluent

1. Start by launching ANSYS Workbench. Double click on Fluid Flow (Fluent) under Analysis Systems in the Toolbox. Select Units>>Metric (tonne, mm, s, …) from the menu.

Figure 18.1 Selecting Fluent

## D. Launching ANSYS DesignModeler

2. Right click Geometry and select Properties. In Properties of Schematic A2: Geometry, select Analysis Type 2D under Advanced Geometry Options. Right click on Geometry in the Project Schematic window and select New DesignModeler Geometry. Select millimeter as the desired length unit from the menu (Units>>Millimeter).

Select the Sketching tab and click on Arc by Center. Click on Look at Face/Plane/Sketch . Draw in the upper two quadrants a half-circle centered at the origin of the coordinate system in the graphics window. Click on the Dimensions tab and select Radius. Click on the half-circle in the graphics window and enter 25 mm for the radius. Draw a line between the two end points of the half-circle.

Select Concepts>>Surfaces from Sketches from the menu. Control select the half-circle and the line in the graphics window, and select Apply for Base Objects in Details View. Click on Generate.

Figure 18.2a) Arc by center

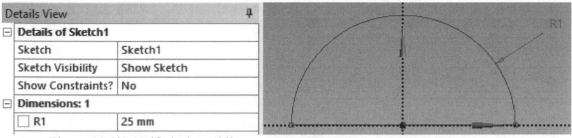

| Details View | 屮 |
|---|---|
| **Details of Sketch1** | |
| Sketch | Sketch1 |
| Sketch Visibility | Show Sketch |
| Show Constraints? | No |
| **Dimensions: 1** | |
| R1 | 25 mm |

Figure 18.2b) Half-circle and line

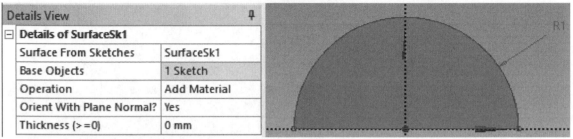

| Details View | 屮 |
|---|---|
| **Details of SurfaceSk1** | |
| Surface From Sketches | SurfaceSk1 |
| Base Objects | 1 Sketch |
| Operation | Add Material |
| Orient With Plane Normal? | Yes |
| Thickness (>=0) | 0 mm |

Figure 18.2c) Finished half-circle

Next, we will be creating the 2D axisymmetric mesh region around the half-sphere. Click on the modeling tab and select the XYPlane in the Tree Outline. Click on ⊡ to generate a new sketch. Select Rectangle by 3 Points from the sketching tools. Click anywhere at the upper left corner of the graphics window, followed by clicking anywhere on the left hand plane on the horizontal axis, and finally click on the right hand plane on the horizontal axis. Select Dimensions, click on Horizontal and click on the vertical edges of the rectangle. Enter 1575 mm as the horizontal length of the rectangle. Click on the vertical axis and the vertical edge of the rectangle on the left hand side. Enter 575 mm as the length. Click on the Vertical dimensioning tool and click on the horizontal edges of the rectangle. Enter 625 mm as the vertical height of the rectangle.

| Details View | 屮 |
|---|---|
| **Details of Sketch2** | |
| Sketch | Sketch2 |
| Sketch Visibility | Show Sketch |
| Show Constraints? | No |
| **Dimensions: 3** | |
| H2 | 1575 mm |
| H3 | 575 mm |
| V4 | 625 mm |

Figure 18.2d) Dimensions for rectangular mesh region around half-sphere

3.  Select Concept>>Surface from Sketches. Click on Sketch2 in the Tree Outline and select Apply for Base Objects in Details View. Select Operation>>Add Frozen in Details View followed by Generate. Select Create>>Boolean from the menu. Select Subtract Operation from the Details View. Click on the mesh region in the graphics window and click on Apply for Target Body. Select the Sphere as the Tool Body and click on Generate.

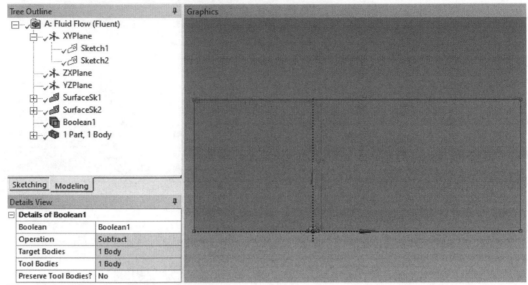

Figure 18.3 Mesh region around sphere

4.  Select XYPlane in the tree outline and create a new sketch ![icon]. Select the Sketching tab and select Line. Draw a vertical line from top to bottom and to the left of the sphere. The vertical line will intersect the entire mesh region. Position the line 75 mm from the vertical axis. Select Concepts>>Lines from Sketches from the menu. Select the newly created vertical line and Apply it as a Base Object in the Details View. Click on Generate.

Create another sketch in the XYPlane with a vertical line 75 mm to the right of the vertical axis and repeat all the different steps as listed above. Repeat these steps one more time with a horizontal line from left to right intersecting the mesh region and positioned 75 mm above the half-sphere centerline.

Figure 18.4a) Lines added to the mesh region

396

Create another sketch in the XYPlane with a vertical line towards the half-sphere as shown in Figure 18.4b). Finally, create the last sketch with two diagonal lines at 45 degrees towards the half-sphere as shown in Figure 18.4b).

Figure 18.4b) Lines added to the mesh region close to the half-sphere

5.  Select Tools>>Projection from the menu. Select Edges on Face as type in Details View. Control-select all 11 line-segments for the 6 lines that you have created and Apply as the Edges in the Details View. Select the mesh region and Apply it as the Target under Details View. Click Generate.

Figure 18.5 Selection of the projection tool

You should now have 9 different regions for meshing. Select File>>Save Project from the menu and save the project with the name "Axisymmetric Sphere Flow Study.wbpj". Close DesignModeler.

## E. Launching ANSYS Meshing

6. Double click on Mesh under Project Schematic in ANSYS Workbench. Click on Mesh in the Outline under Project. Select Home>>Tools>>Units>>Metric (mm, kg, N, …) from the menu. Right click on Mesh under Project in Outline and select Generate Mesh. A coarse mesh is generated.

   Select Mesh under Model (A3) in Project under Outline on the left-hand side. Select the Mesh tab in the menu and Controls>>Face Meshing. Control-select all 9 faces of the mesh. Apply the Geometry under Details of "Face Meshing".

Figure 18.6a) Selection of face meshing

Figure 18.6b) Details of face meshing

   Select Mesh>>Controls>>Sizing from the menu, right-click in the graphics window and select Cursor Mode>>Edge. Control-select the two edges 8 and 19 as shown in Figure 18.6c).

Figure 18.6c) Numbered edges for mesh sizing

Apply the Geometry under Details of "Sizing". Select Number of Divisions as Type under Details of "Sizing". Set the number of Divisions to 100. Set the Behavior to Hard. Select the first Bias Type from the drop-down menu. Enter a Bias Factor of 10.

Figure 18.6d) Details for 1st mesh sizing

Select Mesh Control>>Sizing from the menu. Control-select edges 11 and 22. Apply the Geometry under Details of "Sizing". Select Number of Divisions as Type under Details of "Sizing". Set the number of Divisions to 150. Set the Behavior to Hard. Select the second Bias Type from the drop-down menu. Enter a Bias Factor of 10.

Figure 18.6e) Details for 2nd mesh sizing

Select Mesh Control>>Sizing from the menu. Select edge 1. Apply the Geometry under Details of "Sizing". Select Number of Divisions as Type under Details of "Sizing". Set the number of Divisions to 100. Set the Behavior to Hard. Select the second Bias Type from the drop-down menu. Enter a Bias Factor of 10.

Figure 18.6f) Details for 3rd mesh sizing

Select Mesh Control>>Sizing from the menu. Select edge 3. Apply the Geometry under Details of "Sizing". Select Number of Divisions as Type under Details of "Sizing". Set the number of Divisions to 150. Set the Behavior to Hard. Select the first Bias Type from the drop-down menu. Enter a Bias Factor of 10.

Figure 18.6g) Details for 4th mesh sizing

Select Mesh Control>>Sizing from the menu. Select edge 2. Apply the Geometry under Details of "Sizing". Select Number of Divisions as Type under Details of "Sizing". Set the number of Divisions to 54. Set the Behavior to Hard.

Figure 18.6h) Details for 5th mesh sizing

Select Mesh Control>>Sizing from the menu. Control-select edges 9, 10, 12, 13, 17, 18, and the four parts of the half-circle. Apply the Geometry under Details of "Sizing". Select Number of Divisions as Type under Details of "Sizing". Set the number of Divisions to 27. Set the Behavior to Hard.

Figure 18.6i) Details for 6th mesh sizing

Select Mesh Control>>Sizing from the menu. Control-select the three edges 4, 5, and 6. Apply the Geometry under Details of "Sizing". Select Number of Divisions as Type under Details of "Sizing". Set the number of Divisions to 100. Set the Behavior to Hard. Select the first Bias Type from the drop-down menu. Enter a Bias Factor of 20.

Figure 18.6j) Details for 7th mesh sizing

Select Mesh Control>>Sizing from the menu. Select edge 7. Apply the Geometry under Details of "Sizing". Select Number of Divisions as Type under Details of "Sizing". Set the number of Divisions to 100. Set the Behavior to Hard. Select the second Bias Type from the drop-down menu. Enter a Bias Factor of 20.

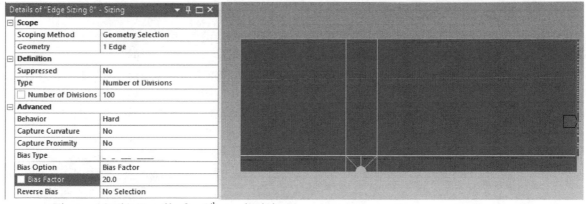

Figure 18.6k) Details for 8th mesh sizing

Select Mesh Control>>Sizing from the menu. Select edges 14, 15, 16, 20, and 21. Apply the Geometry under Details of "Sizing". Select Number of Divisions as Type under Details of "Sizing". Set the number of Divisions to 18. Set the Behavior to Hard.

Figure 18.6l) Details for 9th mesh sizing

Right click on Mesh in the tree outline and select Generate Mesh.

Figure 18.6m) Details of mesh around half-sphere

7. Select geometry in the Outline. Right-click in the graphics window and select Cursor Mode>>Edge. Control select the two vertical edges on the right hand side, right click and select Create Named Selection. Name the edges "outlet" and click OK. Name the two vertical edges to the left "inlet" and the four edges of the sphere with the name "sphere". Name the three horizontal edges at the top "symmetry" and name the four horizontal edges at the bottom "axisymmetry". Export the mesh and save it with the name *flow-past-sphere-mesh.msh*. Open Geometry in the Outline and select Line Body. Right click on Line Body and select Suppress Body. Close the meshing window. Right click on Mesh under Project Schematic in ANSYS Workbench and select Update.

Figure 18.7 Named selections

## F. Launching ANSYS Fluent

8.  Double click on Setup under Project Schematic in ANSYS Workbench. Check the Options box Double Precision. Select Parallel Processing Options and increase the Number of Processes to the same number as computer cores. Click on Show More Options and write down the location of the Working Directory. Click on Start. Select 2D Space Axisymmetric under General on the Task Page.

Figure 18.8a) Launching Fluent

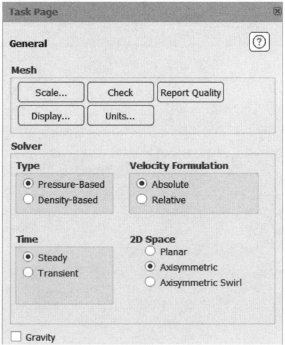

Figure 18.8b) General settings

9. Double click on Models under Setup in the Outline View. Double click on Viscous Model and select Laminar Model. Click on OK to close the Viscous Model window. Double click on Boundary Conditions under Setup in the Outline View. Select the *inlet* Zone under Boundary Conditions on the Task Page. Click on Edit…. Select Components as Velocity Specification Method. Enter 0.02921469 as Axial-Velocity (m/s). This is corresponding to Reynolds number *Re* = 100. Select OK to close the Velocity Inlet window.

Figure 18.9 Velocity inlet settings

10. Double click on Initialization under Solution in the Outline View. Select Standard Initialization. Select Compute from inlet. Click on Initialize. Double click on Reference Values under Setup in the Outline View. Select Compute from inlet and set the reference values for Area (m2) and Length (m) to the values as shown in Figure 18.10b). Set the Reference Zone to *solid-surface_body*.

Figure 18.10a) Solution initialization          Figure 18.10b) Reference values

Double-click on Report Definitions under Solution in the Outline View. Select New>>Force Report>>Lift… from the drop-down menu. Select *sphere* as Wall Zones. Check the boxes for Report File, Report Plot and Print to Console under Create. Enter *lift-report-def* as Name. Click on the OK button to close the Lift Report Definition window. Repeat this step for the Drag and set the Force Vector for X to 1, Y to 0 for the Drag Report Definition. Enter *drag-report-def* as Name. Close the Report Definitions window.

**F** Report Definitions

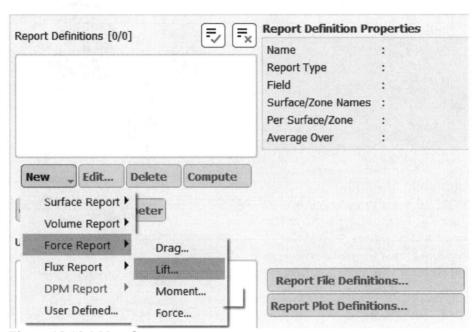

Figure 18.10c) New force report

**F** Lift Report Definition

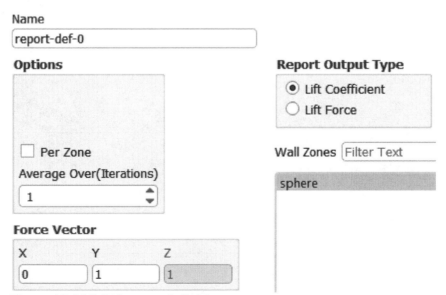

Figure 18.10d) Lift report definition

11. Double click on Monitors and Residual under Solution in the Outline View. Check the boxes for Print to Console and Plot. Set all three Absolute Criteria to 1e-12. Click on OK to exit the Residual Monitors window.

Figure 18.11 Residual monitors

Double click on Run Calculation under Solution in the Outline View. Enter 300 for the Number of Iterations and click on Calculate.

## G. Post-Processing

12. The value of the drag coefficient at $Re = 100$ for the first coarse mesh is $C_d = 1.08922$.

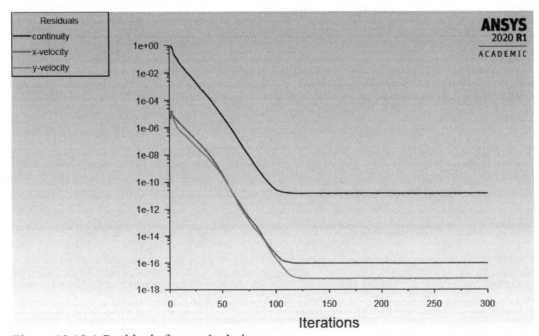

Figure 18.12a) Residuals from calculations

Double-click on Contours in Graphics under Results in the Outline View. Enter *static-pressure* as Contour Name in the Contours window. Select Contours of Pressure… and Static Pressure. Check the box Filled under Options. Deselect all Surfaces and click on Save/Display.

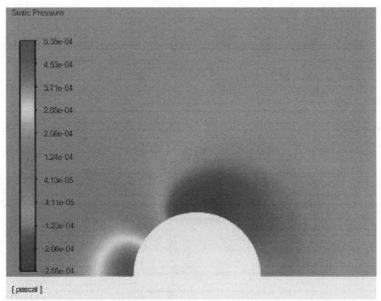

Figure 18.12b) Contours plot for static pressure

Select Contours of Velocity and Axial Velocity. Enter *axial-velocity* as Contour Name in the Contours window. Check the box Filled under Options. Deselect all surfaces and click on Save/Display.

Figure 18.12c) Contours plot for axial velocity

Find the coefficient of drag by double-clicking on Reports under Results in the Outline View. Double-click on Forces under Reports. Click Print and write down the value for the total drag coefficient that you have calculated: 1.0892219.

13. Select the Domain tab in the menu. Select Adapt>>Refine / Coarsen under the Domain tab from the menu. Select Cell Registers>>New>>Region in the Adaption Controls window and enter -0.575 for X Min (m), 1 for X Max (m), 0 for Y Min (m), and 0.625 for Y Max (m). Select Save and Close the Region Register window. Select *region_0* as Refinement Criterion in the Adaption Controls window and click on Adapt. This increases the number of cells by a factor of 4 from 39,094 to 156,376 cells. Select OK to close the Adaption Controls window. Select File>>Export>>Case & Data… from the menu. Save the file in the Working Directory with the name "Axisymmetric Coarse Mesh Flow Past a Sphere at Re = 100.cas".

18.13a) Adaption controls window

18.13b) Region register

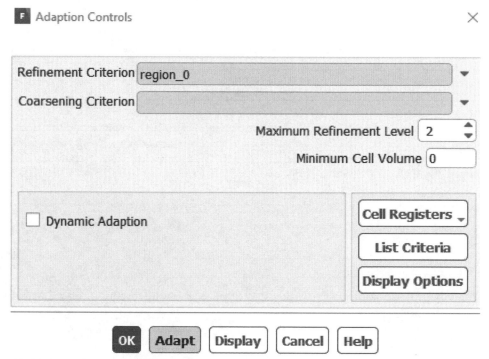

18.13c) Region_0 as refinement criterion

Initialize the flow and run the calculations once again for this new medium mesh. Enter 300 for the Number of Iterations and click on Calculate. The value of the drag coefficient at $Re = 100$ for the medium mesh is $C_d = 1.0955586$.

| Number of Cells | $C_{d, Fluent}$ | $C_{d, Experiment}$ |
|---|---|---|
| 39,094 | 1.0892 | 1.1855 |
| 156,376 | 1.0956 | 1.1855 |

Table 18.1 Drag coefficient before and after refinement of mesh

## H. Theory

14. The drag coefficient from experiments for a smooth sphere is found using the following curve-fit formula:

$$C_{D,Exp} = \frac{24}{Re} + \frac{6}{1+Re^{1/2}} + 0.4 \qquad 0 \le Re \le 200{,}000 \qquad (18.1)$$

We determine the Reynolds number for the flow around the sphere that is defined as

$$Re = Ud/v = 0.02921469 * 0.05 / 1.46 * 10^{-5} = 100 \qquad (18.2)$$

, where $U$ is the magnitude of the free stream velocity, $d$ is the diameter of the sphere, and $v$ is the kinematic viscosity of air at room temperature. The difference between ANSYS Fluent and experiments for the drag coefficient is 7.6%.

## I. References

1. Clift, R., Grace, J.R. and Weber, M.E. "Bubbles, Drops and Particles", Academic Press, New York, (1978).
2. Jones, D.A. and Clarke, D.B. "Simulation of Flow Past a Sphere using the Fluent Code", Australian Government Department of Defence, Defence Science and Technology Organisation, Maritime Platforms Division, DSTO-TR-2232, (2008).
3. Roos, F.W. and Willmarth, W.W. "Some Experimental Results on Sphere and Disk Drag", AIAA Journal, **9**(2), 285-291, (1971).
4. Tabata, M. and Itakura, K., "A Precise Computation of Drag Coefficients of a Sphere", Int. J. Comput. Fluid Dynam. **9**, 303, (1998).

## J. Exercises

18.1 Run ANSYS Fluent Simulations for $Re = 20, 40, 60, 80, 100, 120, 140, 160, 180$ and 200 and compare your results with equation (18.1). Include a plot of drag coefficient versus Reynolds number in this range.

# CHAPTER 19. TAYLOR-COUETTE FLOW

## A. Objectives

- Using ANSYS Meshing to Create the Mesh for 3D Taylor-Couette Flow
- Inserting Wall Boundary Conditions for Rotating Inner Wall
- Running Laminar Steady 3D ANSYS Fluent Simulations
- Using Contour Plots for Visualizations
- Compare Results with Neutral Stability Theory

## B. Problem Description

We will study the flow between two vertical cylinders where the inner wall is rotating at 1.5 rad/s. The inner and outer cylinders have radii of 30 mm and 35 mm, respectively. The height of both cylinders is 100 mm. The centrifugal instability will cause the appearance of counter-rotating vortices at low rotation speeds for the inner wall with a fixed outer wall.

## C. Launching ANSYS Workbench and Selecting Fluent

1.  Start by launching ANSYS Workbench. Double click on Fluid Flow (Fluent) under Analysis Systems in the Toolbox. Select Units>>Metric (tonne, mm, s, …) from the menu.

Figure 19.1 Selecting Fluent

## D. Launching ANSYS DesignModeler

2.  Right click on Geometry in the Project Schematic window and select New DesignModeler Geometry. Select millimeter as the desired length unit from the menu (Units>>Millimeter) in DesignModeler. Select the ZX Plane in the Tree Outline and select Look at Face/Plane/Sketch ⬚. Select the Sketching tab and click on Circle. Draw two circles centered at the origin. Make sure that you see a P next to the cursor before you start drawing the circles from the origin. Click on the Dimensions tab and select Radius. Click on the circles in the graphics window and enter 30 mm and 35 mm for the radii of the circles in Details View.

Figure 19.2a) Circle sketch tool

Figure 19.2b) Dimensions for circles

Select 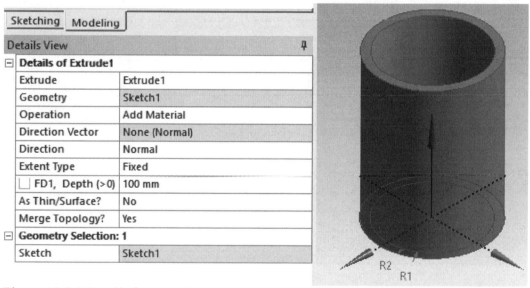Extrude and apply Sketch1 under ZXPlane in the Tree Outline as Geometry in Details View. Enter 100 mm as the FD1, Depth (>0) of the extrusion. Click on Generate and select isometric view in the graphics window. Close the DesignModeler.

Figure 19.2c) Details for extrusion

## E. Launching ANSYS Meshing

3. Double click on Mesh under Project Schematic in ANSYS Workbench. Click on Mesh in the Outline under Project. Select Home>>Tools>>Units>>Metric (mm, kg, N, …) from the menu. Right click on Mesh under Project in Outline and select Generate Mesh. A coarse mesh is generated.

   Set the Element Size under Defaults in Details of Mesh to 0.65 mm. Right click on Mesh under Project in Outline and select Generate Mesh. Under Statistics in Details of Mesh we can see that this mesh has 449190 Nodes and 397936 Elements.

   Right click in the graphics window and select Cursor Mode>>Face. Select the outer cylindrical face, right click and select Create Named Selection. Enter the name *wall_outer* and click on OK to close the Selection Name window. Repeat this for the inner cylindrical face with the name *wall_inner*, the bottom face named *wall_bottom* and the top face named *wall_top*.

Figure 19.3a) Details for Taylor-Couette mesh

Figure 19.3b) Details for named selections

414

Select File>>Export…>>Mesh>>FLUENT Input File>>Export from the menu and save the mesh in the *Working Directory* with the name *cylinder-mesh-taylor-couette-flow.msh*. Select File>>Save Project from the menu and save the project with the name *Taylor-Couette.wbpj*. Close the Meshing window and right-click on Mesh under Project Schematic in ANSYS Workbench and select Update.

## F. Launching ANSYS Fluent

4. Double click on Setup under Project Schematic in ANSYS Workbench. Check the Options box Double Precision. Select Parallel Processing Options and increase the Number of Processes to the same number as computer cores. Click on Start.

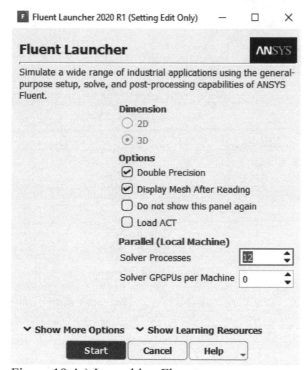

Figure 19.4a) Launching Fluent

Click on Check and Scale… under Mesh in General on the Task Page to verify the Domain Extents. Close the Scale Mesh window. Select Relative Velocity Formulation. Check the box for Gravity. Enter -9.81 as Gravitational Acceleration in the Y direction. Double click on Models and Viscous (SST k-omega) under Setup in the Outline View. Select Laminar as Viscous Model and click OK to close the window.

Figure 19.4b) Domain extents for Taylor-Couette flow mesh

**Task Page**

**General**

**Mesh**

Scale... | Check | Report Quality

Display... | Units...

**Solver**

**Type**
- ● Pressure-Based
- ○ Density-Based

**Velocity Formulation**
- ○ Absolute
- ● Relative

**Time**
- ● Steady
- ○ Transient

✔ Gravity

**Gravitational Acceleration**

X (m/s2) 0

Y (m/s2) -9.81

Z (m/s2) 0

Figure 19.4c) General settings

Double click on Materials under Setup in the Outline View. Click on Create/Edit for Fluid under Materials on the Task Page. Click on Fluent Database in the Create/Edit Materials window. Scroll down and select *water-liquid (h2o<l>)* as the Fluent Fluid Material. Click on Copy and Close the Fluent Database Materials window. Click on Change/Create and Close the Create/Edit Materials window.

**F** Fluent Database Materials                                          ✕

Fluent Fluid Materials [1/563]

Material Type
fluid

vinyl-trichlorosilane (sicl3ch2ch)
vinylidene-chloride (ch2ccl2)
water-liquid (h2o<l>)
water-vapor (h2o)
wood-volatiles (wood_vol)

**Order Materials by**
- ● Name
- ○ Chemical Formula

Figure 19.4d) Selection of water-liquid as fluid

416

5. Open Cell Zone Conditions and Fluid under Setup in the Outline View. Double click on *solid (fluid, id=2)* under Cell Zone Conditions. Select *water-liquid* as Material Name. Check the box for Frame Motion and enter Speed (rad/s) -1.5 as Rotational Velocity. Set the Rotation-Axis Direction as X 0, Y 1, Z 0. Click OK to close the Fluid window.

Figure 19.5a) Selection of water-liquid as fluid and setting for rotational velocity

Double click on Boundary Conditions. Select *wall_inner* under Zone in Boundary Conditions on the Task Page. Click on the Edit… button for wall Type. Select *Moving Wall* under Wall Motion. Check Absolute and Rotational under Motion and enter 1.5 as Speed (rad/s). Set the Rotation-Axis Direction as X 0, Y 1, Z 0, see Figure 19.5b). Click OK to close the window. Repeat this step for the *wall_outer* Zone, use Absolute and Rotational Motion, enter 0 as Speed (rad/s) and set the Rotation-Axis Direction as X 0, Y 1, Z 0, see Figure 19.5b). Do the same for the top and bottom walls, see Figure 19.5b).

Figure 19.5b) Details of wall motion for inner wall, outer wall, top wall and bottom wall

6.  Double click on Initialization under Solution in the Outline View and select Hybrid Initialization. Click on Initialize. Double click on Run Calculation under Solution in the Outline View. Enter 1000 for the Number of Iterations and click on Calculate.

Figure 19.6 Solution initialization

## G. Post-Processing

7.  The residuals are shown in Figure 19.7a). Double-click on Contours in Graphics under Results in the Outline View. Enter *y-velocity* as Contour Name in the Contours window. Select Contours of Velocity... and Y Velocity. Check the box Filled under Options. Uncheck Node Values under Options. Select all Surfaces and click on Save/Display. Select the red X coordinate axis in the graphics window.

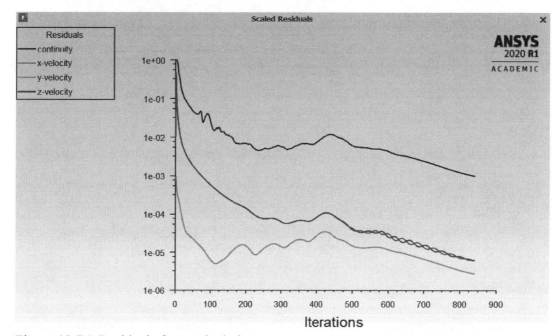

Figure 19.7a) Residuals from calculations

Figure 19.7b) Contours settings

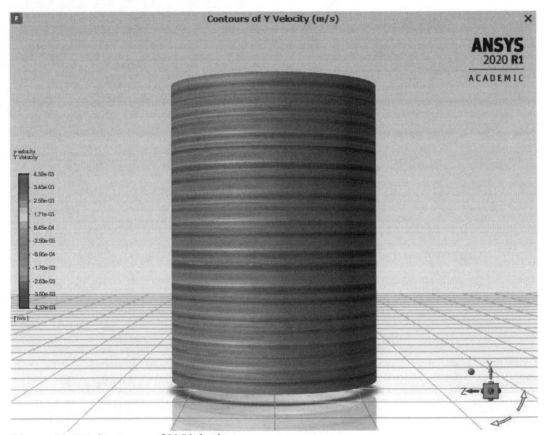

Figure 19.7c) Contours of Y Velocity

## H. Theory

8.  The instability of the flow between two vertical rotating cylinders is governed by the so called Taylor number $Ta$.

$$Ta = \frac{4\Omega_i^2 d^4}{\nu^2} \tag{19.1}$$

where $\Omega_i$ is the rotation rate of the inner cylinder, $d$ is the distance between the cylinders and $\nu$ is the kinematic viscosity of the fluid. Below the critical $Ta_{crit} = 3430$ for a non-rotating outer cylinder, the flow is stable, but instabilities will develop above this Taylor number. The non-dimensional wave number $\alpha$ of the centrifugal instability is determined by

$$\alpha = \frac{2\pi d}{\lambda} \tag{19.2}$$

where $\lambda$ is the spanwise wave length of the instability. The critical wave numbers $\alpha_{crit} = 3.12$ in the narrow gap limit: $\eta \to 1$. The radius ratio is defined as $\eta = r_i/r_o$ where $r_i$ and $r_o$ is the radius of the inner and outer cylinders, respectively. From figure 19.7c), the wave number can be determined to be

$$\alpha = \frac{2\pi \cdot 0.005}{0.008957} = 3.51 \tag{19.3}$$

In order to determine the wave length that is used to determine the wave number in equation (19.3), you can measure the total length in the vertical spanwise direction for twelve red or twelve blue successive bands in figure 19.7c). Next, you take this vertical length and divide by twelve to get the average wave length in the vertical spanwise direction. To get the scale for figure 19.7c), use the total height of the cylinder in the vertical direction in figure 19.7c) that corresponds to the 100 mm height of the cylinder.

The Taylor number in ANSYS Fluent simulations is

$$Ta = \frac{4 \cdot 1.5^2 \cdot 0.005^4}{(1.004 \cdot 10^{-6})^2} = 5580 \tag{19.4}$$

The neutral stability curve can be given to the first approximation, see figure 19.8.

$$Ta = \frac{2\left(\pi^2 + \alpha^2\right)^3}{(1+\mu)\alpha^2 \left\{ 1 - \dfrac{16\alpha\pi^2 \cosh^2\left(\frac{\alpha}{2}\right)}{\left[\left(\pi^2 + \alpha^2\right)^2 (\sinh \alpha + \alpha)\right]} \right\}} \tag{19.5}$$

where $\mu = \Omega_o/\Omega_i$ and $\Omega_o$ is the rotation rate of the outer cylinder.

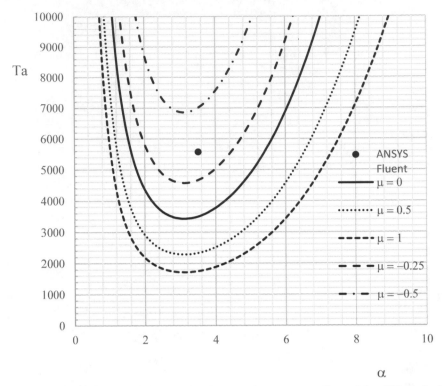

Figure 19.8 Neutral stability curves for Taylor-Couette flow. The filled circle represents result from ANSYS Fluent. The radius ratio is $\eta = \frac{6}{7}$ and $\mu = 0$ in ANSYS Fluent simulations and $\eta = 1$ for the stability curves.

## I. References

1. Chandrasekhar, S., Hydrodynamic and Hydromagnetic Stability, Dover, 1981.
2. Koschmieder, E.L., Benard Cells and Taylor Vortices, Cambridge, 1993.
3. Matsson, J.E, On the Integration of Fluid Flows and Fabrication, *Proceedings of the 2002 American Society for Engineering Education Annual Conference & Exposition.*, Montreal, Canada, (2002).
4. Taylor, G.I., Stability of a Viscous Liquid Contained between Two Rotating Cylinders, *Phil. Trans. Roy. Soc.* London Ser. A, Vol. **223**, (1923).

## J. Exercises

19.1 Run the calculations for the flow in the Taylor-Couette apparatus with only the inner cylinder rotating $\mu = 0$ for Taylor numbers $Ta = 10000$, $20000$ and $30000$ and compare the spanwise wave numbers with the one determined in this chapter for $Ta = 5580$. Include your results in figure 19.8 for comparison with the neutral stability curve.

19.2 Run the calculations for the flow in the Taylor-Couette apparatus with both cylinders rotating $\mu = 1$ and for Taylor numbers $Ta = 3000$, $5000$ and $10000$ and determine the spanwise wave numbers. Include your results in a graph and compare with the neutral stability curve corresponding to $\mu = -1/2$, see equation (19.5).

## CHAPTER 20. DEAN FLOW IN A CURVED CHANNEL

### A. Objectives

- Using ANSYS Meshing to Create the Mesh for 3D Dean Flow in a Curved Channel
- Inserting Wall Boundary Conditions
- Running Laminar Steady 3D ANSYS Fluent Simulations
- Using Contour Plots for Visualizations
- Compare Results with Neutral Stability Theory

### B. Problem Description

Dean flow appears in a curved tube but can also be realized in a narrow gap curved channel. We will therefore study the flow between two curved walls where the inner wall has a radius of 395 mm and the radius of the outer wall is 405 mm. The height of the curved channel is 100 mm. The centrifugal instability will cause the appearance of counter-rotating vortices at low flow rates.

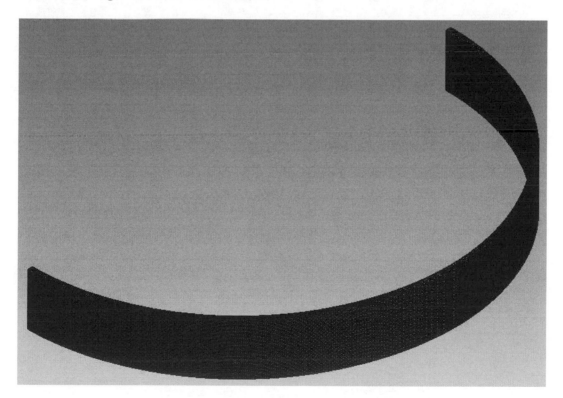

## C. Launching ANSYS Workbench and Selecting Fluent

1. Start by launching ANSYS Workbench. Double click on Fluid Flow (Fluent) under Analysis Systems in the Toolbox. Select Units>>Metric (tonne, mm, s, …) from the menu.

Figure 20.1 Selecting Fluent

## D. Launching ANSYS DesignModeler

2. Right click on Geometry in the Project Schematic window and select New DesignModeler Geometry. Select millimeter as the desired length unit from the menu (Units>>Millimeter) in DesignModeler. Select the ZX Plane in the Tree Outline and select Look at Face/Plane/Sketch ⟦⟧. Select the Sketching tab and click on Arc by Center. Draw two 180 degrees half-circle arcs centered at the origin. Click on the Dimensions tab and select Radius. Click on the arcs in the graphics window and enter 395 mm and 405 mm for the radii of the circles in Details View. Select the Line sketch tool and draw two horizontal lines that connects the ends of the arcs.

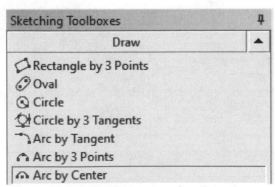

Figure 20.2a) Arc by center sketch tool

424

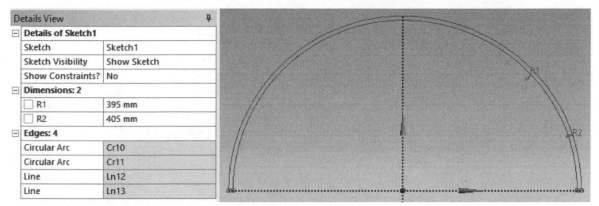

Figure 20.2b) Dimensions for half-circles

Select 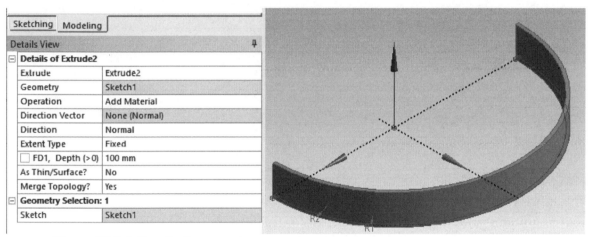 Extrude and apply Sketch1 under ZXPlane in the Tree Outline as Geometry in Details View. Enter 100 mm as the FD1, Depth (>0) of the extrusion. Click on Generate and select isometric view in the graphics window. Close the DesignModeler.

Figure 20.2c) Details for extrusion

## E. Launching ANSYS Meshing

3.  Double click on Mesh under Project Schematic in ANSYS Workbench. Click on Mesh in the Outline under Project. Select Home>>Tools>>Units>>Metric (mm, kg, N, …) from the menu. Right click on Mesh under Project in Outline and select Generate Mesh. A coarse mesh is generated.

    Set the Element Size under Defaults in Details of Mesh to 1.4 mm. Right click on Mesh under Project in Outline and select Generate Mesh. Under Statistics in Details of Mesh we can see that this mesh has 517824 Nodes and 446306 Elements.

    Right click in the graphics window and select Cursor Mode>>Face. Control select the outer cylindrical face, inner cylindrical face, top curved face and bottom curved face, right click and select Create Named Selection. Enter the name *wall* and click on OK to close the Selection Name window. Select the flat inlet face and name it *inlet* and select the flat outlet face and name it *outlet*.

Figure 20.3a) Details for curved channel mesh

Figure 20.3b) Details for named selections

Select File>>Export…>>Mesh>>FLUENT Input File>>Export from the menu and save the mesh in the *Working Directory* with the name *curved-channel-mesh-dean-flow.msh*. Select File>>Save Project from the menu and save the project with the name *Dean Flow in Curved Narrow Channel.wbpj*. Close the Meshing window and right-click on Mesh under Project Schematic in ANSYS Workbench and select Update.

## F. Launching ANSYS Fluent

4. Double click on Setup under Project Schematic in ANSYS Workbench. Check the Options box Double Precision. Set the Number of Parallel Processes to the same number as computer cores. Click on Start.

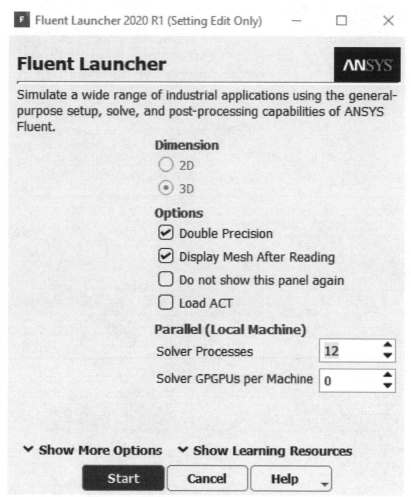

Figure 20.4a) Launching Fluent

Click on Check and Scale… under Mesh in General on the Task Page to verify the Domain Extents. Close the Scale Mesh window. Check the box for Gravity. Enter -9.81 as Gravitational Acceleration in the Y direction. Double click on Models and Viscous (SST k-omega) under Setup in the Outline View. Select Laminar as Viscous Model and click OK to close the window.

**F** Scale Mesh

**Domain Extents**

| | | | |
|---|---|---|---|
| Xmin (m) | 0 | Xmax (m) | 0.405 |
| Ymin (m) | 0 | Ymax (m) | 0.1 |
| Zmin (m) | -0.405 | Zmax (m) | 0.405 |

Figure 20.4b) Domain extents for curved channel flow mesh

427

Figure 20.4c) General settings including gravity

Double click on Materials under Setup in the Outline View. Click on Create/Edit for Fluid under Materials on the Task Page. Click on Fluent Database in the Create/Edit Materials window. Scroll down and select *water-liquid (h2o<l>)* as the Fluent Fluid Material. Click on Copy and Close the Fluent Database Materials window. Click on Change/Create and Close the Create/Edit Materials window.

Figure 20.4d) Selection of water-liquid as fluid

5. Open Cell Zone Conditions and Fluid under Setup in the Outline View. Double click on *solid (fluid, id=2)* under Cell Zone Conditions. Select *water-liquid* as Material Name and enter *water-liquid* as the Zone Name. Click OK to close the Fluid window.

Figure 20.5a) Selection of water-liquid as fluid

Double click on Boundary Conditions. Select *inlet* under Zone in Boundary Conditions on the Task Page. Click on the Edit... button for velocity-inlet Type. Select *Components* as Velocity Specification Method. Select Local Cylindrical (Radial, Tangential, Axial) as Coordinate System. Enter 0.05 as Tangential-Velocity (m/s). Enter X 0, Y 1 and Z 0 as Axis Direction, see figure 20.5b). Select OK to close the Velocity Inlet window.

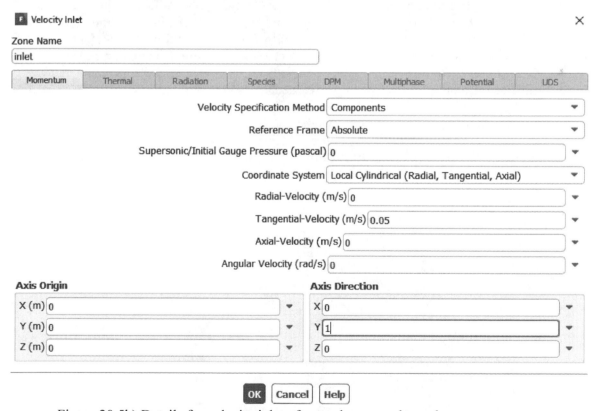

Figure 20.5b) Details for velocity inlet of curved narrow channel

6. Double click on Initialization under Solution in the Outline View and select Hybrid Initialization. Click on Initialize. Double click on Residual under Solution and Monitors in the Outline View. Set the Absolute Criteria to 1e-12 for all Equations. Double click on Run Calculation under Solution in the Outline View. Enter 650 for the Number of Iterations and click on Calculate.

Figure 20.6 Solution initialization

## G. Post-Processing

7. The residuals are shown in Figure 20.7a). Double-click on Contours in Graphics under Results in the Outline View. Enter *y-velocity* as Contour Name in the Contours window. Select Contours of Velocity… and Y Velocity. Check the box Filled under Options. Uncheck Node Values under Options. Select all Surfaces and click on Save/Display. Select the X-Y coordinate system in the graphics window. Select the View tab in the menu and Lights… under Graphics. Set the Direction of the Light to X 0, Y 0, Z -1. Click on Apply and Close the Lights window. Select the Colormap Options… in the Contours window. Select Top as Colormap Alignment, click on Apply and Close the Colormap window. In Figure 20.7c), you can see 4 distinct streaks in the middle of the channel. The streaks indicate the presence of streamwise counter rotating vortices with a wavelength in the spanwise Y direction that can be determined from the figure.

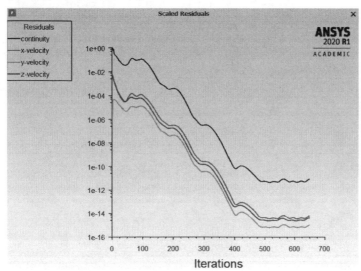

Figure 20.7a) Residuals from calculations

Figure 20.7b) Contours settings

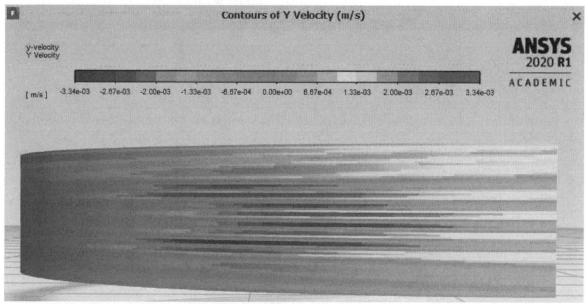

Figure 20.7c) Contours of Y Velocity

## H. Theory

8. The centrifugal instability for the flow in a curved channel is governed by the so called Dean number $De$.

$$De = Re\sqrt{\gamma} = \frac{U_b d}{v}\sqrt{\frac{d}{R}} \tag{20.1}$$

where $U_b$ is the bulk flow velocity in the curved channel, $d$ is the channel width, $R$ its radius of curvature at the channel centerline and $v$ is the kinematic viscosity of the fluid. Below the critical $De_{crit} = 36$, the flow is stable, but instabilities will develop above this Dean number[1,2]. The non-dimensional wave number $\alpha$ of the centrifugal instability is determined by

$$\alpha = \frac{2\pi d}{\lambda} \tag{20.2}$$

where $\lambda$ is the spanwise wave length of the instability. The critical wave numbers $\alpha_{crit} = 3.96$. From figure 20.7c), the wave number can be determined to be

$$\alpha = \frac{2\pi \cdot 0.010}{0.0128} = 4.9 \tag{20.3}$$

In order to determine the wave length that is used to determine the wave number in equation (20.3), you can measure the total length in the vertical spanwise direction for three red or three blue successive bands in figure 20.7c). Next, you take this vertical length and divide by three to get the average wave length in the vertical spanwise direction. To get the scale for figure 20.7c), use the total height of the curved channel in the vertical direction in figure 20.7c) that corresponds to 100 mm height.

The Dean number in the ANSYS Fluent simulations is

$$De = Re\sqrt{\gamma} = \frac{0.05*0.01}{10^{-6}}\sqrt{\frac{0.01}{0.4}} = 79 \tag{20.4}$$

The neutral stability curve can be given to the first approximation[4], see figure 20.8.

$$De = \frac{1}{6\alpha}\left[\frac{(\pi^2+\alpha^2)(4\pi^2+\alpha^2)}{(A-B-C)(D+E-F)}\right]^{1/4} \tag{20.5}$$

where

$$A = \frac{2(640-48\pi^2)}{27\pi^4(\alpha^2+\pi^2)^2} + \frac{64(9\pi^2-56)}{27\pi^2(\alpha^2+\pi^2)^3} - \frac{256(\alpha^2-5\pi^2)}{9\pi^2(\alpha^2+\pi^2)^4} \tag{20.6}$$

$$B = \frac{64\pi^2\left[16\alpha\pi^6+24\alpha\pi^4(\alpha^2+3)+\alpha^3\pi^2(9\alpha^2-38)+\alpha^5(\alpha^2-2)\right]}{(\alpha^2+4\pi^2)^3(\alpha^2+\pi^2)^4(\sinh\alpha+\alpha)} \tag{20.7}$$

$$C = \frac{64\pi^2\{(24\pi^4-34\alpha^2\pi^2-22\alpha^4)\alpha\cosh\alpha+\left[16\pi^4(\pi^2+3)+4\alpha^2\pi^2(8\pi^2-21)+\alpha^4(19\pi^2+36)+3\alpha^6\right]\sinh\alpha\}}{(\alpha^2+4\pi^2)^3(\alpha^2+\pi^2)^4(\sinh\alpha+\alpha)} \tag{20.8}$$

$$D = \frac{2(640-48\pi^2)}{27\pi^4(\alpha^2+4\pi^2)^2} - \frac{64(9\pi^2-104)}{27\pi^2(\alpha^2+4\pi^2)^3} - \frac{256(\alpha^2-20\pi^2)}{9\pi^2(\alpha^2+4\pi^2)^4} \tag{20.9}$$

$$E = \frac{64\pi^2\left[4\alpha\pi^6+9\alpha\pi^4(\alpha^2+8)+2\alpha^3\pi^2(3\alpha^2+59)+\alpha^5(\alpha^2-2)\right]}{(\alpha^2+4\pi^2)^4(\alpha^2+\pi^2)^3(\sinh\alpha-\alpha)} \qquad (20.10)$$

$$F = \frac{64\alpha\pi^2\left\{(24\pi^4-46\alpha^2\pi^2-22\alpha^4)\,\alpha\cosh\alpha+\left[4\pi^4(\pi^2+12)+\alpha^2\pi^2(17\pi^2-156)+4\alpha^4(4\pi^2+9)+3\alpha^6\right]\sinh\alpha\right\}}{(\alpha^2+4\pi^2)^4(\alpha^2+\pi^2)^3(\sinh\alpha-\alpha)} \qquad (20.11)$$

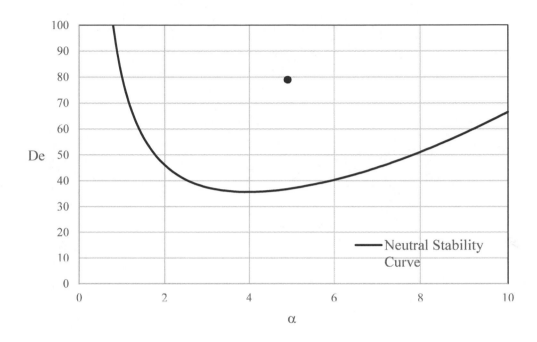

Figure 20.8 Neutral stability curve for Dean flow in a curved channel. The filled circle represents result from ANSYS Fluent.

## I. References

1. Chandrasekhar, S., Hydrodynamic and Hydromagnetic Stability, Dover, 1981.
2. Dean, W.R., Fluid motion in a curved channel. *Proc. Roy. Soc.* A**121**, 402, 1928.
3. Matsson, J.E. and Alfredsson, P.H., Curvature- and rotation induced instabilities in channel flow. *J. Fluid Mech.* **210**, 537, (1990).
4. Reid, W.H., On the stability of viscous flow in a curved channel. Proc. Roy. Soc. A, **244**, 1237, (1958).

## J. Exercises

20.1 Run the calculations for the flow in the curved channel but use the following tangential velocities: 0.03, 0.06, 0.09 and 0.12 m/s and determine the Dean number and the spanwise wave number for each tangential velocity.

20.2 Run the calculations for the flow in the curved channel as shown in this chapter for different mesh sizes using Element Size 1.6, 1.8, 2.0 and 2.2 mm. Determine the spanwise wave number for each case and compare with the critical value.

**K. Notes**

# CHAPTER 21. ROTATING CHANNEL FLOW

## A. Objectives

- Using ANSYS Meshing to Create the Mesh for 3D Plane Channel Flow
- Inserting Boundary Conditions
- Running Laminar Steady 3D ANSYS Fluent Simulations
- Using Contour Plots for Visualizations
- Compare Results with Neutral Stability Theory

## B. Problem Description

In this chapter we will study the appearance of streamwise vortices for the flow in a narrow gap rotating plane channel with rectangular cross section. The height of the rectangular cross section is 100 mm and the channel width is 10 mm. The length of the channel is 1000 mm. The Coriolis force due to spanwise system rotation will cause the appearance of counter-rotating vortices and transition to turbulent flow at much lower Reynolds numbers as compared with the non-rotating plane channel flow case.

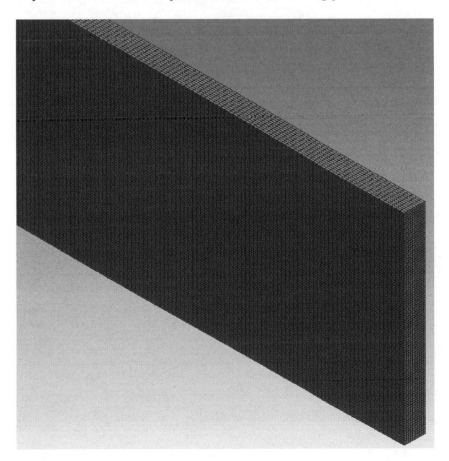

## C. Launching ANSYS Workbench and Selecting Fluent

1. Start by launching ANSYS Workbench. Double click on Fluid Flow (Fluent) under Analysis Systems in the Toolbox. Select Units>>Metric (tonne, mm, s, …) from the menu.

Figure 21.1 Selecting Fluent

## D. Launching ANSYS DesignModeler

2. Right click on Geometry in the Project Schematic window and select New DesignModeler Geometry. Select millimeter as the desired length unit from the menu (Units>>Millimeter) in DesignModeler. Select the YZPlane in the Tree Outline and select Look at Face/Plane/Sketch ![icon]. Select the Sketching tab and click on Rectangle. Draw a rectangle from the origin. Click on the Dimensions tab. Click on the vertical and horizontal sides of the rectangle and enter 10 mm and 100 mm for the vertical and horizontal dimensions in Details View. Select the Line sketch tool and draw two horizontal lines that connect the ends of the arcs.

Figure 21.2a) Rectangle sketch tool

Figure 21.2b) Dimensions for rectangle

Select 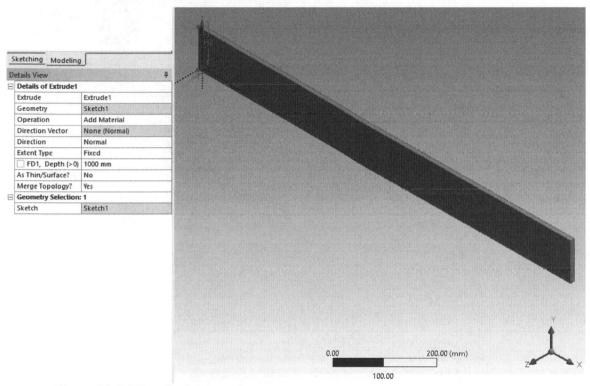 Extrude and apply Sketch1 under YZPlane in the Tree Outline as Geometry in Details View. Enter 1000 mm as the FD1, Depth (>0) of the extrusion. Click on Generate and select isometric view in the graphics window. Close the DesignModeler.

Figure 21.2c) Details for extrusion

## E. Launching ANSYS Meshing

3. Double click on Mesh under Project Schematic in ANSYS Workbench. Click on Mesh in the Outline under Project. Select Home>>Tools>>Units>>Metric (mm, kg, N, …) from the menu. Right click on Mesh under Project in Outline and select Generate Mesh. A coarse mesh is generated.

   Select Mesh>>Controls>>Face Meshing from the menu. Right click in the graphics window and select Cursor Mode>>Face. Control select the six faces of the mesh and apply the faces as Geometry under Scope in Details of "Face Meshing".

Select Mesh>>Controls>>Sizing from the menu. Right click in the graphics window and select Cursor Mode>>Edge. Control select the four edges with the 1000 mm length in the X direction and apply the edges as Geometry under Scope in Details of "Edge Sizing". Set Behavior to Hard. Set the Element Size to 2.0 mm. Repeat this step but select the remaining eight edges of the mesh and set the Element Size to 1.0 mm.

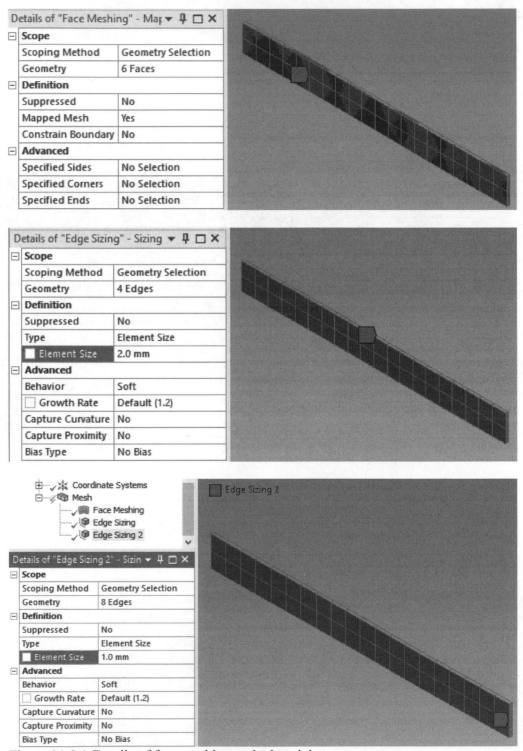

Figure 21.3a) Details of face meshing and edge sizing

Right click on Mesh under Project in Outline and select Generate Mesh. Under Statistics in Details of Mesh we can see that this mesh has 556611 Nodes and 500000 Elements.

Figure 21.3b) Details of finished mesh

Right click in the graphics window and select Cursor Mode>>Face. Control select the four faces with the length 1000 mm in the X direction, right click and select Create Named Selection. Enter the name *wall* and click on OK to close the Selection Name window. Select the inlet face and name it *inlet* and select the outlet face and name it *outlet*, see Figure 21.3c).

Figure 21.3c) Details for named selections

Select File>>Export…>>Mesh>>FLUENT Input File>>Export from the menu and save the mesh in the *Working Directory* with the name *plane-rotating-channel-mesh.msh*. Select File>>Save Project from the menu and save the project with the name *Plane Rotating Channel Flow.wbpj*. Close the Meshing window and right-click on Mesh under Project Schematic in ANSYS Workbench and select Update.

## F. Launching ANSYS Fluent

4. Double click on Setup under Project Schematic in ANSYS Workbench. Check the Options box for Double Precision. Set the Number of Parallel Processes to the same number as computer cores. Click on Start.

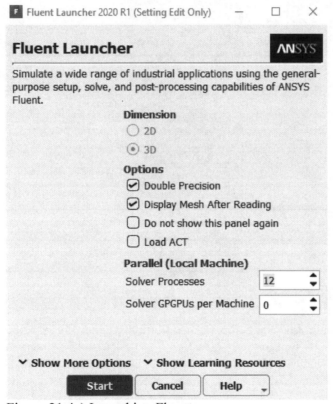

Figure 21.4a) Launching Fluent

Click on Check and Scale… under Mesh in General on the Task Page to verify the Domain Extents. Close the Scale Mesh window. Check the box for Gravity. Enter -9.81 as Gravitational Acceleration in the Y direction.

Figure 21.4b) Domain extents for curved channel flow mesh

440

Figure 21.4c) General settings including gravity

Double click on Models and Viscous under Setup in the Outline View. Set the Viscous Model to Laminar and click OK to close the window.

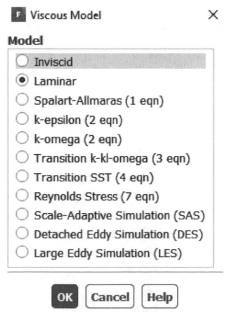

Figure 21.4d) Viscous model

Double click on Materials under Setup in the Outline View. Click on Create/Edit for Fluid under Materials on the Task Page. Click on Fluent Database in the Create/Edit Materials window. Scroll down and select *water-liquid (h2o<l>)* as the Fluent Fluid Material. Click on Copy and Close the Fluent Database Materials window. Click on Change/Create and Close the Create/Edit Materials window.

Figure 21.4e) Selection of water-liquid as fluid

5. Open Cell Zone Conditions and Fluid under Setup in the Outline View. Double click on *solid (fluid, id=2)* under Cell Zone Conditions. Select *water-liquid* as Material Name and enter *water-liquid* as the Zone Name. Check the box for Frame Motion. Set the Rotation-Axis Origin to X (m) 0, Y (m) 0 and Z (m) 0.005. Set the Rotation-Axis Direction to X 0, Y -1, and Z 0. Set the Rotational Velocity Speed (rad/s) to 0.5. Click OK to close the Fluid window.

Figure 21.5a) Selection of water-liquid as fluid and settings for frame motion

Double click on Boundary Conditions. Select *inlet* under Zone in Boundary Conditions on the Task Page. Click on the Edit… button for velocity-inlet Type. Select *Components* as Velocity Specification Method. Enter 0.05 as X-Velocity (m/s). Select OK to close the Velocity Inlet window.

Select *outlet* under Zone in Boundary Conditions on the Task Page. Click on the Edit… button for pressure-outlet Type. Select *From Neighboring Cell* as Backflow Direction Specification Method. Select OK to close the Pressure Outlet window.

Figure 21.5b) Details of velocity inlet

Figure 21.5c) Details of pressure outlet

443

Double click on Methods under Solution in the Outline View. Set the Pressure-Velocity Coupling Scheme to SIMPLE. For Spatial Discretization, set the Gradient to Least Squares Cell Based, set Pressure to PRESTO! and Momentum to First Order Upwind.

Figure 21.5d) Settings for solution methods

Double click on Monitors and Residual under Solution in the Outline View. Set the Absolute Criteria to 1e-12 for all equations and click OK to close the window.

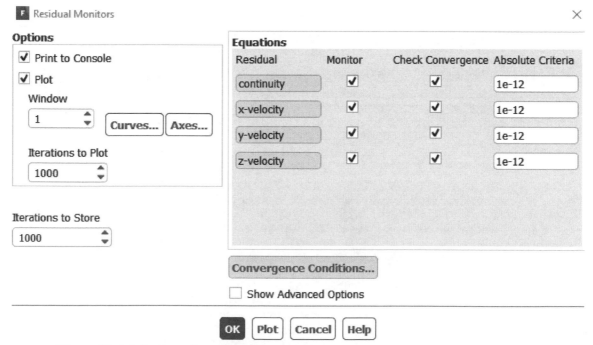

Figure 21.5e) Settings for residual monitors

6. Double click on Initialization under Solution in the Outline View and select Standard Initialization. Select Compute from Inlet. Click on Initialize. Double click on Run Calculation under Solution in the Outline View. Enter 1200 for the Number of Iterations and click on Calculate.

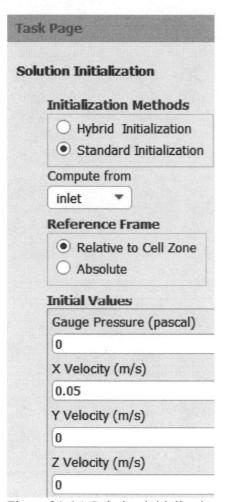

Figure 21.6a) Solution initialization     Figure 21.6b) Running calculations

## G. Post-Processing

7. The residuals are shown in Figure 21.7a). Double-click on Contours in Graphics under Results in the Outline View. Enter *x-velocity* as Contour Name in the Contours window. Select Contours of Velocity… and X Velocity. Check the boxes for Filled, Node Values, Boundary Values, Contour Lines, Global Range and Auto Range under Options. Select News Surface>>Plane… and select XY Plane. Set Z (m) to 0.005. Click on Create and Close the Plane Surface window. Create another plane in the YZ plane and set X (m) to 0.5. Select the Colormap Options… in the Contours window. Select Top as Colormap Alignment, click on Apply and Close the Colormap window. Select all Surfaces except *wall* under Surfaces and click on Save/Display. Select the X-Y coordinate system in the graphics window. In Figures 21.7c) – e), you can see five distinct streaks in the channel. The streaks indicate the presence of streamwise counter rotating vortices with a wavelength in the spanwise Y direction that can be determined from the figure.

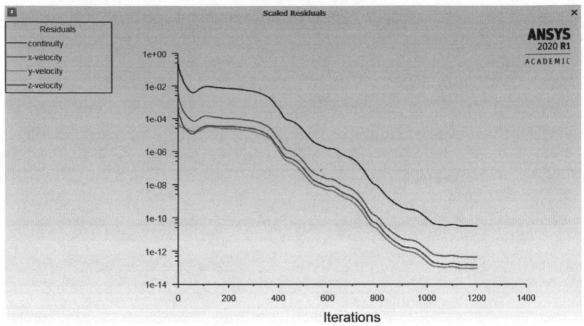

Figure 21.7a) Residuals from calculations

**F** Contours

Contour Name

x-velocity

**Options**                           Contours of

✔ Filled                              Velocity...

✔ Node Values                         X Velocity

✔ Boundary Values                     Min            Max

✔ Contour Lines                       0              0

✔ Global Range

✔ Auto Range                          Surfaces  Filter Text

☐ Clip to Range

☐ Draw Profiles                       inlet
                                      outlet
☐ Draw Mesh                           plane-3
                                      plane-4
**Coloring**                          wall

⦿ Banded

○ Smooth

Colormap Options...

                                      New Surface ‗

Save/Display    Compute    Close    Help

Figure 21.7b) Settings for contours

446

Figure 21.7c) Contours of X Velocity in XY Plane, X = 0 – 1 m (flow from left to right)

Figure 21.7d) Contours of X Velocity in XY Plane, X = 0.5 – 1 m (flow left to right)

Figure 21.7e) Contours of X Velocity in ZY Plane at inlet and outlet of rotating channel

447

## H. Theory

8. The Coriolis instability for the flow in a plane channel with system rotation is governed by the Reynolds number $Re$ and the rotation number $Ro$.

$$Re = \frac{U_b d}{\nu} \tag{21.1}$$

$$Ro = \frac{\Omega d}{U_b} \tag{21.2}$$

where $U_b$ is the bulk flow velocity in the channel, $d$ is the channel width, $\Omega$ is the rotation rate and $\nu$ is the kinematic viscosity of the fluid. The critical Reynolds number $Re_{crit}$ is 5770 caused by Tollmien-Schlichting waves without rotation. Roll cell instabilities will develop below this Reynolds number due to the Coriolis force. The non-dimensional wave number $\alpha$ of the Coriolis instability is determined by

$$\alpha = \frac{2\pi d}{\lambda} \tag{21.3}$$

where $\lambda$ is the spanwise wave-length of the instability. From figures 21.7c), the wave number can be determined to be

$$\alpha = \frac{2\pi \cdot 0.01}{0.01555} = 4.04 \tag{21.4}$$

In order to determine the wave-length that is used to determine the wave number in equation (21.3), you can measure the total length in the vertical spanwise direction for five successive streaks in figures 21.7c) – e). Next, you take this vertical length and divide by four to get the average wave-length in the vertical spanwise direction. To get the scale for figures 21.7c) – e), use the total height of the channel in the vertical direction in figures 21.7c) – e) that corresponds to 100 mm height.

The Reynolds and rotation numbers in the ANSYS Fluent simulations is

$$Re = \frac{U_b d}{\nu} = \frac{0.05*0.01}{10^{-6}} = 500 \tag{21.5}$$

$$Ro = \frac{\Omega d}{U_b} = \frac{0.5*0.01}{0.05} = 0.1 \tag{21.6}$$

## I. References

1. Alfredsson, P.H. and Persson, H., Instabilities in channel flow with system rotation. *J. Fluid Mech.,* **202**, 543, (1989).
2. Chandrasekhar, S., Hydrodynamic and Hydromagnetic Stability, Dover, 1981.
3. Hart, J.E., Instability and secondary motion in a rotating channel flow. *J. Fluid Mech.,* **45**, 341, (1971).
4. Lezius, D.K. and Johnston, J.P., The structure and stability of turbulent boundary layers in rotating channel flow. *J. Fluid Mech.,* **77**, 153, (1976).
5. Speziale, C.G. and Thangam, S., Numerical study of secondary flows and roll-cell instabilities in rotating channel flow. *J. Fluid Mech.,* **130**, 377, (1983).

## J. Exercises

21.1 Run the calculations for the flow in the rotating channel in this chapter but use the following bulk flow velocities: 0.03, 0.06, 0.09 and 0.12 m/s and determine the Reynolds number, rotation number and the spanwise wave number for each velocity.

21.2 Run the calculations for the flow in the rotating channel as shown in this chapter at $Re = 500$ for different rotation numbers $Ro = 0.2, 0.3, 0.4$ and $0.5$. Determine the spanwise wave number for each case and compare with the critical value.

**K. Notes**

## CHAPTER 22. COMPRESSIBLE FLOW PAST A BULLET

### A. Objectives

- Using ICEM CFD to Create the Mesh for 2D Axisymmetric Flow Past a Bullet
- Inserting Boundary Conditions
- Running Turbulent Steady 2D Axisymmetric ANSYS Fluent Simulations
- Using Contour Plots for Visualizations
- Compare Drag Coefficient Results with Experiments

### B. Problem Description

In this chapter we will study the flow around the Berger 7 mm 180 grain VLD bullet. We will be using a parabolic mesh for the compressible airflow at different Mach number past the bullet. Results from simulation drag coefficients will be compared with experiments for the bullet. ICEM CFD is not available in ANSYS Student. Move to step 21 and read the finished mesh directly in ANSYS Fluent standalone mode.

## C. Launching ICEM CFD

1.  Start by launching ICEM CFD. Select Settings>>Model/Units from the menu and check the box for Meters as Length Units. Click on Apply and OK. Select File>>Replay Script>>Replay Control from the menu. The Replay Control window opens.

Figure 22.1a) ICEM CFD main window

Figure 22.1b) Length units

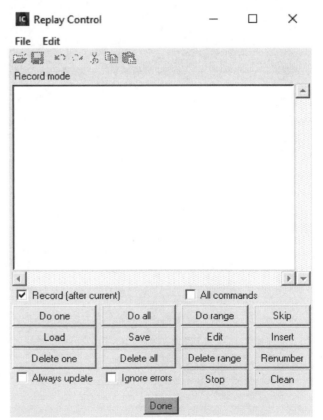

Figure 22.1c) Replay control window

## D. Importing Geometries

2. Select File>>Imported Geometry>>Formatted point data from the menu. Select the file "BergerBullet7mm180grainVLD.dat" and open the file. This file can be downloaded from sdcpublications.com. Set the name for the Curve Part to BULLET. Check the boxes for Import Points, Import Curves and Import Surfaces. Click on Apply.

Figure 22.2a) Import of formatted input point data for bullet

Figure 22.2b) Imported curve for Berger 7mm 180grain VLD

3. Select File>>Imported Geometry>>Formatted point data from the menu. Select the file "farfield.dat" and open the file. This file can be downloaded from sdcpublications.com. Check the boxes for Import Points, Import Curves and Import Surfaces. Enter the name GEOM for Point Part, FARFIELD for Curve Part and the name FLUID for Surface Part. Click on Apply. Select Merge when you get the message Geometry Already Exists.

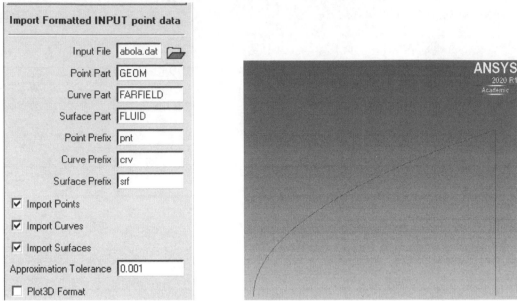

Figure 22.3a) Imported curve for mesh    Figure 22.3b) Imported curve for mesh

Check the box for Points located under Model and Geometry in the tree to the left of the graphics window. Select the Geometry tab below the menu and click on Create/Modify Curve. Uncheck the box for Inherit Part and name the Part AXIS. Select From Points and click on the lower end point for the parabola in the graphics window. Zoom in on the bullet using Box Zoom. Next, click on the lower front end point of the bullet and click on the mouse scroll wheel. Select the lower front end point of the bullet once again. Select the lower rear end point of the bullet and click on the mouse scroll wheel. Select the lower rear end point of the bullet once again and zoom out and select the lower end point of the vertical line to the right. Click on the mouse scroll wheel. Click on Apply and OK. Uncheck the box for Points. This creates three line segments for the horizontal AXIS.

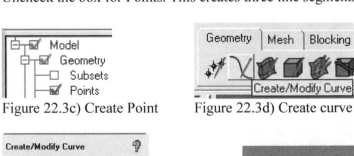

Figure 22.3c) Create Point    Figure 22.3d) Create curve

Figure 22.3e) Create curve from points    Figure 22.3f) Completed geometry

## E. Creating Blocks

4. Select the Blocking tab under the menu and select Create Block. Select FLUID as Part under Create Block. Select 2D Planar as Type under Initialize Blocks. Click on Apply.

Figure 22.4a) Initializing blocking

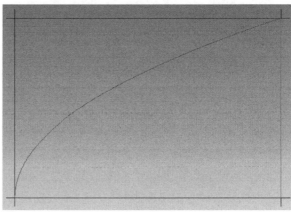

Figure 22.4b) Settings for blocking    Figure 22.4c) Initial block

5. Select the Blocking tab under the menu and select Associate. Select Associate Edge to Curve under Edit Association for Blocking Associations. Select the right vertical edge of the block and click on the mouse scroll wheel. Select the right vertical curve of the mesh and click on the mouse scroll wheel.

   Select the lower horizontal edge of the block and click on the mouse scroll wheel. Select the three parts of the horizontal AXIS curve of the mesh and click on the mouse scroll wheel. You may need to zoom in to select the short middle section.

   Select the remaining two edges of the block (one vertical and one horizontal edge) and click on the mouse scroll wheel. Select the remaining parabolic curve of the mesh and click on the mouse scroll wheel. The edges of the block have now turned green.

Figure 22.5a) Selecting associate          Figure 22.5b) Selecting associate edge to curve

Figure 22.5c) Block and mesh after completed association

6. Select Snap Project Vertices under Edit Association for Blocking Associations. Click on Apply.

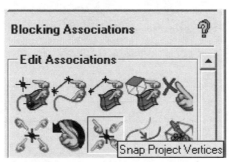

Figure 22.6a) Selecting snap project vertices

Figure 22.6b) Completed snapping of vertices

456

### F. Setting Max Mesh Size

7. Select the Mesh tab under the menu and select Part Mesh Setup. Set Maximum size for AXIS and FARFIELD to 0.1 and Maximum size for BULLET to 0.02. Click on Apply and Dismiss. Select the Blocking tab under the menu and select Pre-Mesh Params. Click on Apply. Check the box for Pre-Mesh located under Model and Blocking in the tree to the left of the graphics window. Answer Yes when you get the question to recompute.

Figure 22.7a) Part mesh setup

**IC** Part Mesh Setup

| Part △ | Prism | Hexa-core | Maximum size |
|---|---|---|---|
| AXIS | ☐ | | 0.1 |
| BULLET | ☐ | | 0.02 |
| FARFIELD | ☐ | | 0.1 |

Figure 22.7b) Entering maximum sizes

Figure 22.7c) Pre-mesh          Figure 22.7d) Mesh

### G. Splitting Blocks

8. Uncheck the Pre-Mesh box and check the Blocks box under Model and Blocking in the tree next to the graphics window. Select the Blocking tab under the menu and select Split Block. Select Ogrid block under Split Block. Select Block under Ogrid Block. Select block number 4 in the graphics window and click on the mouse scroll wheel. Click on Apply.

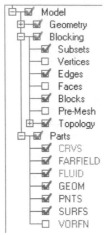

Figure 22.8a) Tree including pre-mesh and blocks

Figure 22.8b) Selecting split block

Figure 22.8c) Selecting ogrid block

Figure 22.8d) Selecting block

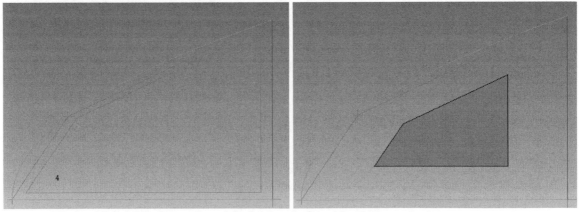

Figure 22.8e) Block number 4 before and after selection

## H. Deleting Blocks

9.  Select the Blocking tab under the menu and select Delete Block. Select block 11 as shown in Figure 22.9b). Click on the mouse scroll wheel. Click on Apply and OK.

Figure 22.9a) Deleting blocks

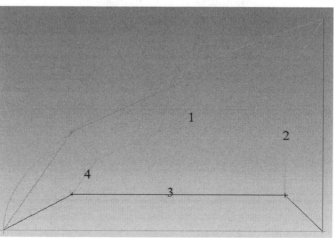

Figure 22.9b) Before and after deletion of block 11

## I. Blocking Associations

10. Uncheck Blocks under Model and Blocking in the tree to the left of the graphics window. Select the Blocking tab under the menu and select Associate. Select Associate Edge to Curve under Edit Association for Blocking Associations. Check the box for Project vertices. Select edges 1 - 4 as shown in Figure 22.10b). Click on the mouse scroll wheel. Zoom in on the bullet using Box Zoom, see Figure 22.10c). Select all edges of the bullet except the lower horizontal edge that belongs to axis, see Figure 22.10d). Click on the mouse scroll wheel. You can also use the mouse scroll wheel to zoom in and out if needed.

Figure 22.10a) Project vertices

Figure 22.10b) Selection of edges 1-4

Figure 22.10c) Box zoom

Figure 22.10d) Selected edges for bullet

Figure 22.10e) After completion of the associations

## J. Moving Vertices

11. Select the Blocking tab under the menu and select Move Vertex. Select Move Vertex under Move Vertices and select and move the rightmost vertex to the lower right corner of the bullet as shown in Figure 22.11c). In the same way, move the left vertex to the lower left corner of the bullet. Finally, move the second vertex on the right hand side a little bit to the next corner as shown in Figure 22.11e). Click on Apply and Dismiss. Zoom in on the vertices to make sure they are lined up exactly in the correct corner locations. If not, repeat this step.

Figure 22.11a) Move Vertex

Figure 22.11b) Move Vertices

Figure 22.11c) After completed movement of the rightmost vertex

Figure 22.11d) After completed movement of a left vertex

Figure 22.11e) After completed movement of all vertices

12. Select the Blocking tab under the menu and select Edit Edge. Select Split Edge under Edit Edge and select Method as Automatic Linear under Split Edge. Select line 5 as shown in Figure 22.12c). Click on the mouse scroll wheel.

Figure 22.12a) Edit edge          Figure 22.12b) Automatic Spline split edge method

Figure 22.12c) Selection of line 5 for split edge

Figure 22.12d) After completed automatic linear split of line 5

Select Linear as Method under Split Edge and zoom in on corner 6 as shown in Figure 22.12d). Select Split Edge and click on the green line segment next to the red corner point. Click on Apply and Dismiss. Zoom in on the different corners to make sure they are lined up exactly in the correct corner locations. If not, repeat this step.

Figure 22.12e) Selection of linear split edge method

Figure 22.12f) Corner 6 before linear split

Figure 22.12g) Corner 6 after linear split

13. Check Blocks under Model and Blocking in the tree to the left of the graphics window. Select the Blocking tab under the menu and select Delete Block. Select block under Delete Block and select block 4 as shown in Figure 22.13b). Click on the mouse scroll wheel. Click on Apply. Uncheck Blocks under Model and Blocking in the tree to the left of the graphics window.

Figure 22.13a) Deleting blocks

Figure 22.13b) Selection of block 4 for deletion

## K. Computing Wall Spacing

14. Go to the website https://www.pointwise.com/yplus/. Enter the values as shown in the left column as Input. Click on "Compute Wall Spacing". Notice the value for wall spacing 4.1015095901749715e-7 m.

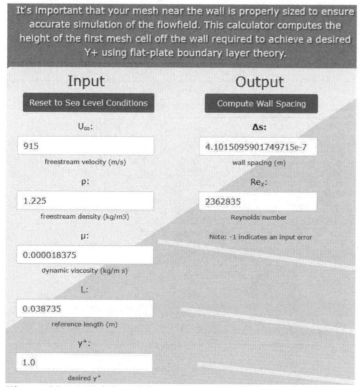

Figure 22.14 Height of first mesh cell off the wall

## L. Pre-Mesh Parameters

15. Select the Blocking tab under the menu and select Pre-Mesh Params. Select Edge Params as Meshing Parameter under Pre-Mesh Params. Click on Fit Window under the menu, see Figure 22.15c). Select edge 6 as shown in Figure 22.15d). Enter 60 as the number of Nodes. Enter 4.1e-7 as Spacing 2. Set Ratio 2 to 1.2. Check the box for Copy Parameters. Click on Apply. Check the Pre-Mesh box under Model and Blocking in the tree next to the graphics window. Answer Yes when you get the question to recompute.

Figure 22.15a) Pre-mesh parameters   Figure 22.15b) Edge parameters

Figure 22.15c) Fit window

Figure 22.15d) Lines for edge parameters

Figure 22.15e) Pre-mesh parameters

Figure 22.15f) Edge settings

Figure 22.15g) Incorrect mesh

Select the Blocking tab under the menu and select Associate. Select Associate Edge to Curve under Edit Association for Blocking Associations. Check the box for Project vertices. Select horizontal edges 7 and 8 as shown in Figure 22.15g). Click on the mouse scroll wheel. Select edges 7 and 8 once again. Click on the mouse scroll wheel. Answer Yes to the question to recompute.

Figure 22.15h) Updated mesh after association with axis

466

**M. Matching Edges**

16. Select the Blocking tab under the menu and select Pre-Mesh Params. Select Match Edges as Meshing Parameter under Pre-Mesh Params. Zoom in around the front of the bullet, see Figure 22.16b). Select the front vertical edge of the bullet as reference edge. Select the inclined top edge of the bullet as the target edge. Click on the mouse scroll wheel. Select Edge Params as Meshing Parameter under Pre-Mesh Params. Select the top edge of the bullet once again. Enter 1.2 as Ratio 1. Click on Apply. Uncheck and check the Pre-Mesh box under Model and Blocking in the tree next to the graphics window. Answer Yes when you get the question to recompute. Repeat this step to match the edges at the rear of the bullet.

Figure 22.16a) Matching edges

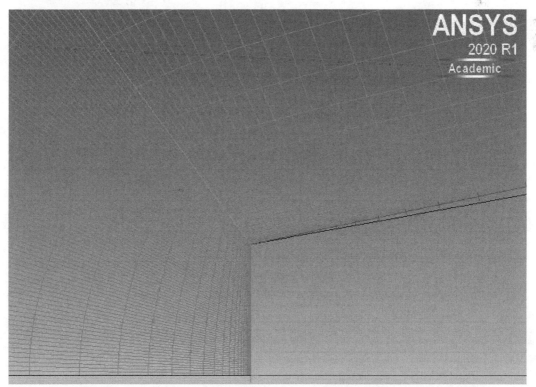

Figure 22.16b) Mesh at the front end of the bullet with matched edges

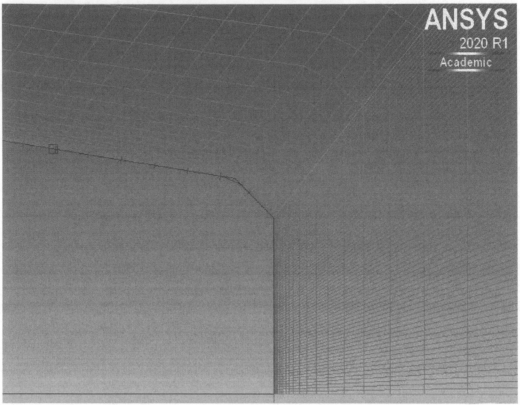

Figure 22.16c) Mesh at the rear end of the bullet with matched edges

## N. Pre-Mesh Quality

17. Select the Blocking tab under the menu and select Pre-Mesh Quality Histograms. Select Aspect Ratio as Criterion and click on Apply. The aspect ratio is in between 1.02 and 1080. One way to lower the maximum aspect ratio is to have a finer mesh. However, since the mesh is very fine close to the surface of the bullet, it will require a much finer mesh to substantially lower the aspect ratio. Select Quality as the Criterion and click on Apply. The Quality is in between 0.775 and 1 which is good since the minimum quality is not close to zero.

Figure 22.17a) Pre-mesh quality

Figure 22.17b) Aspect ratio criterion

Figure 22.17c) Aspect ratio values

Figure 22.17d) Quality values

## O. Converting to Unstructured Mesh and Selection of Solver

18. Right click on Pre-Mesh under Model and Blocking in the tree next to graphics window. Select Convert to Unstruct Mesh. Select the Output Mesh tab under the menu. Click on Select solver. Select ANSYS Fluent as Output Solver under Solver Setup. Check the box Set As Default. Click on Apply.

Figure 22.18a) Convert to Unstruct Mesh

Figure 22.18b) Selection of solver

## P. Boundary Conditions

19. Select the Output Mesh tab under the menu and select Boundary conditions. Click on plus sign next to Edges and FARFIELD. Select Create new under FARFIELD and select *pressure far-field* as boundary condition type. Click Okay in the selection window.

    Click on plus signs next to surfaces, ? Mixed/unknown and FLUID. Select Create new under FLUID and select *fluid* as boundary condition type. Click Okay in the selection window.

    Click on the plus sign next to Edges and AXIS. Select Create new under AXIS and select *axis*. Click Okay in the selection window.

    Click on the plus sign next to Edges and BULLET. Select Create new under BULLET and select *wall*. Click Okay in the selection window.

    Click on Accept. Select File Save Project from the menu and save the project with the name "Berger's 7 mm 180 grain VLD".

Figure 22.19a) Selection of boundary conditions

Figure 22.19b) Pressure farfield boundary condition

470

Figure 22.19c) Fluid boundary condition

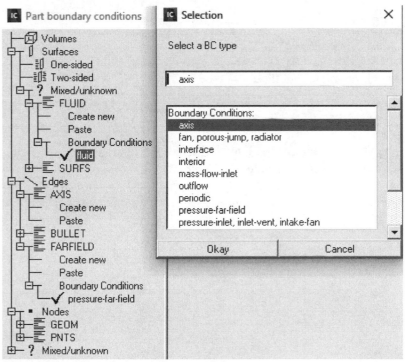

Figure 22.19d) Axis boundary condition

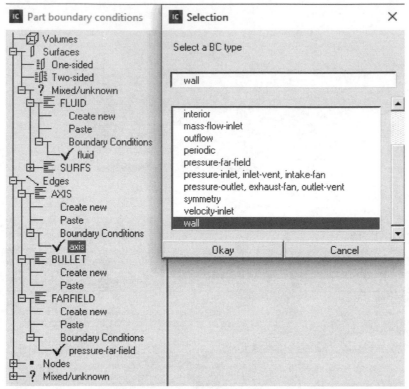

Figure 22.19e) Wall boundary condition

## Q. Saving the Mesh File

20. Select the Output Mesh tab under the menu and select Write input. Answer Yes to the question Save current project first? Select *BergerBullet7mm180grainVLD.uns* and click on Open. Select 2D as Grid dimension. Enter the name for the Output file as *./BergerBullet7mm180grainVLD*, see Figure 22.20b). Click on Done.

Figure 22.20a) Write input    Figure 22.20b) ANSYS Fluent

**R. Setting Up ANSYS Fluent**

21. Start ANSYS Fluent in standalone mode. Click on Mesh. Select *BergerBullet7mm180grainVLD.msh* and click on Open. Select Dimension 2D, Double Precision under Options and set the number of Solver Processes under Parallel (Local Machine) to the same number as the number of computer cores. Click on Start With Selected Options.

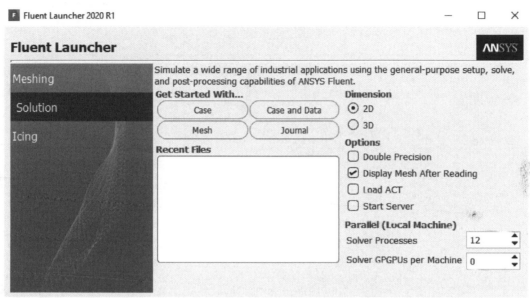

Figure 22.21 Fluent launcher

22. Double click on General under Setup in Outline View. Set 2D Space to Axisymmetric. Double click on Models and Viscous (SST k-omega) under Setup in Outline View. Set Model to Spalart-Allmaras (1 eqn). Select Strain/Vorticity-Based under Spalart-Allmaras Production. Click OK to close the Viscous Model window.

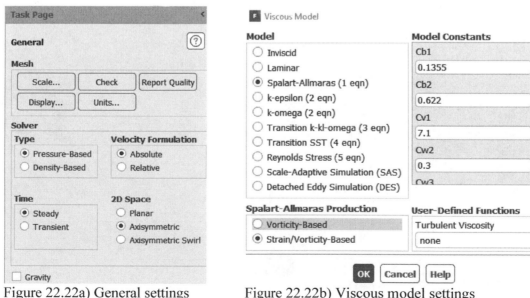

Figure 22.22a) General settings      Figure 22.22b) Viscous model settings

23. Double click on Materials, Fluid and air under Setup in the Outline View. Select ideal-gas for Density and select Sutherland for Viscosity. Select OK to close the Sutherland Law window. Click on Change/Create and Close the Create/Edit Materials window.

Figure 22.23 Create/edit materials

24. Double click on Boundary Conditions under Setup in the Outline View. Select farfield as Zone under Boundary Conditions on the Task Page. Click on Edit. Set Mach number to 2.68 and click OK to close the Pressure Far-Field window.

Figure 22.24 Pressure far-field

25. Double click on Methods under Solution in the Outline View. Select Second Order Upwind for Modified Turbulent Viscosity under Spatial Discretization. Double click on Controls under Solution in the Outline View. Set Density to 0.5 and Modified Turbulent Viscosity to 0.9 under Pseudo Transient Explicit Relaxation Factors.

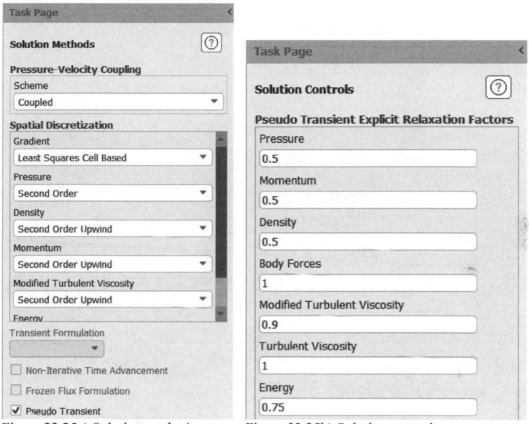

Figure 22.25a) Solution methods     Figure 22.25b) Solution controls

26. Double click on Monitors and Residual under Solution in the Outline View. Set all Residuals to 1e-06. Click OK to close the Residual Monitors window.

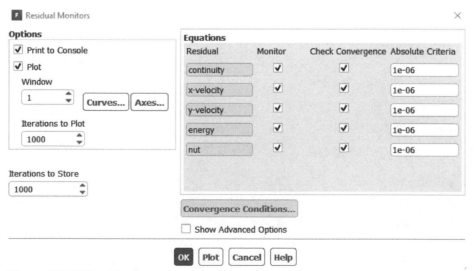

Figure 22.26 Residual monitors

27. Double click on Reference Values under Setup in the Outline View. Select Compute from *farfield* under Reference Values on the Task Page. Set the Area (m2) to 0.0000408894 and set Length (m) to 0.038735. Double click on Report Definitions under Solution in the Outline View. Select New>>Force Report>>Drag in the Report Definitions window. Check the boxes for Report File, Report Plot and Print to Console under Create. Select *bullet* under Wall Zones. Click OK to close the Drag Report Definition window. Close the Report Definitions window.

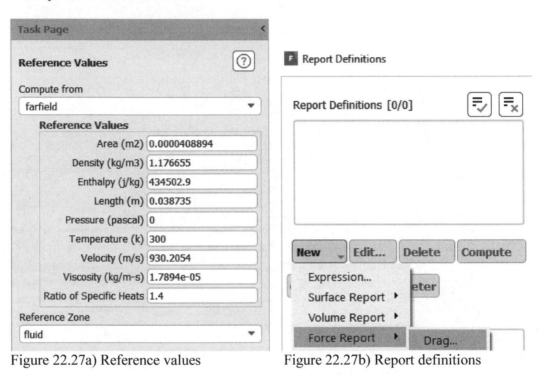

Figure 22.27a) Reference values      Figure 22.27b) Report definitions

Figure 22.27c) Drag report definitions

28. Double click on Initialization under Solution in the Outline View. Select Hybrid Initialization and click on Initialize. Move the cursor to the Console and press enter on the keyboard to get the command prompt. Enter *solve/initialize/set-fmg-initialization* and press enter three times. Enter 100 as number of cycles on level 1 and press enter two times. Enter 100 as number of cycles on level 2 and press enter eight times. Answer yes to the question enable FMG verbose? Enter *solve/initialize/fmg-initialization* and press enter. Answer yes to the question Enable FMG initialization? Select File>>Write Case & Data… from the menu. Save the file as BergerBullet7mm180grainVLD.cas.

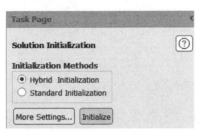

Figure 22.28a) Hybrid initialization

```
> solve/initialize/set-fmg-initialization


Customize your FMG initialization:
  set the number of multigrid levels [5]

  set FMG parameters on levels ..

   residual reduction on level 1 is:  [0.001]
   number of cycles on level 1 is:  [10] 100

   residual reduction on level 2 is:  [0.001]
   number of cycles on level 2 is:  [50] 100

   residual reduction on level 3 is:  [0.001]
   number of cycles on level 3 is:  [100]

   residual reduction on level 4 is:  [0.001]
   number of cycles on level 4 is:  [500]

   residual reduction on level 5 [coarsest grid] is:  [0.001]
   number of cycles on level 5 is:  [500]


 Number of FMG (and FAS  geometric multigrid) levels: 5
* FMG customization summary:
*   residual reduction on level 0 [finest grid] is: 0.001
*   number of cycles on level 0 is: 1
*   residual reduction on level 1 is: 0.001
*   number of cycles on level 1 is: 100
*   residual reduction on level 2 is: 0.001
*   number of cycles on level 2 is: 100
*   residual reduction on level 3 is: 0.001
*   number of cycles on level 3 is: 100
*   residual reduction on level 4 is: 0.001
*   number of cycles on level 4 is: 500
*   residual reduction on level 5 [coarsest grid] is: 0.001
*   number of cycles on level 5 is: 500
* FMG customization complete


  set FMG courant-number [0.75]

  enable FMG verbose? [no] yes

> solve/initialize/fmg-initialization
Enable FMG initialization? [no] yes
```

Figure 22.28b) Full multigrid initialization

29. Double click on Run Calculation under Solution in the Outline View. Enter 400 as Number of Iterations. Click on Calculate.

Figure 22.29a) Running calculations

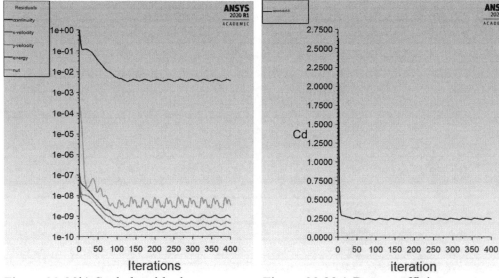

Figure 22.29b) Scaled residuals      Figure 22.29c) Drag coefficient

30. Double click on Graphics and Contours under Results in the Outline View. Select Contours of Pressure and Static Pressure. Deselect all surfaces and use the settings and check boxes as shown in Figure 22.30a). Click on Save/Display. Use the same setting but change to Contours of Velocity and Mach Number. Double click on Reports and Forces under Results in the Outline View. Click on Print in the force Reports window.

Figure 22.30a) Settings for pressure contour plot

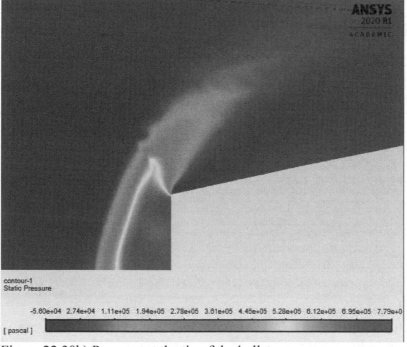

Figure 22.30b) Pressure at the tip of the bullet

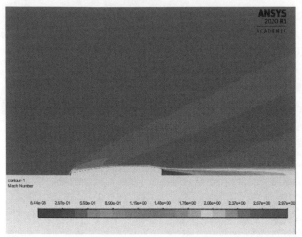

Figure 22.30c) Mach number for flow around bullet

```
Forces - Direction Vector (1 0 0)
                      Forces (n)                                  Coefficients
Zone                  Pressure         Viscous        Total       Pressure       Viscous        Total
bullet                4.1287722        0.8278968      4.956669     0.1983505      0.03977302     0.23812352
--------------        ----------------  -------------- -----------  -------------- -------------- ----------
Net                   4.1287722        0.8278968      4.956669     0.1983505      0.03977302     0.23812352
```

Figure 22.30d) Forces and coefficients at Mach number 2.69

31. Double click on Boundary Conditions and Inlet under Setup in the Outline View. Set the Mach number to 2.23 as shown in Table 22.1. Click OK to exit the Pressure Far-Field window. Double click on Reference Values under Setup in the Outline View. Select Compute from farfield. Make sure that the Velocity (m/s) is set to 774.0142 as shown in Table 22.1. Repeat steps 28 – 30 and determine the drag coefficient for Mach number 2.23. Continue in the same way to repeat this step 31 to determine the drag coefficient at Mach numbers 1.79 and 1.34, see Table 22.1.

| Ma | V (m/s) | $C_{d, G7}$ | $C_{d, Exp.}$ | $C_{d, Fluent}$ | Percent Diff. |
|---|---|---|---|---|---|
| 0.50 | 173.5458 | 0.119 | | 0.139 | 17 |
| 0.60 | 208.2549 | 0.119 | | 0.137 | 15 |
| 0.75 | 260.3187 | 0.122 | | 0.136 | 12 |
| 0.89 | 308.9115 | 0.143 | | 0.144 | 1.2 |
| 0.93 | 322.7952 | 0.174 | | 0.173 | 0.4 |
| 0.95 | 329.7370 | 0.205 | | 0.203 | 1.4 |
| 0.98 | 340.1497 | 0.316 | | 0.250 | 21 |
| 0.985 | 341.8852 | 0.332 | | 0.286 | 14 |
| 0.99 | 343.6206 | 0.348 | | 0.324 | 6.9 |
| 1 | 347.0916 | 0.380 | | 0.370 | 2.6 |
| 1.05 | 364.4461 | 0.404 | | 0.380 | 6.1 |
| 1.12 | 388.7425 | 0.399 | | 0.377 | 5.6 |
| 1.23 | 426.9226 | 0.384 | | 0.368 | 4.1 |
| 1.34 | 465.1027 | | 0.355 | 0.357 | 0.7 |
| 1.79 | 621.2939 | | 0.301 | 0.310 | 2.9 |
| 2.23 | 774.0142 | | 0.266 | 0.272 | 2.4 |
| 2.68 | 930.2054 | | 0.239 | 0.238 | 0.4 |

Table 22.1 Drag coefficient from ANSYS Fluent in comparison with experiments for Berger 7mm 180 grain VLD

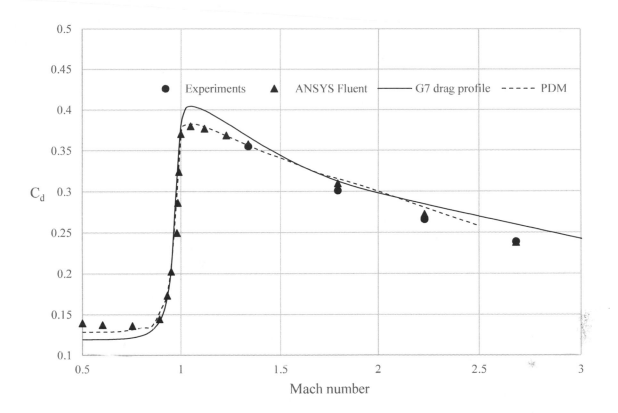

Figure 22.31a) Comparison between ANSYS Fluent, experiments[4], G7 drag profile and Personalized Drag Model (PDM)[2]

| Ma | $i_{G7,Exp.}$ | $BC_{G7,Exp.}$ (lb/in$^2$) | $i_{G7,Fluent}$ | $BC_{G7,Fluent}$ (lb/in$^2$) |
|---|---|---|---|---|
| 0.50 | | | 1.167 | 0.273 |
| 0.60 | | | 1.149 | 0.277 |
| 0.75 | | | 1.120 | 0.284 |
| 0.89 | | | 1.012 | 0.315 |
| 0.93 | | | 0.996 | 0.320 |
| 0.95 | | | 0.986 | 0.323 |
| 0.98 | | | 0.792 | 0.402 |
| 0.985 | | | 0.863 | 0.369 |
| 0.99 | | | 0.931 | 0.342 |
| 1 | | | 0.974 | 0.327 |
| 1.05 | | | 0.939 | 0.339 |
| 1.12 | | | 0.944 | 0.337 |
| 1.23 | | | 0.959 | 0.332 |
| 1.34 | 0.920 | 0.329 | 0.973 | 0.327 |
| 1.79 | 0.963 | 0.331 | 0.991 | 0.321 |
| 2.23 | 0.934 | 0.341 | 0.956 | 0.333 |
| 2.68 | 0.920 | 0.346 | 0.916 | 0.347 |
| Ave. | 0.946 | 0.337 | 0.981 | 0.325 |

Table 22.2 Ballistic coefficient from ANSYS Fluent in comparison with experiments

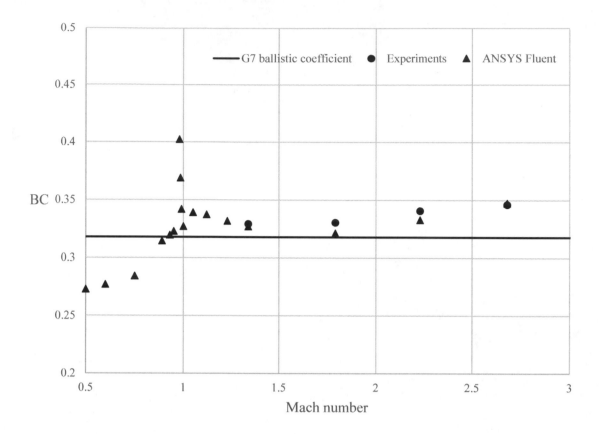

Figure 22.31b) Comparison between ANSYS Fluent, experiments and G7 ballistic coefficients

## S. Theory

32. The drag coefficient for a bullet is defined as

$$C_d = \frac{F_d}{\frac{1}{2}\rho V^2 A} \tag{22.1}$$

where $F_d$ (N) is the drag force on the bullet, $\rho$ (kg/m$^3$) is air density, $V$ (m/s) is the velocity of the bullet and $A$ is frontal area of the bullet. The Mach number $Ma$ is defined as the velocity of the bullet divided by the speed of sound $a$ (m/s) in the air

$$Ma = \frac{V}{a} \tag{22.2}$$

where the speed of sound depends on the absolute temperature of the air $T$ (K), the gas constant $R$ (J/kg-K) and $\gamma$ is the adiabatic index.

$$a = \sqrt{\gamma R T} \tag{22.3}$$

The ballistic coefficient $BC$ (kg/m$^2$) for the bullet is determined from

$$BC = \frac{m}{id^2} \qquad (22.4)$$

where $i$ is the form factor, $m$ (kg) is the bullet mass and $d$ (m) is the diameter of the bullet. The form factor is determined from

$$i = \frac{c_d}{c_{d,GX}} \qquad (22.4)$$

where $c_{d,GX}$ is the drag coefficient from the GX drag profile as shown in Figure 22.31 and Table 22.2 for drag profile G7.

## T. References

1. ANSYS Fluent Tutorial Guide, Release 18.0, January 2017.
2. Beech, D., Aerodynamic Drag Measurement and Modeling for Small Arms – Improving on Ballistic Coefficients, Applied Ballistics, 2019.
3. Litz, B., Ballistic Coefficient Testing of the Sierra .308 155 grain Matchking PALMA Bullet., Applied Ballistics, ABDOC107.2, (2007).
4. Litz, B., Berger's 7 mm VLD Bullets Part 1: Properties and Test Results, Applied Ballistics, ABDOC109.1, (2008).
5. Muruganantham, V.R. and Babin, T., Numerical Investigation of hybrid blend design target bullets, MATEC Web of Conferences **172**, 01006 (2018).

## U. Exercises

22.1 Run the simulations in this chapter for the Berger 7mm 168 VLD bullet. Bullet dimensions in inches are given in Reference 4. Use the file "BergerBullet7mm168grainVLD.dat" to read the geometry for the bullet. This file is available for download at sdcpublications.com. Fill out the missing information in Table 22.3. Draw the G7 drag profile and include comparison with experiments and ANSYS Fluent results in the same graph. The G7 drag profile is also available for download at sdcpublications.com.

| Ma | V (m/s) | $C_d$, Exp. | $C_d$, Fluent | Percent Diff. |
|------|----------|--------|---------|--------|
| 0.89 | 308.9115 | ------ | | ----- |
| 1.12 | 388.7425 | ------ | | ----- |
| 1.34 | 465.1027 | 0.335 | | |
| 1.79 | 621.2939 | 0.297 | | |
| 2.23 | 774.0142 | 0.270 | | |
| 2.69 | 930.2054 | 0.249 | | |

Table 22.3 Drag coefficient from ANSYS Fluent in comparison with experiments for Berger 7mm 168 grain VLD

22.2 Run the simulations in this chapter for the Sierra .30 cal 155 grain PALMA MatchKing. Bullet dimensions in inches are given in Reference 3. Use the file "SierraBullet.30cal155grainPALMAMatchKing.dat" to read the geometry for the bullet. This file is available for download at sdcpublications.com. Fill out the missing information in Table 22.4. Draw the G7 drag profile and include comparison with experiments and ANSYS Fluent results in the same graph. The G7 drag profile is also available for download at sdcpublications.com.

| Ma | V (m/s) | $C_d$, Exp. | $C_d$, Fluent | Percent Diff. |
|------|----------|--------|------|------|
| 0.89 | 308.9115 | ------ |      | ----- |
| 1.12 | 388.7425 | ------ |      | ----- |
| 1.34 | 465.1027 | 0.406  |      |      |
| 1.79 | 621.2939 | 0.348  |      |      |
| 2.23 | 774.0142 | 0.309  |      |      |
| 2.69 | 930.2054 | 0.280  |      |      |

Table 22.4 Drag coefficient from ANSYS Fluent in comparison with experiments for Sierra .30 cal 155 grain PALMA MatchKing

# CHAPTER 23. VERTICAL AXIS WIND TURBINE FLOW

## A. Objectives

- Using Dynamic Mesh and 6DOF Solver
- Inserting Rotating Mesh
- Running Turbulent Transient 3D ANSYS Fluent Simulations for VAWT
- Using Contour Plots for Visualizations
- Comparison of Rotor RPM with Experiments

## B. Problem Description

In this chapter we will study the airflow that causes the drag based helical Savonius rotor VAWT to spin. We will be using a combination of fixed and rotating mesh domains for the incompressible airflow. Results for rotor RPM will be compared with experiments. We will create a mesh with less than 512 000 elements so that the ANSYS Fluent student version can be used. The performance of this rotor has been studied by Zakaria and Ibrahim[1-2] using the commercial code AcuSolve and compared with experiments. The helical rotor has 180-degree sweep angle, height over diameter ratio of 2, an overlap ration of 0.242, and end plates with a diameter that is 10% larger than the rotor diameter of 0.5 m. The helical rotor was modeled in SOLIDWORKS.

## C. Launching ANSYS Workbench and Selecting Fluent

1. Start by launching ANSYS Workbench. Double click on Fluid Flow (Fluent) under Analysis Systems in the Toolbox. Select Units>>Metric (tonne, mm, s, …) from the menu.

Figure 23.1 Selecting Fluent

## D. Launching ANSYS DesignModeler

2. Right click on Geometry in the Project Schematic window and select New DesignModeler Geometry. Select millimeter as the desired length unit from the menu (Units>>Millimeter) in DesignModeler. Select File>>Import External Geometry File … from the menu. Select and Open the file *HSR inside Extrusion.IGS*. This and other files can be downloaded from *sdcpublications.com*. Click on Generate. Figure 23.2b) shows the imported rotor placed inside the rotating domain. The rotating domain has a diameter of 650 mm and a height of 1052 mm. Select Create>>Boolean from the menu. Select Subtract as the Operation is Details View. Apply the cylindrical rotating domain as the Target Body and Apply the rotor as the Tool Body. To select the rotor, you will need to select the second rectangle in the lower left corner of the graphics window. Click on Generate. You will now have 1 Part, 1 Body in the Tree Outline.

Figure 23.2a) Importing geometry

486

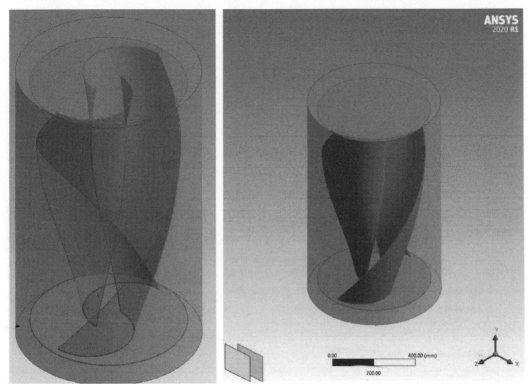

Figure 23.2b) Imported rotor      Figure 23.2c) Subtraction of rotor from domain

3. Select File>>Import External Geometry File … from the menu. Select and Open the file *Fixed Domain for HSR.IGS*. Click on Generate. Figure 23.3a) shows the imported fixed domain with the cylinder in the middle of the fixed domain. The fixed domain has a length of 15,000 mm and a square inlet and outlet with dimension 8,000 mm. Select Create>>Boolean from the menu. Select Subtract as the Operation is Details View. Apply the fixed domain as the Target Body and Apply the cylinder as the Tool Body. To select the cylinder, you will need to select the second or third rectangle in the lower left corner of the graphics window. Click on Generate. You will now have 2 Parts, 2 Bodies in the Tree Outline. Close DesignModeler.

Figure 23.3 Fixed outer domain and rotor

### E. Launching ANSYS Meshing

4. Double click on Mesh under Project Schematic in ANSYS Workbench. Click on Mesh in the Outline under Project. Select Home>>Tools>>Units>>Metric (mm, kg, N, …) from the menu. Right click on Mesh under Project in Outline and select Generate Mesh. A coarse mesh is generated.

   Right click on Coordinate System under Project and Model in the Outline. Select Insert>>Coordinate System. Select Define By Global Coordinates under Origin in Details of "Coordinate System". Set Origin Y to 500 mm. For Axis Y under Orientation About Principal Axis, select Define By Global Z Axis, see Figure 23.4a).

   Right click on the new coordinate system and select Rename. Rename the new coordinate system as Local Coordinate System. Right click on the new Local Coordinate System and select Create Section Plane. Click on Section Plane in the menu, see Figure 23.4b). Right click in the graphics window and select View>>Top. Use your mouse wheel to zoom in and out on the circular rotating domain, see Figure 23.4c). Right click in the graphics window, select Isometric View and zoom out using the mouse wheel. Uncheck the box for Section Plane 1 to show the full mesh.

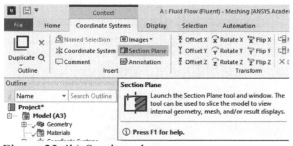

Figure 23.4a) New coordinate system    Figure 23.4b) Section plane

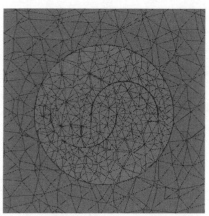

Figure 23.4c) Coarse mesh around the rotor

5.  Select Mesh in the Outline. Select Mesh>>Controls>>Sizing from the menu. Right click in the graphics window and select Cursor Mode>>Body. Select the larger outer fixed domain in the graphics window and Apply as Geometry under Scope in Details of "Body Sizing". Set the Element Size to 900 mm and set Capture Curvature and Capture Proximity to Yes. Right click on Body Sizing under Mesh in the Outline and select Rename. Rename the body sizing to Body Sizing Fixed Domain.

    Open Geometry under Project and Model in the Outline. Right click on the first Solid and select Rename. Rename this Solid as Rotating Domain. Rename the second Solid as Fixed Domain. Right click on Fixed Domain under Geometry and select Hide Body. Select Mesh in the Outline and create another body sizing but this time select the cylindrical rotating domain in the graphics window. Set the Element Size to 50 mm and set Capture Curvature and Capture Proximity to Yes. Rename the body sizing to Body Sizing Rotating Domain. Right click on Fixed Domain under Geometry and select Show Body.

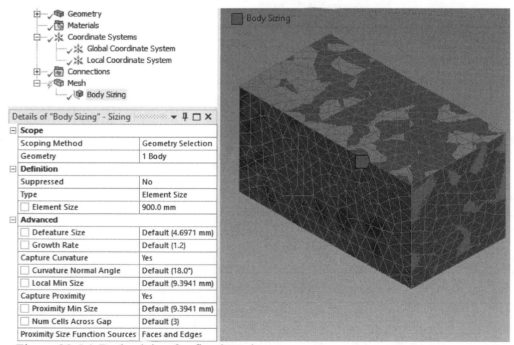

Figure 23.5a) Body sizing for fixed mesh

489

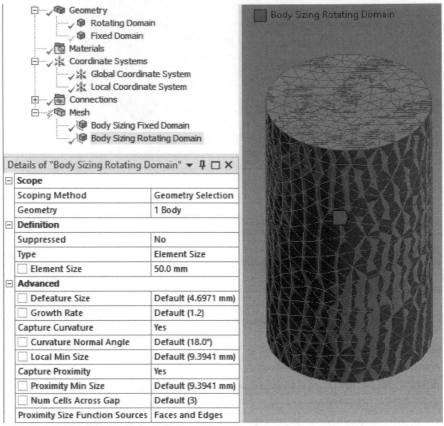

Figure 23.5b) Body sizing for rotating mesh

6. Right click in the graphics window and select Cursor Mode>>Face. Right click in the graphics window and select View>>Left. Zoom out and select the square inlet face, right click and select Create Named Selection…. Enter the name *inlet* as Selection Name and click OK to close the window. Repeat this step but select Right view and name the face *outlet*. Select Isometric View in the graphics window and zoom out. Select Wireframe and hide the mesh from under the menu.

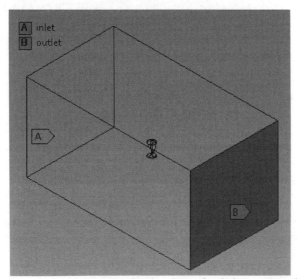

Figure 23.6a) Named selections for inlet and outlet

Right click in the graphics window and select Cursor Mode>>Body. Select the outer fixed domain, right click and select Create Named Selection…. Enter the name *fixed_domain* as Selection Name and click OK to close the window.

Figure 23.6b) Named selections for inlet, outlet and fixed domain

7.  Right click on Fixed Domain under Geometry in the Outline and select Hide Body. Right click in the graphics window and select Cursor Mode>>Box Zoom. Zoom in on the rotating domain, right click in the graphics window and select Cursor Mode>>Face. Right click in the graphics window and select Select All. Control deselect the cylindrical outer face of the rotating domain, control deselect the top circular face of the rotating domain, and finally turn the model around by clicking the mouse wheel and drag the mouse followed by control deselection of the bottom circular face of the rotating domain. Right click in the graphics window and select Create Named Selection…. Enter the name *rotor* as Selection Name and click OK to close the window.

Figure 23.7a) All faces selected, cylindrical face deselected, and top and bottom circular faces deselected

491

Select *rotor* under Named Selections in the Outline. You will have 14 Faces selected as Geometry for the rotor, see Figure 23.7b).

Figure 23.7b) Selected faces for helical Savonius rotor

Right click in the graphics window and select Cursor Mode>>Body. Select the cylindrical rotating domain, right click and select Create Named Selection…. Enter the name *rotating_domain* as Selection Name and click OK to close the window.

Figure 23.7c) Selected body for rotating domain

8.  Select Mesh in the Outline. Select Mesh>>Controls>>Sizing from the menu. Select Named Selection as Scoping Method under Scope in Details of "Face Sizing". Select *rotor* as Named Selection. Set the Element Size to 20.5 mm and set Capture Curvature and Capture Proximity to Yes. Right click on Face Sizing under Mesh in the Outline and select Rename. Rename the face sizing to Face Sizing Rotor.

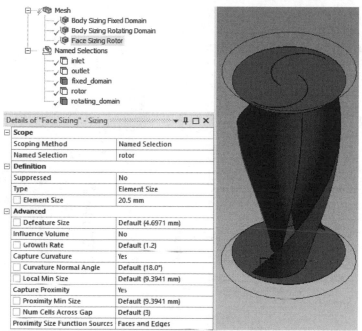

Figure 23.8a) Face sizing of helical Savonius rotor

Select Mesh>>Controls>>Inflation from the menu. Select Named Selection as Scoping Method under Scope in Details of "Inflation". Select *rotating_domain* as Named Selection under Scope. Select Named Selections as Boundary Scoping Method under Definition in Details of "Inflation". Select *rotor* as Boundary under Definition. Select First Layer Thickness as Inflation Option and set First Layer Height to 1.0 mm. Set Maximum Layers to 3 and growth rate to 1.3, see Figure 23.8b).

Figure 23.8b) Inflation settings

9. Right click on Mesh in the Outline and select Generate Mesh. Open Quality in Details of Mesh and select Orthogonal Quality as Mesh Metric. The Min value is 0.14638 which is larger than the minimum recommended value of 0.1, see Figure 23.9a).

Figure 23.9a) Orthogonal quality of the mesh

Open Statistics in Details of "Mesh". The number of Nodes is 122,202 and the number of Elements 511,736. Select File>>Export>>Mesh>>Fluent Input File>>Export from the menu and save the mesh file with the name *helical-savonius-rotor.msh*. Close ANSYS Meshing. Right click on Mesh under Project Schematic in ANSYS Workbench and select Update. Select File>>Save As from the menu in ANSYS Workbench. Save the project with the name *Helical Savonius Rotor Flow.wbpj*.

Figure 23.9b) Finished mesh around the rotor

10. Right click on Setup under Project Schematic in ANSYS Workbench and select Edit…. Check the box for Double Precision and set the number of Parallel Solver Processes equal to the number of CPUs. Click on Start.

Figure 23.10 Fluent launcher

11. Double click on General under Setup in the Outline View. Select Transient as Time on the Task Page. Double click on Models and Viscous (SST k-omega). Select the Spalart-Allmaras (1 eqn) Viscous Model and click on OK to close the window.

Figure 23.11a) Transient time setting

Figure 23.11b) Viscous model selection

12. Open Boundary Conditions and Inlet under Setup in the Outline View. Double click on inlet (velocity-inlet, id = 8), select Components as Velocity Specification Method and set X-Velocity (m/s) to 5. Click OK to close the Velocity Inlet window. Open Wall under Boundary Conditions. Double click on wall-fixed_domain (wall, id=7) and select Specified Shear as Shear Condition. Click OK to close the Wall window.

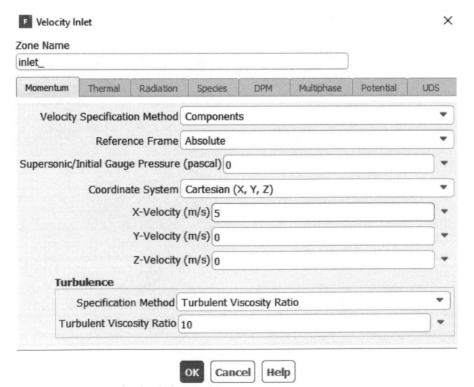

Figure 23.12a) Velocity inlet settings

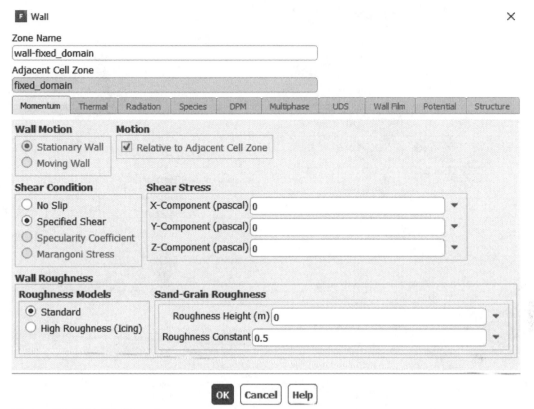

Figure 23.12b) Wall settings

13. Double click on Dynamic Mesh under Setup in the Outline View. Check the box for Dynamic Mesh, uncheck Smoothing under Mesh Methods and check the box for Six DOF under Options. Click on Settings… under Options. Select Create/Edit … in the Options window. Check the box for One DOF Rotation and set the Mass (kg) to 4.013. Set the Axis under One DOF to X 0, Y 1, Z 0. Set the Center of Rotation to X (m) 0, Y (m) 0.5, Z (m) 0. Set Moment of Inertia (kg/m2) to 0.1374. Enter *one-dof-rotation* as Name. Click on Create and Close the Six DOF Properties window. Check the box for Write Motion History. Enter *HSR Motion History* as File Name and direct the File Name to your *Working Directory*. Click OK to close the Options window.

Figure 23.13a) Dynamic mesh          Figure 23.13b) Six DOF properties

Figure 23.13c) Options settings

Select Create/Edit… under Dynamic Mesh Zones on the Task Page. Select *fixed_domain* under Zone Names in the Dynamic Mesh Zones window. Select Stationary under Type and click on Create.

Figure 23.13d) Creation of *fixed_domain* dynamic mesh zone

Select *rotating_domain* under Zone Names in the Dynamic Mesh Zones window. Select Rigid Body under Type and check the boxes for On and Passive under Six DOF. Select *one-dof-rotation* under Six DOF UDF/Properties. Click on Create.

Figure 23.13e) Creation of *rotating_domain* dynamic mesh zone

Select *rotor* under Zone Names in the Dynamic Mesh Zones window. Select Rigid Body under Type and uncheck the box for Passive under Six DOF. Select *one-dof-rotation* under Six DOF UDF/Properties. Click on Create. Close the Dynamic Mesh Zones window.

Double click on Reference Values under Setup in the Outline View. Select Compute from *inlet* under Reference Values on the Task Page. Set the Area (m2) to 0.5 and Length (m) to 0.25.

Figure 23.13f) Creation of *rotor* dynamic mesh zone

Figure 23.13g) Reference values

14. Double click on Methods under Solution in the Outline View. Select Second Order Upwind for Modified Turbulent Viscosity and select Second Order Implicit under Transient Formulation. Open Monitors under Solution in the Outline View and double click on Residual. Set the Absolute Criteria for all Residuals to 1e-06. Click on OK to close the Residual Monitors window.

Figure 23.14a) Solution methods

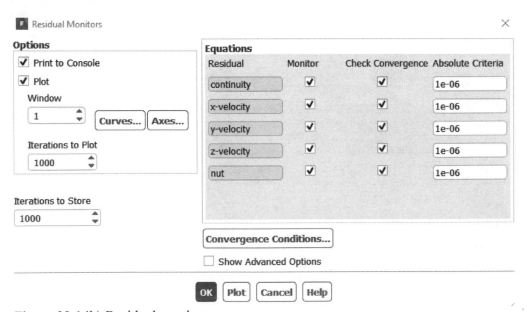

Figure 23.14b) Residual monitors

15. Select New>>Force Report>>Force… in the New report File window. Select the Force Vector as X 1, Y 0 and Z 0. Select *rotor* under Wall Zones. Check the boxes for Report File, Report Plot and Print to Console under Create. Enter force-x as Name. Select OK to close the window.

Figure 23.15a) Force report definition for *force-x*

Select New>>Force Report>>Force… in the New report File window. Select the Force Vector as X 0, Y 0 and Z 1. Select *rotor* under Wall Zones. Check the boxes for Report File, Report Plot and Print to Console under Create. Enter force-z as Name. Select OK to close the window.

Select New>>Force Report>>Drag… in the New report File window. Select Drag Coefficient as Report Output Type. Select the Force Vector as X 1, Y 0 and Z 0. Select *rotor* under Wall Zones. Check the boxes for Report File, Report Plot and Print to Console under Create. Enter *downwind-drag-force-coefficient* as Name. Select OK to close the window.

Figure 23.15b) Force report definition for *force-z*

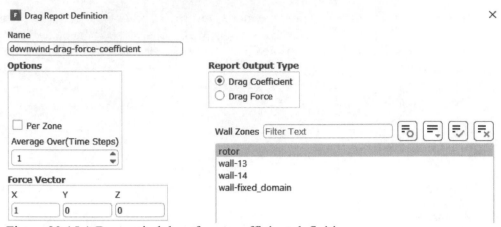

Figure 23.15c) Downwind drag force coefficient definition

Select New>>Force Report>>Lift… in the New report File window. Select Lift
Coefficient as Report Output Type. Select the Force Vector as X 0, Y 0 and Z 1. Select
*rotor* under Wall Zones. Check the boxes for Report File, Report Plot and Print to
Console under Create. Enter *side-force-coefficient* as Name. Select OK to close the
window.

Figure 23.15d) Side force coefficient definition

Select New>>Force Report>>Moment… in the New report File window. Select Moment
as Report Output Type. Select Moment Center as X (m) 0, Y (m) 0.5 and Z (m) 0. Select
Moment Axis as X 0, Y 1 and Z 0. Select *rotor* under Wall Zones. Check the boxes for
Report File, Report Plot and Print to Console under Create. Enter *moment-y* as Name.
Select OK to close the window.

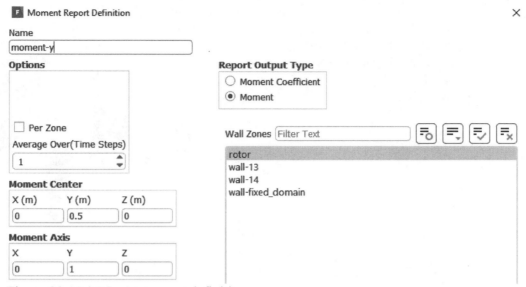

Figure 23.15e) Moment report definition

Select New>>Force Report>>Moment… in the New report File window. Select Moment Coefficient as Report Output Type. Select Moment Center as X (m) 0, Y (m) 0.5 and Z (m) 0. Select Moment Axis as X 0, Y 1 and Z 0. Select *rotor* under Wall Zones. Check the boxes for Report File, Report Plot and Print to Console under Create. Enter *torque-coefficient* as Name. Select OK to close the window. Close the Report File Definitions window.

Figure 23.15f) Torque coefficient definition

16. We are going to define a point at the outer edge of the rotor in the rotating domain. Select the Results tab from the menu and Create Point under Surface. Set the Coordinates to x (m) 0, y (m) 0 and z (m) 0.275. Enter *end-plate-edge-point* as the Name. Click on Create and Close the window.

   Double click on Report Files under Solution and Monitors in the Outline View. Select New… in the Report File Definitions window. Select New>>Surface Report>>Vertex

Average… in the New report File window. Select Velocity and Velocity Magnitude as Field Variable in the Surface Report Definition window. Select *end-plate-edge-point* under Surfaces. Check the boxes for Report File, Report Plot and Print to Console under Create. Enter *end-plate-tip-velocity-magnitude* as Name. Select OK to close the window.

Figure 23.16a) Point definition

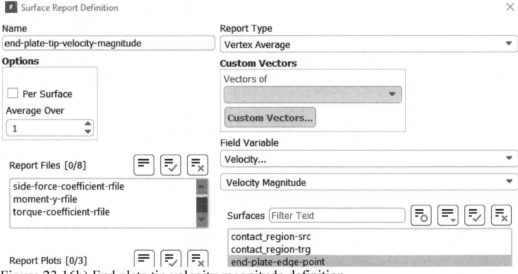

Figure 23.16b) End plate tip velocity magnitude definition

Select New>>Expression in the New report File window. Select *end-plate-tip-velocity-magnitude* from Report Definitions. Divide by the radius of the rotor 0.275. Multiply by 30 and divide by PI to get rotor-rpm, see Figure 23.16c). Enter *end-plate-tip-rpm* as the name. Check the boxes for Report File, Report Plot and Print to Console under Create. Select OK to close the window.

Select New>>Expression in the New report File window. Select *end-plate-edge-velocity-magnitude* from Report Definitions. Divide by the incoming wind velocity 5 to get tip speed ratio. Enter *end-plate-edge-velocity-ratio* as the name. Check the boxes for Report File, Report Plot and Print to Console under Create. Select OK to close the window.

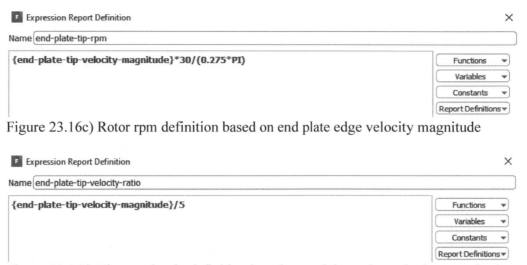

Figure 23.16c) Rotor rpm definition based on end plate edge velocity magnitude

Figure 23.16d) Tip speed ratio definition based on endplate edge velocity magnitude

17. Double click on Initialization under Solution in the Outline View. Set X Velocity (m/s) to 5 and click on Initialize. Select Hybrid Initialization and click on Initialize once again. Answer OK to the question. Open Calculation Activities and double click on Autosave (Every Time Steps). Set Save Data File Every to 25 Time Steps. Click OK to close the window. Double click on Solution Animations under Calculation Activities. Select New Object>>Contours…. Select Contours of Velocity and Velocity Magnitude. Check the box for Filled under Options. Select *rotor* under Surfaces. Enter *velocity-magnitude* as Contour Name and select Save/Display. Select *velocity-magnitude* as Animation Object. Name the animation as *velocity-magnitude-animation*. Select OK to close the window.

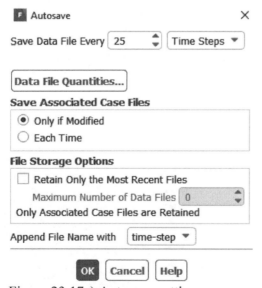

Figure 23.17a) Autosave settings

**Contours** ✕

Contour Name

velocity-magnitude

**Options**

☑ Filled
☑ Node Values
☑ Boundary Values
☐ Contour Lines
☑ Global Range
☑ Auto Range
☐ Clip to Range
☐ Draw Profiles
☐ Draw Mesh

Contours of

Velocity... ▾

Velocity Magnitude ▾

Min          Max

0            0

Surfaces  Filter Text

contact_region-src
contact_region-trg
inlet_
outlet
rotor
rotor-tip-point
wall-13
wall-14
wall-fixed_domain

**Coloring**

◯ Banded
◉ Smooth

Colormap Options...

New Surface ▾

Save/Display  Compute  Close  Help

Figure 23.17b) Contours settings

**Animation Definition** ✕

Name: velocity-magnitude-animation

Record after every  1  ▲▼  time-step  ▾
Storage Type  HSF File  ▾
Storage Directory  C:/Users/jmatsson  ...
Window Id  14  ▲▼
Animation View  isometric  ▾  Preview  Use Active

Animation Object  ▾

residuals
velocity-magnitude
cp-rplot
rotor-power-rplot
tip-speed-ratio-rplot
rotor-rpm-rplot
rotor-tip-velocity-magnitude-rplot
torque-coefficient-rplot
moment-y-rplot
side-force-coefficient-rplot

New Object ▾  Edit Object...

OK  Cancel  Help

Figure 23.17c) Animation definition

18. Select File>>Save Project from the menu. Select File>>Export>>Case & Data … from the menu. Save the file in your *Working Directory* with the name *Helical Savonius Rotor Flow.cas*. Double click on Run Calculation. Set the Time Step Size (s) to 0.01 and set the Number of Time Steps to 2000. Set Max Iterations/Time Step to 50. Click on Calculate.

Figure 23.18a) Run calculation settings

Figure 23.18b) shows the velocity magnitude at the edge of the rotor end plate during the first 20 seconds. The velocity magnitude levels off at around 7.23 m/s corresponding to a rotor rpm of 251. This value is 21 % higher than the corresponding value of 208 rpm as listed by Zakaria and Ibrahim[1] in their experiments. The end plate edge velocity magnitude level of 7.23 m/s translates to an end plate tip speed ratio of 1.32.

Figure 23.18b) Velocity magnitude at rotor end plate edge during the first 20 seconds

Figure 23.18c) shows the contours of velocity magnitude for the helical Savonius rotor after 20 seconds. It is seen that the velocity magnitude increases as expected further away from the rotation axis up to a maximum value of 7.23 m/s at the edge of the circular end plate.

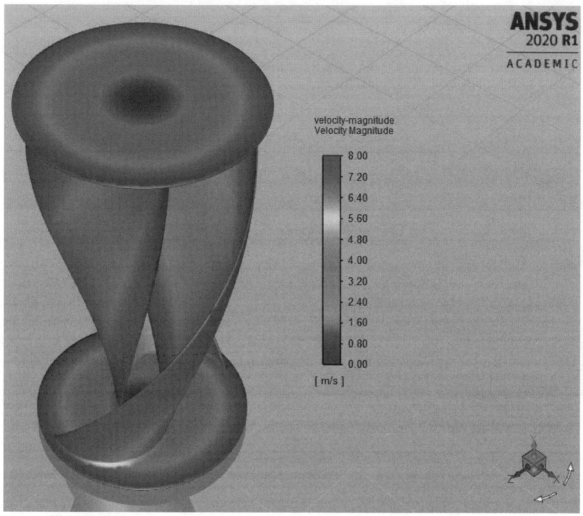

Figure 23.18c) Contours of velocity magnitude for the rotor after 20 seconds

In Figure 23.18d) we see the time signal of the drag and lift coefficients on the rotor during one second. The average value of the corresponding lift force 10.65 N is 13% higher than the average value of the drag force at 9.39 N. The corresponding average values for the drag and lift coefficients are 1.23 and 1.39, correspondingly.

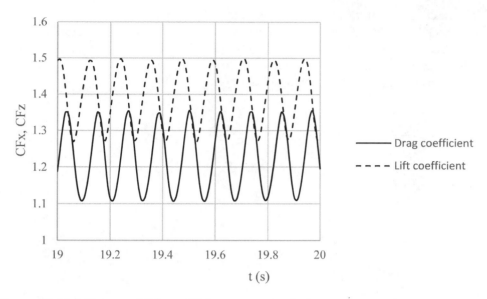

Figure 23.18d) Drag and lift coefficients on rotor during one second

## F. Theory

19. In defining the geometry we follow the approach by Rogowski and Maronski[3]. The cross sectional geometry of the rotor is shown in Figure 23.19.

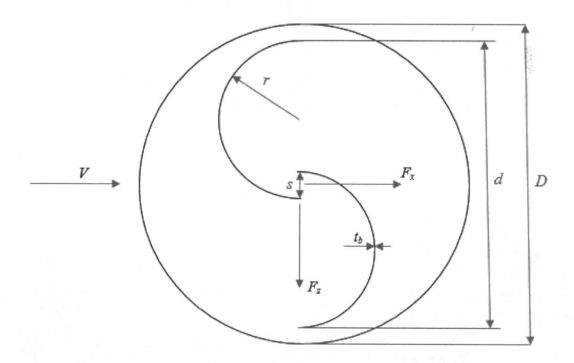

Figure 23.19 Cross sectional geometry for the helical Savonius rotor

The bucket gap width $s$ is 0.121 m and the bucket thickness $t_b$ is 3 mm. The bucket radius $r$ is 0.15525 m and the rotor diameter $d = 4r - s = 0.5$ m. The overlap ratio is $s/d = 0.242$. The twist angle of the helical rotor is 180 degrees. The end plate diameter $D$ is 0.55 m and the end plate thickness $t_e$ is 2 mm. The free stream velocity is $V$ (m/s). The downwind drag force is $F_x$ (N) and the side force or lift force is $F_z$ (N). The rotor swept area is defined as

$$A_s = (4r - s)h \tag{23.1}$$

where $h = 1$ m is the height of the rotor. We define the rotor tip speed $v$ (m/s) and the tip speed ratio $TSR$ as

$$v = \omega d/2 \tag{23.2}$$

$$TSR = \frac{\omega d}{2V} = \frac{v}{V} \tag{23.3}$$

where $\omega$ (rad/s) is the rotational speed of the turbine. The turbine rotational speed $N$ (rpm) is then given by

$$N = \frac{30\omega}{\pi} = \frac{60v}{\pi d} \tag{23.4}$$

The drag and lift coefficients can be defined as

$$C_{F_x} = \frac{F_x}{\frac{1}{2}\rho V^2 A_s} \tag{23.5}$$

$$C_{F_z} = \frac{F_z}{\frac{1}{2}\rho V^2 A_s} \tag{23.6}$$

where $\rho$ (kg/m$^3$) is air density. We can also define the torque coefficient

$$C_T = \frac{4T}{\rho V^2 A_s d} \tag{23.7}$$

where $T$ (Nm) is the turbine torque. Finally, we define the power coefficient as

$$C_P = C_T * TSR \tag{23.8}$$

## G. References

1. Zakaria, A. and Ibrahim, M.S.N., "Analysis of Savonius Rotor Performance Operating at Low Wind Speeds Using Numerical Study.", International Journal of Engineering & Technology, **7**, 1549-1552, 2018.
2. Zakaria, A. and Ibrahim, M.S.N., "Numerical Performance Evaluation of Savonius Rotors by Flow-Driven and Sliding-Mesh Approaches.", International Journal of Advanced Trends in Computer Science and Engineering, **8**, No. 1, 2019.
3. Rogowski, K and Maronski, R, "CFD Computation of the Savonius rotor.", Journal of Theoretical and Applied Mechanics, **53**, 37-45, 2015.
4. Blackwell, B.F., Sheldahl, R.E. and Feltz, L.V.,"Wind Tunnel Performance Data for Two- and Three-Bucket Savonius Rotors, Sandia Laboratories, Report SAND76-0131, 1977.

## H. Exercises

23.1 Run the simulations in this chapter for the helical Savonius rotor at the different free stream velocities as shown in Table 23.1. Fill out the table and plot drag and lift coefficients versus tip speed ratio.

| $V$ (m/s) | $N$ (rpm) | TSR | $F_x$ (N) | $C_{F_x}$ | $F_z$ (N) | $C_{F_z}$ | $N$ (rpm)-Exp. | % diff. | $\Delta t$ (s) | $N_t$ |
|---|---|---|---|---|---|---|---|---|---|---|
| 2 | | | | | | | 83 | | | |
| 3 | | | | | | | 124 | | | |
| 4 | 147 | 0.96 | 4.94 | 1.01 | 4.27 | 0.87 | 170 | 16 | 0.01 | 2000 |
| 5 | 251 | 1.32 | 9.39 | 1.23 | 10.65 | 1.39 | 208 | 21 | 0.01 | 2000 |
| 6 | | | | | | | 230 | | | |

Table 23.1 Turbine rotational speed from ANSYS Fluent in comparison with experiments[1].

**I. Notes**

## INDEX

**Notes:**

**Notes:**